Sarah Purser's portrait of Casement painted over ten sessions in June 1913, donated by William Cadbury in 1930 to the National Gallery of Ireland

ROGER CASEMENT'S GERMAN DIARY 1914-1916

Including 'A Last Page' and associated correspondence

Edited by Jeffrey Dudgeon

BELFAST PRESS

Published by Belfast Press

56 Mount Prospect Park
Belfast
BT9 7BG

Tel (028) 90664111 and 079 2125 1874

First published 2016

Copyright (editorial) © Jeffrey Dudgeon 2016
The moral right of the author has been asserted.

Typeset in Adobe Garamond Pro 11

ISBN 978-0-9539287-5-0 (Paperback)

ISBN 978-0-9539287-6-7 (Kindle)

All rights reserved. Without limiting the rights under copyright reserved above, no part of this publication may be reproduced, stored in or introduced into a retrieval system or transmitted in any form or by any means (electronic, mechanical, photocopying, recording, or otherwise) without the prior permission of the copyright owner.

CONTENTS

Illustrations	vi
Preface	viii
Introduction	x
Roger Casement's German Diary 31 October 1914 to 11 February 1915	1
'A Last Page' 17 March to 8 April 1916 with other documents taking the account to 11 April 1916	175
Appendix 1 *The Nation* 1921-22: eleven chapter outlines edited by Charles Curry using Casement's diary and extracts from letters	270
Appendix 2 John Devoy 1924 articles in the *Gaelic American* on Casement's actions at Easter 1916	282
Appendix 3 *Casement's War in Germany and Ireland 1914-16*: response by Jeffrey Dudgeon to Angus Michell articles in the Field Day Review	293
Appendix 4 *Casement Wars (over The Black Diaries)*: response by Jeffrey Dudgeon to Angus Mitchell's '*Phases of a Dishonourable Phantasy*' in the Field Day Review	303
Appendix 5 Sequel 1: *Casement and the Easter Rising: Berlin, Dublin and British Intelligence* by Jeffrey Dudgeon given at Tralee conference *Roger Casement: The Glocal Imperative*	322
Appendix 6 Sequel 2: Roger Casement letter to his cousin Gertrude Bannister from Pentonville Prison 20 July 1916	333
Appendix 7 Sequel 3: *Casement and Ulster: Seeding Separatism and Misunderstanding* by Jeffrey Dudgeon given at TCD conference: *The North Began? Ulster and the Irish Revolution 1900-25*	337
Bibliography	342
Index	348

The editor, Cllr. Jeffrey Dudgeon at St George's Market, Belfast, 25 February 2016

EDITOR'S BIOGRAPHY

Jeffrey Dudgeon, was born in Belfast in 1946 and educated at local primary schools, Campbell College, Magee University College, and Trinity College, Dublin. He joined the Northern Ireland Labour Party while at school. In the 1970s and 1980s, he was an active member of the Campaign for Labour Representation, and later the Campaign for Equal Citizenship. In 1975, he co-founded the Northern Ireland Gay Rights Association (NIGRA), and in 1981 was the winning plaintiff at the European Court of Human Rights in a seven-year suit against the British Government. This resulted in the decriminalisation of male homosexuality in Northern Ireland in 1982. It was the first successful gay case at Strasbourg and has been a precedent throughout the world, including the Supreme Court of the United States. He continues to work with NIGRA on legal and police issues.

After a stint in shipping at Belfast docks, he was a civil servant for many years, working mostly in pensions. From 1995-8, he was parliamentary adviser and constituency office manager for the UK Unionist MP for North Down, Robert McCartney. For the following two years, he was engaged, full time, in researching his book *Roger Casement: The Black Diaries*, returning in 2000 to the Department of Health at Stormont to deal with health protection issues, including antimicrobial resistance, healthcare-associated infection, and screening. One-time honorary secretary of the Irish Association's northern branch, he stood as a liberal unionist for a Trinity College seat in the Irish Senate in 2011.

Jeffrey Dudgeon was awarded an MBE in the 2012 New Year's Honours List for services to the LGBT community, and, in 2013, was one of the two Ulster Unionist Party representatives at the Haass Talks on Flags, Parading and the Past. In 2014, he was elected to Belfast City Council as a UUP Councillor for the Balmoral area, and chairs the Council's Diversity Working Group. He is also a member of the City Growth and Development, and Licensing Committees.

In Council, he is majoring on achieving the erection of a Belfast Blitz Memorial in the City Hall grounds to commemorate the more than 1,000 victims of the two terrible air raids of April and May 1941. He also works on litter and graffiti problems in the south of the city, and the building of a municipal art gallery in its centre.

The author continues to discuss, write and speak on issues relating to Roger Casement and his global significance, particularly so in this Decade of Centenaries, the high point of which is 2016, because of both the Easter Rising and the Battle of the Somme. The author's email address for contact or comment is: jeffreydudgeon@hotmail.com.

ILLUSTRATIONS

Cover image: Roger Casement in Germany on 17 April 1915 when being 'kinematographed' (also German officers in *Pickelhauben*)

1	Sarah Purser's portrait of Casement in June 1913	*frontispiece*
2	The editor, Jeffrey Dudgeon	iv
3	Casement leaving court in 1916	ix
4	Adler Christensen note to Casement on Findlay dated 26 November	xiii
5	Adler Christensen outdoors	15
6	Joseph McGarrity	16
7	Richard Meyer (*two photographs*)	20
8	Count Georg von Wedel	21
9	Hindenburg and Ludendorff	22
10	Princess Evelyn Blücher	56
11	Count Johann Heinrich von Bernstorff	64
12	Kaiser Wilhelm II and German officers in *Pickelhauben*	68
13	Roger Casement's German passport	74
14	Roger Casement in German Foreign Office photograph; image used on the 50th anniversary of execution Irish stamp in 1966	94
15	St. John Gaffney, US Consul General, Munich	104
16	Luncheon party in Munich 1915: St. John Gaffney, Roger Casement, Dr Curry, Col. and Mrs Edwin Emerson	117
17	Irish Brigade NCOs in Zossen in 1915	127
18	Julius Pokorny when younger and c. 1967 (*two photographs*)	136
19	Roger Casement in Hamburg 26 February 1915	137
20	Bulmer Hobson, when younger, and in 1912	145
21	Adler Christensen signed photograph 24 June 1915	165

22	Roger Casement signed photograph 24 June 1915	166
23	Rudolf Nadolny in uniform	169
24	Roger Casement 22 July 1915	170
25	Roger Casement reading in boat on Ammersee in 1915	172
26	Robert Monteith, full length	173
27	John McGoey	177
28	Roger Casement c. 1915	178
29	Riederau house with commemorative plaque where Casement stayed in 1915	180
30	Irish Brigade in Halbmondlager Camp, July 1915	181
31	Robert Monteith, head and shoulders	184
32	Corporal Michael O'Callaghan's photographic pass	191
33	Irish Brigade machine gunners: Thomas McGrath, Michael McDonagh, Michael O'Callaghan and James Carroll	192
34	Count Curt Haugwitz-Hardenberg-Reventlow	211
35	Adler Christensen's first wife Sadie Weaver (*two photographs*)	225
36	Daniel Julien Beverley (or Bailey)	229
37	Private Charles James McCarthy (Irish Brigade)	231
38	Rudolf Nadolny in civilian clothes	253
39	Roger Casement with hat on Ammersee pier in 1915 and kinsman Hugh Casement on the same jetty some 75 years later (*two photographs*)	271
40	Riederau house plaque	272
41	John Devoy and Roger Casement, August 1914	282
42	Memorial stone with German and Irish inscriptions at McKenna's Fort near Banna Strand where Casement was arrested in 1916 (*two photographs*)	332
43	Irish stamps issued in 2016 to mark the centenary of Casement's execution – 70c and €1.05	336

PREFACE

This is a companion volume to the second edition of my book *Roger Casement: The Black Diaries – with a Study of his Background, Sexuality, and Irish Political Life* which was published in paperback and Kindle form[1] earlier this year. It consists of another, and the last surviving, Casement diary, and deals with that most interesting, dramatic and penultimate period of his life in Germany and Berlin prior to his departure to Ireland for the Easter Rising. It was not a private diary in any sense as Casement left instructions for its future publication. Much of what he wrote was designed to provide a record justifying his time in Germany.

He was of an age to have his eye on history while knowing the accusations of treason he had, and would, face, Casement was desperate to have his actions understood. A secondary prompt in the last months was to indicate just how disgraceful and intransigent the behaviour of the Germans had become and how the decision to start the rebellion in Ireland was something he did not agree with for tactical reasons, and an event he hoped to prevent or at least postpone.

There is a cast of the usual characters that Casement mixed with, political, often aristocratic, although in Germany also frequently military. There were to be none of the street people or lovers that his earlier, more sexual diaries, detailed. In Germany, probably for security reasons and lacking the language, he chose not to go out at night or to cruise for sex. He was also getting on.

Of course his Norwegian companion and betrayer, Adler Christensen, looms large, tricking and twisting his way round Germany and America, while draining much of Casement's time and common sense. (A biography by the Norwegian writer Bjørn Godøy is in preparation revealing much more about Adler including his sad death in Fresnes prison.)

This version, unlike that in the book sub-titled *The Berlin Diary* by Angus Mitchell, is unabridged. It carries Casement's full text while being accompanied by related letters. This makes the narrative vastly easier to follow and assists in understanding both Casement's political thinking, and the manoeuvring by him and his German hosts. Students of Germany during the war can sense the atmosphere of a country in crisis through Casement's frank accounts and colourful descriptions. I must here acknowledge the considerable assistance received from Hugh Casement in translating and clarifying German phrasing, manners and geography.

The text is laid out in as close a way as possible as the actual manuscripts to provide an impression of originality. The appendices include correspondence

---

[1] *Roger Casement: The Black Diaries*: paperback, http://www.amazon.co.uk/dp/095392873X; Kindle http://www.amazon.co.uk/dp/B01AXB9754

and newspaper articles from the time, while bringing the reader up to date with articles on recent discussions in relation to Casement in Germany, the Easter Rising as well as the ongoing Black Diaries authenticity debate which is, if anything, accelerating. That controversy tells of a still contested issue in modern-day Ireland, despite the immense strides made towards gay equality and emancipation, most recently in the Republic.

Jeffrey Dudgeon
Belfast
July 2016

Casement leaving court in 1916

INTRODUCTION

Casement's German or Berlin Diary is in two notebooks in the National Library of Ireland where they are catalogued as NLI 1689 and 1690. The text essentially covers the eight months from July 1914 to February 1915. Separately, 'A Last Page' (NLI 5244) picks the narrative up on 17 March 1916 and runs it to Casement's final days in Berlin. Before the notebook transcription itself commences, Casement's separate account of his departure from Norway on 31 October and first arrival in Germany is given.

The diary actually opens on 7 November 1914 and takes Casement retrospectively from England, to the US and to Germany, and includes a tour of war-torn Belgium, It then backdates the narrative to 2 July 1914 when he left for America and effectively concludes on 11 February 1915 with him in a German sanatorium. At the end, however, there is a brief account dated 28 March 1916 of events later in the previous year.

The NLI gave Accession number 863 to the notebooks (inscribed in the first just beneath "Part I") which were part of an extensive donation in 1930 by Casement's cousin and heir Gertrude Parry. Further items came into the NLI in 1951 after her death. Together, these donations were catalogued as manuscripts 13073-13092 and form most of the NLI's Special Collection List A15 ('Casement Papers 1889-1945'). It consists of some 4,000 documents.

The Hayes 'Sources' volume (now digitised as 'Sources Database') catalogued the two notebooks, as, "Diary of Roger Casement relating largely to his efforts in Germany to obtain arms and help for the Irish Volunteers, Nov. 7, 1914 – March 28, 1916."

The two are described by Dr Charles Emerson Curry in his 1922 book[2] *Sir Roger Casement's Diaries – His Mission to Germany and the Findlay Affair,* on page 197, as "four quarto notebooks of 180 pages each." As only two are in the NLI, the four seem to have been joined and combined.

The sheets in NLI 1689 are numbered 1 to 138 in pencil, by an archivist

---

[2] Published by Arche, Munich, 1922. NLI manuscripts 1689 and 1690 comprise much, but by no means all, of what is in Curry's book. A close American friend, and frequently Casement's host, Dr Curry lived at Riederau on the Ammersee near Munich. He was to become the ultimate custodian in Germany of Casement's papers. In his book, he omits much that was critical of Germany or America, including discussion of the German atrocities in Belgium in 1914 (and Casement's trip to Charleville), many names of those he met, presumably to protect them from possible legal action for treason, and most of Casement's enthusiastic listing of British war casualties. The book was published in Germany as *Meine Mission nach Deutschland während des Krieges und die Findlay-Affaire - Auf Grund der Tagebücher und Korrespondenz dargestellt* von Dr. Charles E. Curry; Stephan Geibel Verlag, Altenburg, Thüringen, n.d. but copyright 1925. Dr Curry died in 1935 and his son Manfred in 1953.

presumably, while NLI 1690 has a series of numbers running from 1 to 80, and then 1 to 81 (again). It therefore contains 161 sheets and has 322 sides.

The first notebook is hard backed in navy blue NLI binding and measures about 10 × 8 inches. There is a Berlin shop stamp in purple ink on the inside back cover in tiny print which seems to read "Bibliographie, Buchdruch".

Casement's text opens "<u>Part</u> 1. Berlin – 7 Nov. <u>1914</u>." The first entries go up to the paragraph on sheet 14 which begins "a connected story". Thereafter, from sheets 15 to 97, entries are the other way up; then upside down again from sheet 98 to the last numbered 138.

Sheet 91 is misnumbered (it should be 97), and blank, and is the back cover of the first of the four notebooks. The following sheet (marked 98) is stuck down and unreadable. The words "1914" II <u>Diary</u> are just visible at the edge.

NLI 1689's last entry is dated Thursday 10 December 1914. The notebook's final back cover page is numbered 138 and carries these notes in ink:

354/6 ½ Rex 12p
<u>Men to go out.</u>
Taylor,
Gleeson,
The Red Cross Corporal – Middlesex Regt.
<u>Murphy 256,</u>

The latter notebook, NLI 1690, is also in navy blue NLI binding with an original cover in black rexine-type card. It starts with notes and cuttings from early December 1914. Entries proper start on 8 December 1914 and run to 11 February 1915, after which there is a time gap of some fourteen months. The text ends with an account taking the story forward from that date but much less extensively than in earlier entries. Footnotes in square brackets below appeared as such in Dr Curry's book.

The entries in NLI 5244, entitled 'A Last Page,' are dated between 17 March and 8 April 1916 while other NLI documents take the account in Germany to 11 April 1916 when Casement left Berlin for the last time.

The Nation[3] between 30 November 1921 and 8 February 1922 published eleven chapters or extracts from Curry's book as 'The Diary of Sir Roger Casement' (see Appendix 1). Chapters II to IV were about the Findlay affair and are not in or from this German Diary. All the other chapters except the last, are in the diary in some form or other. A letter from Casement's sister Nina (Agnes) Newman in Chapter VIII was in response to one from a Canadian woman published on 28 December 1921:

---

[3] *The Nation*, the oldest continuously published weekly magazine in the United States, was founded in 1865 and has been described as "the flagship of the left".

Sir: In this week's Nation a Canadian woman refers to my brother, Roger Casement, as something of a "lady killer." Nothing could be further from the truth. No man had a greater detestation of that unmanly creature, "lady killer," than Roger; and he was much too busy at all times, both when, at home and abroad, to trouble his head concerning woman, – good, bad, or indifferent.

Certainly I as his sister have a vivid recollection of very determined advances made by members of the opposite sex toward him, and also of his very brusque rejection; and I utterly deny he was more popular with women than men. As I lived for many years near our relations in the North, I am personally unaware that he was laughed at by them for his "poses"; but no doubt the Canadian woman knew more about us than we knew about ourselves.

AGNES NEWMAN
Atlantic City,
December 31

Chapter XI of 8 February 1922 reprinted two letters from Princess Blücher, a section of her then recent book, *An English Wife in Berlin*, a famous letter from Casement to Adler Christensen,[4] and one from Casement to Georges Chatterton-Hill.

When forwarding some letters to Casement, again in a sanatorium, Captain Monteith, knowing Casement's tendency to scribble incessantly, had to warn, "I am afraid you are going to start writing again & if I was sure of it, I would not send on these things, a spade and a garden rake would be better."[5]

Similarly, B.L. Reid wrote of how John Devoy, "in his Recollections noted the awkwardness of Casement's habit of writing at great length 'in the plainest terms on large sheets of foolscap' which he sent in very large envelopes usually further swelled out with masses of paper – cuttings, clippings, pamphlets, and documents of all kinds".[6] The renowned Irish author Frank O'Connor wrote of Casement that "the man was a maniac for scribbling." Another biographer, Roger Sawyer, noted his "compulsion" to write, an urge that seems to have been at least as strong as his sexual desires: "He was capable of writing no fewer than three versions of the same day's events, working at his largely self-imposed task long into the night, and into the early hours of the following day."

---

[4] See Curry pp. 206-7 and MacColl p. 152. Letter written by Casement in Hamburg in February 1915: "...Now don't go & be foolish with the money – you will soon have not a cent!...You are fearfully wasteful of money, my dear, faithful old Adler – much more so than I am even – because you buy things you don't need at all – like that rain coat & the gloves &c. I have no gloves & you have about six pairs! – & face & complexion "blooms"! & God knows what. All you need is some healthy, good work to keep your mind occupied."
[5] NLI 13085/24, 1 February 1916
[6] *Recollections of An Irish Rebel* by John Devoy (1842-1928), published in 1929; an account of his long career as an Irish revolutionary.

What follows, in this book, bears out these very similar assessments of a man who wrote too much. He drafted many hundreds of other letters and memos when in Germany of which only a number of the more significant, particularly those related to the arrangements for his departure to Ireland, are reprinted here, along with the full, unabridged diary.

Although the time frame jumps, this transcription sticks to trying to replicate the documents much as they were written down. Being complete in its narrative makes it vastly more readable and comprehensible than an abridged version.

The text of the journals and letters is nearly always interesting, and often informative and provides a rare, insider's view, from a non-German, of life in that country during the First World War, and of the milieu and outlook of its upper and military classes.

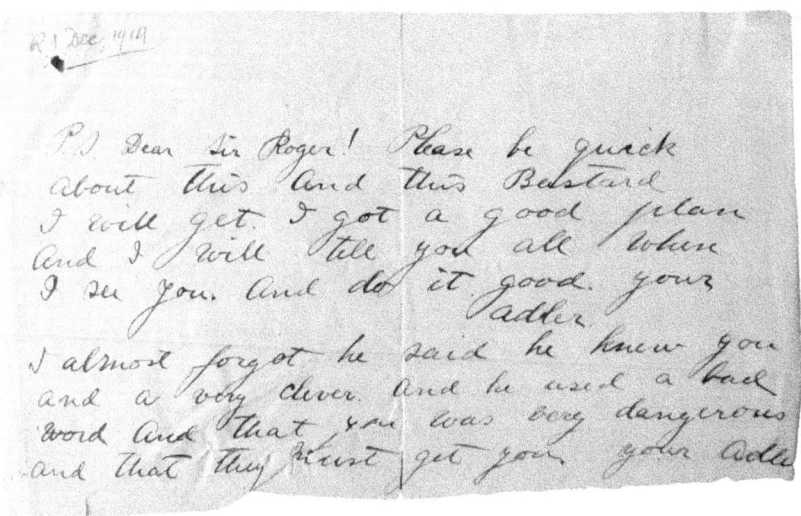

Adler Christensen note to Casement on Findlay[7] dated 26 November 1914 (NLI 13085/17)

---

[7] Mansfeldt de Cardonnel Findlay (1861-1932), British Minister in Christiania (Oslo) 1911-23

ROGER CASEMENT'S
GERMAN DIARY

ROGER CASEMENT'S GERMAN DIARY
31 October 1914 to 11 February 1915

[The days from 31 October to 2 November 1914, when Casement arrives in Berlin and first meets high German officials, including the No. 2 at the Foreign Office, Arthur Zimmerman, are recounted in Chapter V of Curry's book (pp. 65-74). Casement's original manuscript for these days is not to be found in the NLI, or indeed elsewhere:]

Saturday, October 31. 1914.

I could not sleep well in the train. Adler was to watch and make sure I was ready to change carriages at Engelholm at 5.45 a.m. However at 1.40 a.m., I wakened suddenly and opened the door of my carriage and found a guard who told me the time. I found, too, Adler asleep in the top bunk, but he wakened at once. From that time on to Engelholm I did not sleep. We reached it punctually – all the other carriages were closed, the inmates sleeping. The train stopped and we jumped out on the platform shifting the baggage more quickly than any porter. Meyer came from his Traelleborg coach to meet me on the platform; and in four or five minutes I saw with joy the Helsingborg car carried on with its sleeping passengers, while we got into the Traelleborg section that did not continue on its route for some time.

I found an empty sleeping carriage in that section and at last lay down really tired out and slept to Malmö. Here we arrived about 7, and the glimpse of the beautifully clean streets. Fine stone buildings and pleasant faced Swedes was a charming awakening. We had 20 minutes stop for breakfast, which we found excellently laid out, with all manners of nice Swedish dishes in the buffet. Poor Adler, however, got more than he bargained for, for in paying the bill and mine of some four Kronen he gave a 10 Kronen note and could not get the change in time from the smiling Swedish waitress. We had to run for the train, that lady assisting our flight by a bustle of haste and confusion but she kept the 6 Kronen.

At Traelleborg we embarked on the railway steamboat "Queen Victoria" for Sassnitz – on the stormy, white capped Baltic. From Malmö to Traelleborg I did not sleep, but looked out on the flat, well cultivated fields and pleasant homesteads of Swedish farmers. Malmö, looked from the train, a very big town with fine buildings and broad streets as we skirted its suburbs. At Traelleborg Adler took tickets only to Sassnitz. The steamer was very comfortable, but the journey of five hours (or more) to Sassnitz was rough. I got a cabin far down below the water line, and slept some little time.

At Sassnitz we had delay in landing, over the inspection of passports. Had Meyer not been with me, even with the telegram from Berlin, I should have had great difficulty. As it was they wanted to turn out my pockets and Adler's for letters &c. – and even did this with Meyer. These were stupid peasant reservists with "42" on their caps. The higher officials at last got us through, after a very close inspection of "Mr James Landy's" passport, especially of the U.S.A. red seal and the lithographed signature "W. J. Bryan". At length we got away to the train – and Meyer and I into a comfortable first class carriage while Adler was put into a second class compartment in the corridor.

The landing wharf and all along the shore of the island of Ruegen where we landed, was guarded by sentries; rough peasant soldiers of same reserve class. As we passed over the island of Ruegen we got here and there glimpses of fine houses, of farms in plenty and villages – the fields all bare, the shorn stubble of most plentiful wheat crop, and truck loads of a large species of parsnip greeting our view. There were plenty of men about and often – fine young men too, so it is clear Germany has still reserves of manhood left in civil occupations. Here and there a glimpse of the Baltic and some bay of the island was given us before we saw the church towers and semi Byzantine minarets of Stralsund. Our train was run onto a ferry and we crossed the narrow branch of sea into Stralsund, where we had to stay a little time. From that on to Berlin the train filled up – and our carriage, which I think had been reserved for us at Sassnitz, got other occupants. Two of these were Junker landlords. One with an excessive Prussian beard, divided in two extraordinary waves that struck out almost at right angles from each other. Both were ugly. Meyer explained to me that these were typical "small Prussian landowners". Their talk was constant, was of the war and of their families and friends who had all got some one at the front.

Presently I noticed them glaring at me. Meyer whispered that they were discussing the "extraordinary insolence" of an Englishman being there, when one of them was about to call the guard to have me put out of the carriage – so Meyer said. Meyer intervened and explained that I was an American going to Berlin and that he knew all about me. The hatred against the English is so bitter in Germany, Meyer explained that while there is only pity for Belgium, respect for France, frank enmity for Russia, there is for England, "the Cousin", the "good friend", who has betrayed Germany and tried to stab her in the back and to incite the whole world against her, nothing but an extraordinary hatred that exceeds anything felt ever in Germany before for any country with which the Germans were at war. Even Adler a Norwegian found this out in the train, for having gone out to get some coffee, he found his seat – a numbered one taken by an old man on his return. His attempts to recover it were futile and although he showed his numbered ticket and appealed to a non-commissioned infantry man in the car they only sneered so he came to us to complain. Meyer went to the carriage and asked me to go away and in a few minutes returned to say he had got Adler reinstated and the old trespasser evicted. It was all over Adler's use of English in appealing for help! Even although they saw he was in the right no one would intervene on behalf of a man talking in the tongue of treachery.

We reached Berlin at 7.30 or 7.45 and saw some wounded soldiers and an ambulance waiting. A lady who had got in to our carriage on route, saw my "Times" and "Daily News" of 31st October I had bought at Christiania and asked to look at them. She explained to me in excellent English (this only after my American Status had been proclaimed) that she had an aunt, an Englishwoman, now practically a prisoner in Germany and she would like to show the papers to her. So I gave them to bag although I had not read them and was saving them for the dreary nights in Berlin I knew must be before me. This lady told Meyer that her husband was at the front, but was coming from Luxembourg that night, for a few hours in Berlin, and she was going up to meet him just for a brief handshake. She was all smiles, good humour and niceness and had a very friendly little <u>dachshund</u> who nestled against me and eat the remains of my bread and sausage from the wayside station at which we had only been able to hurriedly buy some rolls and hot sausages. The food arrangements were bad worse even than in England I thought. When we got these sausages and rolls, from a hand truck on the platform pushed by a boy, we could not get anything to drink and all was scramble. Further on we could get coffee, with equal rush and scramble, from a boy with a movable tray table trolley but were not allowed to take the cup into the carriage.

Meyer had intended to take me to the Palast Hotel – near the Foreign Office – but on ordering the taxi driver to go there the man looked at him amazed and said it had been closed since the beginning of the war – so we were driven instead to the Continental where Meyer got room for me under the name of "Mr. Hammond." I had decided to bury "Mr. James Landy" on the shores of the Baltic, after we had traversed the Custom inspection there. The management were impressed by Meyer and were all bows – and smiles and so I was duly registered as "Mr. Hammond of New York", and they were told they would be responsible to the German Foreign Office if anything unpleasant occurred to me.

My room was 219 – with a bathroom – and Adler's 240 – close at hand. The prices are rather bewildering. Thus Adler's room, only two doors from mine, is only four marks – a smaller room and without bathroom, while my, by no means, magnificent room is 18 marks.

Meyer soon left me for the Foreign Office to report our arrival and to arrange for me to see some of them tomorrow. He begged me not to go out, or let Adler out, until the police had been advised as English speaking men, without papers &c. and unknown to the police, would surely get into trouble. So we both stayed in the Hotel – and I had a quiet and lonely dinner in the restaurant – and then went to bed after a talk with Adler.

At last in Berlin! The journey done – the effort perhaps only begun. Shall I succeed? Will they see the great cause aright and understand all it may mean to them, no less than to Ireland? Tomorrow will show the beginning."

Sunday 1 November.

The hotel is comfortable and quiet. Very few guests. When I came down to luncheon a man at a table near, hearing my order given in English, glared stealthily and then got up and went out. I knew by instinct he had gone to the office to ask about the visitor who spoke English. Presently he returned and resumed his meal but when I had done mine, he stood up and came over and stood beside me. So I said "Good day" in English and he pointed out a great portrait of the Emperor and two other pictures and walked me round to see them as his English was not much more vigorous than my German we soon bowed and parted.

I did not go out all day. Meyer called twice, to report progress. No one at the Foreign Office at first. The Chancellor, von Bethmann Hollweg, and the Secretary of State, von Jagow, both with the Emperor at the French front – at Charleville I gathered later. At the Foreign Office only the Under Secretary of State, Zimmermann and the Staff. The second visit of Meyer, in the evening, was to tell me that I should be received by the Under Secretary on Monday morning at 11.30 – and that meantime they had discussed Christiania incident and he had shown them the document and the Kronen notes and explained the attempt on me – and that they would like to hear more of it also. Anyhow, he showed me plainly, I was a welcome guest – and I felt as easy in mind, as it is possible to be in so strange a position. Here I am in the heart of the enemy's country – a State guest and almost a State prisoner.

I wrote today to Major Lothes[8] and the young Muller Beeck, and also sent von Skal's letter to Maximilian Harden.[9] I was sorry afterwards I had written

---

[8] [cf. pp. 34 and 37]
[9] Harden, Maximilian (originally Maximilian Witkowski), b. Berlin 1861, d. in Valais (Switzerland) 1927. Actor, political author, essayist, journalist, outspoken critic. Editor of the weekly periodical *Die Zukunft* ('The Future') from 1892 in which he defended Bismarck and criticized Wilhelmian policies. To put a stop to his exposures, he was called up as an army clerk in 1917.

these letters so soon – but the inertia of a whole Sunday in this dreary hotel was too much for me.

The people are very kind in the hotel. They regard me, Adler reports from the Servants' Hall, as an American millionaire – and he added to this belief by saying I had a fine steam yacht.

Monday, 2 November 1914.

Meyer called for me at 11 – and took me on foot to Unter den Linden close at hand – and down it to the Wilhelmstrasse in which, at No. 76 is the Foreign Office. He pointed me out the closed Russian Embassy in Unter den Linden and the equally closed British Embassy in Wilhelmstrasse – and further on in this street the "Palace of the third son of the Kaiser" – a fine building with sentries outside. We met a Prince Fürstenberg in the Wilhelmstrasse whom Meyer knew – a cousin, he said, of the prince whose splendid chateau at Donaueschingen I passed in May 1912 with Dick Morten and Heini.[10]

The Foreign Office, No. 76, is an old fashioned, white, very plain house of the time of Frederick the Great or earlier. You have to ring at a wooden gateway door, and the door opens. We went upstairs and a servant man took our coats, hats and sticks. So different from the London Foreign Office where I have been so often chez moi! The waiting room we were shown into was a fine salon, well furnished and large, with fine oil paintings of King Frederick Wilhelm III[11] and the old Emperor Wilhelm.[12] Meyer told me I was to be received, first by the Under Secretary of State, Herr Zimmermann, and then by Count Georg von Wedel, the "head of the English Department." Meyer left me alone a few minutes. Some Officers came and went, cavalry men in grey.

Strange thoughts were mine, as I sat on a big sofa in this centre of policy of the German Empire. No regrets no fears – well – yes – some regrets, but no fears. I thought of Ireland, the land I should almost fatally never see again. Only a miracle of victory could ever bring me to her shores. That I did not expect – cannot in truth hope for. But, victory or defeat, it is all for Ireland. And she cannot suffer from what I do I may, or must suffer and even those near and dear to me – but my country can only gain from my treason. Whatever comes that must be so. If I win all it is national resurrection – a free Ireland, a world nation after centuries of slavery. A people lost in the Middle Ages refound and returned to Europe. If I fail – if Germany be defeated – still the blow struck today for Ireland must change the course of British policy towards that country. Things will never be again quite the

---

[10] Heinrich d'Oleire, a German working in Batavia. He was interned in Ceylon during the war.
[11] Friedrich Wilhelm III of Prussia, reigned 1797-1840
[12] Wilhelm I, proclaimed German Emperor in Versailles in 1871

same. The "Irish Question" will have been lifted from the mire and mud and petty, false strife of British domestic politics into an international atmosphere. That, at least, I shall have achieved. England can never again play with "the Irish Question." She will <u>have</u> to face the issue once for all. With the clear issue thus raised by me she will have to deal. She must either face a discontented conspiring Ireland – or bind it closer by a grant of far fuller liberties. Coercion she cannot again resume. Laissez faire must go for ever. "Home Rule" must become indeed home rule – and even if all my hopes are doomed to rank failure abroad, at least I shall have given more to Ireland by one bold act [**not the word 'deed' as in Angus Mitchell's *Berlin Diary* long title and in Curry's book**] of open treason than Redmond and Co. after years of talk and spouting treason have gained from England.

England does not mind the "treason" of the orthodox Irish "patriot." She took the true measure of that long ago. She only fears the Irishman who <u>acts</u>; not him who talks. She recognises only action, and respects only deeds. Those men have killed England with their mouth times and again – I am going to hit her with my clenched hand. It is a blow of sincere enmity, based on a wholly impersonal disregard of consequences to myself. Sure alone that it is in truth a blow for Ireland I should be a traitor did I not act as I am doing.

I have often said, and said it without the slightest concealment, that if ever the chance came to strike a blow for Ireland I'd do it. Well the chance has come. I am not responsible for it. The crime is not mine. It is England's own doing. Grey and Asquith are the real traitors. They have surely betrayed <u>their</u> country and her true interests to glut the greedy jealousy of the British commercial mind. Germany's sin has been her efficiency. They chose to build up a league of enmity against the people they feared to assail themselves, and having triumphed in their tortuous, ignoble secret diplomacy they joyfully hurried to the encounter when, at last, sure as they thought of their prey. For them, that so called Liberal administration, I have nothing but unmeasured contempt. A scorn I cannot express. And for the "governing classes" too of the pirate realm. For the people themselves, and for many individual Englishmen, I have only deep sorrow, regret, pity and affection. But as Wilfrid Blunt said to me in Sussex at Newbuilding in May when I lunched with him and that lovely girl (the great granddaughter of Lord Edward Fitzgerald[13]) – the time has come for the break up of the British Empire.

Even as he said he hoped now to live to see it, so I hope to be able to do <u>something</u> to bring it about. That Empire is a monstrosity. The world will be the better, the more sincere the less hypocritical for a British defeat, for a German <u>victory</u>.

---

[13] Anne, a famous horse breeder, and also a granddaughter of Lord Byron

Many thoughts, like these, were with me as I waited. When I was shown into Herr Zimmermann's cabinet, I met a fair haired very good natured face and a warm and close handshake. I liked the man at once. He was <u>warm</u> hearted as well as warm handed. He congratulated me warmly on my <u>safe</u> arrival and spoke of the Christiania episode in fitting terms. He asked me long about it – and I described the whole incident, and his comment was my own – "Dastardly" he said – "but it is what they do and have <u>always</u> done when their interests are at stake. They stick at nothing."

I had written a hasty memorandum, in the morning in my bedroom – in my pyjamas – giving a fresh point of view and drawing in outline the form of declaration I thought the German Government might issue (I append it hereafter). The memorandum briefly recited the cruel calumnies the British Government and their agents were spreading through Ireland, in order to defame Germany and to induce the Irish youth to enlist in their army of plunderers under the pretence that it was a war to protect Belgium and the "small nationalities" – and went on to show that the German Government could quite legitimately defend itself from these atrocious charges of evil intact towards Ireland by making a formal declaration of its attitude towards my country. I read the declaration I suggested to Herr Zimmermann. He agreed with every paragraph and sentence, and when I had done took the whole paper from me and said "I accept it entirely."

After an interview more cheering and full of a spirit of good will than I had ever hoped for, I was taken by Meyer to Count v. Wedel.

Here I found a charming personality – a man of upright build; frank, straight brown eyes and a perfect English accent. Our talk was long and friendly. I told him I had left the memorandum and form of proposed declaration with the Under Secretary of State – and we talked of the Irish soldiers in Germany and the line of action that I hoped to follow there. It is this step that appeals most to the Germans I can see. They perceive its full "moral" value to their cause. Meyer said to me yesterday "If you do that it is worth <u>ten army corps</u> to us!" I made it plain beyond all misconception to Wedel that my efforts with the soldiers must be strictly defined as an effort to strike a blow for Ireland – not an attempt merely to hit England. I described the character of the Irishman and of the Irish soldier, and pointed out that any Irish man might commit treason against England <u>for the sake of Ireland</u>, but that he would not do anything mean or treacherous. He would put his neck in the noose, as I had done, for love of Ireland; he would not "desert to an enemy" or forsake his own colours merely to assail England. In fact he must have an active cause, not a negative. If, thus, Germany, made the declaration I sought as to the fortunes and future of Ireland in the event of

German victory, I had little or no doubt scores, perhaps, hundreds of the Irish prisoners would follow me.

So said Wedel – "It is clearly the declaration first of all." He then discussed with Meyer and myself the steps for my safety in Berlin "not alone from the British but from our own people." He proposed going at once with Meyer to the Chief of the Secret Police and explaining things – and took me back in his taxi as far as the Continental where I got out. Later in the day Meyer returned with a card issued by the Chief of the Political Police, saying that Mr. Hammond of New York was not to be molested... This card I am to carry always and it will ensure me in case of any street trouble or enquiry. Adler is to have no paper, as being a Norwegian he is not an "offensive personage." We both, however, are going to wear little American flags in our button holes and this evening Adler bought them.

I went for a walk after dinner – Adler taking me up to the Kaiser's Palace and round it and then back down Unter den Linden again. We saw the fine buildings of that quarter – so many of them royal or imperial in origin and more than one pertaining actually to the Royal house.

Berlin is not imposing I think – from the glimpses had today but it is fine. It is extraordinarily well kept and clean – and while the buildings are not lofty, they are massive and well built. Unter den Linden is, frankly, disappointing. It is not a fine thoroughfare and the shops do not impress one – neither do the Lindens. The latter are short, and add little to the character of the street so far as I can see – but then I saw them in the beginning of winter. There are too few people visible also. The street is wide and rather empty of any human throng. The cross street Frederickstrasse is, on the contrary, full of life, and I presume the true Berlin is rather this street than Unter den Linden. The Spree is a very insignificant river in the city – one crosses it before reaching the Kaiser's palace and again, a branch of it, on the other side. Now I am fairly launched on Berlin – and today sees me take up a definite position. "Mr. Hammond of New York" – not to be molested.

[There is then a four day gap before Casement commences his diary proper in Berlin on 7 November:]

Part I
Berlin – 7 Nov. 1914

Now that I am safely in Berlin, having arrived here on Saturday evening, 31st October 1914, from Christiania[14] via Traelleborg and Ruegen-Stralsund route I shall put on record facts connected with my journey and its objects

---

[14] Modern Oslo

that may be of use hereafter. For it is not every day that even an Irishman commits High Treason especially one who has been in the service of the Sovereign he discards and not without honour and some fame in that service.

It is true "Colonel" Arthur Lynch,15 now loyalist and repentant M.P. for Clare (the "Banner County" as your blatant Irish "Nationalist" Editor loves to call it), did commit Treason of a sort in the Boer War – but of so minor a degree that his trial in London and "Death Sentence" were about on a par with his election for Clare as an "Irish Nationalist" – unreal shams.

I remember the trial – I was in London at the time and I then thought Lynch was an earnest man and "apologised" for his treason on the ground of his sincerity.

I little thought then – it must have been about 1903 or so he stood his trial – that I should go the whole hog myself – and not to a little Boer Republic – that had once been British territory – but to the mightiest military power in Europe, whose war to the death with England meant destruction to one or other of the combatants.

Lynch's treason was that of an individual and, I fear, a self-seeking individual – mine is the premeditated, clearly thought out treason not of an individual but of a representative of a still remembering people.

When I left Ireland on 2 July last and Glasgow in the "Cassandra" (name of ill omen!) on the 4th as a second class "emigrant" to Montreal, how little did I think of what was before me!

I chose that route in order to avoid publicity and possible interviews at New York, and the quite probable attentions of the British spy bureau, whose agents in Ireland had been so maladroitly pursuing me since the beginning of the year.

I embarked on the "Cassandra" on 4 July in the Clyde as "Mr. R. D. Casement" my right name and initials, but without the prefix my knighthood conferred. No one suspected I was Sir Roger Casement, and one passenger once asked me if I was any relative to that "well known Irish baronet"! I laughed and said I believed I was a near relation and that I knew him well. With the exception of one Irish boy from Cork the passengers were Scotch – and very largely butter scotch. At least they talked it. I know no language that fills me with the sense of nausea that Glasgow or Butter Scotch does. It is like that vile laugh of Harry Lauder's in the gramophone that winds up every verse of every song in his odious repertoire. [**This sentence was**

---

[15] Col. Lynch, an Australian journalist, was convicted of treason in 1903 after being elected an MP for Galway. He was sentenced to death, and lost his seat but reprieved. Later elected for West Clare in 1909, he supported the war in 1914, and rewarded with a colonelcy by London. In the last months of the war, he apparently tried to build up support for an Irish Brigade to fight for the Allies.

omitted by Curry in his book.]

Voyages I have made enough but the "Cassandra's" was very much better than the majority! Barring the butter Scotch I enjoyed myself. The Irish boy became a great friend – from the Clyde mouth even –

On Sunday morning 5 July at 7 a.m. I looked from our port and saw far south the jagged precipices and towers of Tory Island.[16] It was perhaps 12 miles off – and beyond it rose in blue lines Muckish, Errigal and the hills of my heart.

I could almost see Cloghaneely and the shining strand of Magheraroarty, – whence two years before August 1912 – I had gone over to Tory with that famous party the fiddler, the piper and the rest.

So far as I can now recall we were twelve days on the voyage to Montreal, although it may have been only 10-11 – My Diaries had to go overboard on this later voyage on the "Oskar II" – not so very far from Tory either – as will be told when we reach this latter more memorable journey.

The only objects of interest on the "Cassandra" voyage to Canada were the icebergs we passed during two days when near Newfoundland.

These were the first I had ever seen and unlike most "first sights" of much talked of things they more than realised all I had conceived of them in my mind. Great Arctic palaces, green and gold sometimes with a crystal sheen and a dazzling a white as of concentrated snow they sailed past us bound to their doom in the Gulf Stream. At one single point during the second day of the bergs we sighted 17 at the same time from the ship's upper deck from the near at hand "growler" sagging past to the vast domes of white and pale white too outlined against the distance of the calm grey horizon.

Newfoundland's coast line grew clear on our right a pleasant coast in a fine, transparent air.

I forget the towns we passed or dimly sighted – rather fishing settlements than towns – but I remember St. Pierre (and Miquelon), for there we saw the town well enough, where, in 1905, it had been suggested by some friends of Lord MacDonnell's I met at Mrs. Green's[17] one night at dinner that I should go as consul. The post, I think he said, was then vacant and I was purposely idle at the time, having practically retired from the service over the Congo controversy. I had been so anxious to support Morel in his Congo fight – more with the Foreign Office almost than against Leopold – that I had asked to he seconded (without any pay) from Lisbon, whither the Foreign Office had sent me after the publication of my Congo Report in the beginning of 1904.

Lisbon had not agreed with me – still less the FO method of conducting

---

[16] [This small island lies about 8 miles off the coast of Donegal.]
[17] [The famous Irish historian, widow of John Richard Green, and intimate friend of Sir Roger; she took the place of mother and adviser to him.]

the controversy with Leopold which consisted largely in running away from their own charges and offering ~~lame excuses~~ apologies for my report.

So on December 1904 I seconded myself and so remained a free lance, devoting myself to Irish affairs, until in August 1906 Sir E. Grey wrote to suggest my return to the Consular Service, when I went out first to Santos, then to Para and finally to Rio de Janeiro <u>en route</u> to Putumayo.

I thought of these things, as I looked at the little town of St Pierre, and wondered as we steamed past it, what might have been the difference had I accepted the advice that night at Mrs. Green's and "applied" for St. Pierre. Happily I was then so well occupied in Ireland trying to keep Irishmen out of the British Army and dreaming of an Ireland that might yet be free, that I gave no second thought to that after dinner suggestion any more than to a later one of Sir Eric Barrington that "Stockholm was vacant and might be offered me." I was immersed in Irish affairs all through 1905 and right up to the very day of my departure for Santos in August (or was it early in September?) 1906.

It was those 19 months in Ireland when "seconded" from the Consular Service that moulded all my subsequent actions and carried me so far on the road to Mitchell's aspirations **[John Mitchel]** that everything I have since done seems but the natural up growth from the seed then sown.

Some day I may try to write the story of the Congo and how I found Leopold, – of the Putumayo and that abominable London Company, and of the "inordinate wild Irishman", who went out on both quests in the garb of a British official, but with the soul of the Irish felon. If the English had only known the thoughts in my heart and the impulses I had obeyed, when I did the things they took pride in, I wonder would their press have praised my "heroism" and "chivalry" as they did, or would that expatriated patriot, T. P. O'Connor[18], have referred to me at the Reading Election last November "as one of the finest figures in <u>our</u> imperial history"? <u>What</u> will he and the <u>Westminster Gazette</u> and even my poor kind friend the <u>Daily News</u> say, when

---

[18] T.P. O'Connor was born 1848 in Athlone and educated at Queen's College, Galway. T.P. or 'Tay Pay,' joined the staff of Saunders' Newsletter, Dublin, as a cub reporter before moving to London in 1870 where he was a sub-editor on the Daily Telegraph until finding settled employment in the New York Herald's London office. For three years he worked on a biography of Benjamin Disraeli. He was elected as a Parnellite MP for Galway in 1880. From 1885 until his death in 1929, he represented the Scotland division of Liverpool as a member of the nationalist Irish Parliamentary Party. T.P. ended his career as 'Father' of the House of Commons, supporting Ramsay MacDonald's government. He founded a number of newspapers and periodicals including an evening paper *The Star* and *T.P.'s Weekly*, having edited *The Star* from 1887-90. His best known books were *The Parnell Movement* and *Memoirs of an old Parliamentarian,* along with his 1929 autobiography. He became the first British film censor in 1917.

the Christiania catastrophe becomes public in England?

But I am anticipating and must return to the Newfoundland shores and the Bay of Anticosti and the Great Gulf of St. Lawrence.

We sighted the Marconi Station on the New Brunswick shore near Gaspé Bay and next morning were in the "mouth of the St. Lawrence" and steaming close enough to the south shore to the point where the ill fated "Empress of Ireland" went down.

The banks of the river extremely pretty and interesting and in some respects, at a distance, bien entendu, recalling the vistas of the mighty Amazon. But the Amazon is a river – a vast flowing sea of fresh water and this is a gulf of the sea right up to Quebec. Many towns and even cities were passed during the day and finally late at night we reached Quebec. I saw nothing of the city beyond the lights of the streets and those on the lately burnt Frontenac platform or promenade.

We left again early in the morning and then began the true St. Lawrence river, almost at once. Up to Quebec is a seaway – an estuary if you will from the Heights of Abraham it becomes a river – often vast in breadth, with many islands and distant far seen banks, sometimes narrowing to half a mile or a mile.

Again many towns and churches were passed and towards 6.30 p.m. the smoke of Montreal I say smoke advisedly, for of all the filthy approaches to a beautiful <u>site</u> (but not city) Montreal, belching forth the blackest smoke in the world, surely takes first place. From the river little is seen but a noisome line of zinc and corrugated iron horrors – grain stores – of factories and warehouses and a shrieking railway, then the "Docks" more corrugated iron – abominations and above the town the first glimpse of the rapids. We quickly docked and at 8.30 we had rooms at the Queen's Hotel. It was hot and I <u>think</u> the 15 or 16 July 1914.

The next day my Irish friend went on to his sister in Toronto, to enter a bank, poor boy! He had never been out of Ireland and hardly out of Cork County (save for a few weeks at a commercial school in Dublin). I saw him off at 7.30 on his long night journey to Toronto.

Next morning I took train for New York having written old John Devoy to say I hoped to see him at his office on Friday morning (18th or 19th).

The journey was long and hot and quite stifling owing to the American fear of fresh air. The windows of the carriages or "cars" open only a little way up from below and some of them will not remain open, but slide down again slowly and have to be constantly re-hoisted. Mine was one of these – so to breathe at all I had to put a hat box in below the lifted sash – to the scandal of the guards and some very uninteresting passengers. The dullest looking lot imaginable. The scenery compensated for the want of the picturesque in the human environment.

Lake Champlain we skirted for over 100 miles, I was told, often running along the edge of cliffs and precipices above its pellucid, aqua-marine waters. I thought of the days when Mohicans and the Six Nations had here a hunters' paradise.

Poor Indians! you <u>had</u> life – you white destroyers only possess <u>things</u>. That is the vital distinction I take it between the "savage" and the civilised man. The savage <u>is</u> – the whiteman <u>has</u>. The one lives and moves to <u>be</u>; the other toils and dies to <u>have</u>. From the purely human point of view the savage has the happier and purer life – doubtless the civilised toiler makes the greater world. It is "Civilisation" versus the personal joy of life.

We got to New York about 8.30 I think – after a delightful journey from the point of view of scenery down the Hudson river to Manhattan Island. The shores of the Hudson and the Catskills were more lovely than I had expected.

I went to the Belmont Hotel at N. York as it lay just opposite the Station, & from the first moment found Irish faces and Irish voices round me – the lift boys, the outdoor porters and the waiters in the bar and at cash counters were mostly either Irish-born or Irish-descended I thought. Some had even the brogue still lingering round the shores of that broad estuary of smiles, that takes the place of a mouth in the true Milesian face.

Strolling down Broadway in the thought of perhaps locating old points of view, like Ponds'[19] and the hotel he lived in **[two words inserted:]** in 1890, a young Norwegian sailor spoke to me – and him I befriended – and told him to see me next morning. I mention him and this chance meeting, because he is destined to figure largely in the end of this story. His name was Eivind Adler Christensen,[20] 24 years old, of Moss,[21] Norway. He had run away from his father's house after getting a severe beating for playing truant at school, and had stowed away on an English collier. This when he was 12 years old. He was landed at Glasgow and left there, and some Norwegian sailors took him and so he became a fireman on a succession of Norwegian steamers.

When he met me he was out of work, starving almost and homeless.

---

[19] This refers to the 'Celebrity World Tours' office or Lyceum Bureau at Union Square of James B. Pond, 'America's Famous Lecture Impresario.' He specialised in explorers and in 1889 had hired Herbert Ward for an American lecture tour. Casement accompanied Ward in the US from December 1889 to March 1890.

[20] Casement had actually met Adler Christensen before, in Montevideo. He was to betray him twice, once in Norway in 1914 at the British legation and secondly in 1916 at the British consulate in Philadelphia.

[21] [Moss lies on the west coast about 50 miles south of Christiania; it is a railroad station of the line Christiania-Frederickshald.]

He was grateful for my help and I saw him once or twice in New York, where with the help I gave him he got work.

It would take too long to record my early days in New York and at Philadelphia. After meeting old John Devoy on the morrow of my arrival at the "Gaelic American" Office, who took me to luncheon at Moquin's, I met shortly afterwards John Quinn and Bourke Cockran – I then went to Philadelphia and saw Joe McGarrity and stayed with him a night, returning to New York to visit Bourke Cockran at Port Washington – The Ancient Order of Hibernians being in annual session at Norfolk, Virginia, McGarrity begged me to go to their Convention and address them in the name of the Irish Volunteers. I consented if invited – This came by telegraph and as I was asked to get him too, if I could, I motored down with John Quinn to Bourke Cockran's at dinner time and carried him off by assault to Norfolk. Our hurried return to New York to reach the 9 p.m. night train for Norfolk was a record motor run on those roads – and it was a foggy night. Quinn 'phoned up for tickets and we got the train with 5 minutes in hand.

Adler Christensen outdoors (NLI EPH A430, Prints & Drawings)

The journey to Norfolk was interesting during the latter stages across the wide bays, past old Point Comfort to Hampton Roads and the fair, very hot Virginian city of Norfolk. The town was all beflagged with green flags and stars and stripes. No flags anywhere shown save the Irish and American. The Hibernians were in session in a large Theatre – Their President, ex-president and nominees for the presidency for the present Convention's Election met us in a deputation and in a few minutes Cockran and I were seated on the platform as guests of our countrymen, with Patrick Egan alongside us.

I was asked to speak first – and gave a short address, on the spur of the moment, on the situation in Ireland, particularly from the Volunteer standpoint – I avoided purely political references and to some extent I eulogised the Ulster men, to the evident content of the great majority.[22] It was a shirt-sleeves and

---

[22] NYPL Maloney IHP, 2 August 1914, "We owe thanks to the Ulster men for taking up arms. For, if we differ with them on some points, possibly on many, we are at least one with

fan audience. Cockran followed with an oration and Egan spoke a few words too – and then we returned to our hotel and spent the rest of the day (Cockran and I) motoring out to Ocean View Beach until it was time to return by the evg. boat and train. I got off at Philadelphia and stayed with McGarrity.

With him some days were spent awaiting news of my pre-arranged <u>coup</u> for landing the guns at Howth. During the period of waiting for Sunday 26 July (the day I had arranged with Hobson and E. Childers that the two yachts should arrive at Howth[23] and the Dublin Volunteers should march out to meet them and get the rifles) I got a letter from Mrs. Green telling me all was well and that "our friends were on the sea." The threatening situation in Europe

Joseph McGarrity (Carrickmore and Philadelphia)

---

them in this - that it is the right of every free man to bear arms in defense of what he believes to be right.

Ulster, two years ago, broke the spell of British disarmament laid upon Irishmen. It was broken with impunity, for two years ago it was thought that only Ulster and Ulstermen could be armed in defiance of the laws…I said every Irish woman can help. They are doing so at home. Ulster women are helping the Ulster Volunteers; and in Dublin, Cork and Limerick the women are with the men – to a man! The task of Irish women is to inspire and uplift the men. In that they are perhaps best fitted of all the women of the world - for the beauty that is theirs is not of face or brow only, but a beauty of heart and a virtue of soul that have never been wanting."

[23] [A town about nine miles from Dublin on the promontory that lies on the north east entrance to Dublin bay.]

following the cowardly murder of the Austrian Arch Duke Ferdinand and his Consort and the Ultimatum to Servia gave me cause for some anxiety.

At other times I should have been even more anxious – but the fears for the landing of the guns at Howth swallowed up all other fears for the time. I had told only John Devoy and Joe McGarrity of the scheme planned before I left Ireland. It was timed for the forenoon of Sunday 26 July. That Sunday I spent at McGarrity's in great anxiety and on tenterhooks. It was a very hot day. At 7 p.m. Joe and I walked down the fields in front of his house until full twilight fell and darkness came. We lay on the grass and talked of Ireland and often, watch in hand, said, "now it is midnight in Dublin now 1 a.m. soon something must come over the cables." About 9 p.m. one of the sub-editors of a Philadelphia paper I need not name rang up Joe over the 'phone and told him a news message had just come in that instant saying that a landing of rifles for the Irish Volunteers had been effected near Dublin that day, that the British troops had been called out to disarm the Volunteers and had fired on them killing several persons and securing the rifles. Joe flew down to the Hibernia Club. Later on a message came from him to his wife to tell me that the guns had not been captured by the troops but retained by the Volunteers.

We hardly slept that night. Joe returned about 2 a.m. (on the Monday morning) and told me he had <u>already</u> taken the steps necessary to have a great protest meeting for the following Sunday, 2nd August in one of the big Theatres of the City and had announced me as the chief speaker!

So whether I liked it or not I was now in for it up to the neck. I would have wished to keep quiet – but from every national point of view it was necessary this meeting should be held and if held that it should lack no support I could give it, so I reluctantly agreed to a step already taken in my name.

The next day, Monday, 27 July, I was interviewed by some of the Philadelphia papers – and photographed – and the interview appeared in full in the evening papers, – particularly the Bulletin.[24] In this conversation I spoke very strongly of the lawless action of the British Authorities in Ireland, culminating in the murder of women and children in the streets of Dublin – and I put the blame fair and square on the shoulders of Mr. Asquith.

The interview gave general satisfaction to the Irish in the city, while I learned it had greatly incensed the loyalists – some of whom wrote stupidly irate letters to my host.

From this on to Sunday 2nd August McGarrity was busy and more than busy in the arrangements for the Sunday meeting. I was a passive agent in his strong hands. He did everything. The Sunday came and with it a great deal of trepidation on my part.[25]

---

[24] *Philadelphia Evening Bulletin*
[25] [In a foot-note to the above Sir Roger writes: "A connected story to be made out of this

[The writing on the next sheet is the other way up. It comes after a black card cover originating from one of the former notebooks.

The following section on Casement's trip into France and Belgium to the German military HQ on the Western Front in Charleville was not reproduced by Dr Curry, as being outwith "Sir Roger's Mission to Germany and the Findlay Affair", and having no direct bearing to the subject nor being of "general public interest." Curry recommenced transcription of Casement's diary a week after on 24 November 1914.

Angus Mitchell in his *Berlin Diary* omits large chunks of Casement's text, some 20 ellipses mark the gaps in the account of his travels. Many are fine observational paragraphs, and some cast the Germans in a less than perfect light. For whatever reason, these omissions, and many others later in the diary, mar the flow of the text while giving only a partial reflection of Casement's narrative.]

Part I
1914

My journey to the German Headquarters at Charleville Novr. 17 (Tuesday) from Berlin and back there (Friday) 20 Nov.

<u>On Monday 16 Nov.</u> I got a 'phone call from Baron von Berckheim[26] of the General Staff, at 8 Moltke Str. about 1 o'clock asking me "Mr. Hammond" to go round there and see him between 3 and 4.

I went accordingly, in a taxi, to the address given. It is across the big Königsplatz in front of the Reichstag – I was shown up by a young orderly soldier who said he could speak "Italienische" but not "Amerikanische"! After wandering through many corridors, going to various rooms (all wrong) he waylaid a very pretty girl (possibly a typist I imagined) in a hat as if to go out who spoke good English and she directed us to von Berckheim's room, No. 182. He came at length, a young officer with sword and spurs in a grey cavalry uniform with riding boots and greeted me kindly and in good English. He said he had heard about me from Kurt von Lersner,[27] and that he too,

---

as the beginning – then the Christiania incident following it and then the Diary in Berlin up to its end in Feby."]

[26] Graf Philipp von Berckheim, b. Berlin 1883 d. 1945. Doctor of law; Legationssekretär (Second Secretary); Major (GGS). The family was ancient nobility from Alsace.

[27] Kurt von Lersner son of Maj. Alphons and Emmy *née* Jacobson, b. Saarburg 1883, d. 1954, Doctor of law, President of the German delegation to Versailles 1919. Lersner was later categorised a *Mischling ersten Grades* (having two Jewish grandparents) and posted to the German embassy in Turkey.

had been at the Washington Embassy and hoped to return there later on. We found the "waiting room" occupied, so he cleared two servant maids out of a dining room – and there we talked. He explained that the "Headquarters" (at the French front) wished me to go there at once. Von Lersner who knew me already had charge of the affair – was I ready to go? I said "at once." He said that arrangements would be made for my journey on the morrow, to leave Berlin by the night train for Cologne, where an automobile would meet me sent by Lersner to take me straight to Headquarters – I would be accompanied the whole way by an officer, A <u>Graf</u> something, whose name he forgot FOR the moment. Would my military passport be made out for me as Sir Roger Casement or as Mr. Hammond? I said better as Mr. Hammond and he agreed.

He explained that the journey was to be kept quite secret and that the Count who took charge of me would only know me as Mr. H – and knew nothing of the objects. I would be simply Mr. H, an American, going to the front in his charge – He explained that Headquarters wanted to talk with me about the Irish prisoners. We discussed this matter and a few other things. He explained further that there was a possibility that the motor car from Cologne might be full the next night and if so my departure would be for Wednesday night from Berlin but he would let me know at my hotel by noon next day (Tuesday) whether the departure would be for that night or Wednesday.

I left about 4.30 and walked back to the hotel thinking first to go the Foreign Office and tell them there – but I decided to await Meyer[28] at the hotel at 5 and tell him.

He came about 5.30, and on hearing my news said he must go at once to the F.O. and tell them there of this sudden summons – and he hurried off in a taxi – returning later to say he would try to accompany me if possible, to Headquarters and that I should call on von Wedel[29] next evg at 5, to talk things over.

I spent the evening alone, as usual, taking a walk in the Thiergarten after a light "dinner" at Hoffmann's restaurant, as usual, where I am now a recognised habitué.

Saw several detachment of recruits going off today – some in uniform, with flowers in belts and bosoms – some in plain clothes, with packages in hand

---

[28] Richard Meyer (von Achenbach), b. 1883, German Foreign Office liaison officer and Casement's interpreter, later director of the *Politisches Amt*. In 1936, Hitler rejected his application, as a Jew, to retain his rights as a citizen but he was allowed to depart for Sweden in 1939. He died in Stockholm in 1956.

[29] Count (Graf) Georg von Wedel, (1868-1950), expert in the German Foreign Office political department (*Referent in der politischen Abteilung im AA*), and chief of its English Department.

of all sorts and mostly just wrapped in paper – women and friends walking alongside. The men – all young mainly – looked happy and smiling – and many were smoking. The passers by stopped to look with kind eye on the sons of the Fatherland marching sedately to the trenches of death.

A quiet, patient, obedient and sure-hearted people this, if ever Europe had one. There is an entire absence of jingoism – and yet today, confirmation came of rumours of a great victory over the Russians. This is the first outcome of the battle Professor Schiemann told me of on Sunday – von Berckheim gave me the assurance that the news in the Evening papers was exact, and added that

Richard Meyer (German Foreign Office or Auswärtiges Amt)

a much bigger event was expected – viz – a decisive victory in the East. The German retreat towards Thorn was part of a plan with the Austrians – now the advance from Thorn to the Vistula, where fighting was on both banks was part of this plan. It was hoped to drive the Russian centre southwest towards the Austrians at Cracow etc and then for the German forces to close the rear and to capture or destroy a very large force. This engagement was now proceeding in part he explained – but nothing of it was given out to the press and he asked me to regard it as a "secret." The news actually announced however, is excellent for the German arms. In two engagements, one at Soldau, and one on the Vistula at Wloclawek? the Russians have been defeated with a loss of 28.000 prisoners, 70 machine guns, one large gun, and several cannon.

The number of killed and wounded are not stated, or definitely known.

The Hotel manager (Klicks) said "50.000 killed and wounded." Meyer, when he called, later in evening, said they were "now believed to be 70.000." Anyhow it is a considerable victory – and the evening newssheets are being sold rapidly.

Tuesday. 17 Nov:–

Berlin is all beflagged today in honour of the Prussian victory. Von Hindenburg the victor again! He is the hero of the Prussian heart – and rightly too – for this victory cannot fail to greatly aid the cause of Germany.

Today I sent Adler out to buy various things needed for my journeys[30] and arranged all details of his return to Moss on Saturday next (When his teeth are finished, poor boy!) With two faked letters[31] and some pages of my "Diary"[32] he has "stolen".

Count Georg von Wedel (German Foreign Office)

Von Berckheim called on me at noon to say all was arranged for my departure that evening at 9.45 in company with the Count, whose name is still uncertain – and that he would call on me about 7.30 p.m. that evg.

I had nothing to do but to get ready as the tickets, passport &c &c would all be in the hands of the Count who would call for me at about 9 p.m.

Meyer called and told me that I should call on von Wedel at 5 or 5.15 & that he would call for me then to take me to F.O. I went with him at 5, to 76 Wilhelmstrasse & was shown into the Saloon to wait for v. Wedel who was just collared by an earlier caller. In this room I found Professor Schiemann – who was delighted with my story of the "Christiania incident" (I had written out on Monday) which he had in his hand to get typed at F.O. and a copy of it sent with a covering letter to the Emperor.

Schiemann complimented me on the way I had written the "story" – "un vrai roman" – but one that he believed the Emperor would be greatly interest-

---

[30] [Sir Roger's visit to the headquarters of the German General Staff at Charleville]
[31] [cf. pp. 77-82]
[32] [These pages, of which no copies are to be found among Sir Roger's papers were taken from Christensen at the German frontier (Sassnitz).]

Hindenburg and Ludendorff

ed in. He told me that Fräulein Meyer had received a letter from her brother Kuno[33] from Rotterdam saying his "coffre" had not arrived and that he was

---

[33] Kuno Meyer b. 1858 Hamburg, d. 1919 Leipzig. At school in Edinburgh 1874-6. Studied Germanic languages and Sanskrit at University of Leipzig. Reader at Liverpool University; professor 1895. Returned in 1911 to Germany to take up the only German professorship of Celtic studies, in Berlin. Published and financed the periodical *Érin* 1904. He was not Richard Meyer's brother but Antonie (Toni) Meyer was his sister.

sailing without it. Neither Schiemann nor the sister know if this referred to the box of papers or to some ordinary trunk of clothes.

Schiemann was alarmed and I shared his alarm, if it should prove to be Kuno Meyer's box of damaging papers. I pointed out that if, by ill luck, the English got hold of this they would certainly arrest Meyer anywhere at sea – even just outside New York. Schiemann left me in the waiting room to go and see Zimmermann;[34] I waited on until 7 as Meyer came in twice to say that von Wedel was still kept by his urgent visitor. This waiting room of the German F.O. is interesting. It is furnished in crimson red, with claret coloured wall paper. There are two life sized portraits, one of the old Emperor William, the other of his father King Frederick William of Prussia. There are two busts (I don't know of whom) flanking the latter picture; and a photograph of the old Royal castle of Goslar, Schiemann told me had been built by the Emperor Henry IV[35] and is kept up and liked by the present Emperor.

Several visitors came and went while I was waiting for the call from von Wedel. At 7 Meyer came for me – and Wedel told he thought I should see von Jagow[36] and perhaps the Chancellor at the front.

---

[34] Arthur Zimmermann (1854-1940) was appointed Germany's Foreign Secretary in November 1916 and owed his political eminence to his unwavering support for the Third Supreme Command, an effective military dictatorship led by Paul von Hindenburg and Erich Ludendorff. Towards the close of 1916, Zimmermann stated his full support for the military high command's decision to impose a highly controversial policy of unrestricted submarine warfare – the policy which eventually drew the U.S. into the war in April 1917. However he is best-known as the author of the infamous Zimmermann Telegram sent to the German Embassy in Mexico on 19 January 1917. The encrypted telegram effectively comprised an offer of German support for a Mexican invasion of the U.S. The thinking behind the telegram suggested that the U.S. would find itself too concerned with fighting a war with Mexico to direct its energies to the conflict in Europe. The British intercepted the telegram and using a captured German diplomatic codebook passed the contents of the plain-text telegram to President Woodrow Wilson. Its publication was initially met by stunned disbelief in American quarters, its contents widely considered implausible. Unfortunately Zimmermann inexplicably confirmed the authenticity of the telegram shortly afterwards. War between the U.S. and Germany commenced within a month. Zimmermann himself chose 'retirement' in August 1917.

[35] Heinrich IV reigned from 1056 to 1106, in troubled times marked by church and state struggles.

[36] Gottlieb von Jagow (1863-1935) served as Germany's Foreign Minister from 1914-16. With a diplomatic background – envoy to Luxembourg in 1907 and Italy in 1909 – he was appointed Wilhelm II's Foreign Minister after being the Foreign Office chief. He played the role of cautious, indeed pessimistic adviser to the somewhat more excitable Kaiser. An advocate of improved Anglo-German relations – among Germany's pre-war political elite he was almost alone in this approach – he expressed his concerns that Britain might not, as widely expected, remain neutral in the event of a continental European conflict. His role in the July Crisis of 1914 is however ambiguous; while he gave clear backing for Chancellor von Bethmann-Hollweg's support for Austria-Hungary's dealings with Serbia this was per-

He told me to tell Baron von Stumm[37] the chief of the political department of the F.O. whom I should find there "everything."

He then showed me the written copy of the <u>interview and declaration</u>[38] I had sent him on the 11th which had been sent to Headquarters and was now back amended and somewhat shortened. The first two sentences have been struck out altogether and it begins with the general statement of goodwill towards Ireland, and ends with my words "national prosperity and national freedom."

In its amended form it contains all the essentials I desire – and is given a more emphatic character as the opening few lines now reads:

"In reply to this enquiry made to the Under Secretary of State the Imperial Chancellor has directed the following Official Declaration to be issued."

The "interview" part remains as I had penned it save that they prefix to my name "the distinguished Irish nationalist" Sir Roger Casement. **[Inserted in pencil:]** I protested and begged to have this struck out – in vain. **[Above four paragraphs are omitted by Angus Mitchell from his *Berlin Diary*.]**

I got back the Christiania papers from von Wedel to show at the front, if necessary – and then I told him of the loss of Kuno Meyer's trunk and my fears that it might be his box of compromising papers. I pointed out that it might be as well to keep back the issue of the declaration until the truth was known, or even until we were sure that Kuno had reached New York safely. Von Wedel was anxious to issue the Declaration at once and told me he should

---

haps more in the hope that a general conflagration could be avoided via a united front than because he favoured war, although he acknowledged that war with Russia would eventually come. Jagow's background was not especially militaristic: he was sceptical of the Schlieffen Plan (and opposed its necessary invasion of neutral Belgium) and, as the war progressed, he opposed Naval Minister Alfred von Tirpitz's constant lobbying for the adoption of a policy of unrestricted submarine warfare, correctly predicting in the latter case America's ultimate entry into the war. When the German military setback at the first Battle of the Marne brought to an end Army Chief of Staff von Moltke's implementation of the Schlieffen Plan, von Jagow was prompt in urging a negotiated peace; without success. His firm opposition to Tirpitz's strategy of unrestricted submarine warfare ultimately (and predictably) cost him his position in November 1916. He played no further role in political affairs and died in 1935.

[37] Baron Wilhelm August von Stumm, younger son of Friedrich Adolf, industrialist, b. Frankfurt 1869, d. Berlin. 1935. Director of the *Politisches Amt* in the Foreign Office, later Unterstaatssekretär (Second Permanent Secretary), privy councillor and senior pro-war diplomat.

[38] Casement wrote in the margin "this the Declaration of Goodwill to Ireland". It was issued on 20 November 1914 and followed by 'The Treaty' on 28 December 1914 largely concerning the Irish Brigade.

"The declaration was a valuable first step, but it fell short of support for the cause of Irish independence and Casement continued to seek a fuller statement of German commitment. In this he was destined to be disappointed. (Ó Síocháin, p. 399)

like to give it out the next day. I agreed, provided they felt easy about the professor's journey – admitting that I might be over anxious in his regard.

I left von Wedel about 7.30 with his final good wishes for my journey to the front, and his kindly face smiling after me as I turned down the stairs.

Meyer met me outside and told me it was settled that he should accompany me to the front, as there was room in the motor car. He would call for me at 9.30 at the Hotel.

At 9 p.m. von Berckheim came with my guide and guard the Graf von Lüttichau – a baldish headed young Prussian nobleman. He was in uniform, that of the "Volunteer Automobile Corps." All the necessary papers were with him.

Meyer came, and all three came to my room, where we arranged for Adler's passport to be visé, so that he could leave for Moss on Saturday without danger of the "papers" I was giving him for Mr. Findlay's benefit being seized at the Sassnitz frontier on his way out of Germany. Bidding poor old Adler (who nearly wept!) good-bye, "Mr. Hammond", with his uniformed escort of the Baron and Count and his attaché Mr. Meyer, was bowed out of the hall by the manager and staff.

We walked round to the Friedrich Str Station and got our "compartment" with some difficulty and delay. The train was crowded – and a great many soldiers and officers in it – and some wounded going back "cured" – while stretchers were on the platform to have others carried off to the hospitals.

Finally we got off. The Count v. Lüttichau[39] and I in one carriage, Meyer going into a sleeping car as far as Hanover where he said he would have to leave the sleeper and come and disturb us for a seat.

Wednesday, 18 Novr.
We reached Cologne about 7.30 a.m. getting a fine view of the splendid old city from the bridge over the (always) hurrying Rhine. The last time that I had seen the Rhine was at Coblenz in May 1912, with Dick Morten and Brab Lake! What changes! to all the world – and to me.

At Cologne the motor car met us – a Herr Meckle,[40] with a young chauffeur, in the corps uniform, being with it. We got our things in and went at once, to the Dom Hotel on the square, looking out on the splendid Cathedral. The Cathedral is magnificent. Altho' so new, it looks old – and it soars up to heaven as if inspired with all the past of this glorious old city of the Rhine.

We went inside and found the nave filled with the devout – crowds of men and women kneeling and a priest I thought collecting – while far up in the

---

[39] Lüttichau's name is variously written by Casement as Luttachau, Lutterich, Lutterau, Luttenau, and Luttechau. He was Siegfried, Graf von Lüttichau, b. 1877, d. 1965.
[40] Probably Paul Meckel.

lighted chancel one could see and hear the distant chant of the choristers. Cologne they tell me is probably "four fifths Roman Catholic."

After a very hurried dejeuner – coffee and bread and butter – at the Dom Hotel – for which I paid m1.50 – we left for Headquarters. Meyer sat next me in the body of the car – the chauffeur ("Stephan" – an East Prussian youth of 21 or so) on one of the two sliding chair seats – and von Lüttichau in front next Meckle who drove the car. Two Mauser rifles (loaded) were fixed across the barrier in front of us, in a metal stand purposely made. It was bitterly cold – a hard white frost on all the roads – I was the only one without a fur coat – Meckle, von Lüttichau and the chauffeur had fur-lined leather coats – and Meyer a fine fur lined tweed.

We went off at a great rate and kept this up throughout the whole run only stopping once to show the papers to a guard over a railway bridge, at the other military posts, and they were many, the driver was known and allowed to go thro'.

The route taken was over the Eifel region – going high over the tops of that arid region, where snow lay in places, and through northern Luxembourg, into southern Belgium by Bastogne, through Neufchâteau and out into France near Sedan and so to Charleville-Mézières[41] where the Emperor and the Headquarters of the German Army and imperial Government are. The distance traversed they told me was 270 kilometres and as we did it in 6 hours and stopped (only for short spells to find the road or look at the wheels etc) many times our speed must have been fully 50 kilometres (if not more) per hour.

Our route from Cologne lay first to Euskirchen and then through pretty little towns to the high blank ridges of the Eiffel. South of us was Wittlich I had so delighted in with Dick Morten in May 1912[42] – but none of that pleasant region could be seen from this line of country. The cold was intense and despite fur-lined gloves my fingers ached so much I had to take the gloves off and sit on my hands for nearly an hour to restore circulation.

I dare say our highest point was 600 metres. There were many farms on these bare, treeless uplands of the Eifel – but all were wrapped in winter haze and frost covered the ground and the sprouts of "winter wheat" or rye more probably. We passed through small towns and villages to St Vith[43] and soon were going across northern Luxembourg and out into Belgium at Bastogne. Here we first saw houses burnt, roofless and blackened with tumbled walls sometimes – from shellfire. But not many. At Neufchâteau, both on entering and leaving the town there were a few such ruined houses – but these were

---

[41] Charleville-Mézières is the capital of the Ardennes department, in N.E. France, on the Meuse River, in Champagne.

[42] Casement's other companion in 1912 was Heinrich d'Oleire.

[43] St. Vith is now in Belgium but was then in Prussia's Rhine province.

the sole traces of war, beyond the numerous German soldiers at times met on the way, or Red Cross motors, or forage motors, we came across. Such Belgian country people as we met, or saw in the towns were going about their business. It was a day of general prayer, and everywhere there had been numbers of people at early mass. In Neufchâteau the townspeople seemed resigned enough, and save for the half dozen or so ruined houses one could never have guessed that this was a conquered land and people. Boys were playing marbles busily in the square of Neufchâteau.

We entered France by a road thro' Messincourt-Messimpre and were soon in Sedan of many memories.

Here again were very few traces of war or conquest – save that most of the fine houses had the shutters up – the families fled. The poor people who could not fly were there as usual, as along the countryside we had passed through. It was only on leaving Sedan to cross the Meuse we came across the first striking sign of the war. The fine bridge over the river, I remembered from 1912, was in the river – a few French labourers under a guard were repairing it – two tugboats lay also sunk deep on the opposite shore.

At Donchery a few miles out from Sedan, however, we saw the dread evidence of the recent combat. Donchery lay across the Meuse, on our right hand. There was scarcely a house uninjured. The whole town lay there roofless, empty and a mass of ruins. The church in the midst was a shapeless mass. The bridge destroyed – but as at Sedan, a temporary wooden bridge served.

An old priest, who came from the town, passed us with bare head. I would have saluted him, had he looked, but he kept his eyes to the ground. At Charleville and Mézières, we found the town bridges all destroyed, but temporary structures had been run up alongside them.

Here too, on the outskirts, were ruined and roofless houses – but in the two towns themselves – they are really one town divided by the winding Meuse – were but few traces of destruction. Soldiers were here in plenty, and motor cars go leór.[44] We drove to the former Prefecture now the residence of the Headquarters staff of the Great German Armies. Somewhere near, I knew, must be the Emperor himself.

We were shown in first to a room where a Lt. Nicolai (I think) received us where after Graf von Lüttichau and Meckle had retired, Meyer explained who I was. This officer, however, spoke no English. I gathered that the Baron Kurt von Lersner (whom I had last seen in the Ritz-Carlton in Madison Avenue!) would soon arrive – so as we were all of us starving we went to the former dining saloon of the Prefect, where an excellently simple luncheon was served by soldier servants. Other officers entered while we four took of

---

[44] go leór – Irish Gaelic word, origin of English word 'galore'.

the plentiful dish of stewed beef, macaroni and boiled potatoes, with a plain white wine – and then we adjourned to the absent Prefect's drawing-room – furnished in a yellow satin, poor Madame la Préfet – & had our coffee. Here von Lersner found us and after a brief delay Meyer & I went to his room upstairs where we discussed the matter of the "Irish Brigade" which is that nearest the heart of the General Staff I can clearly see.

Lersner told me of the steps being taken to collect the "Irish Catholic soldiers" who are prisoners of war, and to put them in one place where I could visit them. Nothing much has so far been done I gathered – their difficulty being largely that they don't know the difference between an Irishman and an Englishman! All are "Englander" to them. However, after explaining things to von Lersner and discussing too the matter of the chaplain for the Irish prisoners, and even the possibility of sending one or two of the men, released, back to Ireland to try and get a good priest to come here – as well as to tell the Provisional Committee of the Volunteers what I am doing here – I left Lersner with the understanding that, as soon as a few score even, or some hundreds of Irish prisoners – authentic Irish – are collected they will let me know and I shall go to the camp to interview the men.

Leaving Lersner we found von Lüttichau and Meckle and after a quest for "quarters" we got a "billet" for the night in the Hotel de Commerce of Charleville. This we found with some difficulty and found there only one manservant in charge. He was a Luxemburger named Joseph left in charge when the personnel of the hotel had fled at the German approach.

Joseph showed us very cold rooms and said there was no food or hot water, or electric light even in the hotel. All had gone. He got his daily "ration" from somewhere. He had only a few bits of candles and these he doled out to us. We next visited Meckle's quarters, which were in a private house. The family all save one lady had fled, like all the rest of the well-to do Charleville population. Only the poor remained – and as "Joseph" explained to me they were better here with the Germans than starving homeless fugitives in "outlands." They, the poor, had their passes and got their daily food somehow served out to them. For the rest they were in no danger as long as they stayed in their prescribed districts and had their proper papers. He showed me his military "pass" which allowed him to be out till 11 p.m. if he liked. Meckle's landlady lived with some family that had not fled, but came daily to the house where he and some other officers were billeted and sat knitting, poor lady, in her empty salon! This we entered. She was away – but her knitting was on the table. A grand piano was there with a plentiful stock of music – Schubert, Mozart, Beethoven – as I remarked to von Lüttichau "nearly all German music."

Finally I returned with Lüttichau to the Hotel de Commerce – for I was told I must go nowhere by myself. One of the gentlemen had to be always with me – for my own safety. Guards were everywhere through the streets, and patrols – and as my pass was with the General Staff and I could speak no German it was far too dangerous for me to be out alone.

At the Hotel Meyer met me and said he had been to the "Foreign Office" – in a fine building in the Avenue Delafare – where he had arranged for Baron von Stumm the head of the political department to see me at 9.30 a.m. on the morrow. It was decided that after this interview I should return to Berlin – and Lüttichau begged me to try and get thro' my interview with von Stumm by 10.30 a.m. so that we might return by Dinant, Namur and Liège. This, a much longer route back to Cologne would be far more interesting as we should pass thro' some of the most famous spots of the opening stages of the war. Meyer had got a pass for his dinner and mine at one of the officers messes in some private house where his friend at the "Foreign Office" told him to take me early as we should then find it "nearly empty."

On getting there about 6.30 we entered after showing our pass to the grounds of a sort of a large villa or even a Casino[45] it seemed. Here were again military servants one of whom took us in hand and asked many questions about me – He deposited us finally at one of seven long tables – at which I counted in all 128 chairs. There were some 30 or 40 officers already at table – we bowed to them and they to us.

The servant brought a book in which Meyer wrote his name and mine, "Mr. Hammond of New York." I noticed Meyer getting more and more perturbed. At length the servant came and said something to him and he went out, leaving me alone to go on with some tough hard sausage and bread and red wine. In a minute Meyer returned and told me I was "wanted to speak with someone" out in the Hall.

Here I found an old officer in a grey frock coat with General's stripes on his shoulders.

He clicked his heels and bowed formally and I bowed without the heel Klick. He then asked me who I was, where I had come form, what I was doing at the General staff and who had "asked me to come" there. All this in slow, good English. I said I was Mr. H of New York – that I had come from Berlin where Baron von Berckheim had called on me asking me to come to the General Staff and that I believed that I had come at the direct request and invitation of Baron von Lersner whom I knew in America. He then shook hands with me, said he hoped I should be interested and that he would see me again. We then returned to our places at the table, after more

---
[45] Kasino was a German officers' mess

very courteous bows, and Meyer begged me to "hurry up" and get away before any further contretemps arose.

So I left with no more than a bite of cold sausage and a piece of bread and when in the garden Meyer said he was really alarmed for me – and that I must get back to the Hotel at once and stay there in my room till morning. He explained that all explanations <u>might</u> come too late! "You might get arrested by any patrol, and speaking English and with no means of explaining yourself and no papers on you you might very well be shot in a jiffy, before any of us would know." So I was hurried back in the motor car at about 7.30 to the Hotel where I found Joseph in the dreary "Kitchen", a Kitchen with no food! To Joseph I talked for ½ an hour, on the plea I was cold and wanted to get warm before going up to the icy bedroom. Joseph confirmed there was not even coffee in the hotel, and that in the morning, we should have to go to the "Gare" to get our cup of coffee, that was the only place in all Charleville where one could <u>buy</u> a cup of coffee!

After exchanging condolences with Joseph until 8, when his wife and a friend came to give him his evening coffee I went to my bedroom. Fearing the very damp sheets of a very cold, uninhabited inn, I wrapped my woollen comforter round my neck and my Irish rug round my body and then got into bed thus well protected by thick layers of wool from contact with the cold touch of the sheets.

I slept on & off till 8 a.m. on

<u>Thursday</u> 19 Novr (Charleville & back to Cologne & en route to Berlin)

When von Lüttichau came in to call me from his room next door and take me off to the station to get our morning coffee.

We went on foot, and after a dose of truly abominable coffee in the buffet of the station where some officers were already at winis [**work?**] too, we visited a barbers opposite at a small shop, sandwiched in between two wings of the Hotel du Nord. The barber boy was a young German in charge of the (fled) Frenchman's shop. He shaved v. Lüttichau while I bought chocolates and photos of the wrecked bridges over the Meuse at Mézières-Charleville.

At the Hotel I had to wait till nearly 10 for Meyer to come with the car and take me to the "Foreign Office." Here, after a brief delay I was shown into a fine airy big writing room where a clean shaven man of some 48 or 50, I judged, in a brown uniform and riding boots was standing We bowed and shook hands and Meyer left us alone. The conversation that followed was of great interest. Baron von Stumm spoke perfect English and told me of more than one talk he had had with Sir E. Grey. Of Grey's abilities he had a poor opinion – a mediocre intelligence, an inferior man, how is it that they think him so wonderful in England? I confessed I shared very largely his opinion of Grey's abilities, altho' I did not doubt his honesty, to which estimate the Baron subscribed.

Most of the talk was mine. He asked about the Christiania incident and I described it fully and he agreed with me that it was well worth while to try and get Mr. Findlay "caught in the act" through my Man Adler – and then to make the whole story public and try and get him turned out of Norway.

We talked of the Volunteers in Ireland, of Redmond's recruiting dodges; of "Home Rule" and of the prospects of keeping the Irish out of the army. I explained the Irish position to him clearly and closely. He admitted he knew nothing about it – that he had once been in Ireland (on a hunting trip I fancy) but that he knew nothing of the feelings of the people.

I told him of my larger hope – "a dream if you will" – of an independent Ireland emerging from this war and he at once said it would be to Germany's interest to have an independent Ireland. I said "Yes – to the interest of Europe at large." As to the Volunteers and why we were not armed already I explained the situation in Ireland and how the British had "closed the ports" as soon as the Irish Volunteers were started on 15th Nov. 1913 – "just over a year ago." I said that Germany had herself very largely to blame for the position in which she found herself today – and he agreed. I said "Why did you not make friends before the war with those who had reason to oppose England? – why did you not <u>think</u> of Ireland?

He replied – "that is the best proof of our innocence, of our sincerity towards England – we believed she could be kept neutral – while she was plotting against us – Had we known – had we acted as <u>she</u> did we should have had agents in Ireland, in Egypt, in India." As regards my "larger hope" he talked frankly. Germany had no objection, on the contrary only the desire to do it, <u>if possible</u>, but that while he fully expected Germany would win the war against France and Russia, and so conclude a general and, for her, successful peace, he did not know how far she could prosper in her fight with England towards the point of "<u>imposing</u> conditions of peace there." That was all uncertain. There was no immediate or even probable prospect of the German Fleet gaining a great victory, so as to clear the seas and render the transport of men and arms to Ireland possible. Were there, it would not be unlikely.

He believed the war <u>must</u> end soon – that none of the combatants, except England, could carry it on for a long period. France would go first – next Russia – perhaps both together.

And here a trenchant phrase was uttered. "We will make peace with France – we pity them too – they and the Belgians will learn that England is responsible for their miseries – not Germany. <u>But what we hold we will keep</u>"!⁴⁶

It is this phrase rings in my ears. The Baron expressed himself deliberately, and the prospect it offers is, indeed for Belgium and France a dreadful one. "What we hold we will keep"! He was quite emphatic in declaring that the German armies could not be driven back. Where they were they stayed – and it was only a questions of months, possibly weeks, when the French and Russian endurance – and materiel – would give out.

We shall see. I do not think he was over confident as to the powers of resistance or of maintenance of the present lines of the German armies – but I think it is highly possible that to secure a just and binding peace in Europe and so leave Germany free to tackle England – the Sea Serpent – the Baron's chiefs would agree to give up what they hold. Otherwise the war <u>will</u> go on for years – despite his estimate of French weakness – for neither France nor Belgium will agree, one to a dreadful dismemberment – the other to extinction.

I told him England would go on for years – He agreed she might, but asked "What can she do to us? She can't get near Germany. Her fleet is become a laughing stock. Her empire will and must break up – her diplomacy has been childish – for she has risked everything, more than we – and in future any little state like Norway or Holland with a fleet of submarines can bottle all the British navy up in to ports. Thus while she may have been able to destroy our external trade she has not been able to use her fleet against ours or directly against our coasts. She cannot come near us. Her position has become ridiculous." ~~and in the future any small power can hold up her trade with a few submarines.~~

I said that England counted on wearing Germany down "as she did Napoleon" – that she would not care for the destruction of France – she would always counsel France to continue, even a hopeless resistance, as she did the Belgians at Antwerp – and rely on her ability to beget fresh forces for Germany and to redress the injured balance of Power in Europe by calling in Asia, Africa, America. I pointed out that I was <u>sure</u> England counted on getting the United States in the field against Germany in the end – certainly if the war should go on against England. Her steps to this end had already been taken and I was convinced that if by chance the German fleet won a considerable victory (he shrugged his shoulders) There would go up a preconcerted and organised howl throughout the American press on behalf of "the Motherland" – of a threatened "common civilisation" and that England would spare no effort, no money, no means to compelling the Washington administration to take sides on her threatened behalf. Further there was

---

⁴⁶ Probably in the German, "Was wir halten, das behalten wir".

Japan, and the grave possibility of the Japanese being brought to Europe in the end. The danger to Germany was a "war of years" – as England predicted. Von Stumm agreed that Germany could not go on for years as England might, but that there was any possibility of France or Russia holding on, even as long as Germany, he did not agree. Germany must win so far as her land frontiers lay and land forces went – but he was by no means confident of her ability to get at England "this time."

If she did, "my dream" might come true! It would accord with her policy and interests. We discussed briefly, I more than he, the Declaration his Government had made at my instance and which I said I presumed would be issued that very day – I pointed out that while it went far on the road of our wishes it did not say all we wanted – and the fullest fruits could not be hoped from it alone – but that I was not "impossible" and did not want them today to go further than they felt was wise.

We were agreed in aim – and as to the means to attain it I knew this lay on the lap of the gods – and I was content to go on with the hope that the fortune of war would more and more bring about the possible realisation of my larger hope.

Von Stumm was clearly interested in our talk, and it was I who rose to leave and end the interview after fully an hour – He would have even kept me – but I pulled out my watch – it was 11.15 – and said I should not detain him longer – Meyer was waiting outside the door – and after a second farewell in the corridor to which he accompanied me I bade the Baron and the travelling Foreign Office adieu and hurried downstairs and back in the motor car to the Hotel de Commerce to get my things, to pay "Joseph" a pourboire of 5 marks – instead of anything to the Hotel for the nights–lodging – and then to pick up Meckle and von Lüttichau at the rooms of the former.

When these were settled in the car and everything aboard it was nearly noon – and fully midday when altogether we steered out of Charleville on the road to Rocroi. The market place or grand place was showering a sprinkling of women and men with vegetables, carts and country produce – an attempt at a market. The women looked less downcast than the men. Small boys even begged from us smiling for "zehn pfennig!" – in bad German. An old woman with white hair came up to us while waiting outside Meckle's rooms and I heard her pleading voice and the words "dans la misère." I gave her 5 marks in spite of Meckle's protest that "they all do this." I said it might be so – but they were "all in great trouble and misery" to which he and Lüttichau agreed. They remonstrated more at the amount than at the act – saying 50 pfennigs would have been enough.

(I had noticed during the hurried walks the previous evening to and from the officers' mess that townswomen were walking about with, or even waiting for, German soldiers! There was no doubt of it. I noticed more than one case – this to my mind gave convincing proof rather of "misery" than of immorality.) I did not tell my German friends of what I had noticed in this respect – for they would scarcely have understood my feeling I fancy.)

As we left Charleville – the ruined outskirts were often a new source of regret – the road to Rocroi lay northwards and upwards. The frost was strong and enduring, the fields and trees covered with it – and the air still and sharp. A few cabs came past – but as yesterday, the vast majority of vehicles met were either automobiles, like our own, with men in uniform, or large wagon motors of red cross comforts or of provisions, rarely with escorts, usually alone or in troops of cars – but once or twice we met horsemen – going through a strip of wood as we neared Rocroi we met a telegraph party out putting up a new wire through the forest – some trees were felled or being felled – and the second line being stretched along the existing single line.

Rocroi lies high, fully 1,400 feet above the sea. We did not enter the village or the fortress. We skirted the outer dry moat of the grass fortifications, diamond pointed Vauban[47] – constructed may be – and went on through largely abandoned suburbs and damaged houses and into the open hill country looking across the steep valley of the Meuse as it wound into the deep wooded hills of the Ardennes. The view here was splendid – despite mist and wintry gloom.

The steep cleft where the Meuse penetrates the Ardennes lay to our right the wooded hills on the far side being, I judged, close on 1000 feet above the gorge – Tufts of white mist clung to the sides of the hills and of the gorge itself – Every tree and shrub was like a fairy tree – each twig and branch a delicate branch of silver – and afar the frosted trees shone white on the darker ground.

Soon we came to the top of the ridge and the road stretched down before us, with great curves and sweeping angles into Fumay on the Meuse itself. We descended rapidly and ran thro' Fumay without pause. Here were many burnt houses – but the town was peopled again and shops and open and people moving about their affairs – We were soon through this pretty little town and running along a fine smooth road that followed the left bank of the Meuse. The river about 100 yards broad – and deep brown. Every bridge was down. Some totally wrecked – others only partially injured – In some cases the piles alone had been blown up – and the iron superstructure had collapsed in the middle into the river, the two ends standing intact. In nearly all cases where a bridge had been thus destroyed by the retreating French, the

---

[47] Marshall Vauban (1633-1707), Louis XIV's famous military engineer

invaders, (now the occupying tenants) had run up alongside, or in the near vicinity a wooden structure on piles that served all the immediate needs of road transport, but not of railway.

In several cases the wrecked bridges themselves had been already repaired – in one notable case, just before reaching Givet, the entire iron superstructure which had not been injured by the explosion that caused its collapse into the stream had been lifted again, well nigh intact, and as we passed it was being used in the ordinary way. Several of the (older) stone bridges of massive masonry had had only one or two arches blown up and in these cases German Engineers had already bridged the cavities with temporary ironwork and the bridges were again in use.

From Fumay we ran alongside the Meuse almost the whole way when the river made wide curves and the road took the short cut. Villages and little towns on both banks, nearly all showed traces of the havoc wrought no doubt so often by the retreating defenders as by the invading foe. What greatly struck me was that in several cases there were villages in close proximity, or little townships, one of which would be almost entirely destroyed, the burnt and shattered frameworks of roofless and wall-less houses alone marking the site, while less than 400 yards away a similar village would present an entirely undamaged front and its inhabitants were going about their business seemingly unconcerned.

At Givet we came across the first evidence of a shattered fortress. Here on the cliff top more than 150 feet above the river I should say – perhaps 200 feet, the ridge was crowned with the stone wall and turreted bastions of a type of fortification no longer erected I imagine. Fine to look upon but of little use against modern guns. This battlement shows pregnant gaps where the German guns, from the hills across the river had battered it. At its foot, and between the roadway and the river, a long stone building of three stories – fully 250 yards long – which had been the caserne of a considerable French force was riddled with shell fire. Not a window remains – the walls had holes in them a coach and four could have gone through – the floors had often collapsed, and a great part of the roof was piled up in the mounds of debris that choked the basement. Givet itself had not suffered so greatly – although we could not see much of it as our car sped through. It was necessary to hasten, as by this much longer route it would take us all our time to reach Cologne in time for the night train to Berlin.

Soon after leaving Givet we crossed the Frontier into Belgium – the former customs notice at the barrier "Alt Douane" still held out its arm across the road – but we had no customs search to pass for today there is no Belgium!

Several of the road inspection posts here at which we halted an instant were in charge of Saxon troops for the green and white standard of Saxony was often visible. The river cliffs as we drew near Dinant were perfectly charming. Great crags and peaks and pinnacles of grey limestone (I think) often garbed thick with dark green ivy, and crowned with a forest of birch and hazel and aspen trees rose some hundreds of feet sharp from the banks of the Meuse.

We burst two tyres almost together when between Hermiton and Anserem and stopped just at a beautiful chateau that was built right on the roadway with gardens, stables hothouses and a perfect little forest park at the back and sides. Von Lüttichau, who told me he was a landowner himself and farmed all his own lands, went in by the fine gateway to the courtyard. I followed – and he soon found out from some Uhlans quartered there that the chateau belonged to a Belgian Baron "quelconque" who was at the front (in France poor man!) with his King and the remnant of the Belgian army. While Mme. la Baronne still kept house at home for the Uhlans. These were certainly very well behaved. One young trooper came down to the river with a pail for water and von Lüttichau talked with him. He had been invalided home sick, and was not yet recovered – but he had egged to be allowed to return to the front – and here he was with his troop again. We entered the gardens – they were in excellent state – and the hothouse was well heated, and some noble blooms of chrysanthemums in fine flower. Evidently Mme la Baroness had courteous and scrupulous guests.

At Dinant we saw the great fortress (on the right bank) similar to that at Givet, but with no visible signs of wreckage at all. Even the notices "entrée à la forteresse" – "Hotel Lion d'Or" &c &c on the summit of the cliffs were quite undamaged. The cliff drops sheer, a fall of 250 or 300 feet from the centre of the fortress to the town, where at the foot a platform of land lies on which the old church or cathedral stood. It still stands, but it showed many traces of the heavy fire – and the houses in its immediate vicinity are only a shapeless mass of rubble – a pile of dead bricks and mortar. The bridge that connects the two banks, right in front of the Cathedral had been well blown up – but parties of Belgian under guard were repairing it slowly, while a wooden improvised bridge 60 or 70 yards upstream connected the two banks and was full of traffic as we passed. Meyer explained that all the gangs of French or Belgian workers we had seen at work on bridges or roadways were paid for their labour. In many cases I noticed houses that had been greatly damaged by shell fire already well on their way to recovery, floors, windows, roofs &c &c all being put in. The left bank of Dinant had suffered less than the right – and as we passed slowly on out of the town we passed many people some boys were playing see-saw – and we got courteous speech from any one we made enquiry of.

Through similar scenes of destruction tempered by clearest evidence of law and order erected on its base we passed always down the left bank of the Meuse, through many charming resorts, with chateaux old and new and pretty villas and well built villages and townlets to Namur – Here we stopped to lunch (at 3.20 p.m.) in a restaurant that was indicated to Meckle by the headquarters of the Automobile Volunteers Corps at which we first stopped.

The great stone fortress on the cliff or hill rather here – for it was a grassy slope rather than a precipice or at first and Dinant showed absolutely not trace of fire – several bridges were down, but the chief bridge, an old one of stone over the Meuse, had been restored this we were told was the "oldest bridge in Belgium" – we crossed the Sambre too, in leaving the town by a different road with a Bavarian Catholic priest who besought a passage to Liège. (He was in the Army I presume – a chaplain).

The City Hall and buildings near it were terribly shattered – and yet along side these piles of destruction shops were open, people moving about and no sign of war! Little boys were selling picture postcards – and I bought a batch of them from a nice little chap of ten or eleven with whom I talked in French outside the restaurant. Beggars too came – just as usual and besought alms or help from the enemy!

From Namur, we crossed the Meuse to the right bank, and with the priest explaining certain points of interest to the others we hurried on to Andenne. A good part of the destruction we saw was caused by Belgians themselves. Thus all the bridges for instance were their handiwork – and as artillery fire is mutual very much of the damage we saw was caused by the defenders – thus the priest pointed out a ruined factory across the river which the Belgians themselves had destroyed. At Andenne, Meckle stopped the car to show me a gruesome sight and tell a horrible story.

First the story.

After the first passage of the German Army, when Andenne was already in German hands, a long column of German ammunition with a smallish escort was passing through Andenne on its way to the front – the town had already submitted and all the Belgian soldiers were scores of miles away. At a signal, <u>given from the church</u>, the church bells ring out, and from all sides rifle fire was opened on the German column. Many men were killed – the punishment was not as at Louvain to destroy part of the town, but to seize a number of the men and shoot them then and there. Three hundred and fifty men were thus arrested, taken to the river front, lined up against a brick wall surrounding an empty yard and shot, and buried in two long graves between the wall of execution and the river. I was taken to this spot.

[Paragraph omitted by Mitchell:] The wall showed many traces of where the bullets had spattered and broken the brick work – Dashes of lime I fancy on the wall itself and at the foot of it told their own story – the two graves lay a few yards out from the wall – the mound over them were perhaps a couple of feet high and were covered with flowers – chiefly chrysanthemums – some in pots even – and with wreaths while a bedding of lime told the same story of sanitary precaution that was written across the wall. The flowers were accompanied by numberless cards and "in memoriam" writings. Poor wives, sons, daughters, mothers! I nearly wept as I looked at these pitiable evidences of a sorrow that is now, perhaps, the chief national asset of the Belgian people. One card to "notre cher époux et père" I bent over.

There were people there too – some of the mourners doubtless. Two workmen in corduroys were bending over the graves when we came up. They moved off – with averted faces. Some women and children, and a well dressed family were there too – but they slowly withdrew from the spot at the sight of the uniforms. How little these poor folk could have guessed that one man of that group was no German – but was a very "British Consul" who had indicted their sovereign and his abominable Congolese system ten years before.

Sometimes I must confess when the present "Agony of Belgium" confronts me – and it cannot well be minimised it is in truth a national agony – I feel that there may be in their awful lesson to the Belgian people a repayment. All that they now suffer and far more, they, or their king, his government and his officers wreaked on the well nigh defenceless people of the Congo basin. And with no such reason as the Germans. Germany offered Belgium fair terms – she asked only a "right of way" to meet her foemen face to face on French soil. Belgium refused – at the instigation of England and preferred the arbitrament of arms. She relied on English promises and French support. Where are these today? Criminal as he was, Leopold II would never have landed his country in the awful plight this morally better King Albert has placed it in. Leopold before he opposed the German demand by force would have made England show her hand. He would have called her cards. He would have said, "Yes, that's all very well to defend my neutrality! But can I do it? What help can you give? Where is your army – where your guns that are going to ensure the inviolability of Belgium if I resist the Germans?"

And if that question had been put – as it should have been put by the ruler of these betrayed people what answer could England have made? She could not defend "Belgian neutrality" and she knew it right well. She deliberately for her own selfish ends, in order to hinder, damage and weaken the German forces, put Belgium into the fire. However blameable Germany may be from the standpoint of international morality in forcing her way through Belgium, England is infinitely more blameworthy. For England knew she could not help the Belgians. She knew her promises of support were worthless. She knew that if Belgium resisted the weight of an irresistible invasion must crush the Belgian people to the earth and lay waste their thriving and prosperous country. All this she knew and yet Sir E. Grey telegraphs to the Br. Minister in Brussels before war breaks out that he urgently begs the Belgian Govt to "defend its neutrality" at all costs! What a crime! Here, these two graves at Andenne, and the looks in the faces of the population as we pass away from it – dejected, scowling, uneasy and with all the evil of latent ill–will in many glances – should be laid at the feet of the British Minister and I though too of von Stumm's firm statement – "We keep what we hold"!

God in Heaven! What will it mean to these poor conquered people in the end if that be the irrevocable intention of the German Government!

That phrase has been ringing in my ears all the morning since I left Charleville and the "Foreign Office."

There they are – the German legions stretching now from the north sea, almost, on the French frontier (at Nieuport) right down through some of the fairest parts of France, through the chief steel, coal, iron and textile manufacturing districts with a large part of the champagne district in their power to the Vosges near Switzerland. All Belgium, save a tiny strip less in size than Middlesex perhaps, and probably a <u>twelfth</u> part of the area of France with a normal population of 3.500.000 or 4.000.000 of French men and women and that the centre of the principal French industries are now held by German troops. A ring of iron, trenched in blood and bones of a million dead and wounded Germans stretches now from the Channel to almost in sight of Paris, and holds in a hand of steel what France will die rather than give up! How will it end?

Of the German ability to "stay where they are" I have little doubt. All French and British efforts to break that line of blood and iron I believe must fail. And as that line remains, or even perhaps advances, France shrinks. Even the stationary line means a shrinking France. For it is thus.

The, say, 15000 square miles of France now held by Germany represents a very great proportion of French industrial production. The remainder of France, every day growing weaker in blood – and materiel too – is deprived of a part of its framework essential to national well–being. But not only is this rich region in German hands, and so aiding German effort against the rest of France by furnishing its products to German and not to French armies, but the many fugitives from this region are now a charge on the rest of France. Say 1.000.000 (at outside) of the 3. to 4. millions of this region fled at the approach of the Germans. How are they living? At whose expense? They constitute an added burden the remaining 11/12ths of France has to bear in addition to the awful strain of bearing up against that solid wall of steel from Armentières to below Verdun that threatens every week to begin a further move south west. The break may come at any moment, as all my German friends think and say. France, they assert – as von Stumm did – will not be able to support the strain for more than three months longer – Once the break begins, it enlarges – it increases. The break at the front will mean the break at the heart, and a point must be reached where France will be forced to say "Enough" – England may intrigue, may plot, may beseech, may subsidise with gold and food and supplies – but is Men will win the fight.

That is the German gospel of this war. They are sure of their men; confident of their manhood and convinced that "what we hold we can keep." I thought all this and much more as we hurried through the conquered lines of French and Belgian towns and villages. I seemed to see in the eyes of many – in France the dejection of face and bearing was more apparent than in Belgium – of those we passed on the wayside, a question – Their glance was afar. Their hearts, their souls were straining far south and west where by Rheims and Soissons, by Laon and Verdun – and westward by Arras and Amiens, the roar of French gave back shot for shot to German fire.

Will those guns ever draw nearer? – will the boom of cannon come up from the south and west? Will France ever come back? That was the question I thought I saw in every eye – a haunting dreadful, fear that this present nightmare of today would prove to be reality and not a dream! That never again would Charleville or Mézières, or Rocroi or Givet see the red and blue of a French uniform but only the smoke grey coat of the new owner, that never again would French life, French speech, French mirth be in these streets – save as the badge of the conquered. "Joseph" at the Hotel de Commerce I could see had something of this fear – altho' a Luxemburger. He put the blame on England! The education of the conquered goes quickly.

Surely this land I passed through today never saw a stranger sight than that I witnessed! As our car topped the western heights beyond Rocroi and we began the descent towards the great cleft in the wooded hills where I knew the Meuse was clearing its way through the Ardennes I looked out on a scene that Caesar and his legions must once have eyed with something of awe. The vast spread of forested hills was the same probably today as then – the same white frosted trees, the same tufted break of cloud half hiding half showing where the Meuse flowed into the northern hills. Only the men had changed – and these not much in mind. In place of Caesar you have the Kaiser! And Gaul is still the quarry. The Belgae that that first of the Kaisers was then advancing against perhaps by this very gap through Fumay and Givet have heard the tramp of many legions since those of Rome crossed the Meuse.

But what were the wars of Rome, the legions of Caesar compared to those of Berlin, to the army corps of the Kaiser! Germany today, Major Lothes told me last week, has seven millions of men under arms! France, (poor France!)

must have fully four millions. Austria Hungary must have from four to five millions now – to say nothing of the millions she has lost! – While Russia, who can tell what millions of men she has gathered or is gathering for this world slaughter!

And England –.

England that is chiefly responsible for the war, that stands to draw the surest profit from it and already counts the gains of the "captured German trade" – what has England contributed of British flesh and blood to hold up the cause she was the chief instrument in erecting? What has the chief conspirator against Germany given of her own lifeblood to this vast conspiracy of murder directed against the mightiest of European peoples?

According to Mr. Asquith, in a recent speech, she has "sent to the Continent" a force of less than 100.000 men!

It is incredible – and I do not believe it. But, at the outside she has certainly not offered her "allies" more than 200.000 men and fully one third (or more) of them would be Irish and Scotch.

The best test of the sacrifices each party to this awful war has made lies in the mortality returns. The killed and wounded are the evidence that nothing controverts. How does England stand here? Of all the combatants engaged the "British" losses are incredibly the least.

Mr. Asquith is reported in a recent London message to Berlin press to have stated in parliament that the total British losses since the outbreak of the war amounted to 57.000 men – killed, wounded and missing. Lord Newton, I see, in a later speech, denies the accuracy of the Prime Minister's statement and puts the figure at 80.000 men.

But of these, how many are killed? I gather that the death list is well under 10.000 men (on land – the figures, I fancy, are not referable to the sea fighting).

There are no published figures yet of Belgian losses – but we know that the Belgian dead alone must be at least three times, possibly five times the British. A recent German casualty list brought the total of Prussian losses up to 549.247 officers and men killed and wounded – this excluded the losses of the Bavarian, Saxon and Württemberg armies that are estimated at not less than 400.000 and these returns deal only with casualties notified up to the middle of October, while the British return was to date – say 12 November. A recent return (published in the Milan *Corriere de la Sera* of 19 Nov.) gives with precision the Austro–Hungarian losses "during the first three months of the war." Here they are.

<u>Killed</u>
Officers   4,612.
Men   215.175   =   219.787

<u>Wounded</u>
Officers   2111
Men   481.965   =   494.076

Missing i.e. prisoners & dead –
Officers   2252
Men   187.191   =   <u>189.443</u>
            Grand total   903.306.

    The infamy of the English position could scarcely be more clearly defined than by contrasting British losses with British share in provoking the war and the gains to be derived from it with the losses suffered by all the other combatants.

    England is to secure the trade of the world, the destruction of the German navy and of the German mercantile marine, the crippling of German industries and the acquisition of German colonies at the loss of a few thousand of her poorer classes and these, be it noted, to be as carefully drawn from the "Celtic fringe" as the gullibility of the "Celtic" temperament will cheerfully permit. In fine, the "sacrifices" England proposes making are to be mainly those of Irish boys and men – but the "captured" trade will not go to Ireland! The case is so lucidly put by the English themselves that I need only quote from the *Liverpool Daily Post* of 12 September best to establish my argument from the mouth of the enemy himself:–

    Commenting on the then call for 500.000 soldiers made by Kitchener an editorial writer pointed out that they could not be raised <u>in England</u> without "a derangement of its industry." He therefore urged the "signing of the Home Rule Bill" because then the King "could make a triumphal tour of Ireland north, south, east and west and in reply to his personal appeal there would be 300.000 Irishmen of all creeds and classes for the front in less than a week. In <u>England</u> the question becomes more and more important in the interests of the efficiencies of our trade whether we can spare any more skilled mechanics for the ranks of hate, The capture of the German trade is almost as vital to the existence of the Empire as the destruction of Prussian militarism and this can be done solely by maintaining our workshops and plant in the highest state of efficiency."

    Here we have the case put with that charming naiveté so characteristic of the English pickpocket when chez soi. Let an Irishman, a German, an "enemy" accuse England of fighting this war for the sake of commercial profit and he is greeted with the figure of Sir Edward Grey assuring the world that England is inspired by a "high moral purpose, to defend the Public Law of Europe and maintain the sanctity of treaties" – or of that even more contemptible character Asquith fulminating at Edinburgh on behalf of the "small nations" a victorious Prussian militarism would crush beneath the heel of its jack boot. And while these fine speeches are being made, the Govt making them plans, I believe, the biggest fraud ever yet worked off against that "small nation" Ireland – by offering it a post obit "a promissory note payable after death" as I truly called it in my appeal of 17 Sept to the young men of Ireland, in the shape of the Home Rule Bill "placed on the Statute Book" in return for the life blood of all young Ireland. A people who, on the same Government's official return shows, lost over 5.000 of its inhabitants last year (deaths and immigration exceeded the births in 1913 by 5497 – the figures were

1913	Births	100.094
	Deaths	74.894
	Emigrants	30.697

– are to "flock to the colours" in Lord Crewe's phrase because the British Govt has kindly signed a piece of waste paper.

In return for a partial promise to allow Ireland to erect a debating society on the banks of the Liffey at some wholly unspecified future date, Irishmen today are to give 300.000 men to the shambles in France and Flanders in order that the Englishmen, who is too valuable himself to be put in danger may "capture the German trade."

I rejoice mightily in my treason when I read these things – and think of those oleaginous scoundrels, like Haldane – quivering masses of blubber – who are so busy killing the Kaiser with their mouth while trying to seduce my brave hearted countrymen to do the real killing – or be killed themselves.

If my treason does nothing else but save Ireland from this I shall have deserved well of my country. To keep you young men at home, for the future of our own country and for all her needs that is the counsel every true Irishman should give today. Thank God I came to Germany – and God be praised for the aid this people and their Government are giving Ireland today!

But this long digression leaves me between Andenne and Liège – in a hurrying motor car, with cold and darkness gathering in intensity –

We sped on through Huy past many factories, some silent, some at work until moments later we came to the outskirts of Liège – or Lüttich as my German friends call it.

We had some trouble in getting to the bridge – as the two that Meckle first steered for were down, and guarded – but we found a splendid bridge, with four columns of victory winged angels on top, two at each end – and over this we entered the busy part of Liège on the north bank of the Meuse. The river seems to be divided here into separate branches – so that more than one bridge is needed to cross it. The broad reach of the Meuse as we saw it from this big bridge was very fine, looking downstream, with a blaze of light from the city and a shining well lit riverside walk. We left the Bavarian priest at what had been the City Hall I presume – an imposing building on the Grand Place. It is now the headquarters of the German military Governor – and orderlies, autos, motors, soldiers were coming and going. The streets were full of life – the shops well lit and the tram cars running filled with people – In fact, from inside no one could possibly say this city had recently been carried by assault and was now in the hands of a "horde of barbarians" – *vide* the Anglo-Saxon press of England and England's dutiful daughter the United States of North America. Of all the lies England has distributed in recent years throughout the world, by her admirable system called "free trade", I guess this lie of German barbarism and German atrocities is the most wilful, the most perverse and the most evil intentioned.

As we hurried out of Liège, through crowded streets, past well lit windows and along pleasant squares and esplanades I thought of the pictures of Liège I had formed in New York and Philadelphia when the Anglo-Saxon lies were walking the streets of those cities. I suppose there is no people in the world so gullible as the Americans. That is doubtless why they invented poker. But the original poker fact must have come from England – and I am convinced it came in the "Mayflower", with an extraordinary pedigree behind it too and a family bible printed on the backs of the cards.

Leaving Liège, the suburbs, again on the south bank of the Meuse which we recrossed by another bridge lower down stream, we stopped to ask the way from a crowd of workmen, A gendarme officer, a Belgian gendarme bien entendu, replied and offered to guide us.

He jumped on the footboard and we invited him into the car – and he took us up about 2 miles of our way on the road to Aachen – Charlemagne's city of Aix. This gendarme – he was an officer too – explained that the people were "quite tranquil" now, and no trouble threatened. His talk was friendly enough and his manner too. The ordinary civil and criminal courts, Lüttichau and Meyer explained to me were working as usual in Belgium and I noticed the ordinary gendarmes on duty in the streets – without arms or sidearms. The only armed men in Belgium today – east of Ypres and Dixmunde! – are German soldiers. After the treacheries of Louvain, Andenne, Termonde, Tirlemont &c. &c., it would indeed be madness for the army of the conqueror to leave arms in the hands of the population of their representatives. Meckle told me he had been shot at, in his car, at Tirlemont when going with despatches and that his earlier journeys thro' Belgium had been dangerous enough. Meckle speaks good and nice English. He told me he had been a good deal in the States. Meyer tells me he is a well known German automobilist and aviator too – Like many others of his class he is a volunteer. Germany has over a million volunteers under arms now – mostly youths. They, the volunteers, boys mostly, carried Dixmunde the other day by assault singing "Deutschland über alles" which the Anglo-Saxon press of America I see cites as another proof of German intentions against the freedom of the world! Asinine is scarcely the word to apply to the pranks of the so-called American newspapers since this war began. A semi-educated newsboy ought to know that the meaning of this is not that Germany is to be on top of all other countries but that Germany is to be before all else to the German. But just as the Park row style editors beat the daily drum on the "Kaiser's war" and the "War Lord" instead of "Commander in Chief" so they glory in the latest Anglo-Saxon fable, that Germany seeks to conquer the world! Seeing that England has now brought pretty well half the world to her side against the 67.000.000 of Teutons she feared to face alone it would indeed be true to say of England today

"England on top of Everybody."

The disgrace of this war; the shame of it to Englishmen is to me overwhelming. Were I English I should open my veins to let the blood out!

Not content with the 160.000.000 of Russians, the 40.000.000 of French, the 42.000.000 of Great Britons, the 3.000.000 of Servian & Montenegrin cutthroats, to pit against the 120.000.000 of Teuto-Hungarians, England has brought in the 52.000.000 of Japanese, the 300.000.000 Hindoos, the 12.000.000 or 15.000.000 of Canadians, Australians, New Zealanders &c. &c. of the Great Dominions, the millions of African Negroes of her own and the French protectorates – and now I see by the latest telegrams that some "Genuine Red Indians" will form part of the next Canadian contingent; and that a regiment of Fiji Islanders is on the way to support the cause of the "small nationalities." It only remains for King Albert of Belgium, from his new seat of Government – Havre, I believe – today to command a corps d'armée of Congo cannibals to come to the rescue of the Lothaires, Fievez,[48] Fanquis and other expatriated Belgian heroes who are now employing the methods of la compagne Congolaise against the German savage as they once employed them against the rubber runners of the heart of Africa.

---

[48] Adam Hochschild in his book *King Leopold's Ghost* (p. 166) wrote, "An account in 1884 describes the actions of an officer called Fievez taken against those who refused to collect rubber or failed to meet their quota: "I made war against them. One example was enough: a hundred heads cut off, and there have been plenty of supplies ever since. My goal is ultimately humanitarian. I killed a hundred people...but that allowed five hundred others to live."

For the Belgian people I have nothing but pity – for their King and Government hearty contempt. These sacrificed the interests, the life itself of their country, to the interest of England. Léopold deux, with all his criminal career on the Congo, was a far better King for this unhappy people than this good King Albert.

I doubt now if Germany will "give back" Belgium. After von Stumm I doubt it very much. Von Lüttichau confided to me today while we were visiting the garden of the Baroness's chateau near Anseremme, that he was not in favour of retaining any of the conquered territory now held by German troops. His argument is right. He says "What do we want with 7.000.000 of Belgians to hold down? We have enough foreign elements already in our midst – the Poles – the Jews! All we want is a united Germany, ensured against assault absolutely on her own national frontiers."

This opinion certainly prevails among the Germans I talk with – but whether it will prevail with a victorious Germany seeking compensation for the terrible sacrifices in blood and treasure she has been put to by the wicked conspiracy of England, France and Russia is another matter – I doubt it. I guess the German official view may be something like this – "We have lost, say, 2.000.000 of men" (if the war goes on for 6 months these losses may well be that) "we have lost all our colonies; our foreign trade has been ruined; our shipping swept from the seas; our internal industries closed or killed – our losses actual and eventual are colossal.

We need not only guarantees for the future peace of our frontiers and peaceful development of our national and industrial life, but we need some great compensation for all you have wantonly destroyed of ours or deprived us of."

It is true that if Germany beats down French defence she can impose on France a profitable peace – but to make France "pay all" is well nigh impossible. And yet Germany will say "disgorge – not only my stolen colonies, but my ships, my trade, my industries – <u>and</u> an indemnity on top."

England will not be willing to disgorge anything – she entered the war for plunder and that chiefly – that and the destruction of the great rival's "menace" – and Russia has nothing to disgorge and cannot be made to pay anything. Now when it comes to the point of France saying to England "I must give in; I cannot hold out longer" – England will shrug her shoulders – wrap herself in the mantle of the seas and failing to get France to go altogether into the fire of defeat as she has put wretched Belgium she will retire from the conflict with all the German swag and an untroubled conscience – leaving her quondam "ally" to her fate. For France to pay all will mean ruin – in one shape or another. That has come to her in any case. Even if the "allies" win the war, France is done for. She can never regain the lifeblood lost, the cities destroyed, the land depeopled that already three months of devastating horror have brought to her once fair fields.

Germany will either do as von Stumm assured me "Keep what we hold" or release it only on such satisfaction as will reduce France to half a century of impotence. As for Belgium, if she is happy enough to get back her independence it will be a freedom qualified by more than one restraint. Belgium will become a larger Luxembourg. Her port, Antwerp, will surely be kept in German tutelage – her fortresses either dismantled or held in trust for the German Army; her foreign relations controlled from Berlin; her customs possibly also; and in time, her national life subordinated to the dire needs of German future safety and the extension of German <u>rights</u> in the World. For there lies the true cause of the war. Germany claims, demands <u>world rights</u>.

It is this that England has secretly plotted against – it is this assertion of German world interests that is the unpardonable sin to Downing Street – and because it was clear to the intriguing spirits of the British governing classes that, left to herself, Germany must acquire power commensurate with her rights England decided to convert the Franco-Russian agreement from a negative policy of defence into an active policy of offence. [**The seven paragraphs above on Casement's view of Germany's strategic 'needs' are omitted by Angus Mitchell, despite their frankness and accuracy.**]

These and thoughts like them were in my mind all the way from Charleville through ruined Givet, and occupied Namur and Liège until in piercing cold and mist we crossed the German frontier and sped towards Aachen, Jülich and Cologne.

The suburbs of Liège, so far as one could see from our car lamplights in the darkness, were almost all destroyed. We passed through village after village, or suburb after suburb of empty shattered and dismantled houses. Whether by German or Belgian shellfire no one can say now – then came fields – miles of them – and our lamps showed the barbed wire entanglements (like grape vines on low trellises) the Belgians had set up to impede the German advance against the ceinture of forts. None of these forts was visible – it was dark – all we could see was the barbed wire, acre after acre of the most worthless crop ever sowed by the hand of men. The wires were lit by the hoar frost – white and clear a laceworks of death. Meyer told me that the German troops had not crossed the fields but he came by the roads and this wire had served little purpose – at any rate it was still there – intact and useless now. We went thro Aachen without stopping, and thro' Jülich and reached Cologne at 8.50 p.m. The city seemed so peaceful, even gay and pleasant and clean and well lit – after the dark barbed wire fields around Liège.

From the hurried glimpse I have got of it I should think Cologne must be one of the pleasantest cities in Europe to live in. I liked it from the first – and on getting to the station at 9 p.m. my cold tired and hungry I liked it better still. The station was full of life – people of all classes and soldiers innumerable going and coming.

We got a hurried dinner in the Speisesaal and then bidding Meckle adieu with a hearty handshake, Meyer, Von Lüttichau and I settled in sleeping cars for the night. As we crossed the Rhine bridge leaving the city, all the lights in our train went out. Von Lüttichau explained that this was a precaution "leaving the fortress" against horrible air-raids. Two searchlights were sweeping the heavens constantly – our train remained in darkness until we had got well clear of the city defences – and then the lights were turned on and I went to sleep.

Von Lüttichau & Meckle I am sure were told something during the day by Meyer who I really was. They had taken me at first for "Mr. Hammond of New York", but after the long interview at Charleville with the Headquarters staff and the F.O. this pretence was not sustainable – their manner had grown more interested and when we parted, with Meckle at Cologne and with von Lüttichau at Berlin at 8 a.m. on Friday morning our adieux were warm and friendly and almost intimate.[49]

[Curry recommences Casement's diary extracts on p. 85 of his book, shortly after extensive detail on the tiresome Findlay affair in Christiania which Angus Mitchell largely and wisely ignores in his *Berlin Diary*.[50]]

Tuesday. 24 Novr. 1914

On getting back to Berlin last Friday from our hurried visit to the Headquarters I found Adler still here, but prepared to go back to Norway on the morrow – with the sham letters I had written for Mr. de C. Findlay's benefit.

The declaration of the German Government on Ireland was not yet issued

---

[49] B. L. Reid wrote (p. 233) with some justice: "Looking back over the elaborate little junket it was hard to see what it was all about. Nothing had been required of Casement that he could not have performed equally well in Berlin, and the Germans had not delivered their promised interviews with the great men, von Jagow and von Bethmann-Hollweg."

[50] Angus Mitchell wrote in *16 Lives* (p. 232), "The Findlay Affair has become and will doubtless remain an unpleasant dimension in the Casement story and reflects badly on all parties. It propels history into a dimension of conspiracy where facts mutate and historical 'truths' are impossible to determine." However in *The Berlin Diary* he writes in the introduction (p. 4), "Understanding this conspiracy between Casement and the British Government is fundamental to unlocking the deeper truths about the complications that emerged over Casement's own entangled legacy and the 'Black Diaries' controversy' that has come to dominate and determine his historical interpretation." In other words, Casement was forging documents and that creates a problem.

– and I wondered throughout the forenoon and after lunch at the cause of the delay, as von Wedel had told me on Tuesday last, before I left for Charleville, that it would be given to the press on Wednesday last. However, about 3 I happened to see the Midday Gazette – the "*B.Z. am Mittag*"[51] – & there it was.

> "*Deutsche Sympathie-Erklärung für Irland.*
> Sir Roger Casement in Berlin."

It was placed in big type & in the most prominent part of the paper – as a central "inset" on the front page. Over columns was an article headed: "<u>Sir Roger's Aktion</u> – <u>Zu Seinem Berliner Besuche</u>", which was not only a sort of biography of me, but a eulogy as well.

I append both here to save further writing –

[Two cuttings from *B.Z. am Mittag* Freitag, 20 Novr 1914 are then tipped in on page numbered 43 but after a *Continental News* cutting and before one from the *Telegraphischer Bericht*.]

All the evening papers as they came out had it in too – some with comment, others without. It had been issued first, I saw, in the morning in the semi-official "North German Gazette."[52]

At 5.30 von Wedel rang me up and asked if I could go to him at F.O. I went at 7 and he read me first a despatch from the German Ambassador at the Vatican saying that two good "nationalist" Irish Priests had been got – thro' Mon. O'Riordan of the Irish College – one named Canice O'Gorman (a good enough name) the other Crotty. Both were ready to come for the work of the Irish soldiers.

Next von Wedel read a letter he had got from a lady named Fulton [? – **name blurred**] now but born Ryan transmitting the article of 20 Nov in *Vorwärts* on Ireland I had already sent to von Wedel

– This she endorsed to the full "as an Irishwoman" and said she hoped to be allowed in that capacity & as the wife of a German to help her adopted country. I took her address – it will always be useful to find an Irishwoman here – & one of the right stamp too. **[The previous two paragraphs were omitted by Curry.]**

The "<u>Continental News</u>" of Friday also has the Declaration in full – I give it here too. I have asked the Foreign Office to order 3.000 extra copies of the edition of the paper for the Irish soldiers later on –

---

[51] *B.Z.* am Mittag - *Berliner Zeitung* at midday. Curry dates it "Freitag, 20. November."
[52] *Norddeutsche Allgemeine Zeitung*

"Continental News" Friday – 20 Nov 1914 and in all the Berlin evening press. **[Note written down the side of the *Continental News* cutting:]** The first five words were put in by the German Govt. – I objected, but they insisted. R.C. **[It reads:]** November 20, 1914.

The well known Irish Nationalist,[53] Sir Roger Casement, who has arrived in Berlin from the United States, has been received at the Foreign Office.

Sir Roger Casement pointed out that statements were being published in Ireland, apparently with the authority of the British Government behind them, to the effect that a German victory would inflict great loss upon the Irish people, whose homes, churches, priests, and lands would be at the mercy of an invading army actuated only by motives of pillage and conquest. Recent utterances of Mr. Redmond on his recruiting tour in Ireland and many pronouncements of the British Press in Ireland to the above effect have been widely circulated, Sir Roger pointed out, and have caused natural apprehension among Irishmen as to the German attitude towards Ireland in the event of a German victory in the present war.

Sir Roger sought a convincing statement of German intentions towards Ireland that might reassure his country men all over the world, and particularly in Ireland and America, in view of these disquieting statements emanating from responsible British quarters.

In reply to this inquiry, the Acting Secretary of State at the Foreign Office, by order of the Imperial Chancellor, has made the following official declaration:

Official Statement

> The German Government repudiates the evil intentions attributed to it in the statements referred to by Sir Roger Casement, and takes this opportunity to give a categoric assurance that the German Government desires only the welfare of the Irish people, their country, and their institutions.
>
> The Imperial Government formally declares that under no circumstances would Germany invade Ireland with a view to its conquest or the overthrow of any native institutions in that country.
>
> Should the fortune of this great war, that was not of Germany's seeking, ever bring in its course German troops to the shores of Ireland, they would land there, not as an army of invaders to pillage and destroy, but as the forces of a Government that is inspired by goodwill towards a country and a people for whom Germany desires only national prosperity and national freedom.

The English sea losses are printed – I see in reply to a question of Lord Chas.

---

[53] Casement has stroked out in pencil the first five words in the clipping, "The well known Irish nationalist."

Beresford. The Admiralty give them as follows – London 18 Nov. 1914

	Officers	Men (mostly drowned, poor chaps!)		
Killed	222	3455.		
Wounded	37	428.		
Missing	5	1		Total
	264	3,884	=	4,148

To these must be added

lost in "Good Hope"	875		
Lost "in action" at Antwerp of the 1st Naval Brigade	1000.	=	1875
Interned in Holland about	1800	=	1800
.. .. Chile or Brazil – "Glasgow" or killed – but lost to the British fleet say	540		540
Grand total			8363.
			officers and men

[The 4th cutting, from *Telegraphischer Bericht*, is tipped in here and inscribed '8 Uhr Abendblatt Friday 20 Nov 1914'. It is headlined '*Englands Verluste zur See*' (England's Sea Losses), London 18 November. A second, similar list of casualty numbers is also present:]

Killed.

Officers			Men
222			3455
Say	20	Good Hope	875
247.			4330
Killed Sea [?] Brigade Holland			247
			4577.
~~Interned~~ say ~~1200~~			1000.
			5577
Interned in Holland say			1500
[ditto] Chile			480
			7557
Add wounded & hurt			
officers		men	
42		429	471
			8028
			15

Officers & men out of action   40140
                                      8078
                                    120.420.

These are very heavy losses indeed for three months of a war that has been, so far as the Navies go, only a matter of coast blockade commerce chasing and skirmishes.

The two actual sea fights that off Heligoland where the British with overwhelming forces destroyed three small German cruisers, and that off Chile where the forces were nearly equal with the advantage on the German side when the Germans destroyed two great 1st class British cruisers and caused a third (2nd class vessel) to take fight and be "interred", are the only two fleet engagements that have taken place – and both were of wholly minor scope. And yet the British have lost actually one twelfth or one thirteenth of their effective sea personnel – and a seaman takes years to make – unlike Kitchener's "2 millions of soldiers" that the "Daily Mail" and the Guildhall veterans are proudly noising of. I wish they had heard von Stumm on Kitchener's "millions of men"! – or the same baron on Sir Edward Grey and "English Diplomacy"!

Von Stumm respected, in other words, what Wilfrid Blunt said to me in May last that what England might achieve in this war was not the ruin of Germany, as she conceived, but the "break-up of the British Empire."

And certainly with the Caliph out on holy war, with the Turkish army advancing on Egypt and nearing the Suez Canal, with Beyers, Christian de Wit and many more brave Boer leaders in the field for "South African Republic" the days I prophesied a year ago – and more! – when the "new Goths and Huns" would emerge on the horizon, seems now very near indeed. It will be a blessed thing for mankind if that conglomerate mass "Great Britain" should indeed be confined to its rightful and natural limits, and become in truth and fact the Kingdom of Great Britain. Then the British race, reduced to the normal limits that island could happily sustain, might achieve true greatness in other fields of effort than those of organised piracy, termed "Empire building," and systematic pillage termed "foreign investments."

The English people in England – "little England" – might even become a good people, and little England might become again "Happy England" as it was before the Tudor pirates seized its throne. The commercial envy of Henry VII began the thing, and the plunder of the monasteries by his son laid a sure foundation on which to achieve the "founding of Empire" – and then with the Union with Ireland – Henry VIII first "King of Ireland" – came the material, physical and even intellectual means to accomplish the stupendous event. If Germany should, indeed, succeed in striking a blow at this monstrosity not Ireland only – but all the small nations of the world should rise up and shout for joy.

On Sunday I saw Adler off at 11.18 to Sassnitz with two faked letters and two "stolen" pages of "my Diary" giving hints at impending invasion of Ireland by myself and friends here (50.000) "by end of December." It should make Findlay's hair – such as remains of it – rise up and bless him and the day he got hold of Adler Christensen!

I spent the day quietly and met Kiliani in the afternoon who told me he had found the Baroness von Nordenflycht[54] in Berlin.

Von Wedel tells me that Mr. Gerard, the U.S. Ambassador, and the Councillor of the Embassy have been making pressing enquiries to know "where Sir Roger Casement is." The Councillor came to the Foreign Office and the attaché who saw him was told by von Wedel to say "they did not know"!

He suggested my giving them "Mr. Landy's" passport & letter of introduction from the Under Secretary at Washington to return to the owner in New York. This I did later on & wrote with them a long account of all Christiania, the Declaration etc. & my private affairs to be given to Cohalan[55] – They go by a special messenger via Rotterdam.

On Monday 23rd <u>Nov</u> I lunched with von Wedel's mother the Countess Groeben, at 3 Fürst Bismarck Str. A charming & and beautiful old lady – perfectly delightful. She greeted with extreme warmth in the most clear English. There were also at lunch Georg, her son, Count and Countess Oppersdorff,[56] he a Bavarian Catholic a member of "the Centre" in the Reichstag and his wife née a Polish Lithuanian Princess. The Count spoke little or no English – but French (his mother was a Talleyrand-Périgord) but the Countess spoke excellent English. There was also present a tall dark German I did not catch the name of – he a good English speaker. He met me on the stairs going up

---

[54] Ferdinand Nordenflycht was born in Berlin 4 Apr. 1850; d. 23 July 1931. Envoy extraordinary and minister plenipotentiary; captain in the Landwehr or militia. He married on 5 June 1884, at Constantinople, Adelheid Mühlig (1863-1933), dau. of the personal physician to the Ottoman emperor. They had two sons and two daughters, the younger being Augusta, nicknamed Gussy: she is evidently the "Baroness Gussie" in the diary. The Nordenflychts were originally Swedish barons. Casement knew him from Rio de Janeiro where he was German Consul-General, appearing in the Black Diaries of 1910 and 1911. The Baron had previously served in New Orleans and later as German Minister in Montevideo.

[55] Daniel Cohalan, b. 1867, New York Supreme Court Judge

[56] 'Opernstock' is struck out and replaced with 'Operndorf'. Count Hans von Oppersdorff was a son of Elisabeth, née de Talleyrand-Périgord; b. 1866; d. at Lourdes 1948; m. 1895 Dorothea Princess Radziwill (1871-1947). They had six sons and five daughters, which doesn't add up to the thirteen later stated by Casement. Perhaps a couple had died in infancy. The family was ancient Silesian aristocracy.

at 1.30 and at once began to speak in English. He had been in India and knew the "Gaelic American" for when he saw my copy he said it had been excluded from India when he was there.

Count Opernstock full of sympathy for Ireland, largely on Catholic grounds, & very anxious to get the German Declaration in there thro' Church channels. **[Note inserted at top of page:]** (He was German Minister in Belgium before the war.)

I suggested Rome and he said naturally and that he would also try through Brittany!

The Countess (who <u>looks</u> 25) told me she had thirteen children! Two of her sons, 18 & 19 are going to the front in a few days as volunteers. I am to go and see them before they leave. I liked her greatly & we became fast friends & she talked much of Ireland – asking of the old Gaelic families & of the Irish language as did the others – Opernstock knew much about it.

At 5 the Nordenflychts called on me – the Baroness & Gussie - but just then came a wire from poor Adler detained at Sassnitz begging me to see von Wedel, – so I had to hurry off to the F.O. & ask him to telegraph to Sassnitz. I also 'phoned & wrote to Meyer to same effect – & then walked a bit & dined, at Hoffman's Kellner.

On Tuesday, today, I was to go to the Baroness von N – but got a 'phone to say she was in bed with cold – & just then a 'phone came from Blücher[57] (Gebhard) at the Esplanade Hotel – to my great joy, & I hurried off to lunch with him there.

<u>Thursday</u> 26 Novr. (Berlin)

After my lunch with Blücher on Tuesday I talked with the Countess.[58] She is in great distress for her young brother left with two broken legs in a captured trench.

Blücher will try and arrange lunch with von Jagow & me – the Secry of S. whom he knows well. Von Jagow arrived in Berlin from the front a few days ago & the Chancellor comes too I hear for the Reichstag debates.

I worked a good deal in evening of Tuesday – it was very cold.

The papers from Countess are very interesting – I made out lists of some 300 Dublin Fusiliers "missing" & see that hundreds of other Irish are captured. So much the better. The English fear of Ireland is clearly rising! Sir

---

[57] Prince Gebhard Blücher died on 19 August 1931 in Bournemouth and was buried in Rainhill, Lancs, his wife's family home.

[58] Blücher, p. 42, "My husband went to him shortly after his arrival and tried to show him what a false position he had put himself in, and that he had better leave the country as quickly as possible, but it was no use. So after that we refused to see him or have anything more to do with him."

E. Grey's "Ireland the one bright spot." of 4 Augt. is a strange commentary on the terror and world wide activities they are displaying to keep Ireland "quiet." For every day fresh evidence comes to hand. I see by the English press of 11 Nov. – that the White Star "mid week vessels now will go straight from Liverpool to New York with mails" &c. So a further nail in the Irish coffin!

To be completely shut off from all contact with the outside world. Then the news that the "Olympic" which was kept for four days in a secluded part of Lough Swilly Oct 29-Nov 3 (I think) on the pretext that she could not get to Liverpool owing to "German mines" was not allowed to hold any touch with the shore – Only one passenger out of many, the Mr. Schob of Commerce I fancy was permitted to land and proceed to London. The reason now partly transpires – the "Olympic" is said to have witnessed the sinking of the British Super Dreadnought "Audacious" off the coast of Ireland on Oct 28-29. The report of the loss of Audacious came out Tuesday night in Berlin – she is a ship of 27.000 tons – one of the very latest of her type. She is supposed to have struck a mine or possibly to have been submarined off the Irish coast. The "Olympia" came to assist the survivors[59] – and it is said now she retained her passengers on board until she got undertaking they would not speak of the matter – and in any case, <u>no one was allowed to land in Ireland</u>, save the neutral Mr. Schob!

But the best of all is the news that now appears in the Berlin press that England wishes to establish a diplomatic post at the Vatican! Shades of Persico and Leo XIII![60] Who will he be? Possibly the Earl of Kenmare – a loyal "Irishman"! The report is qualified here by the press assertions that the Pope[61] has refused the offer. The form it was said to have taken was that "during the course of the war England would like to have a diplomatic channel with

---

[59] All aboard survived but, somewhat pointlessly, her sinking by a mine was kept secret in Britain until November 1918.

[60] Pope Leo XIII, gathered together those he felt best suited to understand the plight of poor Irish tenants and sent Cardinal Persico, a Jesuit-educated Neapolitan, on a fact finding mission in 1887. He went with little notice and without consulting Archbishop Walsh of Dublin. Persico's secretary, Enrico Gualdi, another Italian and one time priest of Cardinal Manning, supplied the necessary English language skills. However Gualdi fell ill on the expedition, which prematurely curtailed it. On Persico's return to Rome, his report was considered in the Inquisition by the Sicilian Cardinal Rampolla, (who later became its head), and Andreas Steinhuber a former Jesuit theologian from Innsbruck, the tribunal's legal consultant. The Inquisition's decree of April 1888 declared that the Pope, "fearing justice should be perverted in consequence of the Plan of Campaign also Boycotting" commissioned the Inquisition to make the matter the subject of grace and careful examination. The Irish bishops attempted to delay the implementing of the decree fearing a mass exodus and loss of control, but Rome's will was final.

[61] Benedict XV

the Vatican established" – and that the Papal FO replied that it saw no good purpose to be served or reason for a <u>temporary</u> connection at this period.

The Pope probably wants to secure permanent diplomatic relations with England – and as "the one bright spot" is clearly the object in view of British diplomacy His Holiness will probably obtain, from English fears of the bright spot becoming brighter the creation of <u>permanent</u> official relations between the Holy See and St. James's – It will be a triumph for the Vatican – and achieved moreover, over the spiritual and political heirs of the author of "Vaticanism"! As to Ireland – the purpose to be served is clearly a harmful one. It is today as in the time of Parnell a fresh British intrigue against the spirit of Irish nationality. The Pope is to be enlisted on the side of British rule in Ireland – even as the Irish won't enlist to spread that rule abroad! But it is clear proof of the strength and reality of the national soul again uprising in Ireland. More even the British announcement of the Vatican <u>Entente</u> comes after the publication of the German Govt's Declaration of Goodwill towards Ireland.

Countess Blücher hopes sincerely I may succeed in raising a real good

Princess Evelyn Blücher von Wahlstatt

rebellion in Ireland – & so bring peace by terrifying the British Government.

I dined last night (Wed) with Professor Schiemann his wife & 2 daughters. He had got copies of New York papers for me G.A. several & the new issue of my brochure with the footnote about the Prince of Wales's "going to the front" – to Brentwood Barracks (I see the poor boy has at length "joined his regiment" in France!) Schiemann also had a letter from Freeman in New York with news – not very first hand I imagine – of Ireland – & a statement that of the "recent lot of recruits taken from Ireland to the front, 3000 had gone over prepared to go over to Germany at first chance." If only these people were less machine made they could get every Irish regiment in the British army to join my Brigade! But they will proceed only by machinery and not by individual intelligence.

Here is a fine tribute to the inherent qualities of the British Tommy taken from the Continental Times of 16th. It recalls the description of the English crews off Dunkirk & Calais in Elizabeth's reign when their French "Allies" lost their ear rings, rings, jewellery and purses on board the English royal ships! I remember in 1905-6, a series of articles in the "Morning Post" on the Army and, incidentally, it was pointed out that "every man steals from every other man" – in the barrack life picture drawn. In the present instance, it is the Belgian "comrades" who appear to have enjoyed this universal proclivity of the British soldier.

[Newspaper cutting tipped in and headlined:] 'The English Huns'

The semi official "Nord Allg Zeitung" [***Norddeutsche Allgemeine Zeitung***] has published the following communication "The German civil government have ordered that an accurate calculation be made of the damage done by the English in the way of desecration and plundering of private property immediately previous to the surrender of the fortress of Antwerp. Up to the present the investigations have resulted in showing that "according to Brussels private reports Belgian and neutral commercial firms alone have suffered damage amounting to 200 million francs at least. The losses of German firms are considerably less. The English destroyed and stole everything they could lay hands on within the port and the wharves without stopping to consider to whom the goods belonged."

What a piquant little affair! Poor "Winnie" Churchill has already been shown up by his own countrymen for despatching to Antwerp at the eleventh hour a newly-recruited naval brigade that could no more fight than fly. Now it appears that they had very strong natural talents although these lay in a peculiar direction. A nice mob they must have been. By the way, if any corroboration of Tommy's bad behaviour was needed, it is to be found in the order of the day (a copy of which was discovered upon a fallen English officer) issued to the 2nd Battalion Royal Scotch Fusiliers which runs: "Many cases having occurred of houses occupied by British troops being plundered and much damage done, it shall be recalled that our troops are operating at present in the country of our allies."

So they are not to rob their dear friends and allies. With other words: "should they ever reach German territory they would be allowed to pillage for all they are worth! **[end of cutting]**
Continental News. 16 Nov. 1914

[Down the side of cutting:] Of course the story may be untrue. But remembering the Boer war & my brother's experiences (and the looting in China and Benin!) when even Lady MacD – & Sir C[62] too, I was assured, took furious part & came home with much trophy, I incline to greatly credit this German version of who it was pillaged best at Antwerp.

Another act (aimed at me I fancy) is just what I predicted wd take place – after Christiania. I see in the D.T. [***Daily Telegraph*** inserted] of 16 Nov. 1914 a telegram from Washington saying that the Br. Ambassador had made representations about the spy Lody's[63] passport which was that of an American named Charles H. Inglis – In consequence enquiry is being instituted at Berlin & further "new and strict rules regarding the obtaining of American passports for use abroad come into effect today (Nov 14) by an order signed by President Wilson having been issued, for the purpose of preventing foreign agents from securing passports for the purpose of espionage or for other reasons." (Reuters)

---

[62] Sir Claude MacDonald who Casement knew well in Nigeria was later Ambassador in Tokyo 1900-12

[63] Carl Lody (1877-1914) was shot as a German spy at the Tower of London on 6 November 1914. His spying began prior to the outbreak of war. Appearing in Britain as a travel guide by the name of Charles A. Inglis, using a stolen U.S. passport, Lody made careful note of Royal Navy establishments in Britain, subsequently providing reports to Berlin. When war broke out in August 1914 Karl Boy-Ed, the German U.S. naval attaché, selected him as an ideal agent in Britain. From there he sent back reports upon London's state of air defences, in addition to notes concerning the Rosyth naval base. Having spent some time in Liverpool, Lody embarked for Ireland where he was finally arrested in Killarney. Given his possession of incriminating documents, his conviction at the Old Bailey in early November 1914 was a virtual formality, although he felt his trial to have been fairly handled. Lody had nevertheless pleaded not guilty to the two counts under the Defence of the Realm Act. He was subsequently found to be responsible for the sinking of a British cruiser following a report to Berlin of its sailing. On the morning of his death at the Tower of London, Lody addressed the Assistant Provost-Marshal who came to take him from his cell with the words, "I suppose that you will not care to shake hands with a German spy?" Impressed by Lody's bearing throughout his imprisonment, he replied, "No. But I will shake hands with a brave man." Aside from being the first German spy to be executed in Britain during the war, Lody's was also the first execution at the Tower of London in 150 years.

I guess the "Oscar II" & the passenger she brought to Christiania is one of the principal "other reasons"!

Schiemann tells me that Kuno Meyer arrived safely in New York yesterday – 25 Nov. – so that now we may shortly expect the first blows in our double campaign. The Declaration of the German Govt should have been with the press of U.S.A. at latest on Sunday last – probably Saturday 21st. I hope my two letters, sent by Meyer to be posted in R'dam arrive safely also.

I wrote to von Wedel y'day asking him to get some Irish flags and metal badges too for the troops – the Continental News has my appeal to the Irish people on both Monday (23rd) and Wednesday (25) issues. Here it is as printed there.

I have ordered 2.000 copies extra for the prisoners and I send some to Rome as well.

Meyer called at 12 & I discussed this latest effort at "Vaticanism" on the part of Mr. Bull against Ireland – A minute after he left Count von Wedel rang me up to say the two priests had arrived from Rome and had been with him at the Foreign Office. They are in charge of a Dominican father, who will get them rooms in some quiet Hotel and then I am to see them. Wedel says they knew "who I was" but did not know me personally No, they did not but I hope their views may become as mine before we part. <u>Nous verrons</u>. I told v. W. not to allow them to visit the Irish prisoners until I had seen them, and been there first.

Last night when I left Schiemann and walked up the <u>broad</u> and beautiful Tauentzienstrasse to the Zoo – & to the Station there I stopped at the tram junction & bought a special "Lokal <u>Anzeiger</u>" – giving news of an important Austro-Hungarian victory over the Russians 29.000 prisoners taken and 42 guns!

This is excellent – & I am particularly pleased it comes to Austria's turn to have a real big success – following the German capture of 28.000 Russians last week – this gives with other smaller captures noted at intervals – nearly 70.000 Russians taken prisoner in the last fortnight – or will as some 5000 Servians – & fully 150 guns of different kinds. If the killed and wounded be added, the Russians total loss of men <u>hors de combat</u> cannot be much short of 200.000 men inside of 16 or 17 days. No army, not even the "Russian myriads" can support losses of that kind indefinitely. Turkey too, is accounting for a fair sprinkling of damages in the Kaukasas, Armenia and Northern Persia.

At this rate the Russian "break" may come before that of France possibly – for France have England, the sea, the U.S.A. and all the world markets and supplies to fall back on – Russia is "bottled up" now almost as completely as Germany. She has only the extreme far east left open to obtain things needed – and this only by the good will of Japan – and possibly of China.

The Russian losses are probably the highest of any belligerent. She has been fighting two powerful armies, and despite initial success against Austria, her losses at Tannenberg, at Przemysl, in Poland, Galicia and the Carpathians must amount now to far over 1.000.000 of men. Blücher says that Tannenberg "wiped out" 300.000 men – but this is obviously an exaggeration – possibly 180.000 men or even 200.000 may have been lost all told in those awful carnages in and around the Masurian Lakes.

I enjoyed my walk to and back from Schiemann's last night – especially the walk home from the Zoo and thus round by Potsdamer Str. Plenty of people in Berlin streets at night – not like London. I walked y'day afternoon (in rain) to Stettiner Str. and met lots of wounded soldiers with such kind faced German nurses and "guides" accompanying them. Part of the scheme of convalescence seems to be to have the men taken out and to theatres and shows, with such kind faced, smiling affectionate nurses acting as friends. Crowds of kind eyed people go with them often and press things on them and all are so full of courtesy, real affection and love for the soldiers that every day I feel more and more in love with German manhood and womanhood. A great people a good people.

No news yet from Adler. Meyer says he is certain he got away all safe and sound from Sassnitz on Tuesday (24th) after noon at 4.56. That means he should have been at Moss yesterday at 11 a.m. & perhaps today he may begin operations with "*ce cher ministre.*" Schiemann is anxious for me to publish the whole story to the world and quickly.

Coming out from lunch at 3 from "Hoffmann's" Kellar the newsmen (not boys here, but <u>men</u>) were rushing thro' the streets with the *B.Z. am Mittag* with the (official) news from Headquarters that the Russians had been defeated near Lódz and 40.000 prisoners taken. The streets were full of pleased faces, hand shaking & smiles and flags were out in a trice from many shops and homes. The newsmen did a roaring trade, surrounded by crowds. But no jingoism or offensive hilarity!

They take their victories as they do their losses – with quiet repose of manner and expression – And yet this is a great victory and a big step on the road to final triumph, or a sound peace. These 40.000 prisoners follow the 29.000 Austria took y'day, in the Carpathians, and that followed the 28.000 Germany captured some ten days ago = 97.000 prisoners, to say nothing of odds and ends mopped up in minor fights the last fortnight coming fully to 15.000 more – so that in a fortnight, say, Russia has lost some 110.000 prisoners, <u>many guns</u>, war material & equipment – & no doubt more than 150.000 killed & wounded – put it at a quarter of a million men <u>hors de</u>

combat in well under three weeks.

No army can continue to advance or win with such losses delaying its "victorious march"! The breaking point may come soon in Russia. I see by the evg. papers that this victory in Poland is a great one. The 40.000 prisoners are stated to be "unwounded",[64] the despatch says the killed and wounded are not yet known. In addition to this whole Army Corps of prisoners 70 cannon were captured, 30 cannon destroyed, 156 machine guns captured and 160 ammunition wagons captured. A few more victories of this kind and the Russian steam roller will back down.

Baroness von Nordenflycht called at 5 & brought me the 1st edition of <u>B.Z. am Mittag</u> with report of Larkin's arrival in U.S.A. denouncing England and saying that there were no "loyalists" in Ireland. Some Daily Mails and D.T.s of 20 Nov. to hand also. Furious and absurd statements about "German gold" and "German-American gold" spent on "the Irish sedition mongers" who it is seen have stopped recruiting. Questions "in the House" about an article in the "Irish Volunteer" of 7 Nov. – saying the only hope for Ireland was "the downfall of the Br. Empire." John Redmond denounced the "<u>Irish Volunteer</u>" & disclaimed all connection with it. I like the "<u>German</u>-American gold"! It used to be "<u>Irish</u>-American gold!" – & when Redmond won the 1911 Election we remember the "Dollar Dictator" campaign! But now – things are changed. Redmond is a jingo imperialist – quite "one of us" – and it would be impolite to speak of "Irish-American" anything now. Besides, there are no "<u>Irish</u> Americans" now! They too are merged in the great loyal mass of friends of freedom fighting for the small nationalities – & there only remain such malignants as a handful of German-gold sustained Boers – like de Wet – and the German American offal in U.S.A. All the rest of humanity – including the Fijians, the Emirs of Nigeria, the Dyaks & headhunters of Borneo, the Esquimaux incidentals, and the Presidents of Liberia, Haiti, Nicaragua and Venezuela are burning to join the forces of the "Allies" in defence of the public laws of Europe and the existence and liberty of the small nations.

These outbreaks of jaundice, produced clearly by German gold, were on Friday last 20th – the very day the German Official Declaration came out here in Berlin.

It will indeed be interesting (soon) to read the comments of the Times, The Daily Mail, the D.T. & the rest when that statement – the interview with "Sir Roger Casement" are permitted by the British censor to appear. I wonder when that will be?

Or will they not be stopped? I fancy they will not allow the Br. Press to publish the Declaration – but they will instead begin an increasing volume

---

[64] *Unverletzt* – uninjured

of "dénigrement" of me preparing for the day when the cat has to leap out of the bag. Anyhow, I have given them now some nice thrills that will certainly cause Sir E. Grey to revise his opinion that "Ireland is the one bright spot." Poor Ireland! if all I dream of comes to pass she will indeed be a bright spot on the map of Europe – in the chart of world peoples.

Friday – 27 Novr.
I walked a good deal last evening – and wound up in the Thiergarten, Siegesallee and a seat in the pleasant garden. Not very cold yesterday – many were without greatcoats – a remarkable rise since Monday & Tuesday.

This morning, papers have more about Ireland – and quote a long article from the Times of 24th Nov. – attacking vigorously "Irish Freedom" and the "Irish Volunteer." The latter enemy is the article of 7th Nov. I referred to y'day as having been denounced in "the House."

My waiter translated it for me. – here is his handiwork **[Nothing is present.]**

All of the servants & people here in the Hotel now know quite well who I am but I remain "Mr. Hammond" still officially – All enquiries for Sir R. C. in Berlin have failed! No one knows where he is. I walk about with an American flag in my buttonhole and often go past the U.S. Embassy on my way to the Wilhelmstrasse. As soon as I have visited the Irish soldiers in their camp I shall return to Berlin to another Hotel and "descend" there as Sir Roger Casement. Poor "Mr. Hammond" will disappear, like Mr. Landy "knocked on the head" in a more effective way than Mr. Findlay, H.B.M. Envoy Extraordinary achieved through Adler! I did succeed in knocking Mr. Landy on the head but the Holy Government failed in its Holy War on Sir R. C.

I see the real Holy War goes well – "Territorials" have been sent to India! The Turks with 76.000 men and 10.000 Bedouins (and 5.000 camels) are reported as near the Suez Canal. General Maxwell, the British Commander in Egypt is said to have 70.000 men all told – but some of them will be Indians and the majority Egyptians – and in the end the latter will surely follow the green flag.

If Turkey breaks thro' the Canal as I think she may do it may indeed bring about the downfall of the Fr. Empire – as Wilfrid Blunt prayed for it in May.

With the Canal gone Egypt goes – and with both gone I look for such an outbreak in India as must tax "the Empire" to its limit, and with Germany at the gates of Calais, and the Irish Declaration out I do not think Master John can spare many men, ships or guns for India.

To hold down India he will have to appeal to Japan – and that spells his own sure and certain eviction from Asia later on. Once India falls the whole house collapses – for it is chiefly on India and her plunder the Colonial scheme of robbery depends. On re-reading the letter in the Daily Mail of 20 Nov. on "German-American gold in Ireland" I feel it should be kept – It is too good to omit – especially the "agent whose name I was given." That's me!!! for they can't know of Pat.

Daily Mail
20 Novr. 1914

Meyer came at 12 & said the two Irish priests (from Rome) were out "for a walk" and could not be found so I can't go till tomorrow. He tells me that in their interview with von Wedel yesterday they show that they had been given strict instructions to abstain from all politics! Good if they keep to that. Meyer said the German F.O. are now convinced that England is going to accredit an envoy to the Vatican! The name is even mentioned – possibly Sir Charles Howard.[65] I knew the instant I saw the telegram in the *Corriere della Sera* three days ago, that it would be done. Blücher y'day was convinced it would not be done – that the Pope would refuse to receive an envoy during the war! I laughed at such amazing faith. The Pope himself in such a matter is like Sir E Grey – "a fly on the wheel." If England offers the Vatican diplomatic relations the Vatican will accept with the joy of 3½ centuries of exclusion, breaking out in a Hosanna of triumph.

I said to Meyer that the fact that England was driven to this course was the clearest proof of the justice of my point of view. Ireland, instead of being as the English proclaim it "loyal" is the danger point – now that I am in Berlin and have got the German Govt to speak out. They are going to do today what they never looked at 1560! Meyer is greatly alarmed and asks how we are to meet this English move – I say by giving on steadily with our plans on behalf of Ireland and proclaiming them all thro' the world. We must get the news into Ireland of the German Declaration – & at all costs get the Irish Brigade formed. I wired as follows to Cohalan to go by von Bernstorff[66] in

---

[65] In December 1914, more than three centuries after relations were severed, Britain re-established diplomatic ties with the Vatican. Sir Henry Howard (not Charles as Casement initially calls him), a Catholic diplomat, was chosen to head the Mission as Minister. The Foreign Office had qualms about appointing a Catholic while hardline Protestant opinion was also enraged at the resumption of diplomatic relations at all.

[66] Count Johann Heinrich von Bernstorff (b. 1862) served as German Ambassador to the United States from 1908 until his recall in 1917. He quickly established a popular reputation in Washington for his apparent moderation (a rarity in Kaiser Wilhelm II's Germany). With an American wife, Bernstorff also demonstrated pro-British views. Favouring a negotiated peace with Germany (particularly after the Schlieffen Plan's failure at the Battle of the Marne in September 1914) he was regarded positively by the peaceable President Wilson. Bernstorff

code – Have you sent special messenger to Ireland & if so wire me the date of arrival there – also have you sent priest here? Cable through Bernstorff. Casement.

Count Johann Heinrich von Bernstorff

How to meet the Papal danger is not yet clear. The best way is to make it clear that Germany will free Ireland if she wins the war and let England intrigue as much as she likes against that!

At the worst we can kill the recruiting – at the best we may get to Ireland

views were however disparaged in Berlin. Despite his personal magnetism, Bernstorff found his position in Washington strained by Germany's policy of unrestricted submarine warfare, which exacted a heavy toll on American merchant shipping (and which Bernstorff opposed). Added to this, the espionage activities of military attaché Franz von Papen and naval attaché Karl Boy-Ed made his position untenable and he was recalled to Berlin in 1917. Although awarded another Ambassadorship in September the same year – to Turkey - he was viewed with great displeasure by both the Kaiser and by the military Third Supreme Command (Hindenburg and Ludendorff). With revolution in the air in November 1918, he was offered – by Friedrich Ebert – control of the Foreign Office, but declined. Instead he chose diplomatic retirement, serving from 1921 to 1928 as a Deputy in the Reichstag for the *Deutsche Demokratische Partei*. He went into exile to Switzerland in 1933 and died in 1939.

with guns & officers & raise a first rate rebellion. The German Declaration is highly moral! – The British reply is prompt & highly moral too! Where Sir George Errington failed against Parnell – will Sir C. Howard or another succeed against R.C. & the Irish Volunteers?

The <u>Continental Times</u> today has more about Ireland – & a further eulogy of me – & a notice about the 2 priests (O'Gorman and Crotty) from Rome. These two men may be a danger – I'll see tomorrow. If they are going to be agents of the British Govt then they shall not get to the Irish soldiers at all –

Saturday, 28. Nov.
I walked nearly all the way to the Baroness von N's last night in Hohenzollern Avenue – a long walk half way across Berlin – & I came back at 11 also nearly all way on foot. The streets are full of life long after midnight and I had a cup of coffee nearly at 1 am in Friedrichstr – the Regent's Street or Piccadilly of Berlin.

Today the papers give details of the destruction of the Br. battleship "Bulwark" at Sheerness, a fearful explosion and down she went, having sunk before the smoke cleared away. The houses in Chatham were shaken and windows smashed. The cause unknown, about 700 men lost some 22 (or 28) officers gone – god help them and their people. This, following the "Audacious" and the possible sinking of the "Canopus" by von Spee's squadron spells dreadful naval loss to England.

Meyer came at my request at 11 and read over the letter I propose sending to Ireland by the channel Princess Pless tells Countess Blücher of. He agreed to its wording and I gave it him to get typed at Foreign Office.

Then to Blücher and the Countess till nearly 2 p.m. I refused to see the princess yet. She is anxious to meet me, says she is Irish – (I believe her mother was Irish but the Cornwallis West family are just what we know – English of the English.) The Countess B. is fine. She really would like to see England get not an overthrow, but a good birching from Germany.

I walked in the Thiergarten at 10.30 to 11.15 a.m. – lovely sun & soft air today & then I walked again back from Esplanade to my Hotel at 2. A message to go and see Father O'Gorman & Crotty at 4. They are in the Nord west Hotel in the Micaville – at Thurmstr 7.

The bar man told me that the evg paper *B.Z. am Mittag* had "something about the big[67] Irishman Sir Roger Casement" – & coming to my room I found it already on the table with a translation by my waiter. Here are both – interesting errors.

---

[67] Should be 'tall' not 'big' Irishman.

B.Z. am Mittag 28 Nov. 1914
[The cutting is then tipped in, while on the facing page on Continental Hotel stationery is the handwritten translation:]

Ulster gegen Casement ['**Ulster against Casement**']
   Daily Mail writes, that the Parliamenter John Lonsdale is going to ask at the English Parliament what the Government intends to do against Sir Robert Casement. –
   Lonsdale is secretary of the Irish Unionist party. –
   – Sir Roger Casement was shortly in Berlin and made the german Government to public, that they don't intend to fall into Ireland.

   So! – as the Germans say.
   So they have actually allowed, or not been able to prevent the Declaration of the German Govt getting out!
   And it is the Ulster Unionists who ask what is to be my "punishment"?
   How funny they are! And dear John R. will be in a devil of a stew – for it will take all <u>his</u> skill to depict me as a traitor to Ireland for coming here to get Germany to say that she will <u>never</u> injure Ireland & only desires her freedom!
   It will be funny to see how the Govt will answer Lonsdale – & what J.R. will contribute to the discussion – & what the Anglomaniac organs will say! Gee! – how they will foam at the mouth!
   Now for Fathers O'Gorman and Crotty.

<u>Monday</u>. 30. Novr Berlin.
   I went to the Holymen at 4.30 & found Father O'Gorman a loyalist nationalist and Father Crotty, the Dominican (thank God!), a raging Fenian! <u>Both</u> promised me <u>not</u> to be "agents of the British Government", as I asked them but to confine themselves strictly to their holy business. They are to be entirely 'non political.' The question is <u>will</u> they?
   [The next six paragraphs were omitted by Curry.] Will they not tell the men that their allegiance to King George V is a moral & religious obligation – if the men consult them? Fr. Crotty will not influence the men against my point of view – that I am sure – but Fr. O'Gorman may. Both, however, are here (at my request too!) as spiritual guides only. If they stick to that all is well. I told them of the Vatican <u>demarche</u> & Fr. Crotty said "<u>That</u> will not help England in Ireland!"
   I told them of Christiania & many other things – Fr. Crotty is a splendid big Irishman with the broad Milesian face – a relative of sorts of Leslie Crotty the singer – & I touched on him.
   Fr. O'Gorman is chiefly influenced, I think, by the Belgian aspect of the

case – the violation of Belgian neutrality & the alleged excesses there & destruction of life and churches. Had he seen Donchery with its ruined church in the midst of a desolation of ruined houses I wonder what he would have said. Donchery was quite the most obliterated town I passed.

Meyer called on me at 9 p.m. to say that the military authorities report that they have already found 2300 Catholic Irish soldiers among the prisoners! as I told them. They thought less than one thousand would be the limit – I told them all along England fights with Irishmen. Here is but proof of it. By the last official figures they had 15400 privates of the British Army as prisoners of war – Since that return they have captured some 1500 – 2000 more at outside – so that of a possible 17.000 to 18.000 men they have already – with only a preliminary search too – got 2300 Catholic Irish soldiers! If we add those passed over, inevitably, in a search of this kind, conducted by foreigners, and the Protestant Irish we should certainly find that well over 3000 (possibly 4000) of the "British" prisoners of war are Irishmen – or about one fourth of the whole.

It points one way or the other – either there are many more Irish in the Army (as I have always said) than the Br. Govt admits – or else the Irish Regiments have been in the posts of danger from the first. Both explanations are true. The number of Irish soldiers is greatly swelled by enlisting in England and Scotland of Irish born boys or sons of Irish parents. Meyer, I think, told me that this preliminary search, however, was through Irish Regiments only! Already 300 or 400 have been collected into a special camp at Limburg near Frankfurt on the Maine – whither I am to go on Tuesday night to see the men.

I go before the priests go & will sow my seed first – & leave them papers & words of love.

On Sunday Blücher called & left me a "Daily Mail" with notice (21 November) of the pro-German demonstration of the Medical College of the National University of Ireland – the inaugural meeting. There were, it seems, wild cheers for the Kaiser and the German Army and hooting for Kitchener & the "President of the Royal College of Surgeons and other gentlemen" had to withdraw! Mr. Newman, it appears, raised the question in Parliament & wants to know what action will be taken. His words are:

> "In view of this discouragement to recruiting and encouragement to the enemies of this country" will the Irish Secretary "take vigorous action to deal with these constant exhibitions of anti-British feeling."
> Good – things are moving in Ireland. Wait for my "Irish Brigade"!

Blücher & I to Eden Hotel to see rooms there for Sir Roger Casement when he returns to Berlin. Then he and **[word omitted]** to the Zoo a fine place, with good tigers and lions – & the Tea Room enormous.

There must have been 1500 to 2000 people in the two big halls (at 4.30) & a good band playing – men, women & children & I could not believe it was the centre of a city beset by more than half the world in arms against the soldier boys of their people we saw so peacefully & happily at tea. Truly they are a great, calm, proud & <u>manly</u> race.

Kaiser Wilhelm II with officers in Pickelhauben outside a Field Post Office

The evg papers announce that the Kaiser had gone to the Polish front! Is that good or bad?

I fear bad news. This morning telegrams say that the cable from Libau to Frederica has been cut, because it served Russian war purposes. That looks as if the news in Friday's <u>Corriere della Sera</u> (to hand today) may be true. This is that the Germans are getting the worst of it on the Vistula & that two army corps are surrounded & will have to surrender! Kitchener announced a great Russian victory in the Lords!

It may be so indeed. The last German wires confessed that the enemy had fresh "enormous forces that prevented the Germans from profiting from their victory over the Russians at Lódz-Lociewieza." I hope and pray it is no disaster. As I write the Prussian guard detachment that daily changes guard at 1 o'clock is marching past (12.30) up Dorotheenstr. to the Palace & the band is playing – "God save the King"!

I had a delightful walk last evening in the Thiergarten – to the Konzertsaal by the Zelten & on to Moabit Bridge & back. Thousands of young soldiers out for the day – Unter den Linden swarming with them – handsome, strong, fine young fellows.   All waiting only for the word.

[Two sentences inserted at bottom of page:] I walked with a young German lad whose brother an officer and another killed – & 4 cousins in the war. A young guardsman.

Blücher says he heard from von Jagow to whom be had written asking him to lunch to meet me.

Jagow replied that he was off with the Emperor on Saturday night – & could not come & added things about Ireland & my mission that by Blücher's showing were not very favourable. But Blücher is extraordinarily inaccurate in his versions of happenings. It is "untruth by defect." He does not intend to misstate, but he does.

He tells me Lay, the U.S. Consul General, showed him the pamphlet "from New York" on Ireland & Germany & they had discussed it. Lay thinks it came from America! I posted it to him on Friday evening.

Tuesday 1 December – Berlin
To Blücher at Esplanade at 6 & left a letter for Eoin MacN – inclosed in one to Mrs. G. – & this in one to Wambersin & Son, Rotterdam – this finally to go to Herr Ballin[68] in Hamburg, who can get it through to England unopened – So B. says – this is the route Princess of Pless takes & it is on her advice.

Met a Graf something or other, a friend of B.'s who is trying to arrange a meeting for me with a powerful member of the Reichstag.

This Graf Praschma[69] is a Catholic deputy too – and of course a soldier! He has just come back from the Aisne front, near Soissons – and looks rosy, pink and blue eyed and fat! Like a nice big Dutch doll. We discussed many things – in French – and he said the "Audacious" was surely sunk – he added with a sigh – "My daughter danced on the "Audacious" at Kiel"!

B. says that the leading Germans still are not keen for war <u>*à outrance*</u> with England – at least the diplomatic world of Germany, of which von Jagow is the type. They wanted – and want! – English "friendship." The military ma-

---

[68] Albert Ballin (1857-1918), director of the Hamburg-Amerika shipping line. Casement and he had corresponded, perhaps even met, in 1913 on the subject of German liners calling at Cobh/Queenstown. They certainly met in Hamburg in 1915. The only Jewish privy councillor to Wilhelm II, he committed suicide two days before the armistice.
[69] Hans Praschma (1867-1935)

chine, however (and happily), is under no such illusions and desires mightily to get at England – and, as B. truly says, the military mind in Germany dominates the civil power in every way and also has absorbed far the ablest minds of the land so that German intelligence is much better represented in Army and Navy circles than in the Foreign Office and governing administration.

This is evident! If the men who have controlled German "diplomacy" & brought this country to its present state of colossal isolation in the world had had the war machine to run, I guess the French and Russian armies would now be near Potsdam.

[Curry omits the text from here to the end of the 1 December entry. Angus Mitchell also leaves out large chunks. There is no entry for 2 December.] As it is they are still afar – battling for life on their own soil. Last night's war news gives a further 5.100 Russian prisoners and 18 guns in Poland & East Prussia. In the last three weeks Germany and Austria-Hungary have captured not less than 112.000 men of the Russian armies. And yet I see by the Times & other English papers (from B.) that Kitchener announced officially "a great Russian victory" in the House of Lords. The Times admits in editorial comment, however, that "the situation in Poland is somewhat obscure"!

The Times gives many particulars of the "Sedition" in Ireland – questions in the Lords, raised by Desart, Ranfurly and Midleton, with replies by Wimborne & Crewe, winding up with notice of a question by Curzon. They want Irish Freedom, the I. Volunteer, Sinn Fein, & Larkin's paper all prosecuted for their active sedition and comfort to Germany – & for the aid of recruiting. Recruits not coming in!

The last Times to hand is <u>Wed. 25 Nov</u>. – & this still contains nothing about me. It is clear the Govt tried to suppress the German Declaration, but must have failed – as Sir J Lonsdale question (from Amsterdam 28 Nov) shows that by Friday it was public property and had been raised in the Commons. I can have come out only through America.

The wireless message to Sayville on 20-21 Novr. was of course read also by the Marconi Coy. All the German Sayville messages that the English wish to publish I find given in full in the <u>Times</u> as having been read by the Marconi Coy. en route.

With regard to my coming here further interesting news about American passports is in both Times & the local <u>Continental News</u> – Here is the cutting Continental News – 30 Nov. 1914

[Two newspaper cuttings are tipped in side-by-side and headlined 'New Passports for Americans' but the text is unreadable.]

The "Times" notice is very similar – The photograph of the bearer affixed beneath the U.S. seal in each case – and the warning very similar.

[Newspaper cutting headlined 'England and Her Indian Troops':]

England is proud of her Indian troops in France and long articles in the press are devoted to the courage and bravery of Ghurkhas and Sikhs. The fighting of natives and whites side by side against a white enemy was not always appreciated in this way. One of the Mutiny veterans for instance Mr. L.E. Runtz Rees, in his "Memories of the Siege of Lucknow" condemns that the Indian artillery was apparently commanded by a European, for the English could distinctly see several white men moving about in the enemy ranks. "I cannot understand" the author says "how it is possible for white men to make common cause with black cut-throats with barbarians who fight like wild beasts, not like human beings. No punishment is great enough for those abominable traitors to their own blood." This was written in 1858. In 1914 English papers describe in glowing terms how – it is their own version, not ours – the Germans were fleeing in Flanders before the knifes of the Indians!

The above is badly presented by the paper – but the quotation is highly interesting. It is an extraordinary thing the way the English deceive themselves. Their "moral appetite is fed on falsehood" as Michael Davitt truly said. The people who blew these same Indian soldiers from the cannon's mouth when they dared to fight against <u>them</u>, 60 years ago now by all their leading "statesmen" proclaim these same soldiers as "civilising agents" to instruct the Germans in "chivalry, humanity and regard for the rules of war" (vide Lord Crewe's speech).

[The text goes upside down from here to the end of the manuscript. Sheet 98 is stuck to a cardboard divider and the writing on the page is largely covered. Only odd words such as 'darkness', 'Berlin', 'Adler', 'is bad enough', 'malicious' and 'disgusted' and the last two words 'machine guns' are currently visible.]

END OF PART I

1914

PART II <u>DIARY</u>

Thursday, 3. December. Frankfurt on Main.

I got here this morning at 7.10 in darkness. My train left the Anhalt Station at Berlin at 10.20 last night. The Crown Princess travelled too by the first part of the same train. I saw her arrive – very little ceremony, but all hats off.

There has been little to record the last few days. Tuesday I was unwell and stayed in my room all day. Professor Schiemann; called late at night with disquieting statements about Adler that were unwarranted and malicious. Poor Adler! God knows he is bad enough without these professional inquests on him. I was annoyed beyond words – and disgusted. **[Curry omits these two words and the next two paragraphs.]** machine guns.

Altogether since 11 Nov. the Germans have taken over 80.000 Russian prisoners and the Austrians 40.000 – say 3 army corps in 3 weeks! The killed and wounded must be fully equal – so that Russia has had 6 army corps wiped out in 3 weeks. What the German & Austrian losses may have been, we don't know. Doubtless heavy too – and the Russians claim to have taken 6.000 prisoners in one batch, 4.000 in another and a few cannon too.

Then last night, Wednesday 2 Dec the fall of Belgrade was announced after over four months' siege. The second capital captured in the war & both by the Germanic armies.

Things look <u>very</u> black for Servia – & there will be little pity for her fate. Her case is different from that of Belgium although the publication of the "Anglo Belgian Military Conventions" of 1906 entirely upsets the Belgian <u>pose</u> of neutrality. She was no more neutral than France – or England. She deliberately allied herself with England 8 years ago – & England in 1912 dared to inform Belgium that she, England, would land troops in Belgium "to defend Belgian Neutrality", whether Belgium consented or not! **[Inserted in pencil:]** This is the masterpiece of the correspondence – & the height of neutrality for you.

I lunched yesterday at the Astoria Hotel with Baron & Baroness von Roeder. He is Court Chamberlain – Master of the Ceremonies – She was a daughter[70] of Lord Rockingham. Of course her English was perfect; but her heart now entirely German and she shared all my views and hopes. Countess Blücher also there. She, poor lady very unhappy and <u>trying</u> to be German – but her heart still with her own land.

---

[70] Actually Lavinia Watson of Rockingham Castle, Northamptonshire, granddaughter of the 2nd Baron Sondes. She married Eugen von Roeder in 1875.

I told Blücher of Schiemann's remark about Adler – & then of the truth – of Adler's confession to me the night before he left. Blücher agrees with me about him, that there is an innate chivalry and sense of honour and courage that make amends. I went to von Wedel at 7 to tell him – as I felt it necessary to be frank. I dined alone with Blücher at the Esplanade & came on to the Anhalt Station at 10.

Blücher is <u>very</u> keen on the Christiania business & says he had a long talk with von Roeder today after I had lunched there who will also take it up. B. proposes getting Herr Ballin interested & employing a special detective to go with Adler to Norway and get the convincing proofs of Findlay's guilt – I agree [**two words then added in pencil:**] with <u>reservations</u>.

[**Inserted later in pencil across the bottom of both pages:**] Blücher had no right to discuss the matter, however, with anyone. I told him to keep it quiet & he has gossiped all through Berlin about it – written about it to von Jagow, the Secretary of State, & now wants to syndicate it – and run it as a sort of private concern!

The letter from Adler of 26 Nov. that Meyer brought me on Monday said that he had "got Findlay sure" – & begged me to write a "fake" letter. This I did on 1 Dec. – an absurd epistle about chartering a boat for $30.000 & hiring two men – & a lot more that Adler suggested.

He says that his plan to catch Findlay is a fine one – Findlay gave him <u>Kronen 500</u> this time – that is 625 Kronen he has got from the Rascal – put the Kroners at 1/2, it gives over £36 the Br. Govt. have disbursed on that branch of their secret service – & I wish them joy of the value received! The "moral and material" gains are, I fear, on the wrong side of the account.

On getting to Frankfurt I came in the dark to the Hessischer Hof (formerly the "Englischer Hof" I see) & took a room. About 9 the manager came to say that the Chief of the General Staff was in the Hotel & would see me at his office at 11 a.m.

This is General ~~von Grafen~~ de Graaff.[71]

I have a letter for him, from the Ministry of War, yesterday signed by the War Minister introducing me as "Sir Roger Casement, an Irishman" & – stating that I am to visit the Irish camp at Limburg & have entire freedom with the Irish prisoners of war.

I also have, for general use, an Imperial Passport No. 2192 issued by the Emperor's "Special Order" and signed for the Imperial Chancellor by one "Dargitz", issued for 3 months from 2 Dec. 1914. The passport is for "travelling in Germany" – and is issued to the "Irishman Sir Roger Casement." I showed it here at the Hotel on registering, and wrote my name, birth place,

---

[71] Probably General de Graeff but Casement spells his name de Graaff or de Graaf.

year & date of birth – & so now thirty four days after I reached Berlin I become myself! Here I am, I presume, the only (unmarried) or male "British subject" at large in Germany, with a special Imperial passport and the full consent and goodwill of the Govt. – & to judge from the manager's face, & the smiles of the waiters, the goodwill of the people themselves.

Roger Casement's German passport (NLI 17590/4)

The <u>Frankfurter Zeitung</u> of this morning has an article on the Irish "Nationalismus" –

I have brought plenty of "literature" for the soldiers – including a lot of copies of the new issue of my pamphlet "Ireland, Germany and the Freedom of the Seas", which the Berlin FO has printed for me under the title "The

Crime against Ireland – and How the War may end it." It is a reprint of the preface and then 6 articles & I have added as a 7th article "The Elsewhere Empire" so that it makes a little book almost. The FO has had 2.000 printed for me – and have done it very well indeed. The type, style, paper & general get up are excellent – I sent a copy to Schiemann – & will send out many to the press & to Americans re here in Germany.

I am now going to change my clothes to go to General de Graaff who, I gather, is to take me on to the camp at Limburg. I expect to stay there over Sunday – and then to return to Berlin and let the two priests go to take up their spiritual duties. I hope the men agree. The FO will agree to all my conditions I gather – that is to the military conditions of the employment of the men as an Irish Brigade – whether they will even go further in a political sense than they have done in the Declaration of 20 Nov. I doubt. I must try to get them – & will try to make that one of the conditions of the men joining my Irish Brigade.

It is hard I can hear <u>nothing</u> – absolutely nothing from America. No reply from Cohalan to the telegram I sent on Friday asking if any special messenger had gone to Ireland & if a priest could come here – No word from Kuno Meyer. No word as to how the Declaration was received in U.S.A. & if any action there has followed. If I knew for sure that the Declaration had produced the effect I hope for it would so greatly strengthen me morally here – & stiffen me in my attitude to the men – & to the German Govt. But for all I know it may have fallen dreadfully flat.

It <u>is</u> strange no word comes from von Bernstorff. Indeed, so far as I can observe it, German "Diplomacy" deserves many of the hard things Billy Tyrrell said of it in the Foreign Office in November 1912 at our historic meeting. But the real German diplomats are not in the Foreign Office, but in the German armies & navy. The brains of the country & its best character are of necessity there & the civil power is left to fish for inferior intelligences with less attractive bait.

Saturday. 5 Decr at Limburg

I found General de Graaff on Thursday at 11.30 a.m. in his office down by the Maine – a very charming man, knowing English well (a friend of the late King Edward VII, formerly, a native of Wiesbaden, I think) & in 5 minutes all was arranged.

He was to take me out to Limburg Friday himself in a motor car going thro Wiesbaden & the lower Taunus – & would visit the Irish camp with me and leave me at Limburg as long as I liked & the car with two orderlies at my disposal.

I returned to the Hotel on foot. General de Graaff assured me I might go about Frankfurt just as I pleased – that every official person had been advised & that he had requested the papers to say nothing about me thinking that for the present I would prefer no comment or interviews.

I walked about Frankfurt a good deal, admiring the broad & beautiful streets and splendid buildings – & the general air of extreme well doing of people, houses & public buildings. The population is generally speaking, darker than the Berlin type – here the Hessian face is the predominant. On the whole the people are nice looking – good deal of Jew in some faces – & have the fine, strong, well shaped bodies I notice all thro' Germany – Soldiers and sailors – very strong, well built young men are in evidence – and many young men & boys I met enough for a division in the streets!

No lack of fine, strong, handsome boys and young men. My old Hotel, the Frankfurter Hof (May 1912) is partly a Hospital – at back I find – The shops filled with Christmas things chiefly "love gifts" for the soldiers and sailors at the front. Everything here in Germany today is simply a gift to the heroic forces defending the fatherland.

The crime and cowardice of England seem to me everyday to be magnified when I contrast her petty, mean, sordid spirit of commercial war and war of conquest over weaker peoples with this heroic spirit of all Germany, to face and overcome by courage, sacrifice and national discipline the hired hordes of Asia and Africa and trained millions of Russia and France too.

I agreed with General de Graaff, at night, after dinner, to leave on Friday at 8.30 for Limburg.

This we did – in beautiful weather for Decr. – The car a fine military motor with a huge War Ministry arms on the panels (the Prussian Eagles wings widespread long) that attracted attention and salutes from every soldier.

We were off at 8.30 and out to Wiesbaden, which we passed through, a perfectly charming town – the gardens well kept – but the smart Hotels shut up.

A big garrison is there (3000 men) & about 4000 wounded, so that there is plenty of military life at present.

We got to Limburg, thro' a beautiful country with sunshine lighting the hills & woods at about 9.45 or 10 a.m. – having come quickly. There, at the Preussischer Hof were the General Exner[72] in charge of the Irish camp & many other officers and among them Prince Leiningen who introduced himself as an "old Harrovian" – He was born at Osborne.

We all went on to the Camp over the Lahn with a glorious view of the

---

[72] Major General Paul Exner d. 1927

Cathedral on its rock right on the river.[73] The camp not finished – a huge wooden encampment, very well put up indeed and with the greatest care being shown for the welfare of the men. About 400 French soldiers working at it & only some 300 "Irish" already collected. They looked a <u>very</u> wretched lot – half clad only in a miserable thin Khaki Stuff – they were pinched with cold, dirty & miserable & I felt ashamed of them beside the better clothed & <u>much</u> finer looking French prisoners.

The German officers (there were nearly 20 with us, following the two Generals) were all struck by the poor starving & generally poor figures of the Irish. I saw about 20 non-commissioned officers first in their room and spoke to them alone. O poor lot – One of them more English than the English themselves – he talked of "getting back to England" – of "squaring it with the Germans when we get them to England" and so forth. Others had the Irish face & eye – & (mostly young men) they had <u>horrid beards</u>.

The men outside looked even worse than the non-coms. and very unpromising material to work on I felt. The scum of Ireland – literally. Thank God for it, from one point of view – it shows so clearly that the blow we have dealt enlisting. Most of the men I saw were from the 18 Royal Irish – with a few S. Lancashires! & Middlesex! & one I saw of the Leinsters. The General said that some "English" soldiers had got themselves smuggled in as Irish and wd. have to be weeded out.

I talked to the non-coms for about 10 minutes – told them who I was & all about the "Home Rule" fake & the Irish in America & that I was going to try to get arms & men into Ireland to join the Volunteers – but I said "I don't think any of you are brave enough to do what I've done." Some had themselves said they'd "join the Volunteers" or "go to America" when the war is over –

The worst was a young handsome lad only of the 18th – the one who spoke of "England" & of "us" all the time – & the "lies of the Germans." I saw <u>some</u> good Irish eyes – & one poor fellow outside among the privates, asked if I was Irish & when I said yes – he said "God bless you, you look Irish too."

I left them after only a few minutes talk promising to return tomorrow. I gave them the pictures of the Pope I brought from New York and lots of papers – including the Continental News with the Declaration of the German Govt – & my "Appeal to the Irish People" – & some English papers too with the usual lies. I left more for the 1800 others I heard were coming – and

---

[73] The unique position of the Limburger Dom at the edge of town on a rock rather than in the city centre is due to its origins as a castle chapel dedicated to St. George. The castle was probably built in Merovingian times (8th century or earlier) and the chapel added in the early 9th century.

gave them to Major Grunert in charge of the camp under General Exner.

Then I visited with the Generals the kitchens. Excellent – clean & well built with huge boilers – in one kitchen half a dozen French soldiers were cooking – I tasted the food – a mixture of maccaroni, potatoes & herbs. very good and <u>very</u> hot. One of the young French soldiers cooking was a splendid young fellow – about 6 feet, fair, strong – in blue puttee's showing splendid calves & with the figure of a young Hercules.

His face was fixed, no smile – Blue eyes, civil & polite to the questions of his captors – but Oh! such a far off look! His heart in France – only his hatred here. I felt deep pity for the French. They were the men of a nation – a national army, citizens under arms – fighting for France. When I looked at them I understood the German pity and respect for the French.

For the Irish I <u>could</u> have no such feeling. They were <u>not</u> fighting for their country – they were indeed, as they are always called on the Continent, "a mercenary army." No spark of patriotism to fire the eye – The Crime Against Ireland stood there before me in these poor sodden sick faces. Demoralised into the ranks of the one <u>anti</u>-national army in all the world. God! <u>what</u> a crime it is:

I left the camp with a sense of despair. We all lunched together at the "Prussischer Hof" in Limburg after General de Graaff (with Prince Leiningen) called on the Bishop to tell him the two Irish priests from Rome were coming as chaplains of the Irish soldiers. A 'phone to the General from Berlin asked if I had any objection to the two priests coming at once – and I said none at all – so de Graaff 'phoned back to say send them at once & they should be here on Sunday morning.

Sunday night – 6 Decr. – (Frankfurt.)

The Friday (4 Dec) afternoon, General de Graaff, his ADC & Prince Leiningen and I went on in the motor car to visit another Prison camp being put up at Wetzlar – on the Lahn. The journey through a beautiful country – the heart of Hesse-Cassell up the valley of the Lahn. We saw afar off some splendid old towers on isolated hills – something like the Roman castles one sees outside of Rome – ruined messages from medieval Germany. At Brauenfels a very fine schloss on the cliff over the Lahn – a huge building belonging I gathered to a Prince Zolms or Solms[74] I think.

Wetzlar, too, very picturesque with a fine old castle – and the river running through it.

The new camp being constructed, to hold at a pinch 20.000 men – is all

---

[74] Solms is the correct spelling: Prince Solms-Braunfels.

of wood – not so solid as the camp at Limburg. Mostly French prisoners here – but 6 English soldiers – a poor looking lot – and six Russians.

A young Belgian "cadet", very smart, tried to get de Graaff to order his treatment as an officer – but de Graaff was civil, smiling and – obdurate.

He said "you <u>are</u> not an officer – you were going to be one – but we can only take cognisance of your actual status" – so the very smart bold hero young fellow got no comfort.

Leiningen spoke to the English prisoners – all had been wounded – with shrapnel but now recovered – and they did <u>not</u> look happy I must say.

Some of the French prisoners were handsome young fellows – tall & strong –with good faces and well built. Two Algerians – Turcos there – & answering the General de Graaff – said they were "volunteers."

We left the camp and on to Giessen – a fine town on the Lahn of 60.000 people and a University.

Full of life – schoolboys & students & some peasant girls in the charming country costume and some of the young men too in the <u>national</u> Hessian garb. The General and the two others got off at the station to wait for a train for Frankfurt and I stayed on in the motor which then set out to return to Limburg.

It was dark & the road uninteresting for that reason. We returned by Wetzlar and Braunfels & got to Limburg at 7 (or 6.40) where I had a quiet dinner & went to bed with a bad sore throat at the Preussischer Hof – it is a very comfortable clean, good Hotel – and extraordinarily cheap.

My excellent bedroom <u>with</u> ample breakfast – coffee, rolls, butter & honey (fruhstück) costs only 3 marks.

Bath free, and the bath is large, clean and airy.

A headwaiter who speaks good English and has young waiters, both boys, who speak only German. But all very civil, clean, smiling and pleasant faced.

The town of Limburg is quite charming – delightful old houses and streets round the Cathedral – and such a fine faced, strong, well shaped bodied population. Literally hundreds of young men and boys here still – and the more I see of Germany the clearer it becomes that she must win the war. One never hears a boast or a bragging word. There is simply quiet calm confidence in the power of the army (and the navy too!) and the patriotism of the whole nation. I gave away several copies of the "Crime against Ireland" to the German officers. The chief interpreter of the camp is a "Professor" Brezien who speaks fairly good English – but will not leave me alone. He is constantly coming to see me on all manner of trifles and is, in fact, dreadfully officious – But well meaning. At the outbreak of the war he had been in France teaching and was locked up in a concentration camp at Sables d'Olonne – He was then released as he is past 60.

A Major Grunert of the camp also speaks very good English – better than either General de Graaff or Professor B – He and the Professor have been in U.S.A. Brezien much at Philadelphia and Grunert at Washington.

On Saturday forenoon at 11 a.m. I went up to the prisoners with Major Grunert & the Professor – & spoke <u>alone</u> to some of the men & non-coms – They seemed already to guess the end in view and began saying they'd like to fight for Ireland. I told them of my plans and several of the non–coms said that "very little persuasion would be needed." that practically all would agree. One man came up & said "How is Father O'Daly?" & then added "I paraded in front of you, Sir Roger, at Six Mile Cross."

I remember it well – the parade, not the man – that dreary Sunday evg in June last at the RC Church & the huge turn out – & Eoin MacNeill & I, & Pat MacCartan standing on the wall & speaking to the men before the evening service. We left that for Dundalk that night in Pat McC's motor car – getting in at 11.30 p.m. to Dundalk – And now here is one of those Volunteers – a British soldier and a prisoner of war!

A good looking young man with a huge fair thick beard – & good blue eyes & a smiling brow. Some of the faces were good – those of soft hearted Irish boys – but many are not good and some are depraved and vicious. They look anaemic and sick mostly and say they were not well treated at Hameln or Hamblen[75] and there they got "English" fare – being "English" prisoners of war! They said that the Irish Regts had been put in the front & sacrificed & that what the <u>G. American</u> said was true in one of the copies I had left in the camp the previous day.

I asked if it was true that the Munsters had fired into the King's Own Scottish Borderers at the end and they said they had heard so, & they thought it was true.

Many said they had "surrendered on purpose"! One young 78th man said "We threw down our rifles at Lille – 400 of us"!

There is plenty of anti-English feeling – but <u>no</u> pro-German!

There is the trouble – they were well fed up with the lies of John Bull's press bureau before starting & then all the destruction they saw in France – especially of churches – they believe was wantonly inflicted by the Germans.

I left two exercise books with Sergeant MacMurrough of the Leinsters and with Timothy Quinlisk[76] of the 18th to fill up with names of all men

---

[75] Actually Hameln

[76] Timothy Quinlisk was appointed quartermaster sergeant by the German naval staffer, H.W. Boehm, who noted that this "while tickling his ambition eliminates him as much as possible." (NLI 13085/17) He was later to be shot in Co. Cork in February 1920, appar-

and regiments. These two are keen for the Brigade – <u>so they say</u>. Mac M is a dark-eyed, black bearded Sergeant of the Leinsters from Belfast ~~originally~~ & once a postal clerk! He admitted his enlistment was due to "financial trouble"!* **[footnote:]** *I expect it was! & that he would not return to Ireland "with a red coat."

Quinlisk is a boy, only 18 & 9 months, from Wexford – a corporal, I think. He writes well & is intelligent & <u>says</u> he will gladly join the Brigade.

Mac M is 32. Both say they have read "The Crime against Ireland," and like it much.

After a few words here & there & telling them I'd come up to Mass at 9 a.m. where as they said there was already an Irish priest to officiate! This I found rests <u>on</u> some opinion the men have that there is "an old Tipperary man," a clergyman here at Limburg.

In the afternoon I went in the car to Coblenz via Montabaur & other small towns. Prof Brezien came with me as *cicerone*. One of the two chauffeurs is a Doctor – studied at Jena for many years.

Both he & the other, a young Prussian type, steel-blue eyed young man, are volunteers like Lüttichau & Meckle. The car is the Staff car of the 18th. Army Corps Headquarters at Frankfurt & is left by the General with me for as long as I need it.

We crossed the Rhine from Ehrenbreits by the bridge of boats to Coblenz & went to the Coblenzer Hof where all four had coffee, wine, beer & cakes for 4.70 all told – very cheap indeed. The Hotel café fairly full of life.

The return journey was in darkness & I got to Limburg at 6 or so & to bed directly after dinner – the small waiter bringing me coffee and hot water at 9 p.m. His name is Rudolf Kuekelberg or some such – & walks with a military strut. All the small boys down to 4 and 5 play at soldiers & salute the car as we pass with a haughty Prussian pride. I bought some fine photos of Limburg today – showing the wonderfully placed Cathedral well poised on its rock.

I got a telegram from Gen. de Graaff saying the two Irish priests arrived by train at 9.17 & I arranged to go to the camp at 8.20 a.m. & then send the car for the priests & while they were at the Hotel I would gather all the men & talk to them of the Irish Brigade.

On Sunday, 8 Decr. [**actually Sunday 6 December**]

---

ently on the orders of Michael Collins, as a spy or British agent (see KV2/6 in The National Archives). In a 1932 letter from John Ryan in New York (NLI 17432) it is stated that Harry Quinliss (Timothy Quinlisk) was recruited by the British in Berlin and sent to Michael Collins. Alerted about his recruitment, a trap was laid and sprung by the IRA. This is not the case, according to recent research.

I went up to the camp at 8.15 (2 Doctors with me) & got from MacMurrough & Quinlisk 383 names of Irish prisoners. Some few, it seems are really English Catholics, children of Irish-born parents, but themselves born in England – Several belong to the Middlesex and S Lancashire regiments. I got all gathered in one room – & told them of my idea of the Irish Brigade, and read out the conditions, roughly, that I should propose to the German Govt. I pointed out all the risks & dangers & said I wanted them to think it over & that I would come again in about a week to hear their answers. They said nothing. All kept quiet. I then returned to Limburg & picked up Fathers O'Gorman and Crotty at their Hotel & took them up to the camp.

They saw a good many of the men several of whom knew Fr Crotty or his brother, a priest it seems, once at Kilkenny.

I had both priests to lunch with me at my Hotel. We talked of the war & of Ireland & of the recent action taken there against the Irish national papers.

They are both well disposed more so than ever.

I decided to go to Frankfurt today & see General de Graaff to get further liberties for the men – & to allow the two Sergeants to come down & see me at my Hotel.

We left in the car at 2.45 or so – I alone in the car & the two chauffeurs. They chose a different road from that by which de Graaff & I had come. The route now taken was right up over the Taunus range leaving Wiesbaden well on the right. The towns and villages passed through were all of interest – particularly one with a fine ruined keep on a hill & a modern Schloss near – I think this was Cronberg – We passed one quite remarkable village down in the valley before going up the Taunus of quite medieval houses the external walls of the houses all joining & being erected on a rocky cliff. They gave the appearance of a vast fortified wall. In the middle ages these walls would have constituted a veritable defence. A ruined tower peered over the <u>straw</u> roofs – dark brown straw – of the high, fortified farm houses, all with their gables & beams & joists of dark wood.

Up in the Taunus pine woods there was snow & frost and these gave very striking character to the otherwise sombre woods.

From Cronberg we ran through a fine big village or town whence I saw a signpost pointing to "Homburg, 3 Kms" – & we got into Frankfurt about 4.30. I found Prince Leiningen at ten, & he took me down to the General Staff headquarters where I had a long talk with de Graaff.

I told him the men were seemingly willing to join the Brigade, but that the matter would have to be worked very carefully & I should want fuller powers to do as I pleased with the men.

I advised soap, shaving, tobacco to begin with – He agreed to all & wrote a letter to General Exner to this effect which I was to take back by the early train (7.57 a.m.) to Limburg.

De Graaff advised me to see either Bethmann Hollweg or von Jagow quickly & not to be content with von Wedel. He said that von W. was merely a "letter carrier" – & I should insist on the heads of the Govt. seeing me.

I wrote to von Wedel letter saying something of this. Here it is x x **[at top of page but no letter present:]** (insert here my letter) and I sent it off by special post at 7.40 a.m. on the Monday morning.

I walked about Frankfurt a bit this Sunday after I left de Graaff and did not return to the Hotel until 9.15 to supper.

This meal cost me 10.40 say 10/6. I could live for the whole day and night at Limburg for less than I pay here for one meal. The room is 14 marks – so that the room & supper come to 25/–

Prices vary so much in Germany. In the big cities you have foreigner's prices, like these quoted, or my 18 mark bedroom at the Continental in Berlin. As soon as you leave the big towns or fashionable resorts and get to the real Germany as at Limburg, you get the prices of a very thrifty, saving people.

The Preussischer Hof at Limburg is not at all a bad hotel – It must have some 60 bedrooms at least – & all good – One front room was offered me yesterday for 3 marks that was a finer room than my 18 marks room in Berlin – without the private bathroom.

Frankfurt was crammed with life this Sunday evening – the Kaiserstrasse & the streets I remember from May 1912 were packed with people – men, women and children – & soldiers.

De Graaff & Prince L. were dining with 3 ladies – speaking English mostly. De Graaff's wife, one of these I find is an American – which accounts for something of his English.

De Graaff himself is quite the most charming of the German officers I have met. His manner is that of a Frenchman or a very polished Dutchman – lively, straight and gentle – his face is handsome, clean cut, grey hair and always a pleasant smile.

He tells me the General in command at Frankfurt, Freiherr von Gall, is interested in me – & I am getting a card from that old gentleman who is a pompous old soldier Leiningen tells me. The card came in due course. I had replied with a copy of my pamphlet "The Crime Against Ireland" – & am also sending a card with my name written on it. I had to explain to de Graaff that I had no cards yet as I had been under a false name at Berlin.

Leiningen presses me to go & see him at Heidelberg "after the war."

Mavrone – for me there is no after the war – or hereafter at all. All I am & have & shall be is here now.

It is all for Ireland – & I refuse to think of anything else or of any personal consequences.

My cold is very much worse and while de Graaff gave me Formamint – a harmless and useless medicament – Leiningen sent a vial of drops to my room with word to try 15 drops on sugar before going to bed. I did – the result was nil. I tried them again twice, during the night, but hardly slept and had a very bad night of it with a cough that rasped me to pieces.

I did not sleep at all – but lay awake wondering what would happen. I have decided, perhaps finally, on one thing. It is that I shall insist on seeing either von Jagow or the Chancellor. Both are in Berlin I believe ~~with the Emperor who has arrived there from the Russian front~~. If I cannot get an interview with them, I shall take it as proof that the German Govt. is not sufficiently in earnest for me to go on further.

I will not accept the responsibility for putting a couple of thousand Irish soldiers into the high treason pot, unless I get very precise and sure promises both in their regard & for the political future of Ireland.

If I learn that neither Bethmann Hollweg nor von Jagow can see me, & I care not what the reason assigned may be, I shall decline to continue our "Conversations" and shall ask for a passport to enable me to go to Norway or Sweden.

These thoughts hardened during the night. I am not at all pleased with their attitude towards Christiania & from Blücher's (& Schiemann's) remarks it is clear they do <u>not</u> accept my view of the Findlay affair. I told Meyer so – & he got very red & shuffled, but from von Wedel's remarks about Adler – when I left the letter to be forwarded, it is clear they want me to drop the Christiania affair altogether & to drop Adler.

Now I am quite determined to do neither. I shall go on with the case against Findlay by every means in my power & I shall do all I can to help poor Adler to live a better life.

From the point of view of the Irish Cause I am not sure that the case against Findlay is not more telling than would be even the formation of an Irish Brigade. Of course for the Germans, the Irish Brigade is most important. It <u>shames</u> John Bull's army & it knocks recruiting on the head in Ireland.

The Findlay business has no interest for them – & they do not appreciate its significance rightly or the vast effect it would have on public opinion in Ireland & U.S.A. But even if they did, it would be for me only – & not for them; & they are keen only on the things I can do that will help them. Quite naturally. But equally, quite naturally, I mean to convict John Bull's Govt. of being what I have always termed it a criminal conspiracy.

Then as regards the Irish Brigade the difficulties are appalling – De Graaff approves the Egyptian idea greatly – but thinks I could get the men off to Egypt without the German press knowing anything! He is afraid of a "hell of a row" in the press any day about the "special treatment" being shown the Irish prisoners of war. Even if the men all agree – the difficulties then only begin. How is discipline to be maintained – what are they going to do? Officers? By and by want of money? both for them and me. I shall soon be penniless. The expenses have been far heavier than I anticipated – and one's hand is always in one's pocket. ~~I thought it well to bring Mac M and Quinlisk some clothes &c on Monday when they were here with me at the Hotel~~ Travelling, changes of hotel and tips take up constant sums. The servants are <u>not</u> paid by the <u>big Hotels</u> at all! The waiter at the Continental in Berlin on my floor has to pay his sub-waiter 20 marks a month to help him. He told me none of the servants on my floor were paid, but that the others "had no expenses!"

These are aspects of German method that are wholly repugnant to me. A callous disregard for the employed and a cynical disregard for the patrons too. For it is obvious if the servants are not <u>paid</u> by those engaging them they will not discharge their duties very brilliantly & if not well tipped by those entitled to proper service for nothing they will leave those who fail to tip them to whistle.

On the whole I find that with the exception of table waiting (which is a German science or philosophy of life in itself embracing a study of languages along with the art of laying plates & knives, always at the cost of the other party!) the service in German Hotels is greatly inferior to that in English – Bedrooms are not looked after nearly so well and valeting is a farce. The Hotels are clean – but the rooms neglected and there is no briskness of service as one sees in a big London Hotel upstairs – where the maids are bright intelligent and quick. Here they look listless, cross grained and ever expectant. By contrast the table service is always good – clean and fairly quick and the man or boy always polite and polished in manner, with a bow that no English gentleman could better and very few approach in grace or dignity.

With regard to the Christiania affair I am more and more determined to go on with it, just as I perceive the reluctance of the German authorities to my proceeding increases. I owe it to myself now. After Schiemann's disgraceful reference to Adler – and von Jagow's letter to Blücher that the latter told me held doubts as to the authenticity of the interview between Findlay & Adler I should be admitting the justice of these views were I now to withdraw. Besides there are the letters I wrote to J. McGarrity & "Pat" & sent by Adler, which were handed by him to Findlay.

Those letters have long since been handed to the Foreign Office & constitute for Downing St. overwhelming proof of my guilt. To now retire from the affair, merely because Wilhelmstrasse does not like it, would be to make the Br. Government a present of my character indeed & enable them to poison the ears of everyone in Ireland and USA. against me & <u>to prove their charges from my own writings</u>.

No I must launch the charge against them – I must be first in the field with the accusation and part of the accusation itself must consist of those very letters on which they are now relying to base their charges of horrible treason against me. And no time should be lost either.

The Irish Brigade will have to wait. In any case the Germans can't complain of delay there. The proposition to separate Irish from British prisoners of war was made by me in August, early in August. It was accepted again & again & urged in the letter sent to John Kenny[77] that he handed the German Ambassador in Rome on 3rd or 4 September. Without exception all the German authorities jumped at the idea from the start – but altho' it had this highest backing no action was taken until long after I had landed in Berlin.

Instead of finding the Irish camp already long since formed on my arrival in Germany as I had expected and had even been led to expect before leaving New York, no single step had been taken of any kind.

On the contrary I am forced to take a long and exposed journey to the Headquarters to say again there what had already been said many times before, before an order is issued to collect the Irish prisoners – and then it is only on the thirty fourth day after I land in Berlin that I am permitted to set out to see the first batch of men so collected – and only the thirty-fifth day when I see a few of them for the first time. Today it is six weeks since I came to Germany – & I have seen a few of the men in a make shift way with <u>no prior</u> preparation of them.

Part of my plan had always been that they should have been got into a receptive frame of mind, by literature, special treatment &c. before I came in person on the scene. Then the men's minds would have been already enlightened before I came. Their hearts would have been heated and their imaginations awake. I would have been in their minds as the only Irishman at large in Germany, the open foe of England – & when they were told that "Sir RC was coming to visit the camp" I would have been sure of a hearty welcome; & anything I had said of treason felony would have met with an instant response.

But these Germans cannot deal with the human understanding & they have mismanaged the thing as they do with all their "Diplomacy."

I have had to introduce myself to a gang of poor devils; distribute the

---

[77] John Kenny was the President of Clan na Gael and had been sent earlier to Germany.

literature; point out my "speeches" &c., &c. – & generally stand out from the first moment as an agent provocateur trying to stir up pro-German sympathies. It will take a great deal of careful work to undo the ill already done – & I don't see where the care is to come from.

The military authorities in charge of the prisoners know absolutely nothing of the purpose of the camp or the reasons for special treatment of Irish prisoners of war. & I am begged to <u>hide from them</u> all idea of any of my true purpose in visiting the camp! It cannot work like that. It is quite impossible. For me to get by stealth & in secret the adhesion of 2000 men to a propaganda of treason, conducted with <u>closed doors</u> in a military camp & with the officers in command ignorant of the game is a pretty fair sample of how these people (the Germans) mismanage their <u>human</u> problems!

<u>Monday</u>. 7 <u>Decr</u>. Frankfurt-Limburg.
  I left Frankfurt at 7.57 in darkness.
  I wrote von Wedel to say should require to see either the Chancellor or von Jagow before I committed the men – they will follow – but I don't go unless I get clear promises.
  This morning's *Frankfurter Zeitung* has a telegram from London, 6 Dec – saying that (D Telegraph reports) the police have seized "Irish Worker" and the press & edition confiscated & there is also something about "<u>Sinn Fein</u>" I cannot translate. Fr Crotty said yesterday the "Leader" had been seized as well as "<u>Irish Freedom</u>." The suppression of the "Leader" will put all the clergy "agin the Govt." Good! Last night de Graaf said there was a "hell of a row" in Dublin – lots about me & the seizure of Irish Freedom and probably "much more really than we saw in print."
  The journey to Limburg is thro' a beautiful country – some of it near the country we passed yesterday up to the Taunus. A great <u>schloss</u> at Idstein, a huge place with an isolated ruined tower at Idstein flies the red cross flag.
  Further on we pass the extraordinarily picturesque village (with its ruined tower) I passed yesterday with the old house. It lies between Idstein & Cronberg & is in Nassau. There is no sign of snow on the hills today – but heavy rain in night and inky clouds. I shall go to bed at Limburg & send the letter to General Exner & ask to have MacMurrough & the young corporal brought down to my room where I'll fit them out & give them a good feed.
  Father Crotty said yesterday "The first thing is that England should be beaten!" I said almost the same to the poor Fürst zu Leiningen last night. He is most unhappy – He would really prefer to be in England! I can see that. He does <u>not</u> sympathise in his heart with Germany – or shall I say, his true feeling is with England & he wants only peace between them.

English pride and prestige must be sinking – even the capture of De Wett[78] (reported I am told in recent papers) cannot restore it.

My defection is a serious blow to their pride – and if the Irish & Germans in U.S.A. are doing what I expect & hope I think we may put John Bull in the wrong box even in America!

At Eschhofen I see an old Church perched on a rock something like the beautiful Cathedral at Limburg – It is on the Lahn too, and we are now traversing its left bank going down to Limburg. This is the heart of Germany! – & as I write the spires & fortress like mass of Limburg cathedral rises close at hand.

Now to the Hotel & bed to my treason felony!

I sent the letter to Gen Exner & then got the interpreter Professor Brezien to come & give him a letter for Exner – who had gone to the camp – asking for Sergeant MacMurrough & the young Sergeant to be sent down to me at the Hotel – I am in bed here – my cold much worse.

I found a letter from von Wedel returning me my letter to Adler left with him on 2nd, to send to Christiania! He declines to send it on. I am getting very tired of the German official! The amount of mistrust & suspicion they move in is colossal.

I wrote to von Wedel this morning from Frankfurt, saying I should require to see either the Chancellor or Secretary of State before I proceeded further with the Irish Brigade.

I now write again to inclose a harmless letter to Adler, asking him to return at once as I had "fresh instructions." I asked that this should be sent at once by the Legation in Christiania – if not that it might be put into German & posted in the ordinary way.

I am very much annoyed!

I dare say they have been employing the "Berlin" on clandestine mine laying, so that Adler's bolt at London went home.

The Professor brought MacM and Quinlisk down to me about 12. I got him to bring them warm things, books & gave them a good dinner each. They talked long with me & it now seems there is much doubt whether any men will volunteer for the Brigade. They are very anti-German and think it is a German trick to get them to fight for Germany – So in one day they have changed their minds! MacMurrough and Q say there is much diversity of opinion – but they would not commit themselves to say how many would

---

[78] Christiaan de Wet: On the outbreak of World War I, de Wet opposed South Africa's decision to take over German South West Africa (now Namibia). His efforts to organize a rebellion led to his capture (December 1914) and a sentence of six years in prison for treason. After serving a year, however, he was released and allowed to live quietly on his farm.

agree to join the Brigade.

They "wanted time." I left them still with the list of names of 383 men & told them to try and find out & put a mark against each man – I was in bed all the time, with a throat with a band of red hot iron round it. General Exner came to see me at 2.30 with the Professor to interpret as he speaks neither French nor English – & he promised to do all I asked him to do for the men and to aid in any way possible.

I sent MacM and Q. back with the Professor at 3 – after many smokes & tea & cake. Neither impressed me very favourably. Both look rogues – especially MacMurrough. I may be wrong but I should think his enlistment was due to some serious defalcation – He says he had been a postal clerk – Quinlisk is only a boy – born in Wexford – but of a R.I.C. stock! Father & grandfather both sold to the British Govt.

The doubts I felt so strongly at the first glimpse of the prisoners here all revived. How could anything truly Irish really survive the free entry into the British army. No, these are not Irishmen but English soldiers – that is all.

The two priests came to see me at 3 or so and stayed a long time. I told them of the Brigade idea – since while they were with me Major Grunert came and actually suggested to <u>them</u> that the Irish should be formed into an "Irish Legion"! I lay in bed and chuckled – while this silly German Major expatiated on his theme. He was wound up – clearly my pamphlet had made a deep impression.

He confessed later it had – and that he saw now that the Irish was "a European question"! So – at last a real student.

The Professor came to report that he had left the two men in camp & I took copious doses of formamint & tried to sleep.

Thursday. 10 Decr.

I am now in the train returning from Limburg to Berlin. We are going by Fulda, where artillery is being exercised as we pass. I left Limburg at 9 and got to Frankfurt at 11.07 & had to wait there till 12.58 to get this train, the direct express for Berlin.

My War Minister's ticket has secured me a compartment to myself & I shall get to Berlin about 8.40 & drive to the Eden Hotel as "Sir Roger Casement."

The carriages are overheated – but are comfortable with a splendid big plate glass window so unlike the horrible barred "eyeholes" in U.S.A.

Yesterday & the day before I spent ill in Limburg. I stayed in bed all day Tuesday 7 got an army Doctor to come to me & he gave me a good dose to stop the cough – some drops tasting of almonds, 6 times a day.

I wrote to de Graaf on Monday telling him of the difficulties in the way of the Brigade – of <u>some</u> of them – by no means all.

They increase & multiply – as my cold grows worse! I am by no means hopeful. Indeed I have really lost all hope.

All Tuesday I lay in bed coughing and pondering – no word from America beyond the telegram about my friend Mr. Clarke of Chicago declaring that <u>he</u> knew all my plans! & would reveal them at the "Irish-German meetings in Chicago."

He declares (so these telegrams say) that "the German Emperor has promised Sir Roger Casement the liberation of Ireland if Germany wins the war!"

And this is one of the party that half caste "Irish" whole-hog politician Medill McCormick[79] arranged to meet me in Chicago on 25 Sept last – a party that impressed me so unfavourably that I said I had come to "meet Irish nationalists I thought, but found myself in an English party gathering." "Mr. Clarke of Chicago" evidently thinks I <u>may</u> represent the more popular side in Irish-American politics & so he wishes to be in the first flight – but the cool audacity of this windy old Humbug saying <u>he</u> knew what were the intentions of Germany towards Ireland & publishing that firm lie about the Emperor & myself is – well it <u>is</u> Chicago.

There have been several, in fact, daily references to Ireland in the press – both the petty local papers of Limburg & the Cologne *Zeitung* & *Frankfurter Zeitung*, showing how German interest is growing. (Just passing Hersfeld & lots of young recruits & soldiers here too – the country is <u>full</u> of men!)

One telegram says that six Irish papers are suppressed – four (Leader, I. Worker, I Freedom & I. Volunteer) by direct act of the military, who have seized the plant of some – & two, "Ireland" & "Sinn Fein" "have ceased to appear."

(I see a fine river[80] here just past Hersfeld – we are passing along its left bank. It is like the Lahn at Limburg or bigger, flowing through a broad meadow with pine clad hills on the right bank.)

"Ireland" is a new paper to me – new since I left Ireland. I fancy (it is only a guess) it is Bulmer Hobson's new paper – its life has been a short one.

Last night the *Colnische Volkszeitung* had an account of a speech of Redmond at Tuam that puts the cap on his treason to Ireland – I give it here (see <u>last</u> page of this vol.)

"130.000 Irishmen" according to this English scoundrel to take part in the most cowardly war even England ever waged for her selfish ends. Certainly if Ireland follows Redmond she deserves the doom of slavery, & degrading death so clearly the reward for helping England to assail Germany.

---

[79] [Joseph Medill McCormick (1877-1925) a Representative and Senator from Illinois.]
[80] The Fulda river.

I went up to the Camp yesterday afternoon (Wed. 9 Dec) with the two fathers at 5 p.m. They were going to confess some of the men.

(At Bebra here – a railway centre I see from the many sheds and much smoke.) I just went to talk with the Tyrone Volunteer – His name McGar (he says). He looked frightened when I spoke to him. MacMurrough said to be in bed ill – probably shamming – Many of the men came round to tell me "<u>all they wanted</u>" was tobacco! I told them there was some for them for Christmas – that I had given Fr Crotty 20 marks for buying it.

The more I see of these alleged Irishmen – the less I think of them as being Irish. They are the black blot on our claim to nationality – these same so-called "Irish Soldiers" in the English army.

After supper I went round to see Frs. Crotty & O'Gorman to bid them good bye.

The former told me, when Father O'G had gone away for a moment – that Msgr O'Riordan was strongly against the recruiting of Redmond and co. – & that the Sub Rector of the Irish College in Rome who is a better nationalist than Mgsr O'Riordan had got him, Fr Crotty, to come "to be a check on Father O'Gorman." He said – quickly – he was in full sympathy with my aims.

So far so good. Father O'Gorman has to return to Rome not later than 25 January – & then Father Crotty will have the men to himself.

But if I can't get 200 or 400 before that out of 2.400 I'm not much use – or rather the men are not much Irishmen.

Several of them gathered round me with friendly eyes – mostly young men – & even a questioning look – Was it – Ireland – or tobacco? Ireland is well represented –

<u>In</u> Ireland, the Loyalist Mr. Redmond imploring 100.000 Irishmen to go out and die for England, while England seizes the only free national organs of opinion in Ireland. Last night's telegrams <u>also</u> contained one from a Basel (Swiss) paper on the "New Enemy" of England!

The Swiss paper commented on the outbreak of Irish sedition & the threatening aspect of this new attack on England. It said that "what particularly attracted attention was that England, the home of free speech & of a free press, should now be violating both in Ireland."

Bravo! My passage through Christiania has borne plenty of fruit already! The panic of these Scoundrels, the British Ministry is illustrated by their prohibiting arms & all armaments in Dublin & other steps against Irishmen having guns. Thus while Irishmen are to be armed <u>out</u> of Ireland, to do the work Englishmen themselves cannot or will not do, it is to be high treason to dare to bear arms <u>in</u> Ireland! What consummate tricksters and hypocrites the English are – and what eternal slaves and fools the Irish!

From Bebra we have turned and are now travelling up the course of a fine river with beautiful pine clad hills and innumerable picturesque villages with gable ended farm houses – lofty & old fashioned with a great many timbers showing. Many are straw thatched but others tiled.

On the whole I feel my week (or nearly so) at Limburg has been a failure.

The chances of forming an Irish Brigade are poor enough – and if I cannot do that I may as well leave Germany – for there is nothing else to do here for Ireland but that.

We have just passed a wonderful old ruined Castle on a hill across the river – a huge ruined wall with several battered towers the remains of some great stronghold of the Middle Ages.

(4.20 p.m.) We have just arrived at Eisenach – a fine town. The houses are well built, lofty and surrounding hills covered with towers, schlosses and other buildings – a really beautiful situation – The river, I see from the map, must be the upper <u>Weser</u>. Our line runs on to Erfurt, Halle & Berlin – It will soon be dark & I shall see no more.

What fools the English are too! Here is the "Pall Mall Gazette" (my old friend J.L. Garvin) quoted in the *Corriere de la Sera* of 7 Dec, boasting about "the ring of iron" the British fleet has drawn round Germany

And here, in the heart of Germany, I pass through the best tilled lands I've seen in Europe – not a square yard wasted – the best fed people one can find in the world & this once quiet, university, medieval town, a large thriving, bustling city full of life, of industry & <u>smoke</u>! No <u>one</u> would dream this people was at war; the life of the country – as I saw it at Limburg – goes on the same and food is as plentiful & as cheap today as when on 2 Augt this war of devils was loosed against Germany.

When I look at this people, at their manliness of brow & bearing, their calm front and resolute strong chests turned to a world of Enemies, & then read the English columns of trash about Prussian barbarism & English heroism, I regret I am <u>not</u> a German.

I used to be proud to be Irish. Since I saw the "Irish" soldiers & read Redmond's speeches I feel ashamed to belong to so contemptible a race.

Bethmann Hollweg's speech at the opening of the Reichstag is given in bad English in the "Continental Times" of Dec 7. 1914, I got at Frankfurt.

It is a fine speech – but too late. He recognises <u>now</u>, after the event, that England made the war!

And I, in Aug 1911, wrote on my way to the Putumayo[81] that, if & when

---

[81] Casement wrote *Ireland, Germany and the Freedom of the Seas* partly "on board the SS Thames on my way out to Barbados to go up the Putumayo". (Text also to be found within *The Crime Against Europe*).

war came, it would be, it was already England's war. I was not only 3 years before the Chancellor, but I saw in peace what he has learned only through war. [**This sentence is unclear being obscured by the new binding.**]

In the (Catholic) *Kölnische Volkszeitung* (no. 1056) of 9 Decr is a telegram from Amsterdam of 8 Decr. says that Redmond at Tuam spoke as follows: [**as mentioned above**]

"The interest of Ireland is that the war should soon be ended. He stated that on 30 Nov. there were <u>89.000</u> Irish of whom 52.000 Catholics were in the <u>English</u> army – the <u>Irish</u> recruiting in England had given many more and some 10.000 Irish in the Colonies – He estimated the total of Irishmen now with "the colours" at 130.000 – & "this was only a beginning" – This is the new Irish <u>patriotism</u>!

[The first notebook in NLI 1689 ends here and the second notebook in NLI 1690 now begins.

Letter tipped inside front cover on Irish Brigade headed paper:]

IRISH BRIGADE (1915)
(Jrische Brigade

<u>Private</u>

In the event of my death, or when the war is over, if I am absent to be sent to

Joseph McGarrity
5412 Springfield Avenue
Pennsylvania. PA

To whom all my letters, books, papers &c in Germany or elsewhere are committed.

Roger Casement

Dresden
3. January 1916.

Roger Casement in German Foreign Office photograph; image used on the 50th anniversary of execution Irish stamp in 1966

At <u>Limburg</u> Camp!
Dec 6-8 1914

[Four newspaper cuttings are tipped in here, back to back. The first is hand-inscribed 'F.Z. 4 Dec/14.' and headlined '*Der deutsch-irische Bund*'. The second is hand-inscribed '*Frankfurter Zeitung* 7 Dec 1914.' and has two headlines:

X   *Die irische Gefahr.*
X   *Der , Burenaufstand*

A third is hand-inscribed '*B. Tageblatt* 4 Dec/14' and headlined *'Die Iren und der Krieg'*. The fourth is marked 'Basel. 9. Dez.' but has no newspaper name. It is also headlined with *'Die irische Gefahr'*].

The following Irish prisoners of war, captured by the German army and now detained in the camp at Limburg, province of Hesse, Germany, voluntarily agree to enter the Irish Brigade on the following conditions.

1. That the purpose of the Irish Brigade now being formed in Germany shall be solely to achieve the independence of Ireland.
2. That the members of the Irish Brigade are enrolled in it solely to serve Ireland and to fight in behalf of ~~the cause~~ the complete freedom of Ireland.

[Two more tipped-in news cuttings are to be found at this point, hand-inscribed '*F. Zeitung* Dec. 3. 1914' and headlined, respectively, '*Der irische Nationalismus.*' and '*Deutschland und Irland.*']

3. That no man entering the Irish Brigade does so for any pay, monetary reward or promise of such hereafter but solely as a volunteer in the service of Ireland with entire willingness to give his life and all he stands for freely and without reserve in his country's cause.
4. That the Irish Brigade, once constituted, while it shall be devoted solely to the purposes stated, with a view to securing the independence of Ireland by force of arms, shall during its stay in Germany be subject to the military discipline and control of the German War Office, and all members of the Irish Brigade shall be bound to obey all orders given to them by the competent German military authorities, whether officers of the Irish Brigade or not, and shall, in all respects, behave themselves with the same obedience and respect for German military authority as if they were German soldiers.
5. That the Irish Brigade shall be equipped by the German Govt. with a special <u>uniform</u>, having special Irish badge and that the Brigade colours shall be the Irish flag, the National Ensign as carried in 1798.
6. That as far as possible the officers of the Irish Brigade shall be Irish, or Irish Americans, but until such time as it may be possible to obtain the services of Irishmen with the necessary military training, the members of the Irish Brigade will obey whatever officers the German authorities may place over them, with the consent of Sir Roger Casement.
7. That Sir Roger Casement shall be in supreme command of the move-

ments of the Irish Brigade – shall be responsible for its active employment in the field and shall accompany it in its active operations.
8. That a formal undertaking in writing, embodying these conditions in the name of the German government, and providing for the despatch of the Irish Brigade to Ireland with officers and military equipment to arm the Irish Volunteers, at the first opportunity, when it might be possible to despatch a body of men to Ireland, shall be drawn up and signed by the proper German Authority in the name of the German government – and by Sir Roger Casement for the Irish Brigade and Irish Volunteers.

Limburg. Sunday 6 December 1914

9. That in the event of it being possible to send the Irish Brigade to Ireland whether after a German naval victory or from other cause, the German Government will aid to the best of its ability to make that movement successful and will do all in its power to assist the Irish People, the Irish Volunteers and the Irish Brigade to establish a national government in Ireland.
10. That in the event of the Irish Brigade failing to reach Ireland, or in the event of peace being restored between Germany and Great Britain with Ireland still in its present relation to Great Britain then the German govt will send every member of the Irish Brigade to the United States of America at its own expense and enable him to land in that country.

I read these provisions out to the men on Sunday morning (Dec 6) before Mass at the Camp. Sergt. MacMurrough has drawn up a list. 383 of them.

He & the young sergeant say that all the men will go.

On Monday 7 Dec – Sergeant MacMurrough & Sgt Quinlisk were brought to my Hotel where I was ill in bed. They then sounded doubtful about the men going & did not want to commit themselves – The objections being raised were two fold – 1st. that they would be used to fight for Germany and next that their hearts were really with England and against Germany – because England "had given them Home Rule" (!) and because Germany had burnt and pillaged the R.C. churches and wantonly attacked little Belgium.

I drew up another set of suggestions and gave the original to Sergt. MacMurrough to take back to camp and use among the men. I obtained him freedom to go about among them.

On Wednesday Evg (9 Dec) when I visited the camp with the two Fathers I saw neither MacM nor Quinlisk – The professor said former was malingering – pretending to have fever – so as not to be obliged to point out the English soldiers on the list whom I wish to have turned out of the camp. It is highly probable & I told the Professor he must not expect MacM to do that & so get into very bad odour with the rest of the men. I despair of any patriotic act coming from such men – they are incapable of any deep thought, and only want all responsibility to be borne by others.

My proposal brings individual responsibility to each man and the last thing a real Irish ~~Catholic~~ "nationalist" wants is to be compelled to think straight and act straight. As they left Ireland "to fight for Home Rule," it is good enough and they won't look beneath or beyond.

Friday – Dec 11 – in Berlin.

I got to Berlin at 8.50 and drove to the Eden Hotel, where they were expecting me. Got a very showy and uncomfortable room.

Two beds but no chest of drawers, mirror or any receptacle at all for collars – hkfs and small things – simply two cupboards with coat rests in them – the two beds stretched across one entire side of the room – and the rest is a sitting room – a bathroom attached.

Price not stated. Very noisy tram line outside – so the windows shut – I walked a few minutes in Tauentzienstr.

Countess Hahn in the Hotel they told me and asking for me.

I slept badly and this morning's news is bad. It is "rumoured" (but alas too true!) that the German overseas squadron, the Gneisenau, Scharnhorst and Leipzig have been sunk off the Falkland Islands and the Leipzig and Dresden captured. It was inevitable but still is depressing. There were fully 70 warships, British, French and Japanese chasing these five splendid German cruisers and sooner or later they were bound to be caught and done for.

No details yet – so far as my ignorance of German permits me to follow the press reports, but I shall hear doubtless all that is known today at the F.O. – or with Blücher.

I will send a card to Countess Hahn and find out when she can see me and then go to Blücher and on to Wedel.

There ought to be some news from America – and possibly some from poor Adler.

I am wholly undecided what is best to do first. I think the Findlay business should be settled and done for, before anything else.

Saturday. 12 Dec.

I went to Foreign Office at 1.30 y'day & saw von Wedel. We agreed 1st that I should proceed as I thought best about Christiania. He had forwarded my letter from Limburg to Adler thro' the post, telling the Police to allow it to go thro' in the ordinary way. He said an Irish trainer "in prison" in

Ruhleben was a "furious Irish Nationalist. I asked for his release to go to the camp to the Irish soldiers as my man. Also I asked for Miss Zittel to be sent to me – and for 100 copies of Continental Times to be sent each issue to the men thro' Fr. Crotty.

We did not discuss my wish, expressed by letter from Frankfurt, to see either the Chancellor or von Jagow. I told him I would draw up in writing the conditions on which I proposed the Irish Brigade sold be enrolled and he said all right.

I called twice on Blücher – not in – but got a 'phone to dine with him and the von Roeders at an Italian restaurant.

Meyer called at 6.30 and told me the Irish badges were too dear! They would cost 1500 marks (say £60!) – and were not worth it. If this is the measure of their good intentions towards the Irish question the sooner I end with them the better.

How can trust any promises that rest on such a niggardly conception of their obligations as this shying at £60 for badging 2.000 men (say 6d per badge) represents.

I suggested a possible telegram to U.S.A. announcing the intended formation of the Brigade to Meyer and gave him a draft of it to show Wedel – but I am not sure it is wise yet.

Wedel read me a telegram that he had received from v. Bernstorff saying

1st that Cohalan* – a trusty messenger had reached Ireland at end Novbr. –

2nd that the Declaration of the German govt had "produced an excellent impression" –

3rd that Cohalan advised I should make no public statement about Christiania until I had clear proof.

This is all good news – so far as it goes. The bad news is in the public press. The German sea squadron of 5 ships – Gneisenau, Scharnhorst, Leipzig, Nürnberg and Dresden has been overwhelmed by a huge allied squadron off the Falkland islands – the Gneisenau, Scharnhorst, Leipzig, (and Nürnberg later) were sunk – the Dresden still in flight. All hands lost – including Admiral Spee and his two sons!

It is said the British had 38 ships gathered to meet this gallant little fleet of five! Another splendid triumph for British pluck! Asquith's "We only ask for a fair fight" at the Guildhall is well illustrated in this encounter. The British were more than 7 to 1 and six of their vessels are said to have been battleships! What cowards!

I called on Countess Hahn at 4 and talked long with her and a Mrs. Behrens came in and wanted me to meet Herr Ballin and asked me to go to Hamburg and stay with her and she would bring us together.

At dinner 7.30 to 10 with von Roeder and the Baroness we discussed the war and nothing but the war with a Countess Oppersdorff – a sister of the Count I met at Countess Groeben's. The more I see of the "governing classes" in Germany the less highly I estimate their intelligence. They are "not in it" with the English – that is certain.

Today Blücher came to lunch at 1, after Schiemann had come with many "<u>Gaelic Americans</u>", and Meyer.

Blücher is quite impossible. He has arranged for me to meet the "Minister of Colonies" (I put it in italics because German colonies today are mainly British possessions or Japanese, or French) tonight at 6. I was to have met Erstberger, [**should be Erzberger**][82] an influential Reichstag deputy, tomorrow, but as I refused to discuss the Irish Brigade with him – having no liberty to do so – he got very "huffy" and talked angry nonsense and altogether behaved as I expected. Blücher's interest is solely in himself and his chances of besting his unscrupulous old father, the Prince, and getting control of the Palace and Estates while the father is interned at Herm.

He has quite dropped the Christiania business – finding it is not popular at the F.O. – and wants now to find some fresh means of exploiting me, or my presence in Berlin for his own personal ends. His interest in Ireland is <u>nil</u>.

Today, however, he let several cats out of the bag – 1st and biggest was that Jagow had "<u>sent for him</u>" and they had discussed me and the Irish matter. I was not to hope for any full declaration of German policy about Ireland

---

[82] Matthias Erzberger (1875-1921) was a moderate German politician who led calls for a negotiated peace in the Reichstag in 1917. On the left of the Catholic Party, Erzberger was elected to the Reichstag in 1903, a confirmed monarchist and patriot yet a moderate reformer. Erzberger was given the task of organising overseas German propaganda in 1914-15. In the latter year he travelled to Italy as a member of the mission intended to maintain Italy's neutrality - ultimately unsuccessful, as Italy entered the war on the side of the Allies on 23 May that year. Over the course of the next year, Erzberger's publicly stated war aims underwent a transformation. As late as 1915 he was calling for significant territorial annexations as the price of German peace (largely in France and Belgium). During the course of 1916 and early 1917 however he came to believe that a negotiated peace was not only desirable but necessary. A firm opponent of unrestricted submarine warfare (along with many moderates in the Reichstag), Erzberger introduced the July 1917 Peace Resolution that led to the fall of Chancellor Bethmann-Hollweg. His publication of a secret memo authored by Austro-Hungarian Foreign Minister Ottokar Czernin, which was decidedly gloomy in its view of the conduct of the war, merely earned Erzberger the ultimately fatal enmity of right-wing groups without altering the course of the war. Finally brought into Prince Max von Baden's government of October 1918, albeit without portfolio, Erzberger was a member of the German delegation that finally agreed the armistice terms on 11 November 1918. Remaining in the cabinet following the 1919 elections – as Minister of Finance – Erzberger worked hard to gain recognition of the widely reviled Treaty of Versailles. He was however obliged to resign in 1920 in the wake of financial allegations. The following year, in August, he was murdered by a right-winger in Berlin.

— that was the angry cat escaped from the bag of wounded vanity, when I declined to discuss all my business with him. Jagow had told him this They (the German govt) were not going to "make themselves ridiculous" and say things they had no intention of carrying out, or attempting.

I knew this all along — or guessed it, but I am glad to have it straight and clear. There is a confirmation of it (to some extent) in the Times of 4th Dec. which I found in the Hotel y'day. There is, in this Times, a long telegram from New York giving the gist of some "extraordinary conditions of peace" posed by Dr. Dernburg[83] in an interview with an American newspaper. The IX (ninth) of Dernburg's possible German conditions of peace is as follows:

"All small Nations, such as Finland, Poland, and the Boers of South Africa, if they support Germany, must have the right to frame their own destinies, while Egypt is to be returned, if she desires it, to Turkey."

I quoted this statement to von Wedel yesterday at the F.O. and said I was surprised that Dr. Dernburg should have omitted Ireland from the list. I pointed out that the Irish people had already given a much warmer and fuller support to the German cause than either Poles or Finns — that both Poles and Finns, no less than Irish, were in the armies now attacking Germany and that if it came to public evidences of goodwill and "value received" Ireland had done much more than either "Poland" or Finland for Germany. Von Wedel agreed with me at once, but said he did not believe the *Times* statement was true — or that Dernburg had said anything of the kind. I said the statement in the *Times* was given categorically, as the report of a public utterance, and was not offered as an "opinion."

I have no doubt Dernburg said it and that the omission of Ireland from his list of friendly "States" was intentional, and a part of the *mot d'ordre* to commit themselves as little as possible to the Irish cause in public so that retreat and "accommodation with England" may always be possible.

When, today, at lunch here I said to Blücher that if neither the Chancellor nor von Jagow cared to receive me I thought my right course would be to leave Germany, he was already furious at my refusal to unfold all my plans to him and said that this was "only vanity on my part." I passed over the silly rudeness because I do not choose to quarrel with him — and said that I was entitled to the assurance of the highest quarter — and that if I did not get it, I should seriously reconsider my whole position and attitude towards

---

[83] Bernhard Dernburg, 1865-1937, German financier and public official. As Colonial Secretary (1907-10), he was responsible for reforms improving the economy, educational system, and administration of the German colonies. His efforts (1914-15) to act as German propagandist in the United States were offset by the sinking of the Lusitania. Dernburg was finance minister in the Scheidemann cabinet (1919) but resigned in protest against the Treaty of Versailles. He served (1920-30) in the Reichstag.

Germany and might find it my duty to leave the country.

In my heart I am <u>very</u> sorry I came! I do not think the German govt has any soul for great enterprises – it lacks the divine spark of imagination that has ennobled British piracy.

The sea <u>may</u> be freed by these people – but I doubt it. They will do it in their sleep – and without intending to achieve anything so great.

England <u>enslaved</u> the seas of set design and far-seeing purpose and has held them in subjection with a resolute and unscrupulous will beyond all praise in themselves. These people, whose supreme interest it should be to have complete freedom and equality at sea, will not take the necessary steps in the direction needed beyond mere ship-building. That is an essential but other things, too, are needed to free the seas besides ships – just as other things are needed to hold them. England supplies all the necessaries – ships <u>and</u> brains – Germany thinks to do it by ships alone without brains and resolute, far-seeing purpose. A fixed, unchanging Irish policy is essential to freedom at sea of every power competing with England. That is the first rule to master.

These things I should like to say to the Colonial Minister this evening – but I shall be wholly debarred from saying them by the presence and constant interruption of Blücher, who has become a very tyrant of speech too. He talks without pause – and mostly irrelevancies.

Sunday – 13 Decr.

A card from Fraulein [**Antonie**] Meyer asking me to call and see her – she has "important letters" to show me. After Blücher left me at 3 yesterday (very angry) I talked to Countess Hahn who said Mrs. Behrens told her the Irish Regiments were surrendering on purpose at the front – and she has a list of recent such surrenders. I doubt it greatly.

The F.O. announced in answer to Lonsdale's question as to "what would be done to Sir Roger Casement" – that they must await evidence and no steps to withdraw his pension (ha! ha!) could be taken without evidence to submit to a Court.

The Spectator feels "confident Sir Roger can give an explanation that will satisfy his friends"! Does it?

Meantime it is confirmed absolutely that the F.O. has appointed Sir H. Howard as Minister to the Vatican! The Pope has accepted – as of course was certain – And where <u>now</u> is the pretence of Irish Loyalty? This is really the most convincing proof of the far reaching character of my coup. I have actually forced them to a step hateful "to every good Englishman" and to reverse the Reformation! It is an unprecedented step and if the German govt had <u>brains</u> they would see how deep they had already struck.

A batch of New York papers ("The Sun" mostly) to hand by Schiemann – but nothing of interest or use either. How badly they are edited – and how dull they seem!

A lot of G. Americans with Larkin's speech at New York on the Manchester Martyrs celebration. Mr. Redmond has announced that his visit to U.S.A. has been "postponed"!

At 6 I went with Blücher to call on Dr. Solf,[84] the Minister of the German Colonies. Found him (after long wait) a fine type. Once Governor of Samoa. Knew Nigeria too. Very charming, great big, strong good man. I told him they would <u>have</u> to knock England out – there was nothing for it but that – and they must use all their brains and intelligence for that.

He agreed and confessed their brains diplomatically, were inferior to the English and that they were not trained to cope with English statesmen, "pirates in evening dress."

(I had called them "very charming men, hereditary pirates of long descent" – and he had laughed approval and said "Yes – I see, pirates in evening dress.")

I got a better impression of the German official world from Solf than from any of them. He confessed, too, that they had <u>all</u> been deceived by English "nice manners" and "hearty hospitality" and cited his own reception in Nigeria many years ago and the speeches of goodwill and "<u>cousinship</u>" exchanged – or professed rather by the Br. officials. I assured him that was all part of the game – and said it would have paid Germany well to have engaged a few Irishmen as guides to the British character in international affairs! An Irish Imperial Chancellor would not have let John Bull wall up the German Michael[85] as we now see him.

---

[84] Wilhelm Heinrich Solf (1862-1936) served as Germany's Colonial Secretary from 1911 and, briefly, as its last Imperial Foreign Minister. A firm advocate and supporter of Kaiser Wilhelm II's desire to construct a German empire to compete with Europe's other major colonial powers, Britain and France, Solf served from 1900-11 as Governor of Western Samoa. Upon his return from Samoa, Solf he became Imperial Colonial Secretary. Unfortunately the outbreak of the First World War actually led to Germany's colonies in Africa and in the Pacific, going to Britain and Japan respectively. In consequence, Solf lobbied for a negotiated peace settlement in 1917 and 1918 which would restore Germany's African colonies while ceding her gains in the west since 1914. Since the declaration of war, Solf had been firm in his opposition to an annexationist policy in the west. He further came out in opposition to unrestricted submarine warfare, a disastrous policy move which directly led to U.S. entry into the war in April 1917. With military defeat imminent, Solf was appointed Imperial Foreign Minister in October 1918. In this capacity he undertook negotiations for an armistice with the Allies. He resigned on 13 December 1918 with the onset of the German revolution. From 1920-28 he served as German Ambassador to Japan in Tokyo, helping to negotiate the German-Japan treaty of 1927. He died in 1936.

[85] *Der deutsche Michel* – country boy, German equivalent of John Bull, despite the French name.

Dr. Solf had read the manuscript of "Ireland, Germany and Freedom of the Seas," when it first came from Rome! He had it in his drawers he said – the mss – brought by Schiemann – and of course had read the translation the "Achilles Heel of England."[86]

He was greatly interested in my explanation of the international value of Ireland to Europe and the freedom of the seas. He said he would speak to von Jagow and arrange a meeting. Jagow returns to Charleville on Tuesday he said.

I left him only at 8.30 p.m. – having previously met Frau Solf at his private house (in 66 Wilhelmstrasse). The Colonial Office is just like a private house – 62 Wilhelmstrasse – with nothing inside or outside that gave the least indication of its being the head of a great Department.

Solf said that the Declaration about Ireland was "an entirely new departure in German foreign policy" – that until that statement was issued Germany had never said or done anything that implied a desire even to meddle in the "internal affairs of another country."

It is a new departure indeed. It was followed, as he admitted, by his own Declaration about South Africa – inspired Blücher says by my old friend Dr. Leyds, who is living at The Hague. Leyds had been so struck by the Irish Declaration, he got Solf to issue the statement that appeared recently in the press defining Germany's wishes and intentions towards the South African Union.

Dr. Solf said to me "Why did Ireland never approach Germany before?" – and I laughed and said "Why did you, in your own interests, never think of Ireland or seek first hand information as to the state of feeling in Ireland? You should have had an Irish policy, as part of your plan of defence against English aggression."

He agreed entirely and we parted the very best of friends.

I went and dined with poor old Blücher at the Esplanade till 10.30 and then walked home by Potsdamerstr and the Spreebank to my Hotel – a delightful walk – the rain of the earlier day and afternoon now gone.

This morning Mrs. White of the Continental Times called on me – just back from Vienna at 11 a.m. She is a Viennese married to an Englishman. She was "charming" and told me that in Vienna they were very anxious to meet me. At the F.O. where she had been, Berchtold and others of the F.O. staff were all hoping I would visit Vienna. So she said. They had read my "Appeal to the Irish People" and were in <u>full</u> sympathy she said.

---

[86] Schiemann, a Professor of east European history at Berlin University, published his translation in 1915 under the title Die Achillesferse Englands: aus dem Englischen übersetzt und eingeleitet. A German political agent, he was a conservative nationalist and enthusiastic supporter of Irish separatism.

She has arranged a small dinner for Thursday with the American war correspondents – Wiegand, A. Stanhope and another – to meet me. She says that Gaffney the U.S. Consul General at Munich is a great friend of Germany, Ireland – and wants to meet me much – that he would come to Berlin to see me, if she wired. Shall I?[87]

St. John Gaffney, US Consul General, Munich (NLI 17014)

Berlin Monday, 14 Dec.

Meyer came at 2.30 – after I had lunched with Mrs. Behrens the friend of Ballin. She wants me to go to Hamburg stay with her and meet Ballin – she says he can get <u>any</u> letter I want into Ireland.

The report about the Irish soldiers surrendering in Flanders "because they did not want to shoot at Germans" was discussed at the luncheon. Two officers were there – one had it from the front – but it is all vague –and is probably the same story Blücher told me 2 weeks ago – I shall hear the truth

---

[87] Thomas St. John Gaffney, b. Limerick 1864, US Consul General, Munich (formerly, from 1905, Dresden) appointed by Theodore Roosevelt; friend of Parnell, Secretary of the McKinley League New York 1896; a foreign policy writer, decorated by King Leopold of Belgium 1905; d. New York 1945.

from the men themselves when I go back to Limburg.

At 4 I went to Mrs. Meyer's rooms in Nassauische Str. She has no word from Kuno yet. But she had an interesting card to him written by a young Irishman in Ruhleben camp begging to be released on the ground that he is Irish and the son of a Fenian! His name is Bryan A. Kelly of Dublin, an official of the University Gaelic Society who had come to Berlin to study and is now locked up as "a British subject." I will get him out, interview him, and if he is a loyal man send him first to Limburg to the soldiers and <u>then</u> to Ireland itself as my messenger.[88]

Another was a letter about a Lt. Col McMicking (a friend of Mrs. Green's) of the Royal Scots who is wounded and a prisoner somewhere. I refused to take steps there – as the Enquiry should come thro' someone else.

I shall draft today my proposals to the German govt. for the formation of the Irish Brigade. The idea is I formulate the conditions in writing, and they reply in writing agreeing and sign it by the Chancellor or von Jagow. Latter returns to the front on Tuesday.

A fresh success yesterday in Poland – the Russians again defeated with loss of 11.000 prisoners and 43 machine guns.

This morning's news too is interesting. The King [**the next 3 words are inserted above:**] George of England gave an interview to the new extraordinary envoy to the Vatican, Sir H. Howard – and the latter takes with him my friend J.D. Gregory[89] as his secretary!

Ghosts of the Putumayo Indians! – how strange it all is!

Gregory, who collaborated with me in the F.O. to get the Franciscan Mission sent out by the Vatican and who was first in belauding me at Rome and in London – now goes to Rome to aid in ~~assailing~~ belabouring me and in enslaving Ireland!

English rule is assuredly the masterpiece of dissimulation of the world.

I await with amusement the forthcoming comments of the English world on my "treason" – but oh! <u>God save Ireland!</u>

The Pope has issued some rescript on "Religion and the Fatherland" I gather – I wonder what it is?

<u>Berlin. Wednesday, 16 Decr</u>

Adler returned last night at 7. I went to the Continental Hotel about my trunk and while there in he came. He had come in response to my wire of

---

[88] See NLI 31783. "Report to Dublin Castle by Bryan A. Kelly, a student in Germany, on his meetings there with Roger Casement, 8 February 1915 also covering letter by Sir Matthew Nathan, 11 February 1915. Photocopy, original in Public Record Office, London."

[89] John Duncan Gregory (1878-1951), a British diplomat who was ultimately dismissed for financial misbehaviour.

Friday last – but had not received my letter from Limburg sent through Wedel.

He reports Findlay in a state of abnormal excitement over my (reported!) doings. Adler spun a delightful web of lies! He talked vaguely, he says, of the "Secret Society" in U.S.A., of its widespread organisation, of the wealthy accessions to its ranks of late, since the war, of the rich Irish American with his big steam yacht ready; of my commission to him, Adler, to charter two sailing yachts in Norway to meet me on the coast of Schleswig at an early date; of my complete system of intelligence, how I got "word" from Ireland three hours after anything happened there"; how I had agents "in the Navy itself" – and how I was certainly going to get into Ireland with the American contingent in the yacht at an early date – probably, he said, I intended the Norwegian chartered boats for transhipment "at sea."

Findlay, he says, was pale, with beads of perspiration rolling off him and walked up and down the room in a state of wild excitement. He called him a very nasty name & said I was "very clever – and a very dangerous son of a b."!

He promised Adler £10.000 for my capture! I am mounting up in value! He said it would be more than that – but that sure.

Adler implicated two great bankers he says – one in Norway & one in U.S.A. – and Findlay asked him if it was Armours yacht. ~~Chicago Beef man~~ (the Kaiser's friend) I had got! So they think Armour is a Fenian too! It is quite delicious – I am to hear more today. I told Adler to stay at the Continental last night and I'd send for him today. He says that if I go to Norway, Findlay will "go bug house" (an American euphemism, I believe, for "going off his chump"). I may have to go to Norway before long – in any case – We shall see.

Professor Schiemann called y'day too – He read parts of a letter from Kuno Meyer saying all well there. He had seen my friends and was to dine with Cohalan. Had met Joe – The "Crime against Europe" had been delayed – but would be out "very soon." His letter was 26th Novr. He urged extreme caution in exposing Findlay, on account of "Mr. L". Poor Mr. L.! [**Casement's pseudonym, James Landy**]

The Ambassador had telegraphed in similar terms to F.O. here on behalf of Cohalan asking me to publish nothing about Christiania unless I had clear "proof".

Thursday, 17 Decr. Berlin

Yesterday afternoon Mr. Gaffney the U.S. Consul at Munich called with Aubrey Stanhope[90]. Former has just returned from Ireland where he went

---

[90] Editor of the *Continental Times*, published in Berlin and described as a pro-German newspaper for Americans in Europe.

to visit his brother, the Crown Solicitor of Limerick. He reports the country "with Redmond" – but admits he was only some 48 hours in Ireland and "saw no one" but his brother and a few friends at Limerick. His letters, addressed to him, had been opened by the Br. Censor altho' sent in U.S. Embassy conveying to page. Gaffney agrees that Redmond is betraying Ireland and is unworthy of support – but says the people hear nothing but lies and are "fed up" with "glorious British victories" and with equally atrocious German crimes.

I went today with Meyer to a Military tailors to order a "sample" uniform[91] for the Irish Brigade – A pale grey with a touch of green running thro' the warp – & then with emerald green facings, cuffs and collar & a harp on collar flaps & a harp with shamrock above on the cap on a green band.

I guess it will be a terror.

It is only to see what it looks like. I may try it on Bryan A Kelly, the young Irish student, from Ruhleben who wrote to Kuno Meyer to get released on ground his father was a Fenian – and whose release and despatch to myself I have asked – Also I have sought the release of a (Mayo?) trainer named Browne who is a "furious nationalist" I am told.

Adler spent most of the day with me here in this Hotel and told me of his plots with Findlay. Findlay admitted I was "a gentleman." "He is a gentleman," he said, "But a very clever dangerous son of a b......" And I must be caught and my dear Foreign Office will pay £10.000 to Adler, if he can get me over to their hands!

"Truth" of 2 Dec. I see has some imprudent paragraphs all lies too! – about me – I append the article **[not now appended to this manuscript]** – Gaffney gave it to me – It is a tissue of misrepresentation and error when not deliberately false.

It is a pity I have no copy of my "friend" Conan Doyle's letter referred to in the Daily Chronicle wherein my mental malady is diagnosed! What strange people the English are! When I served them I was a hero "the most chivalrous public servant in the service of the Empire" &c. &c.

Now that I dare to cut myself off from them & to do a far braver thing & surely more chivalrous one I am at "the most charitable view" a lunatic – and in my case "a rampant traitor."

I like that – as if I ever owed any loyalty to that cowardly Cringing Bully the British Empire!

Friday, 18 December.

Today (and yesterday) have been great days. Many things have happened.

---

[91] Apparently based on the uniform of a German infantryman

I must try to put them down while Adler is out shopping for me.

At luncheon y'day (about 2 p.m.) I heard the church bells ring out suddenly – a peal of joyful news to all Berlin, I could not at first think what it might be – as I did not think these people rang the church bells for public festivity. In a few minutes I saw, from the restaurant window, the flags springing out from every parapet and window and streaming far and wide – I knew then. A great victory somewhere, but where? The waitress came with the "tape" – It was brief, direct and positive. The Headquarters announced that the "whole Russian front against Posen and Silesia, from north to south Poland had been completely broken and was in full flight with the German armies in close pursuit"! There it was! This is the "news" I had been hearing rumours of for three days – from Schiemann and others. He told me several days ago that they "hoped to corner eleven Russian army corps" – i.e. 440.000 men. It looks as if they have done this. There was no doubt. Everywhere I found men sure, with a deep certainty in Hindenburg that he had done the trick and smashed completely the entire Russian offensive with overwhelming loss.

The evening press gave no further details, but said that today would be a public school holiday, for all the Berlin schools, in honour of the great victory. Everyone knew it was coming, and was only waiting the announcement of the Staff that it had come.

Jesco von Puttkamer,[92] the old Governor of Cameroons, called on me this morning. I had not seen him since March or Feby 1895 – in Cameroon, when I was his guest and when I climbed the great peak with "Gyp" my dear little fox terrier. He is old and white – but just married & full of life & hope still – and wished me all luck for Ireland.

In the afternoon I had a long talk with Adler about Christiania & put down the gist of his two interviews with Findlay on the last visit to Norway and the scheme devised.

It briefly is that I should be represented as putting to sea off the coast of Schleswig to join "the American yacht" and that Findlay will have British cruisers there to catch me and – we catch them!

I'll see if the F.O. here and Coy. will be men enough to follow it up.

At 8 I went to Mrs. White's to dinner expecting to meet only Gaffney (the U.S. Consul of Munich) Aubrey Stanhope and Karl Wiegand[93] – but met in addition Puttkamer and Mrs P. – and many more, all invited to meet me

---

[92] Jesco von Puttkamer (1855-1917), nine times Governor of Kamerun, later a League of Nations mandate.

[93] Karl H. von Wiegand, Berlin correspondent of *United Press*. His graphic dispatch on the October 1914 battle of Wirbollen is at http://www.lib.byu.edu/%7Erdh/wwi/1914/wirballen.html

as the "Guest of Germany." The dinner was delightful, especially I liked one German officer, a Major Herwarth v Bittenfeld[94] of the Headquarters General Staff. He had been at Washington as Military Attaché and spoke very good English and talked with great charm and good sense.

Puttkamer told me the victory in Russia was "decisive." It would "end the war"! The Russians had been completely smashed and were in full flight and Hindenburg hoped to get the whole lot. They talk already of 200.000 prisoners – but all details are withheld still – Today the entire city is beflagged as I have not seen it yet. Everywhere streamers flying and a look of joy and content on every face.

On getting back from Mrs. White's at midnight I found a letter from von Wedel asking me to go to the Imperial Chancellor at 12 (today) as Bethmann Hollweg wished to see me.

[Inserted at top of page:] (This letter left with Dr Curry Mch 29 1916.[95])

I also got a letter from Meyer at 6 p.m. saying that news had been received from my friends in U.S.A. saying that Revd Father Nicholson of Philadelphia was sailing for Naples on 18 Dec. (today) to take up his duties with the <u>Irish Brigade</u>.

I could arrange nothing with Adler until I saw F.O. today and he was very downcast at thought that all our plans against Findlay would come to naught owing to these people being so weak as not to take advantage. I talked to him till 7.30 and sent him away very despondent and I was greatly cast down too.

The dinner revived me and the many sane views I met there. Mrs. White says I am sure of a hearty welcome in Vienna – the Austrians will be glad to help Ireland. A Colonel Emerson[96] and his wife – American war correspondent – also there. He goes to U.S.A. on 9 January on a special mission of enlightenment. He told me he had read my pamphlet and liked it immensely – and hoped it had gone all thro' Ireland.

Today the morning was clear and delicious and all Berlin in joy for the decisive overthrow of the "Russian Steamroller."

It ought to bring the war towards the sight of an honourable ending for

---

[94] Hans-Wolfgang Herwarth von Bittenfeld, b. 1871, ended his career in the Propaganda Ministry where he was tasked by Joseph Goebbels in 1939 with writing a special brochure on Nostradamus's prediction of England's disappearance.
[95] Now in NLI 13085/27 dated 17 December 1914
[96] Edwin Emerson b. Dresden 1870, experienced war correspondent, served in the Spanish-American war 1898; Venezuelan colonel in war with Colombia 1901; Russo-Japanese war 1905 (Japanese POW);, from 1914 to 1917, editor of the *English Continental News*, published by the German government to carry on pro-German propaganda among English-speaking soldiers. Emerson was to be Hitler and the NSDAP's initial representative in America.

Germany. The morning press also gives a list of the officers killed, wounded and prisoners of the British Army. Here it is. It is taken from the London press.

Killed	1133.
Wounded	2225.
Prisoners or missing	<u>513</u>
	3871.

It is "colossal" – for so small an army. If the proportion of men be as, say, 30 to 1 officer it means a British loss of some 120.000 men so far.

I went at 11.15 to von Wedel at F.O. who was more than friendly and told me they agreed to all my conditions as to the Irish Brigade.

The document I drew up on 15th last they had considered fully and with the exception of the following words dealing with German officers – they would sign it. The international law authorities at the F.O. ad had it under consideration and found no flaw in it. It was not contrary to the rights of nations. There were precedents for it – apart from exiting cases of the same thing in the present war. The precedents von Wedel cited were two – a Hanoverian legion formed in 1870 to aid the French in Paris, and a Hungarian legion that in 1866 fought for Prussia against Austria.

Von Wedel gave me a mass of London press references to myself – *Morning Post* and *Manchester Guardian* are very loquacious and latter speaks of my visit to Berlin as an "act of monstrous baseness at first thought incredible." Also as an "act of treason to England and of double dyed treason to Ireland." He also gave me a copy of the open letter to Lord Northcliffe sent out by my (former) friend Gardiner of the *Daily News* which Gaffney so volubly assured me (and I see assures the readers of the Continental Times) is written by Garvin.

Of Gaffney's wisdom I have not a high opinion and much too loquacious and not capable of thinking things out for himself.

Wedel took me round himself to the Chancellor's official residence next door to the Foreign Office. A fine palace. I was received and shown upstairs and sending in my card in a moment I was admitted to a large room where the Chancellor, in a grey uniform, was standing up. He advanced to meet me, shook me warmly by the hand, and led me to a chair. We smoked cigarettes. He spoke in French, in English, by agreement. I did most of the talking and discussed Ireland, the Irish in America and my hopes or "dreams" of a free Ireland. Either now or later – but some day. He agreed that an independent Ireland, if possible of achievement, would be a good thing for Germany and for the freedoms of the seas – and a desirable thing to attempt. I said I was aware, fully aware that today, with the British Fleet barring the way and keeping all Ireland in jail, to think of an independent Ireland was "fantastic" and he agreed to that – But I begged him to have an Irish policy for Germany in the future – for the next war would be a war for the seas, and then the cause of Ireland would indeed be the cause of Germany. He agreed. I spoke also of the Irish Brigade and of my hope that by its formation "at least a hard blow could be struck at recruiting in Ireland" to which the Chancellor assented and said that that would be of great service.

We discussed at his request "Christiania" and Mr. Findlay and the extraordinary later developments with Findlay's present offer of £10.000 for me "anywhere in the North Sea or Skagerrak" and his entrusting the key of the back door of the British Legation at C. to my rascal Adler!

This latter act of Findlay's has possibly, more amaze the German officials and more aided to convince them of the truth of the whole story than all the rest. Von Wedel (truly) said to me this morning "It is incredible – a man in Findlay's position to so act with an unknown, with your servant!"

I said "Yes – but that is the English character. You see I know them much better than you. To get me, to crush an Irish national movement they would commit any crime today, as in the past – they have no conscience when it comes to collective dealing – individually the Englishman is a gentleman often and frequently very charming – collectively they're a most dangerous compound and form a national type that has no parallel in humanity. Like certain chemicals – apart harmless, brought together you get an infernal explosive or a deadly poison."

He laughed and agreed that my diagnosis applied to the disease.

I stayed with the Chancellor fully half an hour. He was interested and showed it and on my leaving he shook me warmly by the hand and wished me "all success in your aims and projects."

I returned to von Wedel at the F.O. next door and talked long with him over Ireland, Gardiner's "open letter" to Northcliffe, which I think is the first sign of retreat.

It is the first clutch at the door handle hand behind the back. The victory over Russia in Poland will make the hand turn the handle. The bombardment of Scarborough, Whitby and Hartlepool and the heavy loss of life caused there and the destruction of property will add to the effect. There was panic at Scarborough, Whitby etc. and the whole towns tried to escape by train.

The German cruisers that carried out this raid moreover have returned with the loss of only one man wounded! They sank two torpedo boat destroyers and perhaps a third and saw no sign of the British Fleet!

Who now are the "rats in their holes?"

Von Wedel was more friendly than ever. He said they would support me in every way and give me all the assurances I needed and that the Chancellor's reception of me was to convince me of their friendship and regard and that I might trust them fully and to show that they trusted me.

I told von Wedel of the Hamburg-Amerika incident at Cork in January and of my conviction that the London F.O. had stopped it though the Emperor. He said he thought it highly probable and would find out – that he was in very intimate touch with the Kaiser, frequently with him and could see him when he liked. In any case Wedel said in answer to me that whatever the immediate outcome of the war and fate of Ireland might be, I might rest assured they would pursue a policy of goodwill to Ireland commercially if they could not achieve a positive act of political assistance.

I then discussed with von Wedel the possibility of the Navy getting something out of Findlay's insane projects against myself, as reported by Adler. All is fair in war, and, if these fine gentleman will stick at nothing to catch me, why not take advantage of their trap and use it for our common interest.

He agreed and said he would at once go to the Admiralty and discuss it and let me know and in any case I had better keep Adler longer than tomorrow.

At 6 I got a 'phone message from him to say the Admiralty were considering the matter – that at first they were naturally "surprised at such a bombshell" but were now apprised of the particulars and he thought would take it up and so I was to keep Adler longer.

Otherwise Adler was returning to Moss tomorrow, with another sham letter and some further invented "atrocities" of mine against England to keep poor Mr. Findlay at a white heat of "criminal invention" against myself until such time as I might arrange for my own going to Norway to get him caught *in flagrante delicto*.

Now, the project is a twofold one to catch Findlay and catch some vessels of the British Navy at same time!

Findlay's hope is that I will embark off the coast of Schleswig in a sailing boat to join the phantom American yacht (Armour's or some one else's) at an assigned locality in the North Sea. Adler is to get copy of my plans and learn the exact spot, and let Findlay know the time to have British vessels there to waylay me. The scheme is simple. The answer is to arrange a spot with the German Admiralty, when they too, shall be there – and instead of the British cruisers catching me they catch a submarine Tartar – a Diodon in fact! This is the thought today. How far it may go I can't say. Personally I don't like it. It is too British!

Also I am <u>not</u> sure of Adler! His air and manner have changed greatly since he came back or rather since he went away. He confesses that he now "admires" Findlay! Findlay "is a man" "he sticks at nothing. He would roll these God d–d Germans up." For the Germans now, since they held him up at Sassnitz, Adler has scorn and a sense of outraged pride. They treated him badly there stripped him, split his gloves open, took his gold coin and gave him paper money, extorted 7 Marks per meal, while he was detained 48 hours their prisoner pending the order from Berlin to release him, and read aloud to the crowd my letters to my American friends. This last extraordinary piece of stupidity it was that chiefly affects Adler. He says they "are fools" and trying to fool me and get advantage of me and Ireland and give nothing in return but empty words.

There is also the recent German action Adler reports from Norway of the condemnation by the Kiel Prize Court of some Norwegian vessels with cargoes of timber that had been seized at the beginning of the war. These "prizes of war" mean much to their Norwegian owners little to wealthy Germany, and Adler says public feeling in Norway is aroused at the decision of the German Prize Court and for his part he has become "anti-German."

Therefore with myself out of the issue his sympathies would be against Germany and on the side of "the man" Findlay, "who sticks at nothing."

There is also the resentment he feels, the very deep resentment at the allegations against himself and his conduct while in Berlin, to which Schiemann referred and which Blücher told me had been conveyed in a police report to the F.O. I told Adler of this report last night – giving it as the reason why I found it impossible to take him on with me to Limburg and the Irish Brigade.

It makes him exceedingly bitter against the Germans and he is vowing vengeance. Knowing <u>now</u> all I do of his character, of its extraordinary complexity, I should feel gravely disposed to mistrust his fidelity in a matter, whence German ships were the issue as against British ships. I should even, now, be indisposed to trust myself to his schemes!

He is clearly beginning to feel that Findlay is a bolder, more uncompromising and reckless rascal than myself and Adler's deepest affection is won by extreme rascaldom. Utter unscrupulousness of action, so long as it succeeds, is his ideal he confesses. He was won to my side, he admits, only by my extreme trust in himself. Seeing how fully I trusted him on the voyage over, his honour (or what corresponds to it) came to the top and he determined to be true as steel to me.

Now that he sees me going off on my Irish "journey" and he not to take part any more in my efforts, and this due to the evil (and indeed quite untruthful) reports of the Berlin police as to his conduct here, his rage against the Germans is almost swallowing up his affection for me. His face is changed. The old, boyish eyes and smile are gone and he does not look me openly in the face.

I think he is in <u>his</u> heart really regretting that – but no! I will not think that even. But I must see that he is ill disposed to the German cause and losing interest in mine, since he can no longer be associated with me in it and since he is aware that the Germans have "scandalised" him so much. Therefore, I feel it would be far safer for all concerned to send Adler back to Norway and let him return to U.S.A. to work there. I told him much of this last night and said I would try to get him good work there, if he would promise to go straight and quite give up doing the things he confessed to me the last night before he returned to Moss he had done. And so there I left him this night.

[**Crossed out:**] Father Nicholson sails today.

This *B. Z. am Mittag* has a telegram from Brussels about Ireland, saying that a veritable reign of terror exists there and that the govt are arresting all they suspect! Here is the cutting (I have omitted it. It said that the govt was striking wildly in Ireland prohibiting public meetings and arresting.)

[Casement did include the cuttings which are in German; the following translation is from Curry's book. Words inscribed:] *B.Z. am Mittag* Freitag, 18 December 1914

"Reign of Terror in Ireland
Telegram of the *Magdeburger Zeitung*

Brussels, 17 December.

London reports reaching here leave no doubts as to the reign of terror that exists in Ireland. All national Irish newspapers are being suppressed and their editors and many other Irishmen thrown into prison. Public assemblies are allowed only when attended by a Government commissioner. Instead of drawing on Ireland for volunteers, the English Government are obliged to strengthen their Irish garrisons. The London papers give one the impression that the agitation hostile to England is increasing in Ireland."

This follows naturally on Adler's fearful stories of my intentions to Findlay. Findlay has spun some magnificent tale to the Foreign Office; and so they are now panicking through Ireland and trying to get hold of the "dangerous" men before my attempted landing comes off. The bombardment of the Yorkshire towns will also have helped and will probably be attributed to my malign influence here in Berlin. Findlay will think I got some information by my secret service agency, on which Adler dilated so much, that had shown the Germans that the coast was clear and the British ships were all bottled up. Adler says he assured Findlay I had men devoted to me in the British Navy and that this conspiracy would do them incalculable harm if they did not capture me. I wish I could get word from Ireland – I sent a letter now 2 weeks ago via my friend here for Eoin MacNeill to go thro' Mrs. Green – but even if it reaches her hands safely I doubt now that she would dare (poor brave but frail lady) to send it on to Dublin. It would be too dangerous for herself and for the Professor. Besides they may have him locked up.

My only hope is that in their fury of rage and fear combined they (the British Government) will show their hand so openly against Irish nationality that Redmond and his gang of traitors will have to either repudiate England openly or repudiate the cause they have so grossly misrepresented for years and finally so cruelly betrayed.

In any case I hope all that is sincere and true in Irish nationality will be outraged by the attacks of the Government and that out of this accursed war of English greed against Germany shall be born once more in tribulation, in jail, in repression, the spirit of Irish revolt against English tyranny. May it be so!

Saturday. 19 Dec. (Berlin).

Still no details of the Russian overthrow. It is clear that they are completely routed for the Austrian War Office accounts correspond with the German and say that along the whole front from Galicia to East Prussia the combined Austro-German pursuit of the enemy is taking place.

At the Esplanade Hotel last night a young German told me he had seen y'day morning already many trainloads of soldiers being brought back from the East front & going thro' to the west.

They were dirty and with beards he said & looked as if they "hadn't washed", but were cheering & waving their hands & shouting "Now for the English."

The Emperor, too, I was told was leaving Berlin again for the front last night – I presume for Charleville. If, as everyone now is convinced, the Russian offensive has been completely broken, it should mean the return of a very large force of victorious troops and many guns and officers of ability for the renewed assault on Calais – Dover and Paris. I hope so.

Bethmann Hollweg said to me yesterday that "Germany could not be beaten" – that not Russia, France & England would succeed in defeating her! I said I feared only the long continuance of the war possibly sapping German strength and allowing England's vast resources in the end to turn the tide. He replied that France would not be able to hold out, whatever England might do – and so the end must come sooner or later with a peace inspired, if not dictated, by Germany.

He said that he had never doubted England would join the others. He did not think England actually wanted this war at the moment[97], or was actively responsible for it coming just when it did, but that she could not resist the opportunity, <u>when it came</u>, of trying to get Germany down and destroy her.

He was convinced that England could have stopped the war but would not because she thought it gave her the chance of years of coming in with every prospect of success to destroy the German menace.

As to the pretext of Belgian neutrality that deceived no one now he thought, "If had not been Belgium, it would have been something else. – I agreed and said: "The detained British vessels in Hamburg perhaps" – "Very likely indeed," he replied!

I left the Chancellor about 12.40 and returned to von Wedel and discussed the Hamburg-Amerika Line and the abortive attempt to open trade intercourse with Cork last January. I told him the particulars and he promised to find out fully and in any case to do all he could (when in attendance again) and the Govt to see that, in all events, after the war there might be set up trade dealings and steamship accommodation with Ireland. He said he thought the Admiralty would take up Adler's suggestion and arrange a surprise for Mr. Findlay over "my capture" "anywhere in the North Sea or the Skaggerrak."

Adler brought me the <u>key</u> of the back entrance to the Br. Legation in Christiania today – given to him by the Minister so that he might "come in at any time"!

Blücher and Larasch, his cousin, who knows Ireland slightly, came to lunch with me. Latter still a bit pro-English. He has stayed at Kylemore with the Duke of Manchester and visited Achill and likes the Irish in the way that a stranger, under these auspices, would like a people who were "amusing" and nice to look at. But he knows nothing of Irish history and never realised all that lay behind Kylemore and Achill!

Monday, Dec 21

On Saturday evg I was the guest of a Colonel Emerson and his wife at the Hotel. He is here also. He is a war correspondent of the United Press and very pro German and pro Irish and has read my pamphlet "with joy" he says and will "use it to the best advantage." **[The previous sentence is omitted from Curry's book.]** The others were a Mrs. White and a Mr. Callan O'Loughlin, an American and once an Under Secretary of State under some previous Administration. He was profoundly uninteresting. He has come to Europe as the U.S. "Santa Claus" with gifts for the poor victims of the war and is returning very soon via England to U.S.A. He is impressed by German courage, calmness and greatness of soul and admitted so to

---

[97] The opposite of Casement's view

Luncheon party in Munich: Dr Curry, St John Gaffney, Frau von Pfister, Frau Gaffney, Frau Emerson, Oberlt. Emerson, Roger Casement; printed in Suddeutsche Zeitung, and in the New York Times 7 November 1915 (NLI 17014)

me – but he gives the distinct impression none the less of being pro-British at heart and profoundly pro-Belgian. This is the pose of the average good American – Why did Germany "violate Belgian neutrality!" They can get no further than this. That others and particularly England have again and again violated treaties and invaded neutrality they refuse to discuss or admit the bearing of. This war, to them, is simply a war undertaken by "the Allies" to protect Belgium (and possibly Servia!) from Teutonic forceful aggression. While O'Laughlin did not assert this openly it was plain he <u>felt</u> it. He said, too, that "many Germans" in U.S.A. were anti-German and pro-Ally! Also that "the Irish in America were with England" – whereupon I contradicted him flatly and said I believed the vast majority were strongly pro-German and assuredly anti-English and cited in proof of my assertion the cancelling of Redmond's announced visit to U.S.A. the dissolution of the Irish League of America, the change of policy of the Irish World and the repudiation by Mr. M.J. Ryan of Redmond's recruiting mission. He withdrew *instanter* and said I probably know better than he did. I gave him before parting a copy of my pamphlet "The Crime against Ireland" which he promised to read on his way to England the next few days. That he should read it would be indeed a miracle.

I got a letter from Kuno Meyer today telling me (28 Nov) of his views and of his having met Cohalan, McGarrity,[98] Devoy and John Quinn. They

---

[98] Curry noted (p. 140) "Mr McGarrity, at least, expressed great surprise when informed that these (Sir Roger's) views were disapproved by him." The others certainly disapproved.

all disapprove the publication of the Christiania incident – and also of my suggested expedition to Egypt. In the former case I <u>can</u> do nothing at present – in the latter idea I am right and they are wrong – because as Fr Crotty said "The first thing is that England should be beaten." since it is highly improbable that the Irish Brigade (should it ever come to life) could get into Ireland it would be a far more effective blow for Ireland and against England to aid the Egyptian to expel John Bull than to remain idle, railway bridge guards or doing some sham garrison guard in Germany. These are the only alternatives I see – either to go to Egypt with the returning Khedive and expel the English – or to sit down at Limburg an der Lahn till the end of the war.

Of course a great naval victory by Germany would open the door to Ireland – but this is not very likely. The *Lustige Blätter* of tonight has a good cartoon on this very subject – a German sailor and a big fleet bring "Home Rule" to Ireland – while Pat says "I've waited a very long time for that!"

I ordered 100 copies to be sent to the Irish prisoners and more for U.S.A.

I called on von Wedel again at 5.30 gave him K. Meyer's letter and told him of my interview with young Bryan A Kelly who had come to me twice today. Let out of Ruhleben (at my request) he will go to Limburg to convert the soldiers and later go back to Ireland with messages of good cheer to Eoin and others. He will be ostensibly "interred" at Limburg without his own assent asked or given. Wedel agreed to all and will visit Frankfurt and Limburg and Kelly will go down on Tuesday as a "prisoner of war."

I also wrote Frau Nelly Zittel to come & see me – & she came y'day (Sunday) and she too will go to Limburg – ostensibly as a "nurse" and will talk to the men in the right vein. She has been so long out of Ireland, however, (9 years) that her accent is now German and she forgets words and does not realise the great changes (for the worse) that the prolonged "Home Rule" <u>fight</u> on the floor of the House and the "trusting in the Liberals" has had on the heart and spirit of Irish nationality. I told her of these desperate evils and of how Redmond had gone over bag and baggage to the enemy and was now simply John Bull's recruiting sergeant in Ireland. She is a pretty woman, with blue Irish eyes and still a good deal of the gentle kindly Irish voice and brogue in her Germanised English.

The Chancellor left his card on me on Friday evg at the hotel.

Last evg (at 5.30) I went to Mrs. White's and met a number of people chiefly from the press. The chief man of the <u>Lokalanzeiger</u> among them – and one of the principal redacters of the *Vossische Zeitung*.[99] Also a Swede,

---

[99] At the beginning of January 1914, Berlin's Ullstein Publishing Company took over the long-established *Vossische Zeitung*. Founded in 1704 as the *Berlinisch Ordinaire Zeitung*, the liberal paper could count among its editors such outstanding literati as Gotthold Ephraim

the representative in Germany of the chief Swedish press – all were more than friendly and the *Vossische Zeitung* man particularly. He said they were only waiting for the naval fight to send an expedition, with me, to Ireland.

<u>Wednesday, Dec 23</u>.
On Monday evening I called again on Wedel at F.O. and arranged definitely about Kelly and Mrs. Zittel going to Limburg. She came in to see Wedel while I was there and we three discussed the matter fully – she will go after Christmas day – probably next Monday. I wrote General De Graaff about Kelly. Kelly is to go down today and at Limburg to report himself to the police and be "interred" with the soldiers.

I also called to bid Major Lothes good bye. He goes out again to Chile to try and take 200 reservists to a certain place I will not put it down here even. I wish I were going too. I fancy the English may have already got hold of his idea for I see the U.S.A. authorities have held up a consignment of stores etc. for that place being shipped from San Francisco and yesterday I was told the English had seized the Chile mail to Germany on a neutral ship off Montevideo and thrown it overboard! A fine regard for the sanctity of treaties. These same English are shrieking to all the world against the bombardment of the Yorkshire towns and batteries. As I have always predicted they are now setting up a concerted yell in U.S.A. to try and get that country dragged in on their side. It will take <u>all</u> the strength of the Irish and Germans yet, in America, to keep Mr. Wilson "neutral."[100] England will stick at nothing when the war she so selfishly aimed at Germany comes nearer and nearer her own shores.

Yesterday, Tuesday, I went by appointment to see Dr Karl Vollmoeller[101] at the Adlon Hotel. He had sent a telephone call to me on Saturday through Count Palby (a cousin of my former friend in London) begging me to call on him as he was sick in bed and wanted to meet me very much.

I found a fair haired, spectacled young German – or <u>almost a German American</u>. He is a journalist and a dramatic writer and I gathered had also helped in the Embassies of England and U.S.A. at times.

He wanted to help the Irish cause and write it up in the Berlin press and do all he could to advance "my cause."

I gave him my pamphlet – Puttkamer writes me that he has read the pamphlet and is so anxious to write an article on it in "Der Tag" and to discuss

---

Lessing and Theodor Fontane. In 1935, the National Socialists forbade its publication.
[100] In the event, President Woodrow Wilson was seriously uninterested in approaching London to reprieve Casement, not least because of his involvement in sabotage in the US.
[101] Dr Karl Gustav Vollmoeller (1878-1948) was a car and aircraft designer, dramatist, lyricist, novelist, and translator who wrote the screenplay for The Blue Angel.

this he comes to see me today.

When leaving Vollmoeller at 12.30 I saw a small gathering at the front door of the Hotel and out on the step a tall dark, Egyptian-faced man with slight beard. A fez with white turban round it and long black robe. Beside him a fezzed gentleman in morning suit. Just as I came out the guard was marching up Unter den Linden and as they passed the Adlon the order was given and all "eyes right" turned on him. I guessed it was the Khedive but was not sure. He was darker than I anticipated a true Egyptian face. In the evening I learned it was the Khedive who had just arrived in Berlin from Vienna, at 11.30.

The English have deposed him and he is already to them the ex-Khedive. They have appointed his uncle Hussein Kamel as "<u>Sultan</u> of Egypt" and proclaimed, at the same time, a British Protectorate over Egypt!
[Casement margin note: It was not. It was Abdel Kader.]
And these are the respecters of treaties who began the war solely because Germany had "violated the neutrality" of Belgium! Of all the hypocrisies mankind ever invented surely English greed of Empire has excelled all other frauds in all other ages. Since this war began they have committed truly unpardonable crimes against honour, truth and public law.

The floods of lies against Germany deliberately designed to poison knowledge poured out in America, in Ireland and elsewhere; the "putting of the Home Rule Bill on the Statute Book" in order to entrap Irishmen into the armed attack on Germans; the bringing of Japan into the quarrel of the white men; the insidious and continuous attempts on Italy, on Portugal, on all the small neutral States; the seizure of Cyprus in open violation of their public treaty with Turkey; the seizure of Egypt; the seizure of German mails at sea; the bombardment of the Belgian coast towns and destruction of the lives and property of their wretched "allies", the wanton destruction and bombardment of defenceless villages in Kamerun, at Dar es Salaam and elsewhere –and, finally, the union of thirty-eight ships of war – Japanese as well – to overwhelm von Spee and his <u>five</u> cruisers! Seven to one is Mr. Asquith's idea of a "fair fight"! – "All we ask is a fair fight" (Guildhall speech). A truly despicable record – and it is this bully, coward and scoundrel of the Nations who is howling through the world against the Germans bombarding <u>his</u> coast!

His delightful press has had an orgie of impotent wrath against the German Navy. *The Times* called the bombardment an "act of vulgar ferocity" and all of them ask "will not the U.S.A. now decide that the time has come for all <u>neutral</u> States to enter the ring on the side of the Allies?"

I am to go at 3 today to call on Captain Isendahl[102] at the Admiralty to

---

[102] Later Konteradmiral (Rear-Admiral) Walther Isendahl

discuss the ways and means of the Christiania incident and how to get Findlay. I don't think anything will come out of it. It can only be carried to success by my going into it personally and that would conflict with the Irish Brigade.

Last night I went to Professor Edward Meyer[103] at Gross Lichterfelde West Weg and met a party of professors there – among them the Director of the Berlin Museum – an officer in uniform covered with medal ribbons – Major Wiegand.[104] He knew Mrs. Green – 18 years ago! Had gone on horseback with her to Troy! He had found her charming and said she spoke "excellent German."

Thursday. Dec 24.

I went at 3 to the Reichsmarineamt General Staff and found Captain Isendahl and another officer waiting. We discussed Findlay at length – and it was settled that "Mr. Hammond" will embark at Gothenburg for Christiania direct (avoiding Kragerö) on 8 January. After that Adler will know nothing of his intentions. Adler will inform Mr. Findlay of this – and then two sketch outline maps of Ireland and Great Britain with hypothetical "mine fields" were given me (at my request). Two of the mine fields will close the Irish Sea North and South – from Port Patrick to Galloway and from Carnsore over to Wales. These to be laid "about the 15 January." Mr. Findlay's only chance of catching "Mr. Hammond" will be when he travels by this small Danish S/S "Mjölnir" from Gothenburg to Christiania. I asked no questions.

I took the maps to Adler and he traced them on paper and did it well too and brought them to me at 7.30 this morning. Then I arranged the tale he is to spin Findlay in addition to the two maps. Part of the tale is that I left for Vienna today and so allowed Adler home for Christmas. Also that I met the Khedive and "stood beside him" at the salute on Tuesday. That a special messenger arrived from New York last night with good news. This is true for a Dr. Ewald arrived by the Norwegian S/S "Kristianiafjord" (to Bergen) and got to the Eden Hotel last night and at once asked for me and I met him at 11 p.m. on going up to my room. He is vice President of the American Truth Society under Jeremiah O'Leary and told me that all was going splendidly in U.S.A. – the Irish-German alliance there a firm and stern reality for Wilson and all the rest of the Anglo-Saxons. No possibility of getting the U.S.A. "roped in" against Germany now he says – "there would be a revolution." The German American press had come out with great headlines over the Declaration of 20 Nov. and the Stadts Zeitung said the next German

---

[103] Eduard Meyer b. Hamburg 1855, Professor of Ancient History and a brother of Kuno Meyer

[104] Theodor Wiegand (1864-1936), archaeologist and founder of the Pergamon museum in Berlin

Dreadnought should be named "Sir Roger Casement."

I called on Wedel at 6.30 (after seeing Meyer at F.O. and telling him of the "plot") and he brought in Graf Montgelas who is taking his place while he goes off for Xmas. I told him of what Fräulein Meyer had told me of Professor Macran[105] of Dublin University (Trinity) who is here in Charlottenburg and he agreed that if Macran will speak the truth for Germany they will release him and send him home to Dublin. He said it 'all lay with me'– that if I said so they would do it – that anything that I asked for of that kind they would at once assent to. So I shall see Prof Macran soon and if he is a decent Irishman he shall go back to Dublin.

Meyer brought the sample uniform today for "an officer" of the Irish Brigade. It fit me well and I shall wear it!

At 11 as I was going to bed Dr. Ewald came to speak to me having just arrived from New York which he left on 12 Dec. He says all is going well – the Irish and Germans a solid mass and Redmond entirely repudiated and my coming here a subject of great rejoicing to all the Irish and Germans. He wants me to return to U.S.A. "if I can" and take up the direction of the Irish movement there – but that is out of the question. He had not seen Kuno Meyer and only knows J. O'Leary and is not in the "inner circle" – but he can tell of things within public knowledge. The pro-German feeling is growing according to him.

Today at lunch with Countess Hahn, the Princess Hohenlohe who is here in the Hotel brought her sailor boy (about 15) a fine handsome lad – Ctess Bernstorff the wife of the U.S.A. Ambassador, my friend, was also there with her son, a young officer of the Imperial Guard of Cuirassiers – like his father the Ambassador.

The manager of the hotel read a special slip of telegram from the headquarters staff saying that there would be an issue of the Staff Report tomorrow (Christmas Day) at midday. This intimation means good news – probably from Poland where the Russian losses in all the recent tremendous fighting will probably be given out for the Christmas party.

In the West, the Germans have stormed many French-British trenches the last three days and killed large numbers (700 "English dead" at one point) and taken some 2000 to 3000 prisoners. Once the battle in Poland-Galicia is definitely decided in favour of Germany and Austria I expect they will leave the further handling of the Russian hordes to Austria and turn 500.000 victorious men into France and Flanders and break thro' towards Paris and towards the channel at sometime.

Meantime the British "Protectorate" over Egypt is announced with a

---

[105] Professor Henry S. Macran of TCD

"Sultan" of Egypt. The proclamation is signed by Miles Cheetham (my old friend from Rio de Janeiro!) and is a delightful specimen of British hypocrisy and double dealing combined with the arrogance of the successful burglar who has got his victim robbed and bound. John Bull is doing it all "for the welfare of the dear Egyptians!" Equally he has <u>no quarrel with the Caliphate</u> – only with the "usurpers" of power at Constantinople! Everybody who acts for his own interests, except John Bull, is an "usurper", a "traitor", a "lunatic" or a "barbarian."

If Turkey gets into Egypt it will be the beginning of the end!.

<u>Sunday</u>. Dec 27$^{th.}$ in Berlin.

Christmas & Stephen's Days have come and gone. Adler left for Moss on Christmas Day only – having been detained at last moment on Thursday by Meyer for fear of possible trouble at Sassnitz again. I saw him off.

The name of the steamer is the "Mjölnir" of Copenhagen. Mr. H. will embark on her. A real Mr. H. will go – but not the one Mr. Findlay suspects.

The war news the last few days is disappointing – No real gain in Poland – the Russians had got large reinforcements and are holding the Bzura line 30 miles west of Warsaw.

In Flanders several English attacks repulsed and yesterday's bulletin shows heavy English losses near Nieuport and at Hubert – "over 3000 dead" – 819 soldiers and 19 officers prisoners and 14 guns and some others – During the last week the English losses have been well over 6000 killed and prisoners – the German officers say the new English army is not so good as the first – the regular army. That must be pretty well used up and disposed of now.

The British losses must be fully 150.000 killed, wounded *hors de combat* and prisoners. I suppose the latter now were fully 21.000 or 22.000 in the hands of the Germans – at least that. The Austrians announce 42.000 Russian prisoners from 11 to 20 Decr in Galicia and south Poland.

The prisoners of war now in the allied Teutonic States should be

	Men
Germany – say	650.000
Austria-Hungary	<u>240.000</u>
	890.000
The Russian (and Servian) killed wounded & invalided cannot be less than	<u>2.000.000</u>
	2.890,000

So that there is the best part of 3.000.000 men of the Eastern enemy's side already accounted for.

Can Germany and Austria bear the strain? That's the question. I think they can.

at Limburg a/Lahn <u>1915</u>.
Friday. January 8th.

It is nearly 2 weeks since I wrote in my diary. I have been ill and greatly upset at failure of my hopes.

Adler left for Moss and Christiania on X-mas Day only, which I spent so quietly in Berlin with Countess Hahn in the evening.

From that on I had several interviews with Professor Macran of Dublin University. He promised to be a true and faithful witness to the "truth about Germany" if released – so I obtained that and he and his wife actually left Berlin for Ireland last 6 January. They should now be in Holland, en route via Rotterdam or the Hook of Holland.

Meyer came to me at the end of December to change the instructions for Adler. The new instructions are for him to tell Mr. Findlay that I embark, <u>he does not know where</u>, on the "Mjölnir" for Christiansand – that I am getting her to call in for me at some small port near Gothenburg, & then she will go direct to Christiansand.

She is due to leave Gothenburg today – tonight sometime, and it is tomorrow the "incident" should come to its head. Adler was told in my letter to go straight to Christiansand, to be there on 9th to meet me on arrival of "Mjölnir." This letter was sent by 76 Wilhelmstrasse to Christiania ~~to be sent at once to Adler~~ & a wire sent to him to call at the Legation.

On Tuesday 29 Dec. I went to the Irish prisoners at Ruhleben, near Spandau. There are 163 nominal "Irish" there – Catholics – I saw a few, young sailors from Rush and elsewhere and one charming youth of 17, Paul O'Brien, son of a Cork man and an apprentice on an English steamer. Only 17. I think all should be released as an act of goodwill to Ireland by Germany.

It would make the English and their Govt furiously angry – and would do great good elsewhere – in Ireland and U.S.A. The fact that the German Government had released nearly 200 civil prisoners merely on the ground that Germany wished well to Ireland would make England foam at the mouth – and would make <u>everyone else</u> pleased throughout the world. I have advised this.

I discussed it with Professor Macran who said it would be a "very nasty blow to the Br. Govt.." He has become entirely "rebellious" at heart since our first meeting – & is really sorry not to be in to the neck with me! He told me so – all red in the face. Strange product of Trinity – but the Irish blood will out – even in a Trinity professor. He is to call on Gertrude at

Caversham, on Mrs. Green, on Eoin MacNeill, (through Sarah Purser), on F.J.B. possibly – and of course, too, on Nina – but that is to be arranged thro' Gertrude. I sent £15 (part £5 gold and rest German money) by him for Nina – to hand to Gertrude.

I got the terms of the agreement between the Imperial German Government and myself on the Irish Brigade by a special messenger from F.O. on Monday evening 28 Dec.

I drew up the conditions and by letter on 23 Dec. forwarded them – and they now reply, in due form, accepting them fully in a letter covering my conditions – in English and German – dated 28 December and signed by the Under Secretary of State for Foreign Affairs Zimmermann with the official seal of the F.O.[106]

[Letter from Zimmerman agreeing to the formation of the Irish Brigade "with a view to securing the national freedom of Ireland":]

Dec 28 1914

Dear Sir Roger,
I have the honour to acknowledge the receipt of your letter of the 23rd inst. in which you submitted to the Imperial German Government a proposal for the formation of an Irish Brigade, pledged to fight in the cause of Irish nationality alone and to be formed of such Irishmen, now prisoners of war in Germany, as may be willing to enroll themselves in such a corps.

In reply I have the honour to inform you that the Imperial German Government agrees to your Proposal and accepts the conditions under which the Brigade might possibly be formed, as laid down in the statement annexed to your letter of the 23rd inst. and enclosed herewith.

 I have the honour to be,
 Dear Sir Roger,
 your obedient servant
 (signed) Zimmermann
 Undersecretary of State for Foreign Affairs.
The Honourable
Sir Roger Casement
Eden Hotel
Kürfurstendamm

I left Berlin, after having got this document, which contains a clear acceptance of an independent Ireland and its recognition by Germany, on Wednesday 30 Dec. by the 10.36 a.m. train getting to Frankfurt at 7.30. I

---

[106] NYPL Maloney IHP (copy). Casement referred to this document of 28 December 1914 on the Irish Brigade thereafter as 'The Treaty'. The earlier 'Declaration' was issued on 20 November 1914.

had got a bad cold on me due largely to the sharp thaw after Christmas and the cold at Ruhleben and on getting to Frankfurt I had to go to bed and stayed there in bed till Saturday the 2nd January 1915.

I saw Prince Leiningen once – & then General de Graaff on Saturday evening, to arrange for the release of Bryan Kelly as soon as I wanted it. Kelly had come to Limburg, to be imprisoned on Wednesday 23 Decr – and he is to give me a real view of what the men truly think. That was the plan. On Sunday 3 January I came on to Limburg by the early morning train – still with this bad cold on me. I found the two Irish priests Fathers Crotty and O'Gorman both very well and delighted to see me. The latter confirmed publicly to me that he had "entirely changed his views" and was now fully pro-German and in full sympathy with me and my plans for an independent Ireland through German help. He has repeated this several times and says my brochure did very much to change his views and that he agrees with every word of it.

In the afternoon of Sunday 3 Janry we went, all three, to Balduinstein to call on Pfarrer Berkessel[107] who spent years at Cashel in the old days of Dr. Croke in the early '80s.

We found him quite a delightful man, with a charming mind and person and a warm regard for the Irish – His conversation was altogether delightful, full of reminiscences of Irish (and English) personalities and he entertained us with the greatest good will till the evening train brought us back to Limburg.

On Monday 4 January I changed my hotel – the Nassauer Hof where I found two rooms, one an excellent sitting room – for 4.50 per day.

On Tuesday, 5 January, I got a letter from Adler from Grand Hotel, Christiania, telling me he had seen Mr. Findlay on Sunday 27 December, and that all was going very well and Mr. Findlay was very keen to catch me on my projected "raid" to Ireland. This was in the morning of Tuesday 5 January I got this letter from Christiania.

In the afternoon I went up to the camp, along with the two priests – I very soon saw from the manner of the men that all hope of an Irish Brigade from such a contemptible crew as are there must be entirely abandoned. Some of them insulted me – but all showed clearly the utter slothful indifference of that type of debauched Irishman to any appeal but to his greed. They complained of "ill treatment" of "want of food" and were anxious for tobacco – but were full of ill will to Germany and in many cases "more English than the English themselves." I did not see Kelly and made no inquiry for him – but wrote and telephoned to Frankfurt for his immediate release.

I came down from the camp at 6.16 p.m. in dark and mud – in a very

---

[107] Father Berkessel

Irish Brigade machine gunners Thomas McGrath, Michael McDonagh, Michael O'Callaghan and James Carroll (NLI 18081)

despondent mood after the revelation of Irish depravity I had witnessed among these 2,200 so called "Irishmen."

At 6.20 I got a telephone from the F.O. as follows. Time 2h 10mts. "Following telegram for Hammond just received from Frederikshald. Meet me train arrives 7.24 Berlin, must see you, good news. Christensen."

Very soon after I got 'phone calls from Mr. Meyer asking me what I should do and saying he would go to the train to meet Adler. I said I did not want to go to Berlin unless absolutely necessary and to keep me informed by wire. At 7.20 a.m. on 6 January I got a telegram sent off in the night saying – "your coming not necessary. Christensen returns tomorrow morning."

I wrote to Meyer telling him that I thought there was no hope of getting the soldiers to do anything and asking to be kept informed of the new "plot" against me arranged now – I wonder what Christensen's "good news" is?

I hope it means that these scoundrels have fallen into their despicable plot to kidnap me. The daily papers speak of "English mines laid off the coast of Norway" – and give some details and the names of steamers Norwegian detained by them. This seems clearly part of the British "action" to prevent my contemplated Wolfe Tone descent on the coast of Ireland.[108]

I must possess myself in patience and wait for developments. I hope it may mean several of their pirate craft caught in their own net laid for the one Irishman today they are really afraid of! Good! They are afraid of me. My price has gone up to £10.000 and poor Adler is anxious to get their money "to give me" (poor soul) so that I may fight them with their own "purse." I have laughed at this and told him we must never touch a penny of this money "given" to him.

On Thursday 7 Janry Bryan Kelly presented himself at the Nassauer Hof and after breakfast I went with him to Frankfurt at the request of the General de Graaff by telegram and got him a pass for Berlin where he is asked by phone from the F.O. to call on Friday morning (today) at 11 a.m. and report himself to Mr. Meyer.

I wrote by Kelly to Meyer asking for him to be allowed off at once to Ireland.

I had a long talk with Kelly. He reports the men as "quite contemptible" – that they steal from each other, are despised by the German guards and the French prisoners alike. The latter will not associate with them in any way.

---

[108] Casement wrote later, then aged 52, that Wolfe Tone was "only 33 when he left France for Ireland…My God! – had I been only 33 again when I left Wilhelmshaven for Kerry! The rebellion would have been a different thing – the Steamer, the code and myself would assuredly never have fallen into the hands of the English". (TNA HO 144/1636/311463/32A, 28 May 1916)

Kelly says that the young men, or boys might be got together into a Brigade if one could get them away from the older men. There are many "Englishmen" he says among them – born in England and no more Irish than any ordinary Anglo-Saxon. He says they are in no case to be trusted and that to think of doing anything for Ireland with such creatures is hopeless. He regards them as "hired assassins and cut throats" and says that they boast of the "blood money" they will get on their emancipation and return "to England."

Kelly was to go to Berlin by the night train. I returned to Limburg, after seeing General de Graaff by the 8.30 train that got me in cold and wet at 10.45 p.m.

Today Friday 8 January, the interpreter (at my request) brought young Sergeant Quinlisk down to me at 9.30 a.m. I kept him till 11 when he was taken again to camp – with some papers. He reported that he was assailed by the men – but he would "fight it out." They threaten to inform on him and have him hanged as a traitor on "return to England." He showed no fear – and said he did not care – that he had done his duty to Ireland and was not afraid of them.

He confirmed – only more so – Bryan Kelly's statements and said they were a contemptible cowardly lot of brutes. Both Kelly and I decided yesterday that it would be a great mistake to allow these ruffians out on Sunday to Mass at the Cathedral and I told the General so. He agreed that it would be very unwise. This will greatly disappoint the two priests – especially poor Fr. Crotty. Father O'Gorman returns to Rome in eight days or so and Father Crotty will be alone. However I think it may be best to break up the "Irish camp" at Limburg altogether. There is no reason for it now. All hope of getting these men to strike a blow for Ireland is at an end – and so far as I can see, my mission to Germany too. It will be impossible to expect the German govt. to make any further declaration about Ireland when the only Irishmen in Germany boast that they are English and repudiate with scorn the idea that they should fight for Ireland! How can anything ever be done for such a people? Here are 2200 Irishmen as Quinlisk said this morning, and said himself "not one to fight or work or lift a hand for Ireland."

I said that Quinlisk could not be left to his fate at the hands of these men – He admitted that while he despised them and was quite prepared "to face the music" that he thought it exceedingly likely the men, and the "co-conspirator" MacMorrough especially, would try to have him tried for treason in England. The English government would be delighted to have a victim.

So I said to Quinlisk that I should apply for his release and send him to America and he jumped at the idea. It is the only way to save him. Even so, there are dangers for him – grave dangers, poor boy! He is a fine type – brave and fearless. A Wexford boy from the Christian Brothers school. Only 19. His younger brother, only 17, was shot through the heart he tells me near La Bassie – "10 miles below La Bassie." He saw him killed. Quinlisk's contempt for his comrades is wholehearted.

He asked nothing from me – made no complaint and was quite prepared to be put on trial for high treason.

If Father Nicholson arrives from Philadelphia, as he should do, at any moment, I may be able to get Quinlisk back with him to America. Father Nicholson, we were advised a long time ago, was to have sailed from America for Naples on 18 Dec. He should have gone to Italy by 30 or 31 Dec. and I have been expecting daily to hear, at least, that he is in Rome. I have asked for him to come on here at once to me. I hope they will hurry him up. Of course it is quite possible that the British ruffians at Gibraltar arrested him – American citizen and all as he is – and that he is "held up" there. I shall soon know. If he comes to Berlin, I can surely make arrangements for him to take Quinlisk back with him by the same boat. In any case poor Quinlisk must be saved from the most Christian Government.

Most of my thoughts are very sad – I am very despondent – How lift up & vivify a land that has such cowards as these to represent it! On the other hand both Fr. Crotty and Fr. O'Gorman are splendid – and both give me good news from Ireland. The Rector of the Irish College in Rome, Monsignor O'Riordan returned from Ireland on Xmas eve and reported that the recruiting was "dead." Redmond had failed. He had tried to get up a meeting at Limerick, and no priest would attend. Fr. O'Hagan, the Vice Rector, wrote to Fr. Crotty in similar strains. Also they said that the Irish ecclesiastics in Rome are all against the new British Envoy to the Vatican. Cardinal Gasquet, one of the four Cardinals who live in Rome for international work and who is called "the English Cardinal", gives a grand reception for Sir Henry Howard and the two Fathers tell me the great bulk of the Irish party in Rome will not go near it. They especially say that educated opinion in Ireland is beginning to change.

at Limburg.

<u>Wednesday</u>. 13 January.

I am still at Limburg – there is nothing here to record save continuous rain. I have not been again to the camp – but have had long talks with General Exner about the men and the "Brigade." Also with Fr Berkessel whom I purpose getting an order for to visit the camp when he chooses just as Fr. Crotty. Also to get a Harmonium to play to the men.

I have been waiting daily for some news from Christiania but no word yet. Since I got the telegrams and telephone calls saying Adler had returned so suddenly to Berlin I know nothing and there may have been a grave change of plans. The "Mjölnir" was to have crossed from Gothenburg to Christiansand with "Mr Hammond" on board on the 9th four days ago. So far nothing seems to have transpired. In the House of Lords of London I see Lord Curzon asked about "Sir Roger Casement" and what would be done to him and the "*B. Z. am Mittag*" of Berlin of Sunday last, received last night by post, gives a long article on me. Lord Crewe seems to have said that "very sensible punishment was due to Sir Roger Casement"! Yes.

Meantime I have been delayed in writing a letter to Sir E Grey which I have long contemplated I have drafted some of it. It recounts my own attitude towards Ireland since I left the F. O. Service on 30 June 1913 [**'1913' later inserted in pencil. The rest is in ink.**] & the <u>acts</u> of the previous Br Govt. against Ireland & then it brings the whole charge of the attempted crime of Christiania straight to Grey & the Br Govt.

I propose writing this letter while here at Limburg & sending the original from Berlin, through the American Ambassador, to London, & handing copies formally to the Ambassador himself for transmission to his Govt. – as well as com'mentry copies to the Norwegian Govt. the German & the Austro-Hungarian – & also getting one to the Pope.

Doubtless when the House of Commons meets early in February the enemy will announce his "sensible punishment" of me. It will be well to let him & the world know first that his base attempt against me was known from the first.

Here in Limburg almost daily men proceed for the front. On Monday a number went off with flowers in their rifles – A fine body of young men – 19-21 – 250 strong, in grey uniform paraded on Saturday – splendid types of tall young Germans.

The land is full of men – & full of courage, certitude of victory and absolute faith in the great destiny of Germany.

No one who sees these people close can doubt for a moment in the national greatness of Germany or in the certainty that these people cannot be overthrown.

When the announced "two millions of men" of Lord Kitchener come, as they say, in the spring, Germany will have a new army of 700.000 men in the field and with the help of God she should do more than hold her own against all comers.

A debate on recruiting in Ireland also took place in the House of Lords and it is admitted that all Redmond's efforts have failed and that the "Nationalist districts remain untouched." So far we have won. Lord Mayo attributes the failure to "the seditious literature" that flooded the country. Me! – and friends of Ireland!

Meantime I am urging the release of all Irish prisoners at Ruhleben on the grounds of German goodwill to Ireland. This will please the Irish people and greatly irritate John Bull. If the Germans are wise they will do it as a gracious act to Ireland. Fr. O'Gorman takes many copies of my pamphlet to Rome on Monday. I am writing again today to Berlin to urge the release of the Irish prisoners at Ruhleben.

Thursday. 14 Janry. —

No news from Berlin at all & so none from Christiania or the Skaggerak. I presume either the "Mjölnir" was not molested by Br. cruisers on her journey from Gothenburg to Christiansand and so the coup manqué'd; or that Findlay has, at last! – found out how Adler has been fooling him, or else that Adler's hurried return to Berlin & abrupt departure again for Norway meant a complete change of plan, of which I know nothing yet – & probably now shall know nothing. It is on the other hand, highly probable Findlay and the Foreign Office have found out that I am fooling them and that all Adler's fairy tales are only designed to get fuller proof against the British Legation in Norway of criminal conspiracy.

The last "Gaelic American" to hand has some very foolish utterances on the subject of my journey across the Atlantic showing clearly that the editor knew of an attempt against me. To thus let the cat out of the bag is to give the show away to Washington Embassy and I think it is highly probable Mr. Findlay has decided now to drop his dealings with Adler. But I must wait the latter's return to Berlin and full report on all.

Neither von Wedel nor Meyer have sent me a line. It is amusing, because I am engaged on an "Open Letter" to Sir Grey charging him and his despicable colleagues with my attempted murder, or my waylaying or kidnapping in Norway and letting them and the world, know what is just the moral standing of the British Government in its action towards Irish nationalists. I propose having this letter drafted here while quiet at Limburg and to send it through the U. S. Embassy to Grey on my return to Berlin and to send copies to other Embassies and finally to the press. It is well to be first in the field.

Friday 15 January.   at Limburg.

It still rains. I am daily nearly at the dentists' who is fixing up my teeth well. Father O'Gorman returns to Rome on Monday next, via Würzburg and Lake Constance. This leaves Father Crotty alone with the soldiers. I have secured permission for Father Berkessel of Balduinstein near this to go and come freely in the camp and to hire a harmonium to play Irish songs &c. to the men. He and Father Crotty will collaborate.

I have not been to the camp since the afternoon I went up with the two priests last Tuesday week – and it has rained daily.

I have been waiting here chiefly in the hope that Father Nicholson of Philadelphia would come. He was to have sailed on 18 December for Naples. Last night, however, I got a letter from Mr. Meyer saying they had received a cable from von Bernstorff saying Father Nicholson had not sailed on 18th but would probably go on 30th but they had not heard since if he had actually sailed.

<u>Meyer said nothing of Christiania, so I am as much in the dark as ever as to the meaning for Adler's sudden return and telegram to me and equally sudden return next day. What was the plot? The German F.O. are very peculiar people – and one never knows where one is with them</u> [**Passage underlined in black ink, the rest is in blue ink**].

Meantime Limburg is full of life. Soldiers and recruits come and go daily. This morning a new batch of the New Year's men came by an early train, in the dark, and were singing through the town. They were fine tall young fellows – mostly fair haired boys of 20 or so – big strapping young men – and all looking as simple and happy as if they were going to a fair instead of to a shambles in cold, mud, rain and slush.

The war news is comparatively nil – save for frequent captures of French at Soissons, and along the line and in the Argonne.

On 12th and 13th the Germans took prisoners 3200 French and many guns, and for several days previously it had been pretty much the same. Since the 1st January the French have lost some 6000 to 7000 prisoners and possibly many more killed and wounded, and a great number of guns.

The German advance on Warsaw is held up by the bad weather – but they are within 30 to 35 miles of it.

On the seas there is little to record – German submarines off Dover in this morning's "Frankfurter Zeitung."

The Note of the <u>U.S.A.</u> Government to England is printed in full in the "<u>Continental Times</u>" of a few days ago. It is a slap on both cheeks to the Power that has posed so long as the guardian of the freedom of the seas. Meantime England has replied and apparently sticks to her "rights" which consist in, practically, holding up the trade of the whole world lest, perchance, some of the goods crossing the oceans might possibly find their way to Germany. It is the clearest illustration of the fundamental truths enunciated in my pamphlet "Ireland, Germany and the Freedom of the Seas." I see, by recent

"Gaelic American", that this is going strong in U.S.A. and it seems to furnish the text for many resolutions at the meetings now being held in U.S.A. to protest against the British attitude towards Neutral States. Dr. Dernburg is reported to have spoken lately in New York and to judge from the speech as given in "Continental Times" it was largely based on my argument.

My own course is not at all clear. Now that I have practically abandoned the idea of the Irish Brigade, there seems little object in remaining in Germany. The Government will not want me, I am sure. Once the hope of the Irish Brigade is gone, they will feel little interest in the other aspects of the Irish Question. Those remain for later settlement – when, after this war is over, the great question facing all maritime nations will present itself more acutely than ever. The control of the seas by one power, and that power the least tied to European obligations, is a standing threat to the welfare of all the peoples of Europe. This war will demonstrate that. It has done so already.

I believe Germany will achieve a successful peace as against France and Russia, unless Italy takes the field for the "Allies" (with Roumania possibly too). With Italy remaining neutral and Roumania neutral I agree with von Hindenburg "the nation with the better nerves will win." That nation is Germany. Her greatest resource is that her people are one and united and march, fight and die as one man – prince, Herr and peasant. I believe with the Chancellor that "Germany is unconquerable." With France exhausted and Russia having had enough of it, these two powers must find their interest is in peace – and they will make peace what ever England may say or do when that day comes.

If Germany can only win France to her side she would then be able to settle the question of the seas, too, as well as of her land frontiers.

But France will not forgive quickly or forget easily. She has a bad Government, and no great man or men. The French soldiers at the camp here say openly, I hear, that France has been "put in the fire" by England and for English interests alone. The truth comes slowly to a nation – but quickly to its defeated citizens.

There are now close on 250.000 French prisoners of war in Germany and close on 350.000 Russians. The figures are mounting by thousands each week.

The German navy I am told is ready for the attack on England "by end of January." Part of the programme is said to be the formal notification of a blockade of all the east coast of England. The first time in her history the "Mistress of the Seas" will have had this indignity put upon her! It is von Tirpitz's aim – and he may well be able to carry it out.

'Berliner Tageblatt. 8 Jan. 1915.' [**Newspaper cutting tipped in here, with** name and date inscribed by Casement, and headlined:] '*Die englandfeindliche Bewegung in Irland*' [**The enemy England's transformation in Ireland**]

Saturday. 16 Jan 1915.   Limburg.

A fine morning that turned into a cloudy rainy day. Still at the Dentist.

The last three days have seen a veritable battle at Soissons, where the French attacked the German position north of the Aisne, and after a first success were finally driven south of the river with heavy loss. They left 5200 prisoners between 4 & 5000 killed on the field (and how many wounded is not given) as well as 14 guns, 7 machine guns & a lot of other things. Poor France! She is paying dear indeed for the Entente Cordiale of the defunct King Edward VII.

How long her tenacity will stand the strain is hard to say, but to judge from the French soldiers, prisoners here, there must come a great awakening with defeat. These men will not speak with or associate with the Irish prisoners. They call them, and rightly, "English" and despise them as frankly as their German guards do. On all hands I hear the most unfavourable comparisons between these "alleged Irishmen" and the French prisoners of war. The latter work cheerfully and are civil and well behaved. The "Irish" are lazy, dirty, and have a most forbidding aspect – slouching, hands in pocket, loafing and cheering "dear old England" all the time.

They expect that this Motherland of theirs will arrive with 2.000.000 of men in the spring and smash Germany – when they will be freed in triumph and get "home" to England and get their accumulated "blood money." They have said these things to me and to the two priests, and both Bryan Kelly and young Quinlisk told me this.

The attitude of these men is one of the things that must make an Irishman despair of Irish nationality and almost despise his country. Kelly called them "contemptible." I endorse the opinion to the full. Even Father O'Gorman, who is to some extent "pro-English" thinks them "miserable specimens of Irishmen."

I have just had a long distance call from Berlin from Mr. Meyer saying Kelly has not gone yet but will leave very soon now, & that he, Mr. M, has written me "tonight" a letter "with some things of interest." I presume this will refer chiefly to Adler's return from Christiania and the "plot" there against myself with "ce cher Mon. Findlay". [**later underlining**].

I got from an unknown correspondent today a cutting from some unnamed German paper giving a long article on Ireland by Professor Pokorny[109] of

---

[109] Julius Pokorny (1887-1970) was the foremost Celtic scholar of his generation on the European mainland. Born in Prague, he studied at Vienna University and learned Irish in

Vienna with many quotations from my old *Dublin Review* article of July 1913 on "Ireland, Germany and the Next War." He did not know the writer – but quotes it – and then later on refers to my visit to Berlin.

Julius Pokorny when younger   *Professor Julius Pokorny c. 1967*

I heard today that the Kaiser had been in Limburg lately at the Irish camp incognito. He is said to have been present at the fight at Soissons – so the young waiter in the Preussischer Hof told me today – my young friend Rudolf Koekelberger.

Mayo and Kerry. He was a German nationalist who also became a propagandist for both the Gaelic League and the Irish nationalist cause from 1908. In 1920 he succeeded Kuno Meyer as Professor of Celtic Philology in Berlin. Douglas Hyde, Eoin MacNeill, Myles Dillon and Liam S. Gogan were counted among his friends in Ireland, while Osborn Bergin and T.F. O'Rahilly were among his contemporaries in Celtic scholarship. He translated Pearse, Ó Conaire and *An Seabhac* into German, and is mentioned in Joyce's *Ulysses*, where the belief that the ancient Celts had no concept of hell is attributed to him. In 1935, Pokorny lost his Berlin professorship because the Nazis discovered that, although a Catholic, his parents and grandparents had all been Jews. He led an uncertain existence in Berlin until, in 1943, he fled to Switzerland. The Swiss did not expel him, perhaps because he possessed an Irish visa, issued in 1940 in Berlin on the instructions of de Valera, at the instigation of then President Douglas Hyde. Pokorny taught Celtic at Zurich and Berne Universities and, after 1955, was Honorary Professor of Celtic at Munich University. He met and photographed Casement in Hamburg in February 1915. Later in 1917 he published *Meine Erinnerungen an Sir Roger Casement* in *Irische Blätter* (1, 93-96). Ó Dochartaigh (p. 45) describes the article, written after meeting Casement over several days as a "a sentimental almost mawkish tribute to the man and his political activity on Ireland's behalf."

Roger Casement photographed by Julius Pokorny in Hotel Esplanade, Hamburg, 26 February 1915

ROGER CASEMENT

Dieses bisher nicht veröffentlichte Bild wurde aufgenommen durch Herrn Dr. Julius Pokorny im Hotel Esplanade zu Hamburg am 26. Februar 1915.

The English Sea losses are really remarkable:
>3 Battleships
>12 Cruisers
>1 Gunboat
>and
>several torpedo boats, destroyers & submarines, with certainly not less than 8000 officers & men gone.

Considering how little they have effected against the German Navy it can be truly said that the honours of war at sea are with the German Fleet.

The British losses are as follows

	Tons.	men.
Audacious.	27000	900
Bulwark,	15250	750
Formidable.	15250	750
Cressy,	12200	755
Hague,	12200	755
Aboukir,	12.200	755
Good Hope	14300	900
Monmouth,	9950	540
Hermes	5700	480
Hawke.		
Pegasus,	2200	234
Gloucester,	4900	376
Pathfinder	3000	270
Fearless,	3500	290
Amphion	3500	290
and		
Gunboat Niger		

"*B. Z. am Mittag* Sonntag 10 Jan 1915." **[Marking by Casement on a newspaper cutting tipped in here and headlined:]** '*Englands Rache an Sir Roger Casement.*'

[There are then two ripped out pages after that numbered 80 which is blank on both sides. The next page is numbered 1.]

Continental Times
<u>2 Dec 1914</u>.
The American Embassy at Berlin announces:
  All Americans, at present residing in Germany and in possession of a

passport issued by the American Govt, or American Govt official or consul are hereby requested to report themselves at the American Embassy, Berlin, Wilhelmstrasse (?) or at the nearest Consular office within a fortnight from now, in order to have their passports stamped according to new instructions recently issued by the Government in Washington. To the passport must be fixed a photograph of the holder, which must also bear the official stamp of the Embassy or Consulate. If these instructions are not obeyed, the passport may be declared void, if no sufficient reason for the omission of the stamping can be given.

[On other side of page:] Extracts from the letters of Queen Victoria of Alice –
Grand Duchess of Hesse,
   Princess of Great Britain & Ireland.
   London. John Murray,
<u>Albemarle St. 1884</u>

p. 66. <u>1864</u> <u>Jan 30</u>.

"...... These poor Schleswig-Holsteiners do what they can to liberate themselves from the Danish yoke, and to regain their lawful sovereign Fritz. And why in England, who stands up for freedom of countries, who in Italy, where there was less cause, did what she could to liberate the country from her lawful sovereigns to do what she can to prevent the Schleswig-Holsteiners from **[The extract ends abruptly here with 'from' being the only word on sheet numbered two.]**

[The sheets numbered 3, 4 and 5 are blank. Four German newspaper cuttings are then tipped in on the back of page 5 and the front of page 6, headlined:]
Frankfurter Zeitung Montag 18 Januar 1915. **[Casement's dating]** *'Der deutsche Tagesbericht'* [**'German Bulletin'**]
Frankfurter Nachrichten Diens 19 Jan 1915. **[Casement's dating]** *'Die täglichen Verluste der Engländer'* [**'The day's English losses'**].
[The 3rd and 4th cuttings have no newspaper name mentioned and are dated internally 19. Jan.:] *'153 englische Frachtschiffe durch deutsche Kriegsschiffe vernichtet'* [**153 British freighters destroyed by German warships**] *'Gesunkene englische Schiffe'* [**Sunk English ships**].

<u>1915</u>
Jan 18th. at Limburg a/Lahn

<u>Monday.</u>   <u>Hessen-Nassau.</u>

Cold weather came last night – and it is now freezing and snow. The change from the continuous rain since I arrived on 3 January (my dear brother Tom's birthday) is a very pleasant one.

I have two rooms at the Nassauer Hof looking out on the big square of Limburg, where well nigh every morning troops parade, and detachments of Landsturm[110] or Landwehr or Volunteers in grey, march off either to entrain for the front or on some route march in the neighbourhood – A fine company of 250 young volunteers marched through a few days ago.

The recruits (for 1914) I am told are the most interesting.

They are young men of 20 & so strong, fair and healthy and all with fine limbs – They march off with songs in the early morning to the station while the streets are dark. There are no tearful adieux, or sad faces. They go as if to a great duty, proudly, smiling – and smoking cigars – their friends pressing their hands and smiling too.

Some of the Landsturm have gone with flowers in their rifles.

It is a nation in arms fighting for a nation's life and I find the words of Princess Alice to her mother, the late Queen Victoria, written in 1866 and in 1870 singularly appropriate to the Germans of today.

I have copied out some passages from those letters in this journal.

They have historic value, coming from a British (or English rather) Princess who had married a German.

Of my own affairs there is nothing of much interest. I have seen General Exner thrice about the camp and he has promised to do all in his power to help the cause. But I have no faith in these poor types of "Irishmen" – demoralised and Anglicised.

Even Fr. Crotty, who tried to think well of them, gives them up. They have discovered that he is an out and out nationalist and wants to see Ireland free – and they pass him by rudely now – many of them – or in silence or even make remarks to the effect that "they" are "good Redmondites" – He says they are the scum of Ireland, and richly deserve the sound hiding the Germans gave them.

The German non-commissioned officers and men despise them openly – and draw very invidious comparisons between them, their bearing, and the French prisoners beside them. The latter are men of a country – men knowing the cause they fight for, and citizens of a citizen army just as the German soldiers are. All one great armed community. The "Irish" are sold

---

[110] A conscripted militia similar in function to the Home Guard. Members of this force (aged over 45) were actually Landstürme not Landsturm.

hirelings – hired men, who have no native land, no cause and no object in the war save to win "blood money."

The German Staff Report of today is a mighty interesting one showing French losses of 150.000 in last four weeks. These give 17860 prisoners, 26.000 <u>killed</u> and the rest wounded.

The English lists of killed, wounded & missing for the first 13 days of January shows 6706 officers & men (203 officers).

Father O'Gorman left for Rome this morning, and declares himself a quite convinced pro-German now. He has been won over completely and says he will be a faithful witness in Rome, and will see the Holy Father in private audience.

[One side of page 10 is blank; the next page starts:] in <u>Berlin</u>

<u>Sunday</u>. 24 January 1915. **[There is a second entry for this date below.]**

I got to Berlin yesterday morning at 8.20, having travelled all night from Frankfurt a. M., and came to the Esplanade Hotel to be near Blücher and also Lay, the U.S. Consul General, whom I wish to consult on my proposed letter to Sir E. Grey, denouncing the criminal efforts of H.B.M. Minister at Christiania. I also want to apply for American citizenship and find out what steps I can take in advance to procure it.

I left Limburg an Lahn on Thursday 12.10 having bidden General Exner good bye the previous day. I left a copy of the Agreement with Fr. Crotty to keep safe and sound always. I propose having a certified copy of it too. At Frankfurt on Thursday afternoon I called on General de Graaff and told him of the situation in the camp and he promised to do all he could to help. I got a letter from Meyer on the morning of Monday 18th saying Father Nicholson had arrived in Rome and would leave for Berlin on 19th and that they proposed keeping him there some days.

I should have stayed at Limburg for him, <u>but for my anxiety over Adler and the strange silence of both von Wedel and Meyer in reply to all my requests to be kept posted. The reasons I now find out on arrival here and they are not creditable to the German F.O. Indeed they are very discreditable.</u> They have wilfully kept me in ignorance of a fact of supreme importance to myself and the cause of Ireland and have taken possession of a document they have no more right to than to my purse! Moreover, Adler I find is back in Berlin for two days and this, too, they did not let me know although here there was some excuse since I had wired I was leaving Limburg on Thursday.

But first I will record the sequence of events as I have learned it yesterday from Meyer, then from Wedel and finally from Adler himself, whom, I found at the Continental Hotel[111] at 7.30 last evening.

I wrote Meyer on getting here & sent it by messenger to his house, 3 Sommerstrasse, & got t'phone reply to say he would call on me at noon. He came & at once told me that Adler's sudden return, notified to me by the telegram to Limburg, was due to the fact that he had extracted from Findlay a written promise, "in the name of the British Govt." to pay him, Adler Christensen, the sum of £5000 sterling on my being secured & handed over to the British!

This precious document, signed by Findlay on official Legation paper, Meyer assured me they had at the Foreign Office and would "show me" (!) when I called. I said I should call on Wedel at 5.30. Meyer suggested a plan for catching Findlay's vessels and suggested my seeing Isendahl tomorrow, Sunday. I agreed, pointing out that now that I had got the convincing proof I should have to use it very quickly to forestall the inevitable action the British Government would, I felt sure, announce when Parliament assembles in February.

I went to Wedel at 5.30 and after some delay Meyer brought several bound volumes of official papers (dealing I perceived with my visit to Berlin and having letters of my own filed among them) and in one of these three volumes reposed in a special docket Findlay's pledge to Adler. It had already been numbered and sealed with a paper seal of the Auswärtiges Amt! It promised Adler not only the £5000 for my body "with or without companions" but guaranteed him "immunity for his action" and to send him to U.S.A. if he desired it.

The letter is the most damning piece of evidence, I suppose, ever voluntarily given by a Government against itself!

I told Wedel that the document was mine, my property and that I should use it quickly and outlined my intention of formally charging Grey with responsibility for a dastardly criminal conspiracy – and also of my intention to inform the Norwegian Government and to go personally to Norway to do so. He agreed, in a perfunctory sort of a way; he suggested that they should "pay" all Adler's expenses while engaged in getting this paper from Findlay – to which I declined to assent. I pointed out that the matter was one between me and the British Government and that Adler was my servant and I could not allow him to accept money from the German Government. He has already been given 400 marks to cover his expenses in returning to Christiania to carry out the "Mjölnir" incident – & they say produced "no results" & they don't know why.

---

[111] Adler Christensen seems to have developed a relationship with the head waiter at the Continental Hotel.

I left the F.O. at 7 after a talk with Meyer who gave me a long letter from John Devoy of 1 January in New York and also one from Adler, in pencil, written in the train when he was going back to Christiania from this after bringing the Findlay guarantee. They kept it for nearly three weeks!

I then went on to Adler and found him just writing a long letter to myself to explain things this he gave me unfinished and I add it to the "dossier."

His account of <u>how</u> he got Findlay to give him the written pledge is the most amusing one. He could have got plenty of money instead – £500. as an "advance" – but he swore & said he would not go a step further in the matter unless Findlay gave him a written pledge. This Adler said: "I did for you; you told me not to get money from him, but to do all I could to get him to commit himself in writing – so I held out. I swore at him, cursed him, & told him to ……. himself (a fearful sailor's sarcasm) & left him. He stormed & protested & said his word was that of the Br. Government and he had pledged it to me.

I left the Legation & he sent after me & brought me back & remonstrated again. I stuck to my guns, and was more and more insolent and rude and stalked off. As I got to the gate down the avenue, the footman ran after me & said the minister wished to see me. I told him to tell Mr. Findlay to …… himself & went on. Then a man came to the Grand Hotel & asked me to go to the Legation again – and so I went. Mr. Findlay said he would give me the written promise and I said "All right, but here now, I want to see you write it with your own hand," whereupon he sat down and did it, standing by."

On getting this proof Adler tore back to Berlin, sending me the wire to meet him and informing me of the "good news" I was then at Limburg. **[Inserted:]** 6 Janry.[112] Meyer met him at the station & to him Adler gave the Findlay pledge "<u>to be given to Sir Roger Casement</u>."

<u>Meyer promised to give it to me & took it from him on this condition.</u>

That was on 5th January – and although I wrote repeatedly asking to be informed of the state of affairs I got no reply from Meyer or Wedel. They had determined to stick to the Findlay proof, for their own ends, & to bluff me out of it by offering to pay all Adler's "expenses"!!!

As to the "Mjölnir" voyage it failed because Findlay said that Adler <u>must</u> travel with me, so as to get a hold of my "box of papers" and incriminating documents when the moment came. Findlay said "If Sir Roger is alone, and he sees a man of war coming he will throw the box overboard – so you <u>must</u> be with him to get a hold of it and keep it for us." A wise precaution!

Adler went to Christiansand to meet the "Mjölnir" there on 9 January as I had directed him in the "new instructions." Findlay sent a special man

---
[112] [Erroneously for 5 January]

with him to telegraph my movements, etc. after arrival. When, however, I did not appear on the "Mjölnir" at Christiansand, Adler had to explain the reason to Findlay by letter only that, owing to his refusal to give him (Adler) the guarantee he had warned me that he had warned me that I might not be safe on the "Mjölnir", so I had not travelled by her. This he had done from "revenge." Findlay accepted the explanation and the position is where it was practically when I sent Adler back to Findlay on Christmas day with the "Mjölnir" plot. With this great change – that I now hold the warrant of shame and ignominy His Majesty's Government signed by their own Minister in their name!

Adler says a good plan can still be devised to catch Findlay's ships. *Nous verrons*. I have caught more than that. I have caught the British Govt *in flagrante delicto* – & with all the difficulties put in my way, too, by this stupid, pig-headed German Govt. And now these men actually have the audacity, the bare faced audacity, to seize my proof and regard it as a "State paper" of their wretchedly run Foreign Office! Truly they merit all the opprobriums Billy Tyrrell heaped on them in the London Foreign Office that November day in 1912 when he was discharging his soul into my ears – and Lichnowsky[113] outside the door and announced as he spoke! It is almost impossible to have true dealings with them. You never know their mind save that if there is a wrong way to tackle a <u>human</u> problem they are likely to choose it.

This Zeppelin raid over the East coast is a proof. They rejoice at a silly exploit – that can only damage the German cause in the eyes of the world – for the English will represent it, through all their myriad channels of public perversion, as a "deliberate murder of women and children." I told Wedel so – and after first demurring, he agreed and said that I had expressed his opinion.

In the evg, after leaving Adler, I dined with Blücher and Baron von Roeder (the Emperor's Master of Ceremonies). Von Roeder agreed entirely with my judgment on the Zeppelin raid over East England and said he had that very day been saying this very thing to Count Oppersdorff, the Catholic chief of "the Centre." Oppersdorff had asserted that the raid was a great thing and just what was wanted.

As regards the Irish civil prisoners in Ruhleben, von W. says they cannot release the whole 163 as I had urged, as an "act of good will to Ireland" but would let out some 20 or so if I selected them – as was done with Kelly and Professor Macran. The former got off safely two weeks and more ago & Kelly followed a few days ago.[114]

---

[113] Prince Lichnowsky, German Ambassador in London

[114] For Bryan Kelly's later career and involvement in Gaelic literature see Ó Síocháin, pp. 600-1. He died in Split in 1936.

Bulmer Hobson, 1912   *Bulmer Hobson seated (NLI)*

I got also last night handed me at the Continental Hotel, a letter from New York, from Padraic Colum[115] of 16 Decr. last, forwarding me a letter from Bulmer Hobson of 22 October last, from Dublin. 3 months & 2 days to reach me! Colum said in his very brief covering letter that "the correspondence in the Tribune" which he sent me would amuse me. It did not come. The outer letter was opened – but Bulmer's letter closed. This letter of B's gave me only the Volunteer news of Ireland & showed the quite disgraceful part Redmond and his nominees on the Provisional Committee had been playing since the gun-running at Howth on 26. July.

Dear old John Devoy's letter was a very welcome one – Along with some bad news it had much good. Among other things that a special messenger who had been sent to Ireland (following my request by cable early in ~~Oct~~ Nov) had brought back a satisfactory report and also that my sister had been kept advised and supplied. So my anxiety on her head, poor desolate, lonely old girl, surrounded by sneers, jibes and hatred, is somewhat diminished.

I tried to see Fr. Nicholson all day y'day – but without success. He is at the Excelsior (Station) Hotel, near Anhalt Bahnhof. At 10 past 12 midnight I was rung up from bed by him trying to hold a long yarn with me on the phone – but I cut this form of American disease sharp off by saying it was far too late and asking him to come and see me at 4 p.m. today (Sunday).

---

[115] Padraic Colum, a poet and friend of Casement who wrote *The Cradle Song*

He will go to Limburg this week doubtless – but I fear it is hopeless to expect any patriotic action from the "Irish" soldiers there and that all my hopes of an Irish Brigade are doomed.

I told von Wedel last night that were I sure of getting over I should return to U.S.A. but the risks are too great. And yet I know not what to do. To stay in Berlin or in Germany, idle, inactive and with the huge disappointment of the Irish Brigade failure staring me in the face, and with no hope of further action by the German Govt. anent Ireland is a policy of despair. Besides I have not the means to live here. Life is very expensive and I must stay at expensive hotels and incur constant outlays. It would be better to retire to Norway – convict Findlay up to the hilt – get H.M. Gov't exposed & <u>if necessary</u>, return to Germany, should Father Nicholson succeed with the soldiers.

I shall talk things over with him today – & decide quickly. As I told von W. last night, no time should now be lost. Already three weeks have been deliberately wasted by this wretched crew at the German F.O. in their kidnapping of my Findlay letter. I feel I can <u>not</u> trust them – and that it is useless to rely on such stupid – and selfish – people.

Count Blücher gave me some copies of the "Times" up to 7 January – full of German "atrocities" and plausible accounts of the "Allies" progress in the field. Soissons with its loss of fully 20.000 French and 35 guns had not then come to hand.

Blücher is, (as usual) full of ridiculous stories. He affirms "on absolute authority" that in addition to the "Audacious" the Br. Navy has lost three other Dreadnoughts, submarined on the North Coast of Scotland – the "King George" & the "Ajax" & the "Thunderer", the latter of 23.000 tons, & the two first of 27.000 tons each. "The crews were saved"! Of course it is a taradiddle – Also he says the Germans have lost one of their Dreadnoughts "blown up by her own mines!"

Possibly this last is true.

Also he says the "Karlsruhe", reported lost in the west Atlantic is safely at Kiel! This is <u>the</u> most surprising of all; if true it is a fine exploit in seamanship.

Also that the escaped "Dresden" from the Falkland Islands battle is also safe & sound in Kiel!

For the rest it seems that great pressure is being put on Austria to secure the surrender of the Trentino to Italy.

This to ensure continued Italian neutrality alone! Not to get Italy to fulfil her pledge to the Triple Alliance, but merely to keep out of the fight in the side of the allies & release some of the 600.000 Austrian troops? (? Blücher's figure!) [**The question mark is in a different darker ink.**] said to be guarding the frontiers against possible Italian invasion.

Blücher swallows any yarn told him by the asses in office here. The latest is from an officer I met y'day from the General Staff that the Russians are in full retreat "once more"; that they have abandoned Radom and that Hindenburg will be in Warsaw "very soon." I said "I hope so."

The Germans know splendidly how to fight, how to die; how to conquer even; but they do not know how to handle men or public affairs where brains are essential, and brains keeping pace with the hearts.

Today I shall have long talks with Adler; with Meyer at lunch, then with Isendahl at the Admiralty; and I hope at 4 with Father Nicholson.

In Berlin – Thursday, 11 Febry 1915.

Nearly three weeks since I wrote in my diary – & in many respects the most eventful since I left U.S.A. Full of anxiety, grave disquiet and overwhelming doubt at times. I came out yesterday afternoon from the Continental Hotel where I had been for eight days to this Sanatorium in the Grunewald to be quiet and away from press reporters. I have still a day of quiet before the newspaper war begins and now that a little peace of mind is returning to me although slowly – I will try to briefly record events since the last entry (Sunday 24, Janry in the Esplanade Hotel).

I had reached the Esplanade Hotel on Saturday morning 23 Jan from Frankfurt a.M. – & had gone there on purpose to be in touch with Lay, the U.S.A. Consul General, to whom I wished, if possible, to tell many things. He was reported by Blücher to be friendly to me from old days in Barcelona and Rio & to be anxious to see me. Then on arrival came the thunderbolt – the double one – that Adler had got Findlay's written guarantee and the Germans had bagged it for their own use as a "State paper." I will now try to record by date where I can recall them the incidents of the days that followed up to this.

[The entries from 24-29 January are out of date order.
The second entry for January 24th:] (Sunday 24 Jan) Meyer came to lunch with me (and tried to pay for it although my guest!). We went (with Adler) to the General Staff of the Admiralty, where I saw first Admiral Behncke – & then Captain Isendahl & the other Captain whose name I forget [**Casement later inserted 'Heydell'**]. Adler told them the whole Findlay story to their intense amusement. They asked to see the guarantee and Meyer said "impossible to take it out of the F.O. as it is a State Document" – this in my hearing, but in German; Adler told me of it and looked at me as it was being said! Nothing decided there as to my return to Norway. They will let me know.

I told Wedel y'day that the Findlay letter was mine & I should use it quickly against the British Government not against Findlay, their poor agent. He hummed & hawed & deprecated haste but could offer no real objection and had to say "of course, Sir Roger, the letter is yours when you need it."

Fr. Nicholson came to see me in the morning and had long talk about Philadelphia &c &c. I showed him the agreement about the Irish cause of 23 Dec. which greatly interested him. A historic document he truly called it. I spent the afternoon also with Fr. N and Adler at the Excelsior Hotel & spent the evening with them – Adler removed there from the Continental Hotel & Fr. Nicholson very kind to him.

I was more and more uncertain how to act about Findlay with the Germans silently stealing the letter & practically saying to me "you can use this only as we choose" my hands tied. However I decided to write my letter to Grey. This I had begun in Limburg on 12 January, but had been forced to keep over until I was aware of the end of the "Mjölnir" incident.

I met Lay, the U.S. Consul General today (Sunday). I left my card on him yesterday after arriving and by appointment to talk with him on Monday at 2 in the 'Rotunde' of the hotel.

(Monday 25 Jan.)

Professor Schiemann called, but I got him away quickly as Fr. N. was coming. Latter to lunch with me – and asked him to come at 5 to go to F.O. with me. I intended he should see the Findlay letter without telling them in advance. They are having it photographed for me.

Lay at 2.30 in the big hall of the Hotel. I told him I wanted advice & a Notarial act performed by him as Consul. viz, to copy a document I should produce and attach to it. He was most uneasy and said he would let me know and suggested the Ambassador &c. &c.

I told him it was purely a notarial act of the consulate I wanted a certificate of a certain document having been brought by me and copied by him as Consul. He promised to let me know if he could do it. He clearly thought I wanted help against the Germans! I said I could only tell him the nature of the document when I was sure he could perform the service and so there it stayed for the time.

At 5 I went with Fr. N to F.O. & saw Wedell [sic] at 6.30 only after long wait. He got the Findlay letter from Meyer who brought it in a portfolio (like a baby being nursed & with a look of grave dislike on his Jew face) – & Fr N. read it, while I copied it in pencil on my knees – Wedel turning his face aside but seeing me doing it of course.

I said I wanted to make quite clear the exact terms of it and particularly of the "immunity" granted Adler.

(Tuesday 26 Jan) [**First of two entries for this date:**]

Still in doubt how to act – My wish is to write Grey, renouncing all honours, recounting his crime & go to Norway to send the letter thence & challenge investigation on spot.

Began writing the final form of my letter to Grey, but only a draft of what I think of saying.

Fr. Nicholson in morning – & told him all about the Findlay letter and the F.O. here bagging it & keeping me for 3 weeks entirely ignorant of its existence and how I only learned thro' the fact that Adler had returned unexpectedly & I found him here.

I saw the Baroness von Nordenflycht and Gussie in the afternoon and told them all – not about F.O. here or my doubts of them but only of the Findlay incident & letter.

I dined on return with Fr Nicholson at the Excelsior, giving him last words – He goes Limburg in morning by 8 a.m. train. I back at 1.20 a.m. in deep snow to Esplanade.

(Wednesday 27 Jan) [**First of two entries for this date:**]

I talked to Lay today – but nothing important. Busy most of day on my letter to Grey writing steadily – discarding much. The difficulty is how much to leave out of it – to put in all the details a huge mistake.

Today the Emperor's birthday. I wrote two letters to von Wedel – one on the day – and one about the Irish civil prisoners at Ruhleben, and sent them by special messenger.

(Thursday 28 Jan) 1915.

Writing my letter to Grey all day nearly & discussing things with Blücher – who is very angry at the Foreign Office business here over the letter & says he will tell von Jagow.

I went to F.O. at 6.30 & saw von Wedel & told him I had made up my mind to write Grey fully & to go to Christiania – He agreed. I said I should send the letter ahead by Adler probably and follow as soon as I could and fight the matter out in Christiania. Essential, I pointed out to act quickly as when the London Parliament assembles on 2 February there will be questions about me and then, if the Foreign Office there know they have failed to catch me, they will make a fine show of "moral indignation" against my "treason" & take some overt step. I want to be first in the field and expose Them – before they get the ear of the world.

Wedel agreed and said I must act as I thought right. He is a gentleman & a friend.

(Friday 29 Jan)

Got the Esplanade typist to type three copies of my letter to Grey – finished. Got photos from Meyer of the Findlay letter to inclose.

All hurry and haste now to get ready for the flight to Norway. Decided to go myself on Sunday <u>with</u> Adler. I told Meyer and von Wedel. Former said would get 3 good private detectives to go with me – and so protect me and do all they could to help. Von Roeder and Blücher very much against my going to Norway. Meyer has a silly scheme for me to go there and try and get Findlay to kidnap me and through my three detectives to catch him and his and hand them over to the police. I rejected this on von Roeder's and Blücher's advice – and decided only to go to Norway openly, as myself, to challenge Findlay and invite the Norwegian Government to investigate the whole affair.

(<u>Saturday. 30 Jan</u>)

Busy writing all morning. Gave typed copies of my letter to Grey to Meyer to get typed for me. I want 20 or 25 copies – to send out to various Legations and public quarters, as soon as I have posted to Grey – and I am begging Meyer to see that copies are sent to the Berlin press too. He says they will publish it textually with the photo in "<u>N-D All Zeitung</u>" – and cable it to U.S.A. &c. &c.

I took letter to F.O. at 5 p.m. & gave to Meyer for typing. I went on to tea at Astoria with von Roeder & Baroness von R. to meet a Fräulein de Bunsen, a cousin (but a German) of the Sir M. de Bunsen once at Lisbon or Madrid. A pleasant woman. <u>I did not tell von R</u> I had decided to go to Christiania in morning as he would object I knew. Blücher was there also. I did not tell him either that I was off to Norway.

To Excelsior and told Adler come early and get my baggage and go to the Stettin Bahnhof with (it) for 10.33 train to Sassnitz.

(Sunday <u>31. Janry.</u>)

I left the Esplanade early & walked to Stettin Bahnhof alone in snow and cold over Thiergarten at 9.30 a.m. At Station Adler found that the 10.33 train to Sassnitz misses the boat! A fine change of plan. The train only gets in at 2.59 to Sassnitz <u>town</u>, 20 minutes by train from the wharf, and the boat goes at 2 p.m., a change of hour due to the presence in the Baltic of some (supposed) English submarines. One of these attacked the gunboat "Gazelle" a few days ago off <u>Rügen</u> itself and torpedoed her. So the mailboat to Traelleborg now crosses only by daylight – and owing to this change of plan one has to leave Berlin the night before, sleep at Stralsund, and go on to Sassnitz thence by an early train to catch the boat at 2. Accordingly when Meyer came at 11. with the three detectives the thing had to be all changed.

I returned but to the Continental Hotel where I spent the day in grave doubt.

Meyer brought me the 20 copies of the letter to Grey typed last night at F.O. but so full of errors I had to send them all back. He came at 6.45 p.m. again for me and hurried me off to the Station with the three detectives and Adler. Everything in confusion. He tells me the German Admiralty sent to warn me that the English submarine might stop the mailboat in the Baltic & demand my surrender! The Staff think it possible.

If a spy is at Sassnitz they wd. surely do it. What did I propose?

I said I should go on & if this happened I'd resist & not be taken alive. Wd. the detectives fight too? Meyer said "Surely – they will fight to the death." Adler agreed also. We left at 7.18 – the three detectives in a 2nd class ~~Hotel~~ car. – & Adler with me. At Stralsund at 11.50 and to the Bahnhof Hotel – & to bed in my clothes greatly upset and wondering how best to proceed. Not afraid of the submarine but of the action of the Br Govt. in Norway, their influence there, their power and gold and my own penniless and defenceless position. To go out, single handed, to thus challenge the mightiest Govt. in the world and to charge them publicly with infamous criminal conspiracy through their accredited Representative is a desperate act. I have no money; no friends; no support; no Govt., save that of the One bent on destroying me, to appeal to. They are all-potent and will not sacrifice Findlay without a fight and in that fight they must win. Such were my reflections through the night.

[Casement note:] Skip the ensuing pages and on top Monday Febry 1st at Stralsund

[Second entry for this date which starts on the sheet numbered 28, one side of which is blank:]

Tuesday Jan 26. 1915 Berlin (at Esplanade Hotel)

On Sunday evg. here in the hotel the Barman said "a Prince" (there are several in the hotel) had told him there had been a sea fight between German & English ships near Cuxhaven.

Y'day morning the Admiralty General Staff report appeared and reported that 4 large German cruisers, 4 small cruisers and two torpedo flotillas had been engaged in fight for 3 hours with a superior English squadron of 5 large cruisers, 4 small and 26 destroyers. The report states that the German cruiser *Blücher* had been sunk – but that one large English cruiser had also been sunk. The *Blücher* is a first class cruiser of <u>15,800</u> tons with 887 men.

Yesterday Capt Isendahl of the Naval Staff told me 123 men only were thought to be saved of the *Blücher's* crew. As to the English cruiser sunk, he said it was reported by the Zeppelin Airship No. 9. She had flown to the scene of the fight and reported that "only four large British ships went away." This is not conclusive of the loss of an English ship – since no one on the German side saw her sink. I thought it improbable – and last night the English naval a/c of the fight appeared here in the press. This declares that the German ships retired on seeing the British squadron and that *The Blücher* being slower was overtaken and sunk. The report says that "no English ships were lost." *The Blücher's* 123 saved men were taken to England. The German papers now deny the English a/c and say that one of their torpedoed boats hit an English cruiser twice and she sank and that two English destroyers were also sunk.

The squadrons were as follows – big ships only –

Germany	tons	England	
"Dorflinger"	26.000	Tiger	29.000
"Senlitz"	25.000	Lion	30.000
"Moltke"	23.000	Princess Royal	19.500
Blücher	<u>5.800</u>	New Zealand	19.500
	90.400	Indomitable	<u>20.300</u>
			128.000

A balance of 38.400 tons in favour of the Sea Bully. Another instance of Mr. Asquith "We only ask for a <u>fair</u> fight." The last thing on earth or water, the English had ever engaged in!

<u>Wednesday 27.</u> Janry (Berlin) **[second entry for this date]**

The Emperor's birthday – 56 I think today. I sent a letter to von Wedel and also with him about the release of the Irish prisoners at Ruhleben.

I saw Mr. Lay, the U.S.A. Consul General, at 2.30 & asked if he wrote **[sic]** perform certain notarial duties for me. I want an established record of the Christiania affair – and certified copies of a Declaration (my own) and to deposit copy of the Findlay guarantee. I did not tell him what it was I wanted, beyond to take an affidavit and obtain a certified copy of a document – for purposes of record.

He said he would let me know if his functions as acting British Consul permitted him to do this.

Father Nicholson left for Limburg this morning. I spent most of yesterday with him – and on Monday he was with me the greater part of the day and at 6 I took him to the F.O. to von Wedel to let him see the Findlay document. It was produced and I made a copy of it (on my knees) and showed it to Father Nicholson. Wedel said: "It is yours, Sir Roger: we will keep it for you here for safety, until you want it." This was volunteered in Father Nicholson's presence.

It relieves to a little my anxiety of mind on the matter – but the action taken has been so upsetting that since Saturday I have been so upset I cannot decide what is best to do. Or rather I know what is the right thing to do – but owing to the evident intention of the German Foreign Office to treat the document as a "State paper" belonging to their official archives I am well nigh prevented from acting at all.

On Sunday I visited the Admiralty and again on Monday where I saw Admiral Behnke. A charming man. He spoke of the loss of the "Blücher" in the sea fight.

I told him there of the Findlay "guarantee" and they wished to see the document – but Meyer intervened and said it was "a State Document and could not be removed from the Foreign Office." This was in German and I only knew what he said thro' Adler, who was present telling me afterwards!

I told the whole story, y'day to Fr. Nicholson with Adler present. As he had seen and read the "guarantee" at the F.O. on Monday I thought it well to have a witness on my own side as to the very difficult position I had been put in by the barefaced appropriation of this precious document by this Govt. It leaves me in a state of helplessness all round. I don't know now how far I can place confidence in anything they say to me or even pledge themselves to. On the other hand I have von Wedel's promise to deliver me the document "when I ask for it" – and I trust him and like him – and feel sure he will carry out his promises.

February 1915

Monday. 1 Feb.
After a hardly spent night – I got up at 5.30 and was got off at 6.50 (I think) for Sassnitz.
Arrived there about 9 and to the Monopol Hotel to wait for the boat. There I went over the pros and cons with Adler, burned some papers I found the enemy might seize if I were arrested and finally decided to return to Berlin tomorrow instead of going on. I told the three detectives this and sent wires to Montgelas (Wedel being away at Frankfurt I knew). Spent a miserable day.
The Baltic partly frozen. The Sound between Stralsund and Rügen quite

frozen over hard and passages cut for the boats and train ferry. Sledges with bells in Stralsund. Swedish faces and blue eyes on many. A charming old city.

The three detectives cannot help me really. It is not kidnapping now I fear – but the direct, open assault of the British Government and some demand for my surrender or else a law case in which with all their wealth and power, poor Adler and I would cut a sorry figure.

Tuesday, 2 February.

Left Sassnitz at 9 a.m. & arr. Berlin at 4 p.m. about. To F.O. & saw Wedel & told him why I had returned. He said he thought Findlay would never <u>dare</u> to fight or protest – that the "guarantee" was too damning. I said all the same the risk was far too great of defeat & that I purposed ~~posting out~~ sending my letter to Holland to be posted there and then when that was done & sure of to send out copies to the Govts. here represented. He agreed.

Decided to send Adler back to Moss at once to get his things, see his people & tell them & then return to Germany so as not to be there when the letter comes out or into Grey's hands as they might try to arrest him so as to bluff a poor penniless wretch and <u>compel</u> me to surrender to defend Adler.

Meyer came at 6 or 7 to the Continental Hotel where I took room (again) on 4th. floor this time – I as Sir R.C. – no longer "Mr. Hammond."

Meyer agreed to all. He came twice, at 6 and then again at 8.30.

A cruiser was to have gone over with my boat he said from Sassnitz – to Traelleborg to safeguard me against the lawless submarine.

He told me a pro-Irish Society[116] had been formed in Berlin <u>that very afternoon</u> and had put up 50.000 Marks as a first contribution to the Irish Cause which would be placed at my disposal to spend as I thought best in the interests of Ireland. Generous indeed – but I cannot accept – at any rate it must be left to my friends in U.S.A. to decide.

(Wednesday 3. Feb)

At Continental Hotel. Made a few slight changes in the letter to Grey & sent it to the Esplanade Hotel (typist) to copy for me. 3 copies to be ready by 5 p.m. Meyer undertook to get it off to Holland by special messenger tonight at 8.49 p.m. to be posted in Hague tomorrow. Adler left for Moss at 8.40 this morning via Warnemünde & Copenhagen. He should get there Thursday forenoon and leave at 8 p.m. again to return via Copenhagen and see his sister there.

I took the letter – final typed copy – for Grey to F.O. at 5.30 p.m. & gave

---

[116] ["Die Deutsch-Irische Gesellschaft"] The members included Matthias Erzberger, Freiherr von Richthofen, Graf Kuno von Westarp, Prince Gebhard Blücher von Wahlstatt, George Chatterton-Hill, Thomas St John Gaffney, Eduard Meyer, and Theodor Schiemann.

it to Meyer & a copy to him for translation to German. He promised send it faithfully.

Then to the Hotel Astoria where I dined with the von Roeders & Blücher (whom I had already taken into my confidence) and to whom I told (the Baron and B.) all the change of plan & the new way of procedure against the Hereditary Enemy. Very wretched and miserable all night.

(Thursday. 4 Feb)

At Continental Hotel most of day – gave a second copy of my Grey letter to Meyer for the German FO to have officially. Got 25 copies in all typed by the typist at Esplanade. She is splendid. Got all the letters ready to go out to the Legations & Embassies here with a covering note to each Minister.

Then to the Nordenflychts at 6 & stayed to supper with them. Told them I wanted to stay with them & they offered me a room there.

Meyer thinks the letter will by "out" here by Saturday and I want to escape reporters.

(Friday. 5 Feb)

Two telegrams from Adler. One[117] y'day saying arrd well & one to say he was leaving & wd. be here Saturday or Sunday.

Got all my letters ready for the Legations &c & sent three copies to Rome – one to Mon O'Riordan, one to Dr. O'Hagan & one to Fr. O'Gorman – begging them to use publicly & show Holy Father.

Stayed in hotel all day – busy & very anxious. Meyer told me they would not publish here first. Only after Rome or some country had got it out first. I agreed, as wise.

The letter should have been with Grey today. In the evening paper there is a telegram from Amsterdam, 5 Feb, saying that Grey in the H. of Cs had said in reply to questions – that "Sir R's pension would be suspended pending investigation into his action against Gt Britain" & in reply to another question he said – the public liar! – that "he did not know whether Sir RC was in Germany or not" !!!

Within a few hours of making that statement he should have rec'd my letter from Berlin.

(Saturday. 6 Feb.)

Sent a long letter to John Devoy with Grey letter – also posted one – registered to Bryan & State Dept. & then sent out all the following by head porter in a taxi:

---

[117] [This telegram which is preserved was sent from Moss on 4.2.'15 and reads "Arrived good voyage – Adler." On it is written by Sir Roger "Rec'd 2.10 p.m. Continental Hotel, Berlin 4 Febr. 1915."]

1st To the Norwegian Minister
2. U.S.A. Embassy
3. Italian d.o.
4. Austro-Hungarian d.o.
5. Spanish d.o.
6. Swedish Legation
7. Danish d.o.
8. Dutch d.o.
9. Portuguese d.o.
10. Swiss d.o.
11. Greek d.o.
12. Roumanian d.o.

They were out by 10.30 a.m. to 1 p.m.

I wrote to Graf Larisch at the Austro-H Embassy privately, asking his help to get the letter public in Vienna.

Dinner Blücher came to & said Larisch wanted a copy of the letter – so I write one by hand – all typed copies used.

Wanted to get to Hamburg – as the Nordenflychts cannot have me – the room they promised taken by a sick friend from the front.

Wrote Mrs. Behrens at H'burg saying wd. come to her.

But got a 'phone reply asking me to wait her letter sent in answer.

Told Blücher all my doubts & difficulties.

Wrote C'tss Hahn who called on me at 4 and told her the whole story. I called at Norwegian Legation at 5.20 p.m. & left my card.

(Sunday. 7 Feb.)

Finished copy of letter for Larisch & took it at 1 to 11 Hildebrandstrasse and stayed to lunch there. A Count & Countess Hahn (I think) the mother apparently of Countess Larisch there too. Larisch very friendly – but not very intelligent I fear.

Wire from Adler at 7.50 to say arriving at 10. So went to meet him & took him to Excelsior Hotel.

He reported all well at home. Had told his father all – & the schoolmaster, who is so afraid of being pulled into a "State trial" he pretended he did not remember Adler telling him before in Decr. all about it.

Monday 8 Feb.

Mrs Behrens does not want me yet in Hamburg – says Ballin in Berlin & weather there terrible.

Adler wrote a brief note to the Norwegian Minister, on my advice, and left it in person at about 1 p.m. at the Legation. He offered to call whenever the Minister wished to see him. He wrote (with difficulty) in Norwegian.

(Tuesday 8 Feb) [**Date error made by Casement. It should be 9 February.**]

Adler called at Norwegian Legation and asked for Minister – Not in.

I & he to Potsdam in afternoon where I thought of staying over the press row. But it was wretched & at the Palast Hotel where Klicks the manager of the Continental told me to stay I got such a rude reception when they found I spoke only English that I returned to Berlin in despair. Called on Mrs. White & told her all about Christiania – also on Fräulein Meyer – but she not in. Mrs. White very friendly and wants me to go to Vienna. She recommended me to go out to the Sanatorium in the Grunewald (where I now am) and stay there over the row – I decided to do this.

Got a very courteous reply from the Swedish Minister by this morning's post – & tonight a very discourteous one from the Portuguese Minister. Latter refused to send my letter to Lisbon as it "exceeded the legal rights of his Legation" and he returned it to me. The Swede wrote a charming note saying he had not failed to send my letter to Stockholm.

(Wednesday 9 Feb.) [**Date error made by Casement as it should be 10 February.**]

Meyer came at 11 & carried off the letter of the Portuguese Legation to show to Zimmermann. He said the P. Minister was a "cochon." I agreed.

He said he thought no other Legation wd. treat my request so rudely. He further says he fears publication of my letter in Rome is impossible! They have doubtless heard by wire.

He says all the "neutral" papers in Italy are "pro-ally" & will say nothing against England.

He thinks, however, that the letter will be out "by Friday" & I gather in Vienna. But Meyer is so secretive and lacking in frankness that he tells me nothing. I am treated by him as a sort of tool or agent – to be directed & used – but never kept informed or referred to – or consulted. Only directed. He now wants me to arrange to have Aubrey Stanhope, Karl Wiegand and Conger out to interview me on Friday (but not before!) and tell them all. I said much better do it before, so that they might be ready by Friday, not merely told on Friday. The wretched suspicion and mistrust of everybody that characterises all their conduct of public affairs again revealed here. I decided to go out to the Sanatorium at Grunewald – as "Mr. Hammond" once more. This latter on Meyer's advice. He said he would arrange all with the police. Arranged with the Continental Hotel to forward letters for "Mr. Hammond."

Meyer will make a mess of everything I am convinced. He and his department are the acme of <u>stupidity</u> and <u>blight</u>. I have lost all faith in their good sense and action. They are either always too late or else do the right thing in the wrong way.

I went out to the Grunewald Sanatorium at 3-4, calling on Mrs. White on the way and telling her and asking her to lunch and bring A. Stanhope and Karl Wiegand to lunch.

Then on to the Sanatorium & took a room there – Adler with me but he returns to stay with the Head waiter of the 2nd floor of the Continental Hotel.

I spent a wretched evening in the Sanatorium. The people there largely military – & all very friendly and polite – but I feel so lonely & abandoned & want only to get away from police spies & military and all the rest of it.

Meyer telephoned at 5 to say "<u>not before Friday</u>" to see the U.S.A. correspondents. Meantime I have asked Mrs. White to bring them! I'll adhere to the invitation.

Especially as today's news is that England has prohibited <u>all cables from the Continent</u>!

This is a fine measure of freedom of communication! My God! How much more will the world have to stand from that Bitch & Harlot of the North Sea!

This measure is <u>asserted</u> to be in connection with the transport of Kitchener's army to the Continent. That may be – but if so it would be the <u>other</u> way about and no cable communication <u>to</u> the Continent from England – whereas it is from the Continent to the outside world they have interdicted.

It is much more likely that the measure is a part of their d....d. conspiracy against me. They fear mightily my charge coming out in U.S.A. <u>first</u> & before they have arranged their version and publicly branded me as a "traitor" before I get the public charge brought against them. This will surely be their game.

And while they are arranging that, here I am a semi-prisoner at the Sanatorium under a false name, with a wholly false entry of my name etc. and depending on Mr. Meyer to make all right with the police.

After the various proofs I have had of their hopeless ineptitude I should not wonder if I were arrested in the morning.

<u>Thursday 11 Feb</u>.

I am in my room at the Sanatorium writing up my diary & eating my heart out. An agent of the secret police has just called (11.20 a.m.) to ask for my "military pass". I have none – I gave him the old police card of Mr. Hammond which I happily still have & referred him to the Auswartiges Amt for further information. It is highly possible they will bungle things there and I may be hauled off to jail.

[This entry ends half way down the left hand side of the back of page 41. Fourteen months later, this follows:]

Berlin   M'ch 28. 1916
My "Diary" ended here.
I was so disillusioned & miserable from this on – so utterly out of touch with the monitors of the German F.O. that I saw the whole aim & object of my journey was a failure.

The only thing I had to show for all my sacrifice (& folly –) was the Treaty. This was a historic fact.

Here, in a formal agreement signed with the Seal of State the Imperial Govt. had pledged itself to take certain steps to assist Ireland to gain complete independence & in the event of these proving successful to recognise publicly and support the independent Govt. so established.

All that I stayed on in January for was based on this Treaty. I hoped that, even while I saw the futility of the Treaty since a possible German victory faded away further & further into the limbo of the lost. Still this Treaty justified me – & it did more.

It was, in itself, a Recognition of Ireland in the world – of Ireland a Nation – an extraordinary admission to have obtained in such set official terms from the most arbitrary of Govts.

My only hope – was to have it published –

If that could be done, I saw its value to the Cause of Irish liberty in the future & to the inspiration of those holding up the flag today. Moreover it was the surest means I possessed or could invoke to keep Irishmen out of the war.

Once it was proclaimed *urbi et orbi* it was clear that the real Nationalists of Ireland would have an answer to England & Redmond that no one had dreamed of – It became then, to try & get the Treaty published.

I sent copies of it to U.S.A. – but only in March – as I had been asked by the FO to "keep it quiet" – But it was obvious that if Irishmen in the U.S.A. were to be moved to great effort they must be informed of the basis on which our hopes rested. So at length I got the Treaty sent over & I subsequently learned it had arrived safely – not the original of course, but a copy.

I was almost completely cut off from communication with America. On one occasion nearly four months passed without a letter coming thro'.

And I could not say all I thought or wanted to – because I did not know who would read my letters en route. Thus we were often at cross purposes.

I knew the German offensive had failed on the West front.

It was really broken in Nov. 1914 by Ypern **[Ypres]** & broken by the English!

This fact I realized in the beginning of 1915 – gradually. I saw that all the talk of "getting to Calais" was talk & that the German lines on the west front wd. remain (at the best) where they were & that the war would gradually take on an attitude of "stalemate" unless one thing happened – viz – the Defeat of the Br-French in Turkey & a successful Turkish advance on Egypt with a possible later movement on India. I had never changed my fixed point of view that England was the Enemy & that unless England could be really & vitally threatened Germany must, in the end, be forced to her knees.

I always preached this. My whole German-Irish policy was founded on this perception.

At a luncheon at the very end of March or beginning of April 1915, given in my honour by Graf Haenckel Donnersmarck (brother of my friend Ctess "Tessa" Hahn) there was a Baron von Schroeder,[118] a brother of the Baron in London. This German brother had expressed much earlier a wish to meet me – to the von Roeders.

At length I met him at Haenckel-D's luncheon party in the flat in Kurfürstendamm. I sat between Princess Reuss[119] and Princess Hohenlohe – the Hohenlohe who was daughter of Count Munster[120] I think – a nice woman, the Blüchers called "Baby Hohenlohe." Princess Reuss I had met more than once before.

Baron v. S. talked about the Findlay affair before we went in to the dining room – & also about Ireland. I saw clearly he had no opinion at all of the Irish question – despised it & he almost frankly said so.

I remarked "if the German Govt has no sympathy at all for Ireland or any aim or policy in respect of it I wonder why they issued their Declaration of 20 Novr. last year." He smiled & shrugged his shoulders – I went on – "That being so as I perceive also – I see no reason why I should remain in Germany."

The trouble was & has been always that I had to stay in Germany. I have been virtually a prisoner from the first day I landed. Ringed round by the Br. Fleet!

Once the "Findlay affair" arose there was no return for me. I should have gone back to the U.S. on many occasions – for I saw again & again in the late winter and Spring of 1915 that the German Govt. had no policy at all about Ireland. No hopes, aims or plans.

They fully justified Findlay's statement that "The German govt. don't care a rap about Ireland but they will welcome Sir Roger in order to make trouble

---

[118] This was Kurt von Schröder, later Hitler's banker. His London-based brother was Bruno Schroder.

[119] Princess Hermine Reuss who was to marry Kaiser Wilhelm II in 1922 as his second wife, becoming thereby Empress of Germany (in exile).

[120] Count Alexander Munster was the son of a German Ambassador to London and Lady Muriel Hay, daughter of the 12th Earl of Kinnoull.

for us and use him for their own ends."

That I had long since found out was true – & that (except for the Treaty, where I had completely beaten them at their own game, & committed them to an Irish policy) it was useless for me to remain in Germany – My heart was breaking – I knew I was being fooled & I did not trust a word they said to me.

With the failure to recruit the Irish Brigade & the exposure of the Findlay affair they had got, as they thought, all they could out of me & "the German –Irish Alliance."

They wanted to drop it.

This was amply proved later on, by John Devoy's letters to me – They had squeezed me dry, & they did not want to be committed further.

In April 1915 came P.[121] from Ireland with his great tale of the planned revolution there. I discounted all that – & sat on it and him as vigorously as was possible.

I told him just what I had often told Wedel at the F.O. that no rebellion or rising in Ireland could possibly succeed of its own unaided effort. The *sine qua non* of a successful military movement in Ireland, today far more than in 1798, 1690, 1641 or 1598-1601 was the military (& naval) support of a great Continental power.

To attempt a rising in the streets of Dublin in 1915 I held was worse than folly – it was criminal stupidity.

But I said "if you do it – if you if you are bent on this act of idiocy I will come & join you (if the Germans will send me over) & stand & fall beside you. Only I deprecate it wholly and regard it as the wildest from of boyish folly – I am not responsible for it and while I strongly disapprove it, if these boys break out I could not, in honour, refuse to stand beside them, since however vain & and futile their fight might be, it wd. be a fight – an act, a deed – & not talk, talk, talk."

I who had always stood for action (but not this action & certainly not in these circumstances) could not stay in safety in this land while those in Ireland who cherished a manly soul were laying down their lives for an ideal.

Just before P. arrived in Berlin – it was 16. April he came from Switzerland – Fr. Nicholson who had been at Limburg, since end of January 1915, came up to see me.

---

[121] Joseph Mary Plunkett "spent some eight weeks in Germany. About three and a half weeks were at Limburg and the remainder in Berlin. In both places his diary shows that he spent a lot of time talking to Captain Boehm, the German sabotage man. He appears to have had meetings with Boehm on around 20 days and with Casement on 30 of the 60 days in Germany. In addition there were some ten meetings with Meyer or von Wedel of the German Foreign Office, and a few with Nadolny." – see http://www.irishbrigade.eu/other-men/plunkett/plunkett.html

He said there was a ray of hope of the Brigade being formed after all – that quite a number of men in Camp were listeners & that, in addition to Quinlisk (the young corporal of the 18th R.I. Rgt. who had stepped out the first day) there were two very good men.

Keogh and Dowling,[122] who had been backing up his, Fr Nicholson's, propaganda with great hardihood.

He asked me to see these men, & if I thought it well to then come down to Limburg & perhaps I'd succeed in enrolling enough men to have the treaty proclaimed.

I sent for the men – Quinlisk, Keogh & Dowling.

They were brought to Berlin by order of the Kriegs Ministerium. A Hauptmann van Lübbers was the intermediary – I was then at the Baroness von Nordenflechts with a threatened lung attack, her brother Dr Mahly said – they were kept for ten to 12 days at the Hotel Prinz Wilhelm in Dorotheen Strasse <u>with no one in Berlin knowing</u>!

I asked repeatedly at the FO where they were – no one there knew! Finally, by chance, I learned they had been for two weeks at the little Hotel.

Meantime I had left the Baron von N's & was at the Eden Hotel (once more). The three young soldiers were brought to me (in plain clothes of course) by the soldier guard who had come up with them from Limburg.

I saw them several times at the Hotel and introduced them to P. ("Mr Petre"). They begged me to come down to Limburg, saying they felt convinced that some 200 men at least could be induced to come out.

I explained pretty plainly the position that I did not believe now any military help for Ireland was possible – the seas were closed & held tight by England – but the political value & importance to the Irish Cause of the Treaty remained & if I could succeed in having it published based on the live fact that a body of Irishmen were in arms, under our flag, it would uplift the Irish heart all the World over & revive & restart much of the true national spirit we had been steadily losing under the demoralization of the Parliamentary campaign.

They saw the truth of this & begged me to go down to Limburg & make a final effort.

I agreed.

I told the G.G.S. & F.O. of the hopes of the three young soldiers & Fr. N's

---

[122] Joseph Dowling was later to be sent by U-boat to Ireland to set up a communication channel for the Germans to send arms into Ireland. Landing on 12 April 1918 on Crab Island, Co. Clare, he was rapidly captured and sent to London for court martial. Sentenced to death in July, he was reprieved with the sentence commuted to life imprisonment. He was not released until 1924.

hopes & asked for Captain Boehm to be placed at my disposal to take the three young soldiers back to Limburg & get all the liberties &c &c necessary for a fresh recruiting effort.

This was at length agreed & I asked P to accompany Boehm & the three young men. This I did with the following in mind.

I had more & more come to the conclusion that the German govt. were wholly insincere in their pro-Irish professions – & I hesitated more & more at the thought of getting a body of Irish soldiers to commit treason just for an ideal.

I told many of my doubts & fears to P. I said I wanted him really to be a check on Boehm & to see for himself how things went. I wd. follow in a very short time, but I did not want Boehm to have a free field & no check. And yet Boehm was far the best, more friendly & more capable for the purpose of all German officers I had met.

The G.G.S. & F.O. again wakened up – The mere prospect of getting "the Irish Brigade" formed stirred the dry bones to life.

The Under Secretary of State Zimmermann said he would see me! Assessor Meyer who had not been near me since 1 March called furiously & asked if there was "anything I wanted."

Once again I had become useful – or possibly useful.

I went down to Limburg on 12 May, a day or two after the others had arrived there.

They had got 53 men the first few days – & then things stuck.

A "circular" had been sent out by Boehm off his own bat (which I have never yet seen!) that Keogh told me (long afterwards) had some harm.

I don't even now know what was in it, but I fancy _it_ may be the origin of "a German farm" and "a German wife" the _Graphic_ of 26 Feby attributed to me!

I knew by long experience that in underhand or stupid acts of this kind, off their own bat, the German officials all excelled.

I had seen in March, or the beginning of April the batch of printed questions Wedel & Co had sent out to the men at Limburg without even consulting me. Indeed it was only by chance I heard of this gross act.

I called one day on Wedel & found him with a pile of printed papers before him, which he was looking through. He showed me them – saying –

"It is strange Sir Roger how the answers to these questions seem to be stereotyped" – handing me a batch of the papers.

They consisted of a printed series of questions addressed to the Irish prisoners of war in Limburg – such as "What was the political feeling in Ireland when you left?"

"What was the sentiment in your Regiment to the English govt?"

I was staggered – dumbfounded.

I turned on him & said.

"Is it possible you put such questions to the Irish prisoners?

Why, no wonder you get these answers.

What could the German govt. have been dreaming of?

The men, practically all answer you alike – that it is none of your business & that they don't admit your right to put such questions to them?

They are perfectly right. I might as an Irishman say things to them – but you can't. You have here done your best to convince them that I <u>am</u> a German agent, as the opponents of my movement assert."

Wedel was far too stupid to understand. I think – I presume he, Meyer and the great luminous mind of the G.G.S. or Kriegsministerium had decided that they knew much better than I did the mind of the Irishmen & they would find out themselves the possibility of the movement by this <u>adroit</u> series of questions.

All these things – I can touch here on only a few of my ever growing want of faith in the authorities – convinced me that while it was vitally desirable to proclaim the Treaty & its publication depended on a certain number of men being enrolled, I should not be justified in doing anything more than I had already done to induce men to join. No temptation was to be offered. P. was far less scrupulous. He said once – "We'll have to get them, if we kidnap them". I said – "no – we must continue only & <u>solely</u> to appeal to their patriotism."

On reaching Limburg, Boehm, P & the three young soldiers met me. I had got them uniforms during their stay in Berlin & these they wore in the camp only.

It was arranged I should address a Company of men called "B Company" – & this I did on May 15. I got the gist of my remarks – they were delivered without prior notes or writing – printed & circulated.

One of the stumbling blocks was the oath of allegiance – & there I said every man must decide for himself. I only pointed out that Kings owed a duty to their people quite as much as a people to them. Kings – & I emphasised how false all <u>our</u> sovereigns had been to their trust as Kings of Ireland, no less than of Great Britain.

I was in a very difficult position. In my heart I felt much with the men – & I understood their point of view – on the other hand I saw the great importance of the Treaty to Ireland & the vital need of getting a small force together so that we should be able to publish it. So much might hinge on its publication. Not only in Ireland, where furious efforts were being made to get Irish men into the Army – but in America.

Signed photograph of Adler Christensen dated 24 June 1915 in Berlin

Signed photograph of Roger Casement reading, dated 24 June 1915

So I tried but only within limits I felt to be honourable (for an open rebel).

I refused to bribe or tempt with money offers, beyond the compensation offer "up to say £10" – for any monies a recruit to the Brigade would forfeit. Indeed I failed really just because I would adopt English methods.

England was bribing, corrupting (& intimidating) Irishmen into her army of aggression & plunder – I could only offer the hope of striking a blow for Ireland – & that, too, a problematical one.

When it became clear that no more men would join at present Boehm decided to take the 53 away to Berlin as a beginning. The promise made was that they should be put into uniform at once, armed – & trained, in all respects, according to the Treaty Clauses. This done & assurances thus conveyed to the many waverers in the Camp that the thing was serious – photos were to be sent down of the men in uniform – then we might hope for more – possibly up to 200.

On 200 recruits the Treaty could be published.

I asked P. and the three young recruiting soldiers to stay on at Limburg & keep the fire warm while the 53 were being put into uniform &c &c "at Berlin."

I told P. this was to me a test case. If the G.G.S. agreed to treat the 53 "as soldiers" & carry out the provisions of the Treaty strictly & honourably I'd feel justified in going on with the attempt to get 200 men. But if not, then I should not feel justified in trying to persuade another man.

I would not lift a finger until I saw what was going to be done in this respect.

I wrote to Wedel urging the importance of getting the 53 into uniform &c at once & then I went to Munich to see Gaffney. This journey I had long contemplated.

It was not merely to see Gaffney but to make enquiry on the spot as to an offer to get me back to America that had come from a friendly American there. If the plan was workable I might accept the offer & go.

Meantime I <u>could</u> do nothing at Limburg until I saw which way the War Office lot wd. jump over the 53 first fruits.

After about a week in Munich when the proposed U.S. journey was discussed & the means exposed – I returned to Limburg & found two fresh recruits there & P. anxious to get back to Berlin. I sent him there & stayed on a day or two longer at Limburg – writing Wedel more than once & urging that the Treaty be sent to Bernstorff with instructions to publish on receipt & a cable.

Finally I returned to Berlin early in June – about 6th or 7th I think. I went to Wedel first. He agreed to all my proposals & said he had already sent the desired instructions to Bernstorff. Then to the G.G.S. with P – who was getting ready to return to Ireland via Switzerland.

I wanted P. to see for himself the dead wall of obstinate stupidity one was up against.

The G.G.S. (Nadolny & Frey) were furious at the poor results obtained. "Only 53 men & we had ordered 100 uniforms!" was one of the chivalrous remarks by Nadolny. I very nearly said "Send me the bill."

I urged the vital importance of going on with what had begun – & convincing the men in camp that the Govt were serious & could be trusted – but the petty mind prevailed.

There were furious interviews at the F.O. between the military and the F.O. people. I will not go into the particulars here. P. was present (in an anteroom) at one of these altercations & began (slowly – I fear) to understand.

He asked at the G.G.S. for arms for Ireland. These were contemptuously refused by Nadolny who said that they had plenty of goodwill for Ireland (in his words!) but would give no arms. Arms must be provided by the Irish in America.

P. was raging – & asked me if I could obtain him an interview with the Minister of War!!!

I laughed & said you might as well ask to see the Emperor.

P. left for Switzerland (with a photo of the Treaty in a hollow stick!) towards end of June. As I saw him off I felt the last link with hope was going from me for ever. I knew I was now & henceforth face to face with absolute failure, ending only in death – or contempt & derision & utter failure to understand all the difficulties around me.

I was alone. I had practically ceased to have any hope of the F.O., the German govt. or anything. The 53 were out at Zossen in a sort of convict garb – mixed up with the Mohamedan prisoners.

I kept on urging the fulfilment of the Treaty promises to them – mindful and all as they were – The obligation could not be gainsaid. I insisted on its fulfilment.

Wedel wrote me at very end of June a letter, evidently a sort of severance of diplomatic relations, pointing out that the Irish in America had failed to show sufficient interest in the cause of Ireland & putting the blame on their shoulders.

I replied very courteously rebutting the statement & pointing out that I should be very pleased if I could find in Germany any public expression of opinion about Ireland half so useful as Irish sympathy for Germany had been in America.

I sent copies of both letters over to America & packed up & left Berlin on

Rudolf Nadolny (Abteilung IIIb) in uniform

Roger Casement 22 July 1915

2 July – I hoped perhaps for ever. If possible I would get over to America. I was torn in two of course – for there were always the 53 at Zossen to be provided for & faith kept with them. But I saw that the best way to compel the Govt. to do its duty to them was to get out of Germany first – & once I was free to say just what I thought, then to send them an ultimatum & demand the strict fulfilment of their promises to the men.

In any case I could do nothing by staying in Berlin. I could not advance anything there – for I could scarcely keep my face before these people – and there was nothing, absolutely nothing to discuss,

I knew for an absolute certainty they had no care or thought about Ireland – only for themselves & that when they saw they could get no more out of me – & the poor betrayed 53 – they had no use for us. I was determined to do all I could to make them keep faith with the men at Zossen.

Throughout July & August I was out at Ammersee – writing sometime to urge the action as I desired for the men at Zossen – once I asked for my passport – & within a few days I learned that (on 4 Sept.) the men had been put into uniform & moved to new quarters.

Keogh wrote & begged me to go & see them – I did so – & as money arrived from U.S. at same time I was able to make financial arrangements that were satisfactory for paying them.

The difficulty was that there was nothing for them to do.

When I gave up the attempt to (or thought rather) of going to U.S.A. then I returned to trying to do something with the handful of men at Zossen.

I told them of my idea – viz – of going East with them as provided in two of the clauses of the Treaty. –

I began urging this on the German auths & recd. assurances from Wedel that "as soon as they had opened the road thro' Servia" I might get underway.

And so the thing went on –

Always promising – always delaying –

The want of officers was raised – no German officers available. Meantime no attempt was made to arm the men. They were only in uniform & behind barbed wire in a cage.

Finally when I was again falling into deeper despair, one fine day Adler Christensen turned up bringing over Lt. Monteith from America – a fine piece of smuggling – Christensen has returned to America after I left Berlin for Munich. He had carried messages over from me to J.D. & Joe McG. **[McGarrity]** & had behaved well at first & J.D. got him to smuggle Lt Monteith back safe & sound to me. Monteith arrived about 22 October & after getting him "recognized" I sent him down to Limburg – once again – to see if there was any chance of beating up more recruits. The military auths

Photograph of Casement in 1915 reading on boat; inscription reads 'Irenführer Casement München, Starnberger See', actually the Ammersee (NYPL)

there wd. not allow him to wear his uniform!

That helped more than all else, to convince the men there that the thing was a sham.

After two weeks at Limburg I had to send for Monteith to maintain discipline at Zossen as things were getting worn there – he returned in Novr. 1915 & went out to Zossen to take on the Command there. He has been there ever since – an invaluable man. Loyal, brave, untiring & of a great fidelity.

What I should have done without him I know not. With him in charge at Zossen I was greatly relieved – but the wish to get to work & to get out of Germany & to justify "our treason" was strong on us. I urged again & again the march to the East.

Captain Robert Monteith in Irish Brigade uniform

Early in December I again saw Nadolny – 8 Decr – the first time since the stormy interview with P. assisting towards middle of June.

Frey, too, was there. Nadolny said they were doing all they could to get us down to Turkey.

That Enver Pacha agreed – but the (German ?) Commander-in-Chief at Bagdad refused.

He was trying again – in another direction in Turkey.

[Page 60 ends here. Those pages numbered 61-80 are blank. Casement wrote a final four words inside the back cover on page 81 at the very end of this second volume:]

    Generaloberarzt [**Assistant Medical Director**]
    Westfahl
an Herrn

[The following words and items are not present in the two NLI manuscripts but are mentioned in Curry's book. He wrote on pages 143-144: "The following notes in pencil, "instructions received", are on a slip of paper attached to the inner back cover of the diary from which the above entries are taken." There is no sign of that slip.]

1915 January 18th:

""Mjolnir" Danish flag.
From Copenhagen   7th Jan.
   „   Gothenburg   8th „
Ar.   Christiansand   9th „

    The S/S will not go to Kragerö – but will go straight to Christiansand to deceive the others.
    Send a sham Mr. Hammond at Gothenburg.
    He will go and embark for Christiansand and return.
    He knows nothing."
Instructions received.

[On page 144, Curry also wrote: "On a loose slip of paper in the diary in question is noted partly in Sir Roger's and partly in Christensen's handwriting":]

"280 marks in gold.
  35   „   „ paper
$ 30   „ gold,
that is about 450 Marks – this not including the ticket."

[Curry concluded, "This was evidently the sum of money Christensen received from Sir Roger upon his departure for Norway on 24 December." 'A Last Page' now takes the account forward until Casement left Berlin.]

A Last Page
17 March 1916 – 11 April 1916

Casement's final German diarying before his departure to Ireland, with notes and associated letters (earlier time periods are also dealt with).

Entitled 'A Last Page', this document is in NLI 5244. The entries were written by Casement between 17 March 1916 and 8 April 1916. Despite its name, *A Last Page* actually runs to 134 pre-numbered sides of script in a quarto, stitched notebook which was, possibly, originally, a gummed pad. The black hardback binding may have been the work of the NLI or Dr Charles Curry, its initial custodian. A few handwritten words at the inner edges are unreadable as they are now incorporated into the binding or stitching.

There are additions in NLI 17587/1-2.[123] A typed version of 49 pages is in NLI 17587/3 and another, partial typescript with handwritten corrections (and other typescript items) is in NLI 17587/4.[124] A third typescript is in the New York Public Library's collection of William Maloney Irish Historical Papers (IHP).[125]

NLI 17587/2 consists of four sheets of additional diary entries or notes duplicating the NLI 5244 period from 28 March to 6 April 1916 and is entitled by Casement, "Rough note of last days in Berlin."

NLI 17587/1, the concluding document, consists of ten sheets and takes the narrative from 9 to 11 April, his final full day in Berlin. The pages start with pre-printed numbered page 135 and go up to page 142, and are followed by two final sheets without numbers.

Although *A Last Page* starts on 17 March 1916 the narrative initially goes back several months. This is a key period, as on 7 March 1916, word came to Casement from Lt. Robert Monteith via Count Plunkett in Switzerland,

---

[123] NLI 17587 contains five folders which are catalogued in Hayes Sources Database as, "Pages of Roger Casement's 'A Last Page of My Diary', for April 9-11, and additional entries for other dates in Casement's hand; also typescript by Maloney of the diary and of correspondence between Casement and associates including Count von Wedel and R. Monteith, Dec. 1915-April 1916."

[124] NLI 17587/4 is catalogued as "Maloney typescript copy of Casement's diary and [typed] correspondence, Dec 1915-April 1916" and includes items to and from von Wedel, and to and from 'A friend of James Malcolm' [Count Plunkett] dated 5 April 1916 from Berne, and the reply dated 6 April. NLI 17587/5 is described as, "'The Nation One' and 'The Nation Two' including extracts from Casement's diaries by Charles. E. Curry."

[125] Box 2, Folios 14-15. NYPL Maloney IHP 1857-1965. Mss Col 1854; Series I. Sir Roger Casement (4 boxes, 56 folios). http://archives.nypl.org/uploads/collection/pdf_finding_aid/maloneyihp.pdf,

that a rising was planned for that Easter. The Germans had however known of this since 10 February 1916 from messages via their Washington Embassy.

In places in the documents, Casement has reviewed what he has written and clarified, corrected, added to, or expanded his original script. Some of these amendments are dated. Someone, in another hand, has re-written some of the harder-to-read words above the text.

Other documents intended to be read alongside this diary are described by Casement as being attached. They are no longer present although some press cuttings remain tipped in. Many of those detached items and other documents of this time are to be found in original or copy form in the NYPL, the NLI, and in official German archives such as the Berlin Foreign Ministry (AA). Some are transcribed and incorporated in this text. There are more Casement-related papers covering the period 1914 to 1916 in other archives, notably PRONI in Belfast and The National Archives at Kew.

Casement's industry and written output is prodigious, given the drama and speed of the events he was experiencing. There are numerous other letters, drafts, notes and memos being written by him in these days, not to mention autograph copies made of letters he sent out.

A Last Page is essentially a justification for Casement's actions, made, he would say, under duress, in his last days in Germany, and is frequently an attack on the German Imperial establishment for what he calls its ulterior motives in relation to the imminent Easter Rising. His largely pointless insistence on travelling in a submarine to Ireland – to his death – is also covered.

It has to be said that surprise at German motives is illustrative of a naive side to Casement's usually sharp political understanding. The documents indicate his changing views as the days progress. Although he consistently worked for postponement of the rising, Casement was still determined to get German arms into Ireland.

His decision to send an emissary to Dublin to try and get the rising called off or postponed is a matter of great significance yet seldom remarked upon. The fate of that emissary, the Scottish-born, American-based, John McGoey, had been another mystery. He was said to have been executed by the British in Scotland[126] or notioned to have been murdered by the German military. He certainly did not reach Dublin, nor was he ever heard of again in Irish circles.

Yet McGoey survived the war. That mystery has been partially solved.

---

[126] See Aodogan O'Rahilly's 'Winding the Clock: O'Rahilly and the Easter Rising' pp. 161-185

Electronically-searchable passenger lists from Ellis Island revealed that he had sailed to the United States in 1920. Then the Irish Brigade website of David Grant[127] made known many more and extensive details on McGoey's life, before and after Casement, and his accidental death on 16 November 1925 in Cook County, Illinois. (Spelling of his name varies widely). The mystery remains as to why McGoey when he got to Britain did not tell Dublin of his message from Casement. Perhaps he arrived too late or perhaps he wanted the Rising to happen.

Spellings and punctuation in these documents have been corrected or otherwise made consistent, as have some abbreviations. Missing accents have mostly been reinstated. Items in bold on the title page were pre-printed.

Roger McHugh, in an anthology of contemporary accounts of the Easter Rising, entitled *Dublin 1916* published a chapter which extracted entries from *A Last Page* with a small amount of commentary. The extracts cover the dates of 17 March, and 3, 5 and 7 April with however a number of mis-transcriptions.

John McGoey

---

[127] David Grant's hugely informative, if undistilled, website which details all the Brigade members' past, and their progress after 1914 – http://www.irishbrigade.eu/other-men/goey/goey.html

Roger Casement c. 1915

A Last Page

IRISH BRIGADE (1915)

(Irische Brigade

St. Patrick's Day

Date 17 March 1916

Berlin

To A Page of my Diary

From

I write this beginning of what I feel is a last chapter on Patrick's Day in Berlin this year of war 1916. Last year on Patrick's Day I was also in Berlin, ill in bed, in the house of Baroness von Nordenflycht.[128]

Even then, hope had gone from me – for I realized then, already, that those I trusted here were little to be trusted and that their only interest in me lay in exploiting me, and the Irish cause in their own supposed interests.

Since then a hundred added proofs have accumulated – and yesterday the climax came, and as now but little time is left I begin, today, a hurried record of things that must be stated in order that some day the truth may be known.

In three weeks I shall probably be at sea on the maddest and most ill planned enterprise that the history of Irish revolutionary efforts offers.

But it is not of my choosing, of my planning, or undertaken with my approval. I go because honour calls me to go – and because to stop it now (even if I could stop it) would involve others and perhaps bring greater grief.

Moreover by going with the tiny band [**Casement inserted at top of page:** (12 men probably)] that is to sail on 8 April I _may_ save them – and perhaps Ireland too from a dreadful fate. To stay here in safety while those others go would do no good to Ireland – and would leave me prey to eternal regret.

Thus while I strongly disapprove what is being attempted, and so wretchedly attempted, with a foregone assurance of failure I _must_ lend it my countenance and accompany the forlorn hope.

And now to make a little daylight for the hereafter.

---

[128] Baron von Nordenflycht was still German Minister in Montevideo at this time which explains why Casement does not mention him being present nor seeing him.

Riederau house with commemorative plaque where Casement stayed in 1915 (NLI CAS 12C)

I will confine myself today to dealing with the events only since the beginning of this year, trusting to the few days of quiet I hope still to get at Riederau a/Ammersee to put down earlier happenings, since I stopped keeping a regular diary[129] at the beginning of February last year.

I stopped that diary when I became clear that I was being played with, fooled and used by a most selfish and unscrupulous government for its own sole, petty interests. I did not wish to record the misery I felt or to say the thing my heart prompted. But today it is my head compels me to this unwelcome task.

At the beginning of this year I was staying out at Zossen, the most wretched of men.

The small band of Irish soldiers who had volunteered in May last were there (see the list attached) **[Casement's note is handwritten in pencil at**

---

[129] The earlier journal ran until 11 February 1915 when Casement entered a sanatorium.

the top of the page with a connecting line downwards to 'the list'[130] which is missing] in uniform, but still kept practically as prisoners of war, and Lt. Monteith in command of them. I had gone out to Zossen on 4th December 1915, to be near him and the men, to encourage and cheer them in their bitter disappointment – and always in the hope that our long urged journey to the East, to get into action, might be sanctioned. The General Staff here had promised me repeatedly, in December 1915, that the "Brigade" should be sent East.

Enver Pasha[131] had agreed and it lay only with the German ships in the East to accept the men. The final assurance was given me explicitly on 4 January 1916 (on return from a hurried run to Dresden) at the German Gr. Staff [**Frequently abbreviated by Casement to G.G.S.; the initials stand for *Grosser Generalstab*.**] that the corps would be sent to Syria, and that they would "at once" be trained in the use of machine guns. This promise, like all preceding promises – was not carried out.

Irish Brigade prior to a boxing match in Halbmondlager Camp,[132] July 1915 (National Museum of Ireland, HE 12051)

Day by day I got worse. I had been ill for long – sick at heart and soul,

---

[130] See Doerries pp. 212-14 for a list of Irish Brigade members. There is also a list in NLI 18081/10, their ages, county of origin, previous occupations, preferred future occupations and place of expected migration. Timothy Quinlisk, for example, was 19 and from Wexford while Daniel Beverley (Bailey) was a 28-year-old painter preferring to go to Mobile, Texas or Rio de Janeiro.

[131] Enver Pasha (b. 1881) was a Turkish nationalist and revolutionary. Minister of War from 1914, he fled to Russia in 1918 and was killed in a skirmish in Turkestan in 1922.

[132] Halbmondlager was another name for Zossen Camp. It was where the Germans placed potentially disloyal Muslim, Hindu and Sikh, as well as, Irish prisoners. It was the site of the first ever mosque in Germany, built to further the 'jihad experiment'.

with mind and nerves threatening a complete breakdown. No man was ever in a falser position. The truth I could not tell to my friends in America. I had no means of communicating with them except by letter that had to pass through the hands of those I felt sure would read it – and to expose their perfidy – thus would scarcely work.

Finally I broke down and acting on the advice of a great doctor I went to a "nerve rest" at the Kuranstalt, Neuwittelsbach, Munich. This was on 19 January 1916.

[Casement letter to Mrs. Gaffney about his belongings:]

Zossen
14 Janry 1916

My dear Mrs. Gaffney,

Very many thanks for your letter – and for all your kindnesses to the men here. They need it – poor chaps. Their long period in hopeless idleness is so disastrous for them in every way – and any kindness shown them like yours is a real act of good.

I have been and am very unwell and hope to get a complete change soon – Thank you about the trunk – I don't know if you had to pay anything for it – please let me know, as I can't tell here.

I think you had better open it – and take out the books. All but one are your husband's, and should go back into his bookshelves – the one that is mine I give him too – so all can go.

There is a suit of clothes – I forgot to mention it – put in as packing to keep the books from shaking.

It ought to be taken out and hung up, as it is a useful suit in summer – and will get spoiled in the trunks. Otherwise everything should stay in the trunks – papers and all just as they are – till I claim them or if that never happens for any reason, then to go to my friend in Philadelphia at the end of the war –

His name is
Joseph McGarrity
5412 Springfield Avenue
Philadelphia, Pa.

All my papers I have in Germany I want to go to him if I die "in my tracks" – and in order that no trouble should ever arise I want you to know and be able to deal privately without any legal powers &c. &c. which are always such a nuisance.

I am very grateful to you and all those kind friends in Munich – please thank them again warmly for all they helped to do to brighten the lot of these poor Irish boys here in exile, if ever men were in exile.

I hope you will very soon hear from St. John – and that it will be very good news indeed. Things look so much better in U.S.A. of late – ever since Congress met.

If only peace would come back to the world and the hearts of men, how mighty would be the change!

All kind thought and thanks for you – and for the "family".

I hope they are flourishing – and glad to have them back.
Yours very sincerely,
    Roger Casement

I was very ill on arrival – but I gradually got better. Then, while there, came the return of my friend Gaffney from America. He stayed in Berlin, but wrote me often, and imperatively begged me to go to Berlin, as there was a matter of "great importance" to discuss with me.

After days of delay and doubt I came here to Berlin arriving on 16th February & coming to this Hotel Saxonia, Gaffney and Lt. Monteith meeting me at the station at midnight.

I was ill and unfit to travel – and got worse here.

I stayed here till 26th February, returning again to the Kuranstalt on 27th where I was ill in bed for some days on my return.

Gaffney has asked me to come to Berlin to discuss here the chance of my going over to U.S.A. His project was that by a steamer of the Norwegian line – the "Kristianiafjord" – I would probably be safe. A certain Mr. Schirmer, a Norwegian (of Germanic descent) was constantly travelling by that vessel on "missions" of the German Foreign Office and was entirely trustworthy.

If S. agreed and said the Captain of the "K" agreed to take me I might get over in safety. Mr. S. came to see me several times, but deprecated my going away with him at once on this journey. He was going over to U.S.A. by the "Kristianiafjord" from Bergen on Feb. 23rd to leave Berlin on Sunday 20 February. He said that the best thing to do was to leave him to try to arrange the matter with the captain of the "K" for the following voyage. Gaffney and I agreed. Letters were given to Mr. S. to take over to certain friends in New York pointing out the desirability of my making this attempt.

At same time Gaffney had told me of the forthcoming Irish Convention in New York on 4-5 March and urged me strongly to send over by Mr. Schirmer the original Findlay letter of £5000 bribe for my capture and other papers with it bearing on that disgraceful incident. I was assured these papers would be absolutely safe with Mr. Schirmer. I gave them to him on Saturday evening 19 February, in this hotel, Gaffney being present – and he promised to deliver them in person to Judge Cohalan along with a covering letter from myself.

At the same time, apart from this, I had seen Mary MacFadden, and as she wanted to get back to America I supplied her with the funds (Mks 1750.00) to allow of her sailing by the same boat.

Lt. Monteith helped her to get all her things ready and she too, left on Sunday morning – 20 February – for Bergen and I hope and believe sailed by the "Kristianiafjord" on 23rd. She took only verbal messages, and our hope was that she might reach New York in time to be present at the Convention on 5 March. As matters turned out, the "Kristianiafjord" was "held up" at Kirkwall for two days and reached New York only on 7 March. It was reported here in the German press that – "her mails" had been taken off by the British authorities – and that is all we know.

[Pencilled insert by Casement (text otherwise in ink):] I do not know yet if the Findlay letters arrived safely or if the English got them.

Mr. Schirmer was to have cabled under the name Newman to a friend here in Berlin, J.E. Noeggerath[133] and if the cable had the word "sold" in, I was to know that the matter of my going over to U.S.A. was agreed to. This cable was to arrive here, at latest, by 17 March. That day is here now – and no cable has been received. Mary MacFadden was also to cable on arrival to a friend here, but none has come. So as I write, I do not know whether the Findlay letters &c. have got over safely or have been seized at Kirkwall – and I do not know how my friends in America regard the proposal for my going over. However, in view of what occurred yesterday, I presume they disapproved and think I can be more useful here. They little know the true situation here.

After the departure of Mary MacFadden and Mr. S. I stayed on in Berlin until Saturday 26th being ill most of the time. I went back with Gaffney that night to Munich and to bed again at Kuranstalt.

Captain Robert Monteith

---

[133] Jacob E. Noeggerath, a German-American whom Casement later described as a "confidential agent of the Foreign Office."

On Friday, 3 March, while in bed I got a letter from Lt. Monteith dated 1st March urging my immediate return to Berlin. No reasons were given.

[Monteith letter to Casement:][134]

Hotel Saxonia
Berlin
den 1-3-15 [sic]
[Casement note:] R at Munich from Dr. von Hoesstin at 12. noon
3 March. 1916
Dear Sir Roger
This is to inform you that I am of opinion that you are quite recovered. You must come see me as early as you possibly can – I can't go into details now, <u>but there is work doing</u> and I am not able to manage without you – wire me your train and I will meet you
Sincerely yours
R Monteith
[Casement note:]
This is an impossible letter.
I get it after 5 days <u>solid</u> in bed – since Sunday on return here with high temperature (39 degrees) & am ordered off as if I were a bale of goods.
[On back of letter:] Ill in bed cannot travel. – write full details
Casement
Sent by Gaffney
3.30 pm 3 Mch/16
[A sketch of a noose and trap door is then drawn.]

I answered that I could not travel and begged him to explain the reasons that called me back so hurriedly.

[Casement letter to Monteith:][135]

March 3, 1916
Copy
Kuranstalt. N. Wittelsbach
3 March 1916
Dear Mr. Monteith.
Mr. Gaffney is telegraphing to you at my request as follows.
"Ill in bed, cannot travel, write full details.
Casement."
Also he will telephone to the Saxonia Hotel in hope you may be there to tell you that it is not possible for me to travel yet.

---

[134] NYPL Maloney IHP, Box 2, Folio 1 (copy of handwritten original)
[135] NYPL Maloney IHP, Box 2, Folio 1 and NLI 17587/4 typescript

I have shown your letter to Dr. v Hoesstin, who absolutely refuses to allow me to move.

But I should not go in any case, were I well, in response to such a letter as that. Before I undertake a long journey I am entitled to know the reasons that call for it and to decide whether they justify it - it is not polite to ask me to go so far with no explanation furnished.

Moreover it is your duty to report on anything of importance to me - and if I am well enough to deal with it, as you assume, it is for me to judge how I shall deal with it.

I therefore, request you to furnish me with a full report on the circumstances referred to in your note and I shall decide what action on my part is called for.

    Yours sincerely,
        Roger Casement.

[On back of letter:]
Lt Monteith (original)
to
R.C. - 1 March 1916
R   3 M'ch 1916
    (12 noon)
replied to at once &
then at 6 pm this second
    reply by Eilboten [**express**].

On 6th March a letter from him of 4th came, telling me there was "a move on" that he could not write, or tell to anyone save myself, and that he would come to Munich to see me, arriving the next morning. I was then much better and on the following day, Tuesday, 7th March, he arrived and spent the forenoon with me.

[Monteith letter to Casement:][136]

[Casement note:] R at M.
9 a.m.
6 M'ch / 16

Saturday
4.3.16.
Dear Sir Roger,

Your letter to hand this moment. I am so sorry to hear of your illness – I am afraid you thought my letter abrupt – please pardon me, I would hate to annoy you in the smallest way – I know I have a wretched way of hurling something at a person when I should quietly hand it over – But what I had to say to you cannot be written, at least in my opinion not with safety —

As it stands then I shall come and see you in Munich – I don't want to be mys-

---

[136] NYPL Maloney IHP, Box 2, Folio 1 (copy of handwritten original)

terious in any way, but you see, I must, therefore as soon as I can get a pass I'll go down — I cannot consult either Mr. Gaffney or Mr Noeggerath on this matter —

Now your second letter has just come in and I can see you are fairly mad with me please understand me, Sir Roger – I do not presume to tell you what you may or may not do, nothing was further from my mind – You said certain news and certain actions would cure you and I have the news and promise of action, even better than we thought of, and I thought you would understand my meaning when I said you "were quite recovered" —

I am so sorry for the misunderstanding - of course you must just think of me as the fool I undoubtedly am – but I tender you my most abject apology; please forgive me — And please Sir Roger remember when you want to hurt me good and hard just write me such another letter —

I do hope that your recovery will be speedy – for you are the only one in this land who can help me — I am the best judge of that—

    Best wishes,
        Faithfully yours,
            R. Monteith.

[Casement note:] on Receipt I sent following - to be <u>Translated</u>.
Lt. M. Irländer Abteilung - <u>Zossen</u>.
[Address on envelope reads:]
Lt Monteith
Irländer Abteilung,
Truppenübungs platz
Kommandantur –
Zossen
See Assessor Meyer and if you cannot get pass to come here immediately I will go you tomorrow night, but better come here if possible.
    Wire decision.
        Casement.

The "move" was this.[137]

[Casement note:]
Rough note. Munich.
March 7. 1916.
Tuesday

Lt. Monteith came from Berlin and told me that arms to be sent Ireland in trawlers disguised as Br. mine layers.

Frey sent for Monteith on Tuesday 1 M'ch to tell him a wireless had been rec'd from J.D. to say that "Something was going to happen in Ireland" & to send arms. This to the G. Admiralty. They agreed & sent for M. to tell him that the trawlers wd. go & to ask for best place to land.

Fennit is the best place - in Kerry.

---
[137] NYPL Maloney IHP, Box 2, Folio 17

Frey offered up to 200.000 rifles.

M. said 20.000 rifles with 300 Ctges. per rifle & 20 machine guns to go off at once or Revolver Cannon.

Monteith's possible selection from Brigade for the forlorn hope to go with the arms.

Kehoe,	Granaghan
Beverley	Kavanagh
Dowling	Young O'Callaghan
O'Toole	Kennedy
Delamore	Wilson
Scanlon?	

They say at G.G. Staff that they will send the arms by 23rd or 25 April next to Ireland.

This is a rough Memo of what Monteith came to Munich to the Nursing Home to tell me. He went back to Berlin that night - 7 March with a Memo from me for the General Staff - This I followed up on the following day - Wed. 8 March.

I was in high spirits. There was at length a prospect of action, and of getting out of Germany into Ireland.

All depended obviously on the submarine being put at our disposal to send me ahead to ensure the arrangements being thorough - otherwise failure is so very likely. Also once I got into Ireland I might be able to stop an abortive rising and arrange as for the reception of the rifles.

All these hopes were dashed to the ground on my getting to the General Staff on 16 March & learning that the submarine would not be sent & still again next day on learning at the Admiralty that the Steamer would not be convoyed by submarine.

On the 1st March he had been asked by the G.G.S. to call, where he had seen Lt. Frey. Frey said that a "telegram" had come from Devoy asking for rifles &c. to be sent to Ireland as "something" would happen there shortly of "great importance."

The military here at G.G.S. were willing to give "<u>up to 200.000 rifles</u>" <u>with ammunition</u> Frey said; to land them in Ireland by a given date, probably in trawlers – and Monteith wanted my counsel and help as to what to do.

I said first – "My difficulty is that I don't trust these people in anything they promise – they lie always – they may or may not keep faith to-day – but I have no reason to believe that in anything they do they ever think of us, or of others – but only of themselves. If then they promise to give us <u>200.000 rifles &c.</u> I am forced to seek their real reason. It is not to help us – rest assured of that. They have shown me, so repeatedly, that they cannot keep faith and that they have no feeling about Ireland at all, that in anything they promise now I seek only their real motive and what end of their own they are after.

However, as they offer us this large armament we should be fools not to take it if we can get it – Let us get what we can."

I drew up a memorandum for Monteith to take back with him that night and hand to them the next day in Berlin – promising to follow it, in person, in a few days.

Time was precious. Monteith said that he gathered the "something" in Ireland would occur in April – the arms were to be there in good time. Devoy's telegram had been in a cypher arranged with Bernstorff and said that a letter coming over by first mail would explain details. This letter was due to arrive, Monteith said, in the course of the present week – 13 March to 18 March – and he begged me to try and come to Berlin in good time. I agreed. My memorandum of 7 March (a copy is attached) (Note Monteith kept copies – but burned them for safety here in Berlin he tells me now. I will try to get copies from G.G.S. 8.4.16.) pointed out that it was essential to send over, <u>before the shipment of arms</u>, <u>certain</u> intelligence to our friends <u>in Ireland</u>, so that the landing place or places, might definitely be fixed, the dates &c. and all arrangements made in concert. I pointed out the vital necessity of this step and showed how it could be done by submarine landing me and two of the Irish soldiers I should pick out on the coast near Dublin – the submarine to wait and bring back the messenger I should send back.

At same time Devoy could be told by telegraph, in his code, of what was being done.

Monteith took the 7th March 1916 memorandum **[date inscribed later at the top of the page]** back with him that night to Berlin.

He wrote me next day that he had given it next day to the G.G. Staff and they were "pleased" with it[138]

[Monteith letter to Casement:]

[Casement note:] R. at Munich
<u>Sat. 11. M'ch 1916</u>
I followed this soon to Berlin. My proposals were the Submarine one first of all.
Zossen 10. 3. 1916.
Dear Sir Roger,
    Your urgent letter to hand last night **[inserted date:]** Thursday 9th, on my return from Berlin. I am so glad to hear of your being so well in spirit, the flesh will follow suit –
    On Wednesday afternoon I went to the G.S. and handed in your paper for perusal and arranged to remain in Berlin until yesterday, when they telephoned for me. I went over at once, and they seem <u>more than pleased with your proposals</u>
    I was informed that <u>Dixon's</u> **[Casement note:** J Devoy**]** date for the sports in the homeland is Easter Sunday next and they seem most eager to make the thing a success.
    Above all I was asked **[Casement underlining]** <u>to not worry you</u> in any way, that

---
[138] NYPL Maloney IHP, Box 2, Folio 17

might unfit you for work - so I take it that it is intended that Smith [**Casement note: R.C.**] is to go and go soon –

I am of opinion Sir Roger that you should come here (Berlin) next Tuesday as you said in your proposal – for this reason - In Dixon's [**Casement note: x J Devoys**] wire it said that following by next mail to the F.O. were certain proposals or instructions from the heads of our departments. The G.S. informed me that these proposals when received (and they are now due) would be laid beside and considered in conjunction with yours, and immediate action taken – They will wire me immediately on receipt - don't you think it would be wise to have you on the spot? –

I met G. on Wednesday night he asked me to come and see him yesterday [**Casement inserted day:**] (Thursday.) - I promised, provided I had time, but I did not go - I was afraid he might ask me too many questions - as it was the G.S. had hold of me at the hour appointed —

I am afraid the gentle Mary did not reach land in time for the convention, only if the ship had escaped detention could she have been on the spot —

      Best wishes

          Faithfully Yours

            R Monteith

– I wrote him I should leave for Berlin on Tuesday or Wednesday of this week.

I left the Kuranstalt on Monday, 13th of March [**when he wrote suggestions additional to his memo of 7 March**] – and went to Riederau a/ Ammersee.[139]

[Casement suggestion regarding the arms landing in Kerry:]

Further suggestion I made to the Memo of the 7 March, 1916 I drew up at Munich and gave to Lt. Monteith to lay before the G. General Staff.

The Submarine sent in advance should = 1st = land the messengers at the appointed spot –

2nd visit – Fennet & the coast of Kerry to spy out the shore.

3. await there the return messenger to arrive at Fennet one week after the landing of the first messengers.

The return messenger will go to Fennet & embark there on a fishing boat, the crew of which will have Green jerseys. The Submarine will know the boat by this – green jerseys. That boat will be a friendly boat, will have the return messenger on board – & she will be available later on when the stove pipes* come in the trawlers.

If the messenger returns to Fennet before a week is up so much the better. The Submarine will know him and his boat from the green jerseys & can pick him up after dark off the Bay of Fennit. This is my suggestion. R.C.

Mc'h 13. 1916.

[**He wrote at bottom:**] *rifles

---

[139] NYPL Maloney IHP, Box 2, Folio 17 (original and typescript)

A Last Page

Corporal Michael O'Callaghan's photographic pass

Next day I tried to see Dr. Curry but missed him and had to wait over till Wednesday 15th – when he hurried back to Munich to see me. That evg. while on my way to the station with Dr. C – I got a telegram from Monteith (attached) **[not attached in NLI manuscript but in NYPL]** begging me to hurry to Berlin.[140]

[Telegram from Monteith summoning Casement to Berlin:]

Telegramm 2692...16 MARZ 14 **[14 March 1916]**
casement adr: von hoesslin
kuranstalt neu wittelsback muenchen
Telegramm aus berlin
kommen bitte sofort dringende angelegenheit - telegrafiere mit
welchen zug nach hotel saxonia = monteith =

[Casement note:]
I got this only at 9 p.m. on 15 March 1916 when on my way to the station to come to Berlin with Dr. Curry. I had telegraphed that morning to Lt. Monteith from the Hotel Basler Hof to say I would arrive at Berlin at 8.40 a.m. on 16th – but the porter

---
[140] NYPL. Maloney IHP, Box 2, Folio 17

Irish Brigade machine gunners: Thomas McGrath, Michael McDonagh, Michael O'Callaghan and James Carroll

brought the telegram back in evening saying the Post Office had refused to send it! I then had <u>telephoned</u> to the Hotel Saxonia asking them to inform Lt. Monteith that I would arrive by the morning train.

He met me at the station. 8.40 am. 16 M'ch 1916 & we went to the German General staff at 10 am & saw Captain Nadolny & two other officers who explained the steps they proposed taking to send the things to Ireland – They showed me a copy of J.D's letter of 16 Feby. stating the position in Ireland & the measure of help he & the Irish in U.S.A. asked & explained how little of this they were going to send & the way they intended doing it.

Lt. Monteith was present & heard all. Their proposal was most inadequate & the means they insist on employing can lead, I think, only to a failure. I did not say so. I merely said I should go with the expedition at all costs & Nadolny said of course I must go too – We stayed about 1½ hours there & came away convinced of their entire insincerity. They are trying to do as little as possible at the least cost to themselves regardless of whether the things reach their destination or of the failure or success of the resulting effort.

Their object is clear to me. While pretending to help – so that they can later on claim they complied with our requests within the measure of their means – they are cutting down the help to the lowest limit & taking no prior steps (that I urged again & again) to render even this tiny help of service or to ensure its safe arrival. They are wholly selfish – wholly untrustworthy and to sum it up – not gentlemen.

   R.C. 16.3.16
   Berlin.

[At side] See my memo of 7 Mc'h
- & the added one of 13 Mc'h 1916

I arrived here yesterday morning at 8.40 a.m. being met by Monteith at the station and he told me he had arranged with Captain Nadolny (Abteilung BIII)[141] to receive me at 10 a.m. at the G.G.S.

We went together to the Staff and spent over an hour with Nadolny and two other (junior) officers, Hauptmann v. Huelson[142] and Graf von Haugwitz (Ansbucher Cuirassiers).[143] The proposals <u>now</u> made were the following:–
1st. The Admiralty refused to send me or anyone ahead on the submarine. Their reason was that it was "too dangerous"! Too dangerous for our project. The Irish coast was so closely watched the submarine would be seen and thus the whole project "blown" upon.

I pointed out that this by no means followed, that submarines had been often seen off the Irish coast and nothing followed and it was absurd to say that if one <u>were</u>, by chance, seen it would reveal our plan. But if my advice were followed, she could not be seen and no risk incurred for her – only for us who landed and that was our affair.

Moreover if the watch was so close that a submarine would be seen how then did they hope to land arms from a big steamer?

All the arguments were brushed aside with the statement that the German Admiralty <u>would not agree and there was an end of it</u>.

So then we advanced to the "project" itself. It was this.

The G.G. Staff would load up twenty thousand rifles (not 200.000!)[144]

---

[141] Captain Rudolf Nadolny b. 1873 of Abteilung IIIb (not 'BIII'), *Chef der Sektion für Politik beim Generalstab*, later Ambassador to Turkey in 1924, and Moscow in 1933. Nadolny was Casement's particular bête noir.

[142] Captain Bernhard von Hülsen, who formed the 'Freikorps (von) General Hülsen', a paramilitary unit which took part in the suppression of the Spartacist League in Berlin.

[143] Count Curt Ludwig Heinrich Georg Haugwitz-Hardenberg-Reventlow b. 1885 was from a Danish German family. A brother of his married the Woolworth heiress Barbara Hutton. He had a long relationship with Fermanagh-born Monica Massy-Beresford who died in a German prison camp in 1945 after her death sentence was commuted. His sister Lucy Marie and he were in Dublin in 1947 pleading his case with de Valera. He was about to be deported from Denmark, "as all Germans has been asked to leave that country." He then wrote an account of his dealings with Casement for de Valera, saying Casement had asked him to accompany him to Ireland. "I am afraid – he just did not like us...He asked me, as a personal favour, if I would go over with him to Ireland. I said yes – provided I got permission." Haugwitz talked of Casement trying to get the Rising called off, also writing, "My chiefs and my own views were: That as Germany had promised Ireland her help, we had to keep our word…" (NLI 13774, "Account by Count Reventlow of Roger Casement's stay in Germany, presented to Éamon De Valera in 1947".)

[144] Doerries wrote (1976), "The decision to send only 20,000 captured Russian rifles must be seen in the light of the general German shortage of arms; on the other hand it again shows

with 10 machine guns and 5.000.000 cartridges in trawlers or "on a steamer" and despatch them, with our Irish handful at Zossen by 8th April at latest. The "rising" in Ireland was arranged for Easter Sunday and the guns were to be "in hand" before that date. They reckoned here to allow ten days for the journey – so that this armament should reach the appointed spot (where that might be!) by say 18th April.

Devoy would be informed by wireless and he would have to make the connection with Ireland, to arrange from New York, all details with the Revolutionary Committee in Ireland for the reception of the rifles and guns. <u>No prior word could be sent from this and nothing done from here save inform Devoy in this way</u>. I pointed out all the grave objections to such a very limited, uncertain and round about way of arranging with the men in Ireland – but all in vain.

Nadolny suggested that <u>all</u> the 55 Irish soldiers at Zossen should go, but I said that all could not be trusted, and the selection must be left to Lt. Monteith, to pick out the men he believed in. These, I said, must <u>at once</u>, without an hour's delay be trained in machine gun practice, so that on landing they could use the guns (or some of them) if needed to ward off police attack or rifle fire. As the proposals developed I saw how hopeless and inadequate they were – and I saw how false were all the professions accompanying them. Nadolny said that with this "help" we should surely be in a position to dictate our terms to the British government and secure "<u>at least autonomy!</u>"

The "war" in Ireland would compel England "to surrender" to us! Was there ever such a Mind in the World! If sincere and he believed what he said, he was a bigger fool than any I had yet met – and if not sincere he must have taken me for that man.

I could not say what I thought of it at all. I listened, smiled and looked at Monteith across the table.

I even pretended to concur in these manifestations of lunacy or at least I did not say "you are an ass or a rogue." What else could I do? The guns were of service.

If we could get them to Ireland they would be a reinforcement to the armed men there who had already with such inadequate weapons, compelled Great Britain to exclude Ireland from the Conscription Act.

Twenty thousand more armed men and 5.000.000 cartridges would be an added security to keeping Ireland out of the war – all I was now hoping for. Besides I saw it was all we were to get. If I refused this offer – and pointed out all the absurdities of the plan and the grave risks, I should rob Devoy

---

that Berlin regarded the Irish project only as a diversionary tactic within the scope of the overall strategy".

and the Irish in America and my volunteers in Ireland of the <u>only</u> chance of external help that would ever come from Germany.

The Germans would throw the refusal on me – the Irish in America and at home would do the same. The <u>facts</u>, as I knew them, could never be known – all that would be said or seen would be that this govt had offered "generous help" in response to our request and that I had stood in the way and opposed. So I was bound to seem to agree to what was patently the most despicable offer.

I asked for the documents they had got from Devoy to see what he had actually asked for.

They produced <u>at length</u>, a typed copy of a letter dated "<u>16.2.16</u>" and signed by him as Secretary.

This letter[145] stated what he believed to be the situation in Ireland both as regards the govt. forces available, and the number of Volunteers to be counted on.

The former were put at 40.000 men (30.000 troops and 10.000 police) the troops inferior men with little artillery.

The Volunteers were put at <u>10.000</u> already armed, but only some 200 cartridges per rifle, and many thousands available if arms could be supplied. Devoy asked for these, saying that if <u>100.000 rifles and artillery and German officers</u> and artillery men could be landed, there was no doubt of our ability to defeat the British forces.

He suggested Limerick as the best place for the landing – and said that the "rising" would take place on <u>Easter Sunday</u>. The final paragraph of the letter was a request that I should remain in Germany as the accredited representative till the end of the war of the Irish Revolutionary Body!!! Poor, good, brave old man – And it is to get rid of me, him, Ireland, the Treaty and all their commitments they now send out this shipment.

I pointed out to Nadolny that Devoy laid stress on the presence of German officers and some trained artillerymen, and that they were not sending any but only Lt. Monteith and some 20 men of ours at outside <u>not trained</u> in gun practice.

I said no more. I added that the final paragraph it was my obvious duty to disregard and that I should have to accompany the men. He said "<u>of course – it is impossible</u> for you to remain behind. You must be there with them. Everything forces you to go."

I again urged the dire importance of first sending messengers from here ahead to let the "Supreme Council" in Ireland know exactly what was going to be done.

---

[145] Reproduced in Doerries, pp. 181-184

He refused, and put it all on the Admiralty – pointing out that if we raised difficulties on this score they might refuse the ships &c. and the whole enterprise collapse.

The trawlers would be accompanied by a submarine – that was all! He would cable Devoy, and he, Devoy, would have to arrange everything with the men in Ireland. Meantime he would go to the General at the War Dept, and get the men Lt. Monteith should pick out at <u>once trained</u> in machine gun exercise. I pointed out that this would take some days – to get the permission &c. &c. and that the training could not begin for perhaps a week. He agreed. So that the invasion of Ireland in 1916 is to be with 12 or 20 men, (who are not to be told in advance a word!) and who are to have perhaps a week's practice with a machine gun at Zossen!

We are all to go on the trawlers (dressed as sailors in English made clothes, got from some of the interned British prisoners in Germany) (this was my idea) – "accompanied by a submarine", round by way of Norway &c. &c. to the West coast of Ireland. Or possibly in "a steamer." What a fine party! Was there ever seriously put forward by a great military power in the world such a proposal! And if I point out its stupendous idiocy, its fundamental falsity, its foredoomed failure, I shall be held, to all ages, in Irish history, as a "traitor", as the man who, at the moment of destiny, failed his country's cause and prevented the great German Empire from extending "military help" to revolutionary Ireland. My God! was ever sane man in such a position!

I left the G.G. Staff with Monteith at about 12.10 and walked back with him across the Tiergarten by the pond, behind the hideous and appalling Hohenzollerns of the Sieges Allée. How I loathe that Allée! – how I abhor these grotesque and ponderous monstrosities in marble – fitting types of the line of coarse and selfish heads of this Prussian abortion.

I told Monteith all my fears – but how I saw clearly I <u>had</u> to go. He agreed that I could not stay behind.

He also agreed with me that in any case, without a German army corps, any "rising" in Ireland by ourselves alone is hopeless – worse than hopeless.

But to attempt it with this meagre "help", under such conditions is madness and criminal. He agrees to it and sees the hopelessness, but feels with me it is our duty to try and get the rifles into Ireland. We have no right to stand in the way of that attempt. I explained to him that my only hope in going is to arrive in time to dissuade the leaders at home from the attempt. That if I can only get ashore a little ahead of the rifles I may be able to stop the "rising" and arrange for the safe delivery of the rifles. If this can be done <u>then</u> (and then only) would the thing prove useful. Otherwise it is an awful danger. Of course the chances are we shall never get near the shores of Ireland.

If it is too "dangerous" for a submarine to go off that coast, how do they expect "the steamer" or the trawlers loaded up with rifles &c. to escape observation. The thing is worse than mad – it is dishonest.

The more I think of it, the more I do believe it to be an act of dishonesty. It is to get rid of us – "the Brigade," me, the Treaty with Ireland, and all of their responsibilities to us, founded on their past dealings with me and with the Clan in U.S.A. – on the cheapest possible terms to themselves, under the pretence of complying with our request and furnishing us with the very aid we had asked for.

In any case <u>they</u> stand to lose nothing. The 20.000 rifles &c. will be captured Russian guns probably – so, too, the machine guns – probably English machine guns captured in Flanders. The handful of German sailors who will navigate "the steamer" or trawlers I fully expect will be instructed to take to their boats at the first sign of capture and get off in the "accompanying submarine"! We should be left to our fate.

That is, probably, why she accompanies us, with the added hope that possibly she may succeed in torpedoing the English cruiser, or war vessel that overhauls us. Should we be captured, well and good – Germany has "done her part." She tried, sincerely, to help us "to the best of her ability" under the naval conditions prevailing and the failure was a chance of war. At any rate she <u>tried</u> to fulfil her pledge.

The Irish in America should be assured of this – we should be dead, or in jail and the alliance in U.S.A. would continue to strengthen Bernstorff and impede Wilson and the pro-Britons.

If on the other hand, we arrive in Ireland (by a miracle) then the subsequent events don't concern Germany at all. Our hideous failure – a "rebellion" whiffed out in a few discharges of constabulary rifles, or at best of machine guns – would be our failure – not theirs.

No German officer or man would be in it – and even proof that the arms came from Germany would be wanting – or at least no publicity would attach – as the English government would hush up, for naval reasons, the successful landing, if we succeed in landing.

The only object <u>this</u> government (the German govt.) has in <u>now</u> offering us this meagre and belated help is to continue the fooling of the Irish in America and possibly a far off hope that we <u>may</u> create some little complication for England in Ireland. They know <u>nothing</u> about Ireland – and not much about England. They are incapable of understanding the minds of other men – or of dealing with free men. They have no conception of personal freedom or of how men used to free action and free thought think. Their sole method of dealing with other people is to apply the methods used at home to their own too obedient, servile drilled and disciplined population.

[Casement's note at end of page:] (I was wrong here – they had and have a far worse object – viz, bloodshed in Ireland. The guns are to be a real gift of death. I have seen for days now that no action of mine can stop the guns. They are determined to send them as they have arranged for bloodshed as their price. R.C. 8.4.16)

Certainly from this point of view of foreign government, Germany does not deserve to win this war. Her people do deserve to win – for they are innocent and victims – and England is certainly attacking them not because of Prussian militarism but because of German commercialism. Still, the emperor and the gang around him are a hard nut for the world to deal with.

In some ways I have acquired sympathy for the English standpoint when I contrast the individual candour, truthfulness and straightforwardness of the Englishman with the absence of these qualities in the governing classes here – or indeed in almost any section of the people. Collectively a great nation – individually an undesirable one.

Here comes Gaffney[146] – so I must stop for the present. I have written all the morning nearly – and shall try to go on here and at Munich between this and the 4th or 5th April when I must return to this horrible city to go to my doom. I don't mind that, if only I could feel that there was some way out for Ireland and those at home, who are <u>so</u> misled into believing that "help will come from Germany."

I see no way out. There is nothing for it but to go on to what I know leads only to ghastly failure. I am making an attempt at 3 today, through Captain Heydell[147] of the Admiralty, to still try and get off ahead on the submarine or if that cannot be arranged then to try and send John McGoey to Ireland to warn them clearly of the character of the help and the absurd German support.[148]

---

[146] Casement was writing cover notes for his instructions, one a letter to Mrs Gaffney "to give up the trunks." It ran to eight sides of self-justification: "Far from my getting "German gold" it is the Germans have had "Irish gold"!. I have not found any German I may say (except Mrs. Gaffney's maid!) who has done anything for me for nothing – or for love." As for German diplomats like Count Leiden, "I find their society less agreeable than that of an Ammersee peasant. They would all Klick heels to Findlay tomorrow…I hope the German people <u>whom I love</u>, will one day deal faithfully with German Diplomacy which I despise." He did add, "I write, I fear, sometimes in a bitter mood." (NLI 17020 "Eight pages of pencilled notes by Sir Roger Casement on the accusation that he had "sold himself" to Germany, March 26, 1916.")

[147] Captain Heydel or Heidel, not Heydell as spelt by Casement.

[148] Extract from Dudgeon book (2016, pp. 507-8) on the significance of Casement's prescient forebodings expressed to Dr Curry on 26 March 1916 (the day before this diary commences in real time), about being humiliated and degraded by unnamed charges: "The

A Last Page

<u>Munich</u>. Monday 27 March 1916

It is ten days since I began my "final page" [**actually entitled 'A Last Page'**] at Berlin on 17th March. That afternoon at 3 p.m. I went to the Reichsmarineamt[149] and saw Captain Heydell and two other Captains in room 763 who had charge of the project. <u>I learned much more</u>. Captain Stültzer is the chief officer in charge of the business.

---

problem of the second unofficial trial was one that had to be faced as newspapers started to publish reports of, and comments on, the existence of the diaries. In a sense Casement was well prepared for this eventuality having warned his friends in Germany of exactly that and the likelihood of his being hanged. Writing on 26 March 1916 in "a last word for my true friend Charles Curry," (NLI 17026 "…a secret memo from Casement containing instructions concerning his personal belongings and papers, an account of the Findlay affair and his forebodings of the outcome of his imminent venture to Ireland. Munich" - 45 pages.) Casement explained "The English government will try now most to <u>humiliate</u> and <u>degrade</u> me. They will not honour me with a High Treason trial. I am convinced of that. They will rob Ireland of that and they will charge me with something else – something baser than 'high treason' – God knows what…I feel convinced they will seek through some dastardly means to assail me otherwise and break their vengeance on me and Ireland by a coward's blow…It is the most hopeless position a man was ever in…I go to a show trial to be wounded in my honour, to be defamed and degraded with no chance of defence probably and then to a term of imprisonment that will end my days in jail – a convict. For I should not long support the indignities and miseries I should be subject to." Elsewhere in the letter he mentioned that Adler Christensen had been found to have misbehaved in America, which provides a certain context to his remarks. There is also a strong echo of Oscar Wilde's terrible treatment in prison and a fear of experiencing the same.

Not content with "a last word" Casement wrote Curry "a final word" on 6 April repeating these fears. In justification, he explained, "I am wholly pro-German always for the sake and cause of the German people…It is not my own honour is at stake alone but the cause of Irish nationality in the extreme form I have stood for. The British Government will seek to injure both – and one through the other. By assailing me and my character they will hope to blacken my cause too – at any rate to gravely weaken it." (NLI 17027 "A final word' – Roger Casement's last instructions (to Dr. Curry?) and his reflections prior to his fatal voyage to Ireland. Dated April 6, 1916. 2½ double pages.") These letters, although in some senses just thinking aloud, were an attempt to soften the impact of disclosures which Casement reckoned could not fail to emerge. Even without the diaries there were, he knew, so many other letters and individuals around the world available to incriminate him.

Once the trial started Casement also prepared the ground for his lawyers on the looming homosexual charge. "If they should succeed in insinuating or implying anything discreditable to my character I must bear it – and carry the war into their camp by saying 'allright – you <u>knew</u> all that long ago; yet you suggested my return to your service on 26 October 1914 and three days after were offering a bribe of £5000 for my betrayal and when that failed too you spread this libel or lie about me all over the world. If you believed it how can you justify to the British people your suggestion of 26 October'…If the worst comes to the worst (as I always dread) and my strength can support the ordeal I will save the situation for others – for Ireland and Germany – even if I suffer worse than death." (NLI 31730 "Notes addressed by Roger Casement to his counsel, George Gavan Duffy, during his trial. 1916. Two sheets.")

[149] *Reichsmarineamt,* the Imperial Naval Office.

First, I renewed the appeal for the submarine to take me and two men ahead. They rejected it – peremptorily. I pointed out the grave importance of this step – they met it with alleged naval reasons; the chief being that the Irish coast was very closely watched and the submarine would be <u>caught</u>. How then about the steamer or steamers with the guns? And they said that the shipment would be in "a small steamer of about <u>1000</u> tons, under the Norwegian flag." She would have false papers, of course. <u>She would not be accompanied or convoyed by a submarine</u>! I insisted on this, but Heydell said it would give the thing away. The submarine to keep up with the steamer would have to steam on the surface and then the British cruisers &c. on look out would see the smoke of the submarine alongside and that would damn the steamer and draw closer attention to her. Nothing I could say would change their obstinate refusal to either send anyone ahead by a submarine or to convoy the gun ship by a submarine! This being so I said I should then rely on trying to get a messenger sent over ahead, and I asked them if they would pass John McGoey over the frontier for me. They sent for Captain Isendahl[150] (of last 1915 February reminiscences!) who at once agreed to get McGoey off whenever I brought him in. I said I would have him in there at the Admiralty next afternoon – 18th March. They had a chart (an English Admiralty chart) of the coast of Kerry and pointed out to me where they proposed landing the rifles.

It was to be at Tralee Bay, at Fenit Pier. The steamer with the rifles would come to "Inishtooskert" (the N.W. of the "Seven Hogs"[151] Rocks north of Rough Point), between 20-23 April – and we the Irish were to have a pilot there to bring her in to Fenit. The pilot boat to show 2 green lights (after dark) only for a short time. This information they said had been cabled over to John Devoy and his reply "Allright" dated <u>14 March</u> was shown me!

Now, the previous day, Nadolny at the G.G.S. pretended they had been waiting for me to come to telegraph to Devoy because when I said "you will then cable fully to Devoy" he said "of course" – and yet it is now clear they arranged everything long before I came – for if Devoy's reply is of 14 March when was their cable sent to him? There is a growing mystery in the whole thing – or, rather I see clearer and clearer the game they are playing.

It was on <u>1st March</u> they first told Monteith and he wrote to me the curt letter asking me to go to Berlin at once. They did not tell Monteith immediately they got Devoy's telegram. That is certain. It would be discussed all round. When did Devoy telegraph?

---

[150] Later Konteradmiral [Rear-Admiral] Walther Isendahl, head of Section N of Admiralty staff, to whom the reconnaissance service, counter-espionage, and agents abroad reported.

[151] The Seven Hogs are the Magharee islands, apparently also known as the Seven Hags.

His letter of details was dated 16. Feby 1916 – this followed the telegram. Probably the telegram was sent about the same date as the letter. So that about 18th February or so they had the request for the rifles. Why did they all at once change their studied refusal to supply us with the arms into this gift? Let me think.

Say they got the telegram on 18th Febry it would be discussed by the G.G.S. with the Foreign Office – Both are equally anxious to get out of their Irish obligations – The F.O. bitterly regret the Treaty – the G. Staff "the Irish Brigade." Here was a chance of killing two birds with one stone!

They might ship the Brigade to Ireland with a load of rifles – and as they knew me quite well enough they knew I would go too – and then there would be an end of the whole engagement to help Ireland. I feel more and more convinced this was the scheme. (It was only part of it – a minor part, the real thing was the "Irish rising" 8.4.16)

Why else did Mr. Meyer send me on 29 February "<u>in these times</u>" Robert Emmet's dying speech?

When I got Assessor Meyer's letter and that typed copy of the death speech I was ill in bed at the Kuranstalt. I could not imagine why it was sent to me.

[Casement note at top of page:] Here it <u>is – just as</u> received.[152]

The idea of the German Foreign Office typing Robert Emmet's last speech for me whom they have so often ignored and derided, and after their attempt to evict Father Crotty in January and February too – (<u>his letters herewith too</u>) made me wonder at the time as to their motive.

Now I see it. Certainly, then, by 29 February the Foreign Office and the G.G.S. were agreed that the request of the Clan–na–Gael for rifles was an admirable chance of shipping off the whole Brigade and myself – and getting rid of the galling obligation they had so "chivalrously" assumed of "good will to Ireland." The Robert Emmet letter to me on 29 Febry was to prepare my mind.

Then, when all was decided on and the Admiralty agreed to furnish ship &c. &c. they send for Monteith on 1 March and tell him of the telegram, of the expected letter of details from Devoy, and of their willingness to supply "up to 200.000 rifles." Liars!

Another point – Monteith told me Nadolny had urged him "on no account to worry me lest I might not be well enough to go"! (See Monteith

---

[152] NYPL Maloney IHP, Box 1, Folio 21: Richard Meyer, in a cover note dated 28 February, only wrote, "Dear Sir Roger, I have much pleasure in sending you herewith the last speech of Robert Emmett (1803) which might interest you to read again in these days. With best wishes for your cure." Casement inscribed on it, "R in bed – March 1st, 1916. at Munich. 38.5 tempt. Attached to this letter was a copy of Robert Emmett's Speech in the Dock."

letters). Nadolny's impudent pretence that with these guns I could dictate terms to the British government was really the last straw. The whole thing is dastardly. They are I verily believe, rather hoping we shall all caught and hanged or jailed for life.

Captain Heydell said they thought it likely the steamer might be stopped by a Br. auxiliary cruiser and a prize crew put on board to take her into a British port – in the event he said "your only chance will be to throw the prize crew overboard" and go on with the ship. I said we would go one better. We would try and capture the prize crew and bind them, not kill them, and take their uniforms for the Irish boys who would then become the prize crew!

I left the Admiralty even more hopeless than the G.G.S. the day before. The thing gets plainer and plainer. It is a regular plot to get rid of their Irish obligations on the very cheapest terms to themselves, with the least risk and least publicity.

And what will the Clan be doing? They have been told that a ship will be at Fenit on a certain date (20-23 April) but have they been told she will have only 20.000 rifles and 10 machine guns and no German officers or artillerymen?

I feel sure not. They have been led to believe that Devoy's letter is being favourably considered and the "goods" supplied – while, in truth, they are avoiding the fundamental issues raised by Devoy – our lack of officers in Ireland and of trained artillerymen &c. &c.

I went back to the Saxonia Hotel, in a very despondent mood and sent for John McGoey to be brought in next day.

Here again, in his case the military have behaved with their usual disregard of promise or promises.

I had applied for his release on 28 Febry and no reply had been received – see the accompanying correspondence attached here **[not attached in NLI but in NYPL]**[153]

[Casement to Major von Baerle (with cover letter by Monteith) dated 28 February 1916:]

"I have the honour to transmit the inclosed request from Sir Roger Casement for the discharge of Pte J McGoey from the Irish Brigade at Zossen in order that he may proceed to America on Sir Roger's behalf."

[Casement note:] "No answer was given to this request – the customary form of official courtesy in this country. R.C."

– John McGoey had come over from U.S. as a Volunteer, to help me in

---

[153] NYPL Maloney IHP, Box 1, Folio 5

any way, with strong recommendations from J. McGarrity. As I could do nothing else with him at the time, I sent him out to Zossen to the "Brigade" on the conditions prescribed in the undertaking he signed on 2 December 1915 which provided for him "immediate" release whenever I should need him for other service. In February I wished to send him back to U.S. to warn our friends there of the double dealing and faithlessness of this government – and how little reliance we could place in anything they said.

Now – as the letter for his release had been ignored, I told Monteith just to bring him in to me without anyone being asked good, bad, or indifferent. I would arrange for the War Office being told once I got him out of the country.

McGoey was brought in next day – I explained all the situation to him very fully and pointed out the imperative need of trying to get some one into Ireland to warn them there of the wholly inadequate help being given and to say that I strongly urged no "rising." He (like Monteith) was with me here. McGoey said it would be criminal and that he had long suspected the Germans of playing a double game. He would do anything I asked him to. I told him it was necessary for me to keep silent as to my real opinions before the G.G.S. and that when I took him to the Admiralty he must do the same.

We went at 11.30 o'clock and found the three Captains again – all was explained to John McG. He is to go as an added string to our bow (in addition to the telegram to Devoy) to tell the Dublin Council to have the pilot boat ready at Inishtooskert &c. &c. – but he goes really to try and get the Heads in Ireland to call off the rising and merely try to land the arms safely and distribute these.

My view, sent by John McG., was that we should try to get the arms &c. landed – and once distributed among 20.000 Irish Volunteers. We are so much the stronger as against the Coalition govt and then we might perhaps find means of getting further rifles &c. from Germany. Make them keep Frey's offer of 200.000 rifles!

Captain Isendahl said a police agent would come for McGoey at my hotel that evening, to identify him, and that he would go next morning 19th via Warnemünde – with no papers or passports and be put over into Denmark – I agreed – and that night I gave John McG full instructions. The police agent came at 7 and was to return at 7.30 a.m.

[Casement note to John McGoey:]

Instructions to John McGoey.[154]
19.3.16
Send word from Copenhagen when you start.

---

[154] NLI 17580 and Maloney IHP, Box 2, Folio 17; written on Hotel Saxonia notepaper

This can be done through the German Legation.
The German Minister can send word to the Foreign Office here to let Captain Monteith know when you sailed.

[John McGoey's unfinished farewell letter:][155]

18 March 1916
Dear Comrades:
The hopes of seeing you again and, on let us trust a brighter morning for Ireland and her children, cheers me now. For on that day we will have a fuller and truer conception of the motives that imperatively demanded my apparently cold and feelingless departure. However I full realized that despite my **[ends abruptly]**
[In Casement's handwriting:] John McGoey's farewell to his comrades. 18 March 1916, Berlin

The chief satisfaction I have is to think that I am successful getting John McGoey out of the country over the heads of the War Office and the others – who have been so ill–mannered. If he gets safely through to Dublin he is to seek out Tom Clarke, and through him B. Hobson and try to "call off" the rising and get them to concentrate only on the successful landing of the guns.

The name of the steamer not yet known. They could tell me on Tuesday, but I said it was more important to get John McG off at once than keep two or three days just to learn the name.

He left Sunday morning 7.30 with the Detective – and I can only pray and hope he got across the frontier all right and that he may be able to get a ship at Copenhagen to Scotland.

I gave him (against his will) 300 mks in Danish money – the hotel porter got it changed for me – and then 350 marks in German money – I saw him off at 7.30 on the stairs of the hotel with a last blessing and greeting in Irish.

[Newspaper cutting tipped in with headline, name, date and comment:]
'*Zum Schutz vor "Möwen"* [**'Seagull'**] Augsburger Zeitung, 24 March 1916
(Since the above, the "Greife" has been sunk by the English)

The chance of getting any steamer thro' is enormously lessened by the Möwe's exploit. The English have a ring of patrol boats right across from Orkney to Norway and I don't think there is a ghost of a chance of our getting through. The more one considers the whole thing, the more certain it is that the chief aim of this government is to "cut their losses" – and shuffle out of all dealings with Ireland.

The Emperor had doubtless again changed his mind – or those round him

---

[155] NLI 13085/24 (original); written on Hotel Saxonia notepaper

have changed it for him. Just as he once played with President Kruger – so he is now trying to do with Ireland – blowing hot <u>and</u> cold. But this is more dastardly far than the abandonment of Kruger – because this <u>is</u> the <u>betrayal</u> of me into the hands of the English!

They know well we shall be taken – and they know the fate that means for me surely, and perhaps for the poor young soldier boys.

The only thing I can see is that by going with them I may save them – as the English will be content with catching me and putting the blame all on my shoulders. But I cannot imagine a more cowardly proceeding by any government than this one arranged by three Departments of State to get rid of a handful of poor men they have deceived and of an obligation that has become hurtful to them.

If I live to make all clear – someday – but there is no chance of that. And yet it is only right the truth should be known and told – for history is history, however govts and rulers change their minds – and it is historical fact that the German government made a Treaty with Ireland and promised recognition of complete independence following on the attempt they were pledged to of conveying military aid. And this is the way they try to fulfil the pledge! To invade a great Kingdom with 12 men – dressed as sailors. Was ever such a thing seriously put forward! They are really beneath contempt.

I told Gaffney who was constantly with me that John McG. was going back to Philadelphia to McGarrity.

That Sunday afternoon (19 March) Gaffney and I went out to Zossen to attend the funeral of poor Holohan, the first member of the Brigade to die. He died on Patrick's Eve – and the priest Monteith had got down to confess the men on Patrick's Day arrived 20 minutes before his death – God be praised.

All the poor lads fell on their knees and recited the rosary when they heard of Holohan's death.

Today the funeral was well done, and the Priest who had been in Ireland, preached a fine sermon over the grave. Some of the boys cried. Then Gaffney, Monteith and I went out to the camp and Gaffney sang a stave of "The Boys of Wexford."

We returned at 7 to Berlin.

Of course Gaffney knows nothing.

Nadolny impressed (on 16th March) on Monteith and myself the absolute necessity of "secrecy" – And here is the second part of the proposal. As soon as we are gone with our party, the rest of the Brigade are to be locked up "in prison" Nadolny said, until it is known we are safely across! A fine fate! And who will ever see them out of prison? I said, in answer to this proposal that of course they remembered they were committed to sending the men to America – and he said "of course, of course." It is all "of course" – of a course with much else I have found at their hands.

How can I go with it? What am I to do? Whatever way I turn misery, failure, degradation and no way out. I know not what to do. I have told Monteith the acute fear I have – not physical or for myself, but for Ireland and our national cause. We are being put in an abject position – and this by this great almighty Power.

I left Berlin again on 23rd March for Munich intending to spend some quiet days and write my diary up at Riederau – but I cannot!

I went to Riederau on 24th and stayed over to 25th walking in to Diessen.[156] I returned on Saturday 25th to Munich and decided to go to Berlin on Sunday 26th. Took tickets and packed and at 8.45 when about to leave hotel, a feverish attack came on. I knew it would get worse in night – so at last moment I decided to stay. No use arriving at Zossen ill, with high temperature to go to bed. My last week in Berlin will be a very busy one. So here I am in bed this Monday – better and determined to go in morning by first train.

I shall be in Berlin tomorrow night 7 p.m. and go to "Saxonia" and talk things over with Monteith. He only got the machine gun to begin practice on 25th March – nine days after Nadolny spoke of getting it. They will have a little over a week's training – and it is <u>ten months</u> since they were taken from Limburg with the promise to be "at once" trained and equipped.

I am getting more and more disposed, as I lie in bed here in Munich (with 6 grills [sic] of aspirin in me) to put my foot down and call off the whole thing – so far as I can.

Unless they agree to send a submarine with us – then all might be different. I shall talk it over with Monteith tomorrow night.

Berlin 29 March 1916 – Wednesday

I arrived here last night at 6.50 from Munich. Monteith came. He agreed with my view that the thing is worse than mad. "Dastardly" is his expression – mine too.

He is training the whole 38 men at the machine gun at Zossen but says

---

[156] Dr Curry's descendants still live in the Riederau area of Bavaria, north of Diessen. Hugh Casement wrote of a building, the Seerichterhaus, once a courthouse: The entrance door opened into a large hall running the whole length of the building and two storeys high. Stairs at one end led to a gallery around three sides of the hall. On the staircase was a plaque (one of many) to Roger Casement. This was previously on the outside of the hotel where he stayed in 1915. That guest house no longer exists, being demolished in the 1960s. The plaque had been unveiled by Dr Curry shortly after Casement's execution in 1916 and carried the (translated) text: '*Here in the summer of 1915 lived Sir Roger Casement, a martyr for Ireland's freedom, a generous friend of Germany in difficult times. He sealed the love of his country with his blood*' (see p. 272). It may be in the village museum now.

only about 12 "at outside" can be counted on. I told him my last idea arrived at yesterday while lying ill in Munich waiting for the doctor – viz – to point out the grave wrong (and risk to Germany too) of sending the men. That to do so is a breach of faith of the kind to them and a flagrant breach of the agreement of 28 <u>December</u> 1914. Moreover, it means that once we are captured the men would naturally and rightly point out the falsehood and the trick played on them by the German government and recount the many breaches of faith perpetrated on them. The English government would be pleased, perhaps, to pardon the men to make the perfidy of the German govt. all the stronger and plainer. As to the "rising" itself in Ireland I am and have been always hopeless on that point, or rather absolutely convinced that without serious foreign aid, say 5.000 men <u>at least</u> and plenty of guns &c. &c. it would be worse than a disaster. To attempt it with <u>this</u> help is – well is a masterpiece of idiocy that admits only of one explanation. That explanation is clear. The German govt want to bury the "folly" of the Brigade – the Treaty and all their coquetting with "Irish rebellion" in this paltry gift of 20.000 rifles, leaving us to bear the shock and pay the piper and they want bloodshed in Ireland.

My view is still we should try and get the guns across. If we don't do that we run counter to the strong wish of those at home and in America who are counting on this at least. The guns, if landed, are an asset and to merely land them need not necessarily involve any bloodshed – or serious trouble, if the men in Ireland can act well.

Having sent as I hope John McGoey to Ireland to explain the meagre help coming and the dire need of <u>not</u> rising I feel we should still try and get the guns over – <u>but not at the cost of the lives of these poor chaps at Zossen</u> – the attempt at any rate. This in no wise requires the presence of the 12 boys from Zossen. That part of the proposal is so manifestly a put up game here between the G.G.S. and the Foreign Office to get rid of the embarrassment of the "<u>Irish Brigade</u>" that it does not really fall into the affair at all.

Devoy asked on 16 February for 100.000 rifles, trained artillerymen, officers and plenty of cannon and suggested Limerick as place of landing. They replied to that request (in terms I have not yet seen) **[later ink insert:]** (I have never been shown their reply yet 8.4.16) saying a ship, or ships, would be at Fenit by 20-23 April to which on 14 March he is said to have answered "Allright." I arrived on 16 March in Berlin and saw the G.G.S. at 10.30 a.m. I was not told that they had already telegraphed Devoy and got his reply, but I was led to believe that they would telegraph to him now that I "approved" the plan.

My "approval" consisted of pointing out that I was willing and anxious to go to help my countrymen, being worse than useless here, and for the rest that what they were sending did not tally at all with what Devoy had asked for.

The whole thing was sprung on me and the only clear thought I had was that those making it were false-hearted scoundrels and if I could get out of their clutches soonest this risk I'd go and try to stop the whole thing. Then came the interview at the Admiralty next day, 17 M'ch and following day 18th, with John McGoey and John McGoey's departure on 19th. No news from him yet. I have waited these days, pondering it all, day and night and hoping to get a card from John McGoey saying he was off. Once I am sure he is clear and away I shall feel more free to deal with the situation here. (He was to send a card to "Mr Hammond" at Auswärtiges Amt[157] when sure of getting away from Denmark to England. None came yet 8.4.16) x

Now today 29.3.16 I am sending a note to Captain Heydell to say I wish to see him and I shall go round and tell them there, first, that I object to the soldiers going at all – but am willing to go myself. That I regard the thing as quite hopeless and wish to limit the number of victims to myself. I will draw out a Memo, giving all the overmastering reasons and send to the Admiralty after I have discussed with them.

[At top of page:] M'ch 29. 1916

They are much franker and straighter than the G.G.S. or F.O. and are far more likely to speak the truth. They are merely innocent agents in the matter, carrying out as well as they can the wishes of the German government as represented by the G.G.S. and Foreign Office – whose object is to get rid of us all under pretence of complying with Devoy's request – and above all to ensure bloodshed in Ireland.

I shall not say anything of this to the Admiralty – but merely express my personal objections to sacrificing the men who trusted in me and the Treaty of 28 Dec. 1914.

Monteith agrees entirely – He would go further and stop the rifles too – as likely to provoke bloodshed in Ireland even if successfully landed.

I reply to that, that we are ignorant of all the plans & methods in U.S.A. and Ireland and it is not right to rob them of this tiny offer of help which need not necessarily involve more bloodshed than Howth if the parties to get the guns do their duty. At any rate, as things are I dare not accept the responsibility of stopping the guns, (even if I could do so!) and leaving the men in Ireland in the lurch.

I am sending this note to Heydell:

---

[157] *Auswärtiges Amt* (AA) – German Foreign Office

29 M'ch 1916
Dear Captain Heydell,
I arrived last night (having been detained two days by a return of the influenza attack) and shall be very glad to see you today whenever convenient to you. There are some things of importance to discuss and I will call at any hour you name.
Yours sincerely,
Roger Casement.

The things I jot down for this interview are the following: –

1. To show me the <u>exact</u> text of the cablegram they sent to Devoy to which he replied on 14 March "allright."
   <u>What</u> was the exact offer they made? I know his demand – what have they told him they are doing?
2. To point out the grave risk of sending Lt. M and the men – how it may fatally compromise German honour before the world – and how it is really in direct contradiction with the solemn promises of the German government in the Treaty.
   If the men are captured as is almost inevitable, they would be regarded as victims of German duplicity and the case against Germany would be overwhelming. I shall not say this all out brutally – but let them see the danger – I shall insist that I go with my eyes wide open, knowing I go to a dreadful fate and that I don't intend to have my innocent young countrymen risk their necks too so hopelessly.
   I shall tell them too, I mean to have poison with me – and that I go really so that they here in Germany shall not say I was a coward.
3. To get the name of the steamer, the port she goes from, the date and hour of departure – and when I must go and be on board, if it is still decided that I go after I put my foot down on the shipping of the men.
   It is probable, highly probably, I think, when the G.G.S. and F.O. learn that I am resisting the shipping off of the "Irish Brigade" they will recall the whole thing and give up the attempt even to lend the arms – putting the "blame" for the abandonment on my shoulders. (I was nearly right there! <u>R.C. 8.4.16</u>)
4. I will ask to be allowed to communicate by wireless with John Devoy, (I did not know until Monteith told me in Munich on 7 March that J.D. had any means of communication with Germany in cypher or they with him. Another proof of their double dealing! They <u>never</u> told me they could send messages for me to him in cypher and never once offered – and from the first day I landed they have always used some card or

trick up their sleeve and have never been frank or straightforward. It is a vicious bureaucracy indeed).

[At top of page:] Wednesday 29 M'ch 1916 – Cold

At the Admiralty I was sent to Captain Stultzer.[158] Heydell came and brought in the chief naval officer Captain -??- in charge of the details of the shipment and the Captain of the steamer. Latter young, tall and frank – a fine young fellow.

I told them that I feared to take any of the Irish soldiers – on political grounds – that if captured the men would surely turn "King's evidence" and rightly and blame would be on the German government. They saw the gravity and said I'd better go to the G.G. Staff at once. The <u>whole</u> scheme was controlled and directed from there – The Captain ?? said he would come with me. We rang up Nadolny and went on in Captain ??'s motor car – a gov't one.

At the Abteilung BIII of the G.G.S. I found Nadolny and his two aides – von Hülsen and Haugwitz. The Captain explained my fears about taking the men, and I added some remarks –

Nadolny became very angry and exceedingly rude – and von Hülsen glared at me with bleary eyes and whispered to the Naval Captain. The only one who behaved well and is a gentleman is the young Count von Haugwitz. It was a most unseemly exhibition of German military culture.

I gave back as much as I got and insisted on the whispering stopping and the conversation being conducted in a language I understood, either English or French.

The chief cause of the fury was my having sent John McGoey to Ireland! I nearly laughed in Nadolny's face. He said it was a gross breach of faith. I told him he was a liar. He said he would cable J. Devoy and say that owing to my action the German govt. now refused the rifles. I said he might do so if he pleased – but that his statement would be an obvious falsehood.

I asserted my absolute right to send a messenger to Ireland – that McGoey had come for this <u>very purpose</u> – sent by the Clan – and that unless I was to assume which, with a shrug I said I clearly was – I had entire freedom to communicate with my countrymen in Ireland and America. If Nadolny cabled I presumed I should be permitted the same action – "No" he roared – I will tell your countrymen it is you have robbed them of the guns they asked for – The Naval Captain having had his ears filled by Huelson got up and scarcely looking at me went out – I stayed on and talked more with Haugwitz than the others. Nadolny went and came – so did Huelson – Haugwitz stayed with me – a gentleman. Their fear was that I had sent John McGoey to stop

---

[158] Probably Kapitan Albert Stölzel, not 'Stultzer'.

Count Curt Haugwitz-Hardenberg-Reventlow

the rising! They asked again and again if I had given him instructions to that effect. I said I was not the master of the Irish Revolutionary body and whatever I might say would only be advice or suggestion. I avowed that John McGoey himself was dead against a rising, and the fury was uncontrolled.

How had I dared to send such a man to Ireland without letting them know!

I saw in clear sharp light, the whole devilish game – Devoy was being fooled too – had been fooled I felt convinced by the ass von Papen. Devoy, an old man, of passionate feeling against England, burning for <u>one</u> brave fight before he dies, had been assured of the entire good will of Germany and of strong military aid. His letter of <u>16.2.16</u> showed what he expected <u>at least</u>, and asked for.

These people wanted only bloodshed in Ireland for their own ends – and the fatal steamer was to be the price of the rising. I was being shipped by her, merely to get me out of the scene, tear up the Treaty, and having had their "rising" in Ireland, for what it might be worth to them – then they could wash their hands of all further connection or contact with "the Irish." I had possibly spoiled this game by sending John McGoey across, and at any rate gravely <u>imperilled</u> the "rising" coming off – or "<u>the War in Ireland</u>" as Nadolny termed it!

<u>Wed</u> 29 M'ch

I saw this clearer and clearer – the "rising" was the thing – the only thing really they were after, and it was only for this the ship was going and the rifles. Shipping me on her (and the men at Zossen) was but a side show. They were relieved of the embarrassment of our presence and of the pretence of keeping faith where no faith was. I explained to Haugwitz my entire right to send McGoey – turning my back on Nadolny – and showed how the "breach of faith" was on the side of the War Office and F.O. who tried, I said, "to play battle door [sic] and shuttlecock with me." When I asked for his being put at my disposal in February, as they were bound to do in virtue of the Declaration he signed in 2 December last on entering the camp at Zossen.

They had ignored those repeated requests – mine to F.O. and Monteith to von Baerle.[159]

[Monteith to Casement:]

Hotel Saxonia
Berlin, W 9, den 22.2.16.
[**Casement note:**] R. in Berlin
   Dear Sir Roger.

I forgot to tell you this morning the amount we have in bank, after drawing the amount I handed you this morning and paying the men to date, it is roughly <u>mks 4970</u>. I had to pay mks. <u>143.50</u> for blankets which some of the boys made away with.

   Faithfully yrs,
   R. Monteith.

---

[159] NYPL Maloney IHP, Box 2, Folio 1 (original and typescript); typescript is also in NLI 17587/4.

[**Casement note in pencil:**] Mks 5000. On Feb 22 1916 in Bank at Zossen & with me 3200 Mks

Monteith came in today (a second time) with J.McG. whom I wish to send away – He was kept 1½ hours waiting by Mr. Meyer at F.O. and then whisked off in 2 minutes with a reference to Major v. Baerle (who is an idiot) & told that – "if the War Office agree" (!) then Mr. Meyer will provide J.McG. with papers to go away! So courteous! So full of goodwill – they are Swine and Cads of the first water – not one of them with the Soul of a Rat or the Mind of a Cur –

They certainly deserve to be thoroughly well taught in the first rudiments of Humanity & Kindliness – for as they are, they are lower than the Congo Savages in most things that constitute gentleness of mind, heart or action.

When Monteith had gone to F.O. with my request of 19 Feb for John McG's release, Assessor Meyer had asked first: "Why does Sir Roger want him?" Monteith said he knew nothing – only my orders – Then Meyer said the matter concerned the War Office and if they released McGoey then the F.O. would give him a pass to cross the frontier. I told von Haugwitz he should get my letters on the subject from the War Office and I added with a laugh "I've taught them and your F.O. a lesson in politeness" – He blushed.

Finally – it was two hours or more I had been there – Nadolny who had been going and coming to his other rooms, came and sat down and said "Well Sir Roger Casement, you must promise to do nothing – to move no hand or finger in this matter and to communicate with no one – we shall decide what course we will take." I said: "I can tell no one – you take good care of that – you have me here virtually a prisoner." He laid stress on my not communicating "with America." I said "How can I?" You hold all the channels of my communication with America and anything I send there is read by your people. Let us talk sense.

I shall certainly communicate as I choose with Lt. Monteith – my officer. He started and I saw a look in his eyes – "How can you forbid me to do that?" He is here in command of my men, with the sanction and recognition of your government under my orders – and I shall tell him anything I choose, the only thing I regret is I have not twenty faithful John McGoeys!" He gulped with rage. "Very well" he said – "tomorrow we shall decide what we shall do and act as we think fit." I said "no one can prevent you."

Coming back from this revelation of depravity and cowardice and of worse – of attempted blackmail – I met Gaffney – and he said Noeggerath wanted to see me – so we went together. There – in great distress of mind I made both promise to keep silent and told them all. I did it to enlist Noeggerath's action with F.O. to see if pressure could not be exercised there to see that I got a fair deal and above all that the men at Zossen were spared the ordeal

I had to go thro'!

Noeggerath promised to act at once and telephoned there and then to Undersecretary Zimmermann to seek an appointment for tomorrow. Z. gave it by phone while I was there for the morrow "between 12 and 1" in the Reichstag "to come by the Tiergarten entrance."

I told him what I wanted – to impress on Z. the grave danger of taking the men on board the ship – since they would assuredly be bound to give the German govt. away under question, and expose how it had not kept faith with them. My true reason is to get the men saved as Monteith implores me to do.

They came back to dinner with me at Saxonia and talked till late.

Thursday. 30 M'ch

I did not sleep all last night. I had fever and tossed in misery on my bed.

At 10 a.m. or so I got a telephone call from Nadolny asking me to go to see him soon – I said 3, as I was to see Noeggerath before he went to 2 – Nadolny replied that would be too late, as he would have to decide by 12. Then I said 10.30 and tore off to Noeggerath's office. He came fortunately while I was there. I told him I had to see Nadolny at once. He said "try to gain time and play for that."

I went on to the German Gr. Staff at 10.30 or 40 and found Nadolny alone. He said as follows:–

"The plan of aiding your countrymen in Ireland was proposed to us from your friends in America. We had and have no responsibility in it, beyond trying to the best of our ability to comply with their request. It is not our plan. Your countrymen in Ireland are determined, they assert, to rise on a given day – your friends in U.S.A. appeal to us for help. We knew nothing of it before Mr. Devoy's telegram came and all our subsequent action has been based on that. You know our proposals and we have sent them to Mr. Devoy. He agrees."

Thursday 30 M'ch [At the top of page 63 someone has inscribed, "Where does this corner lead to?" The following paragraph is written down the side of the page:]

He said much more. He said "We have no idealistic interest in Ireland and no revolution, no rifles. If it were not that we hope for a military diversion there we should not give the rifles." I said I could guarantee no revolution and that I sincerely hoped there would be none! I was profoundly against it unless there was great military support and they were giving none – practically three men in a boat to invade a Kingdom. The thing was an insult to my intelligence and either he was a fool or thought I was one to speak as he had once about "autonomy." But as things were I was forced to try and get the rifles to Ireland since they had so planned things that the "rising" seemed certain thro' their promises and these promises I did not know but could guess.

You oppose the project – or you are hindering it. The soldiers are an essential part to its success. The Naval men say so. The machine guns must be ready to come into action as soon as the steamer arrives. We have no other men to send. If they don't go the whole thing may collapse – I shall cable to Mr. Devoy and say owing to your action we are compelled to withdraw from the matter at the eleventh hour, and leave your countrymen in Ireland in the lurch – and all the responsibility falls on your shoulders.

I protested that this was gravely unfair – that they were not, to begin with, complying with Mr. Devoy's request at all – but sending a far smaller consignment of arms than he had asked for <u>and no officers</u> on which he had laid such vital stress. He had never asked, either, for me or for the Irish soldiers. I personally had to go – that was evident and required no further word. I had to stand beside my friends in their resistance whatever it might be and take all the consequences, since I was so largely responsible for the whole situation, although not for this wholly unexpected development. As to the men, I felt a peculiar personal responsibility for their not being captured by the British government. That was my objective today. As to the ship she must go at all costs – I could go alone – but he insisted on the men.

I left him in despair and saw Noeggerath after his interview with Z. He said that Z. had listened very attentively and would act. Also submarines essential.

Monteith had come in to see me before I went to G.G.S. I told him to do so by telephone, by telegram and by special letter. He reported Haugwitz had been out there at 9.30 a.m. ostensibly to see how the men were shooting – really to try and get him, Monteith, to take the men to Ireland over my head. Monteith said it was a clear "try on." He even offered money in shape of "funds for propaganda"! Monteith replied he was here absolutely and solely under the orders of Sir Roger Casement. It was on finding out that they could not capture Monteith (they would then have ignored me completely) that Nadolny phoned me. Haugwitz had come back from Zossen with Monteith – and turned up at the G.G.S. after Nadolny had tried to compel me to assent by his (repeated) threats to denounce me to the Irish in U.S.A. as the man who had stopped the guns and robbed my poor battling countrymen in their hour of need of the only help offered.

I had, apparently, submitted to this threat and left the G.G.S. in complete despair – and I returned to the hotel and saw Noeggerath again, before he went to Zimmermann at the Reichstag. Noeggerath returned at 2 saying he had seen Zimmermann who was interested and said he would look into the matter and do something.

I was in despair – and my fever on me worse than ever. That evening before Monteith returned to Zossen we talked things over. I told him that I should play a last card and write Count Georg Wedel, one of the few men here I had any regard for and tell him just how I saw it all. This with a view to save the men at all costs – that idea was growing firmer and firmer – that they at any rate could not be taken. Monteith begged me to do this – that he thought it infamous to take the men – in any case and especially with the absurd training of only 2 or 3 days already[160] at the machine guns.

He urged me to haste – and I said I'd write that night. I lay awake for hours in despair and at 1 a.m. or 2 a.m. got up and wrote a rough draft of a long letter to Wedel – I did not lie down again until near 5 a.m. and was awake again at 6.30 a.m. 31st.

Von Haugwitz on his return from Zossen apologised to me for going there – saying he had not wished to do anything behind my back.

I absolved him.

He is the only decent man I have met at the G.G.S. the rest are all cads, scoundrels or cowards – and invariable liars.

I have detected Nadolny often, (v. Lübbers once!) Boehm[161] more than once, a Herwarth v. B. &c. &c. There is not one I'd trust out of my sight on any thing.

Friday 31 Mch.

I was ill in bed all day with the Doctor – congestion of lungs threatening – I finished as well as I could the long letter to Wedel. I emphasized so much – and repeatedly the danger of capture to myself because I wanted to excite their fears for themselves. If they could be brought to see that my capture by the British government would reflect on their honour, they would begin to appreciate the importance of my request for the submarine and if I could get that and land in Ireland before this d——d ship and her guns arrive I may stop the whole dreadful thing.

It is for this I will play, but I am so sick and utterly wretched beyond expression. Doctor told me to stay in bed and prescribed usual stuff.

Berlin, Saturday 1 April

---

[160] "(see p. 199)" is inscribed here – no such page exists. This was probably written by an archivist.
[161] Major Hans Boehm helped set up the Irish Brigade and travelled back and forth between the USA and Germany as an agent of Abteilung IIIb. He almost certainly carried messages to and from Clan na Gael as mentioned in Hector C. Bywater, *Strange Intelligence; Memoirs of Naval Secret Service* (London, 1931)

Finished my letter to Wedel[162] – softening down some of the rougher passages. Gaffney came and I read it to him and Lt. Monteith took it (after hearing it) up to Wedel and gave it to him in person. He saw Wedel who said it should have his "immediate attention."

[Casement's cover note to his 30 March letter to Wedel:]

Copy Saturday 1 April 1916.
Dear Count Wedel,
 This letter has been delayed by my continued illness. I am in bed by the Doctor's orders and could write it only in bits at a time. I will get up today and if possible go to Zossen tomorrow. I may say that I wrote this at the wish of Lt Monteith - save that he wishes to accompany me on the ship - but I shall require him to stay with the men.
 They must be looked after when I am gone - it is for their sakes he wished me to write - altho' I had already decided to write you on Thursday before I saw him. If the Gr. Staff wishes to discuss further with me it might be done through Count Hauchwitz [sic] who could come and see me.
 He speaks good English and to some extent I fancy grasps my point of view.
 Personally I shall be delighted to go on this journey, but I cannot bring the men in. Of course Lt. Monteith can come too, if he insists (as I think he will) for he is not in the position the Irish soldiers are in.
    Yours very sincerely,
       Roger Casement.

I was in bed till afternoon when on Drs advice I went out for a very short walk in blazing sun to Thiergarten and then to tea at the Esplanade Hotel with Emerson and my translator Fromme.[163]

 The Zerhusens came – she a dear, kind-eyed Irish woman – Gaffney dined with us.

 I wrote Wedel again today – a short letter pointing out the sole justification I could see for any armed attempt in Ireland – and I was told he had "gone on leave of absence till Thursday."

 I thought he might have gone to the Hauptquartier to intervene and call off the whole thing.

Sunday. 2 April
 Spent day mostly with Gaffney – writing and hoping that Wedel had

---

[162] A copy dated 30 March 1916 consisting of 26 handwritten pages is in NYPL Maloney IHP, Box 2, Folio 6 and in a number of other archives in both manuscript and typed form e.g. NLI 17587/4 and NLI 43227/1. A cover note to the 30 March letter dated 1 April 1916 (original 1 p., and typed copy 1p.) is also in NYPL Maloney IHP, Box 2, Folio 6.
[163] Franz Fromme, Casement's translator who later wrote on Ireland's independence struggle; *Irlands Kampf um die Freiheit* (1933).

taken action of some kind. At near 7 p.m. a phone call from Assessor Meyer to say that Wedel had left my letter to him to read – and they reported that they could do nothing in the matter. It did not concern them – but only the G.G.S. and the Irish in U.S.A. and referred me to the G.G.S. I said that was quite useless – as I always had spoken very plainly there and I saw no object in continuing such uninteresting conversations with those from whom I disagreed so profoundly. He then asked if I would go to the F.O. I said "what is the use of that – if one of you runs away and you have no power in the matter – I shall do nothing. My mind is made up and the men shall not go."

Walked a little bit with Gaffney and dined with him in evening.

Berlin Sunday – 2 April 1916. 6.35 p.m.

This morning I sent a letter (No. 2) to Count Wedel following on that sent yesterday morning (No. 1 of 30 M'ch) – see both.[164]

[Casement 2 April letter to Wedel:]

Berlin 2. April 1916.
Dear Count von Wedel,

After I had sent my letter (of 30th. ult.) to you, I yesterday got a copy of the "Irish World" giving text of Mr. Devoy's speech at the Irish Convention on 4-5 March.

From Mr. Devoy's remarks it is probable that the impending action in Ireland rests on very justifiable grounds and that were I in Ireland I should personally approve it. Mr. Devoy is precise.

He says the American-Irish are not responsible for anything occurring in Ireland - it is Irishmen themselves who will decide their action - all the American-Irish can do is to help if action arises.

This action would depend on that of the British Government. Briefly, Mr. Devoy's contention is:

The 12.000 or so armed Irish Volunteers have forced the British Government to exclude Ireland from the Conscription Bill

The Government are determined to destroy the Irish Volunteers, and once broken up and their leaders in jail, Ireland will be forced by a new Act into the Compulsory Service Camp.

Against this policy the Irish Volunteers are sworn to resistance and will resist. What then should American Irish do? Stand aside - or help?

The answer is clear - help and help largely.

If this be a just statement of the situation I am of Mr. Devoy's way of thinking, and I, too, am most anxious to help, and towards such an effort as this I welcome

---

[164] This letter to von Wedel of 2 April is in the *Politisches Archiv des Auswärtigen Amtes* (PA AA), WK 11k secr., vol. 11 (R 21163) and quoted in full in Doerries pp. 204-5. It was initialled by Wedel on 6 April. Copies are in NYPL Maloney IHP, Box 2, Folio 6 (original 2p. and typed version 1p.), NLI 10880 and TNA HO 144/1637/194A.

the help offered by the German Government. I will very gladly go to Ireland with the arms and do all I can to sustain and support a movement of resistance based on these grounds.

For in this case it is far better for Irishmen to fight at home and resist conscription by force than to be swept into the shambles of England's Continental war and lose their lives in an unworthy cause.

Mr. Devoy's speech removes some of the doubts that had so troubled me.

I, therefore, repeat with greater insistence than in my previous letter - nothing should stop the vessel going next Saturday, with me certainly on board and probably Lt. Monteith.

If he insists I cannot refuse his right. He is not in the position the Irish soldiers are in nor do I incur in his case any responsibility - whereas in theirs I incur the entire responsibility and I must act in their regard in the way that seems right to me.

Believe me, Dear Count Wedel,
Yours sincerely,
    Roger Casement.

The messenger reported that Count Wedel had gone away on "Urlaub"[165] until Thursday next. Gaffney was with me at the time. We both hope that this meant he had gone to the Hauptquartier to try and arrange things as I decided.

I decided to stay here all day, instead of going to Zossen, and now at 6.35 p.m. I get a telephone call from the Auswärtiges Amt from Assessor Meyer –

I record it instantly:–

He said

"Count Wedel left yesterday for some days leave of absence,[166]

[Casement note:] Recd. 30.3.16 in Berlin
Auswärtiges Amt. Berlin, 29th March 1916.
Dear Sir Roger,

I beg to inform you quite confidentially that I have received news from America that a man called Ponsonby Stalleys who pretends to be of Irish descent intends to come over to Germany. As Stalleys is suspected of being a british agent I thought it advisable to warn you, in case he should succeed in reaching Germany.

Believe me, dear Sir Roger
yours sincerely
G. Wedel.

[Casement note:] He runs away on leave of absence – caused by "heart failure"! – on 2 April after getting my letter of 30 M'ch in answer to this – There is a double deceit in this letter. It is to pretend goodwill to me & at the same time ignorance of the fact that I am to be shipped off on 8 April very far indeed from Mr. Ponsonby

---

[165] 'Urlaub' – leave or holiday
[166] NYPL Maloney IHP, Box 2, Folio 6 (original and typed versions)

Stalleys! Poor Wedel – another victim of "soulless efficiency"!
RC

and before going he handed me your letter. He reports he can not do anything in the matter. This has been arranged entirely between the Gr. Staff and the Irish organization in America and we cannot interfere or bring any pressure to bear on them – You must arrange everything with the Gr. Staff and I suggest you seeing Captain Nadolny." I said "I have written very plainly my standpoint and I must abide by it – I cannot and will not be forced into a false position by Captain Nadolny or the Gr. Staff and do what I feel to be wrong."

Mr Meyer said. "We cannot discuss the matter in detail over the telephone" – I agreed – and went on "perhaps you will come here tomorrow and see me?" – I said "What use is there in that, if you the Foreign Office cannot interfere?" – I then asked if he had seen the letter I had written to Count Wedel today – and he said "No – that must be the one lying on his table – I will read it – and then, perhaps I may ring you up tomorrow, but in any case the matter must be settled between you and Captain Nadolny."

I said again that "I am not going to be forced into a wrong position by the Gr. Staff and my last word, or at least my last fixed opinion is expressed in the letter sent to Count Wedel."

So there it stands.

This is the climax of their cowardice and infamy!

The whole thing, so far as they are concerned, is a put up murder plot (in which I am to be one of the victims) and Ireland the chief. Anything more atrocious is hard to conceive.

The war party here – who are supreme, evidently think they had a chance of reaping some military profit from bloodshed in Ireland – and at a very cheap price! (Twelve men in a boat!) – "£200.000" as Nadolny priced it!

The "Irish Brigade" is to be got rid of – and the Treaty with me buried.

The Germans are to have their pound of Irish flesh at all costs.

A more infamous form of blackmail it is hard to conceive.

Wedel runs away on purpose till Thursday! Knowing that by Thursday I shall be "dealt with." What _shall_ I do?

If I go and take the men as the Staff wants me to do – shall _we_ seize the ship and give ourselves up? That is one thought. Anything to punish _these_ scoundrels and ruffians and base, dastardly cowards.

I must see Monteith and talk things over with him tonight.

It _is_ the most damnable position a man was ever put in – and _this_ is the great German government!

My God! What curs and cowards and infamous scoundrels – and these are the ruffians I thought might help Ireland. English rule in Ireland has indeed been a curse – but the English man is a truthful man and a gentleman and his word is sure – and here no one of these men is a gentleman. They don't know the meaning of the name.

11.30 p.m. I saw Monteith and kept him till 11.28 train when he went out to Zossen. We don't know where we are – but we agree that under no circumstances am I to consent to the men going – That M. will accompany me – but we go alone. That is all I can decide.

Tomorrow Meyer will "ring" me up again and say I must see Nadolny &c. I shall decline – and say that they must come to see me – that my mind is made up and I go forward on my terms alone – and part of those are that they come to me to discuss the minor details left. Or if I go to the G. Staff that then I take a witness with me! One or the other. But in no circumstances shall I take any of the soldiers or allow them to go. On that M. and I are fully agreed and beyond that I can dictate nothing. I am already a dead man – but not yet a wholly dishonoured one despite all my mistakes. God knows they were not for self. R.C.

Monday, 3 April 1916

A very bad night. After M. left for Zossen, poor chap, at 11.28 I tried to sleep and did – This morning I wrote a letter more and decided to see a certain lady in whom I could trust. I met her early and told her enough – not anything of the inside matter, merely my awful doubts and the hopeless position in which I was and the use they were trying to make of "the others." I did not say who the others were, and she does not know or guess – but I said I had made up my mind not to budge from my position on that point – and I asked her to keep the two letters (copies) of 30 March and 2 April to W. I handed her these and she promised faithfully to keep them until the end and then to hand them over to the person whose name I gave her and wrote on the cover.[167]

Also I am going to leave my "Diary" as far as it goes with G. I may be arrested, I think, at any moment! The lady said that the Emperor himself was powerless today – he was in the toils too – and was being accused of being "pro-English" – that the whole power of the land was in the hands of Falkenhayn and a small clique and everyone trembled before them. That Falkenhayn was a scoundrel and swayed by "finance" – whatever that means!

---

[167] The lady was Countess, shortly to be Princess, Blücher who passed Casement's letters to British Intelligence in 1918. She was from a very Catholic family in Lancashire and believed Britain needed "a good birching".

She agrees with me that this curse of Prussian militarism is an internal evil that must be fought by the German people themselves and broken from within.

I then saw G. at his quarters – and told him I wanted him to keep papers for me until he could get them in a safe place – if such be in this land today. Everyone is spied on. That is certain. They have had spies on me ever since I came here. She told me of some of the stories circulated against me! She doesn't know half of them.[168]

She does not know the situation I am in – poor lady.

I got at 12 a telephone from von Haugwitz begging me to come to the G.G. Staff at 3 p.m. this afternoon.

I demurred and asked him to come here. He said he could not leave the place – someone was away and it was very desirable we should meet and Captain von Hülsen was not there. I think he said not there. This Captain V.H. is a bleary-eyed pig who has the papers in hand and the whole business is his particular show. Nadolny is the presiding chief of the whole "Political" Department – which is really the Spy Department of the G.G.S. – as things are going and as the time is so short now, I have consented to go at 3 but I feel it is a mistake – yet what can I do? At any rate I must at all costs stick to my guns and help the soldiers here.

Today settles their fate sure – or rather as far as I am concerned that is settled. It settles mine – for ever.

Monday 3 April, 1916

[**This section is stroked out, presumably because it is largely a repetition of the above:**] I called on a lady friend and left a certain paper with her for safety and a brief outline of <u>some</u> of my trouble only.

I had asked Lt. Monteith to wire Fr. Crotty to come at once.

V. Haugwitz begged me by phone to go to G.G.S. this afternoon – very important. I said first you better come here but he said it was impossible and I agreed reluctantly.

I arrived at 3. and found him and von Hülsen there. The first thing they did was to show me a typed paper with the names cut out signed John Devoy

---

[168] Casement also wrote a letter to Curry in NLI 17025 catalogued as, "Photocopy of a letter from Casement to Curry giving instructions on his imminent departure for Ireland and expressing his disillusionment with the German authorities April 3, 1916. Also photocopy of Casement's poem "Treason"."

The letter from the Hotel Saxonia, Berlin opens, "Monday. 3 April 1916. My Dear Dr. Curry, Mr Smith's affairs are in a <u>very</u> bad way and he is the greatest anxiety. He may not be able to write to you again – & if so you will understand the reason. Gaffney knows all about it & can explain to you when he comes if things go as bad as I fear they must go. I see <u>no</u> <u>way out</u>!" It is a hopeless and atrocious situation."

recording Christensen's perfidy in U.S.A. dated Decr. 1915[169]

[Devoy's letter to Casement about Adler Christensen:]

[**Note at top:**] I also enclose letter for Mon[teith] from his wife. It was to have been carried by one of the men who failed to get off. Dec. 19, 1915.
No: 8

Dear Friend: As Joe does not go into particulars about Olsen, [**Adler Christensen**] you will be at a great disadvantage and may think we have nothing definite against him. Unfortunately, the proof is conclusive and overwhelming that he has been swindling us and recklessly and foolishly lying. The reason is a woman whom he brought over with him when he returned here the first time and who is now in a hospital across the river with a new born baby. All his pleas to me for money for his wife – which were in all cases generously responded to – were to keep up the dual establishment. She is the daughter of an official of a Berlin bank.

The first proof we got was when he went to Joe. Early one morning, broken from want of sleep, with a story that he had been robbed of $4.50, a watch and a diamond pen, in a subway train and asked Joe. to lend him the money so that he could pay the passage of three men, for which I had given him $300, as well as $100 for himself. But two nights before he had told me a story which would leave him only $280. Joe. insisted he must tell me and he (Joe.) came on and did so. The robbery story was too ridiculous for me to believe and Joe. did not believe it either, but when Olsen came to me I did not say an angry word and gave him $300 again but told him it placed me in a very bad fix. Then I found he had gone to the man who had given him work and asked $100 to pay for his wife's confinement in a hospital. It so happened that the man knew the doctor who keeps the hospital and I told him his wife[170] could not be in that condition then. He did not give him the money and next day Olsen called again and admitted it was not his wife but a Berlin girl.

Then I found he had got $25 each from three of the men to whom he had seen me give $100 each, so that they might not be short on their arrival. And he told them his money had been stolen in the Hoboken hotel where they all stopped. He said it had been taken out of his trousers pocket which he had hung up in the hall outside the room. One of them was lying awake and saw him take something out of his trousers pocket and then carry the trousers outside. A hotel hand brought it in next morning saying, "This man must walk in his sleep." They did not believe he had been robbed, but they were so anxious to get over that they gave him the money.

He got two men aboard and they were put off in a few minutes. His story of the reason does not hang together at all and does not coincide with theirs – and they are two splendid young men.

They tried the next vessel – staying over there all the time, but failed. For the third vessel, without saying a word to me, he bought third class tickets, giving them Norwegian names, and they were refused admission. They would certainly have been

---

[169] NLI 13073/44/viii
[170] Adler's first wife (of three), Sadie Weaver, in Philadelphia.

taken off, so it was lucky. I had given him the money to pay the boatswain $100 for each. He forgot that he told me the boatswain and now makes him the steward.

I can't go into further details, but all the evidence points to his having made no bargain with any ship's officer, but depended on a Dane who works on the dock to get them in as stowaways, and this man and he are now quarrelling about money the Dane claims is due him.

I had worked for nearly a month, to the neglect of everything else, pledging my word to the men and losing much sleep. I had 35 good men ready, with many more to come, but it is all gone for nothing now and I am discredited and a lot of money thrown away. Of course also the news will spread.

I said nothing harsh to him, not even last night when he came to me with a ridiculous fake about a detective – whom he described as not English, but American, and later called him "this Englishman" – in the presence of two others offering to pay him $2000 cash down and $50 a week if he could keep in with "them" (naming nobody) and report to him. He confessed about the girl and said he wanted to go West and that if I would let him keep the un-expended money, he would ask no more. I told him that on account of his services to you I would give him the money to get away and I am giving him to-morrow morning $100 for the uniform, as I don't him to have it to blackmail other people. I got it from him today.

I did not express to him the slightest doubt of his honesty, but I know he knows what I think of him. I told him I am going away on a long trip, which is true, and I won't see him again.

When he was arriving last time he sent me a wireless from the steamer to the office, under my own name, asking me to deposit $100 with the steamship Company for him, which I did. Of course the wireless was picked up by the British cruisers outside the harbor. Then I paid for him the money with which you had entrusted him. He gave excuses for having had to spend it. He also tried to learn from one of the men how much money we had collected. Of course the man did not know.

     I was near forgetting to say that that one day he told me he was going to see Capt. V.P. [**von Papen**] I told him he could not find him. He said, "Oh Yes I can. Sir Roger told me all about it and the funny times he had going to see them. It is at No. 6 Hanover St." I told him the truth, that they had moved away from there six months ago.

I need not apply names to the man. His conduct speaks for itself. I am sorry to have to tell you, but you must be told the truth. I have to write in a great hurry and have no time to touch on anything else. Joe. is familiar with every little of these facts.

Your sister is to bring me a letter for you to-morrow, which I will enclose.

Yours truly

John Devoy

[Hand annotated on reverse by Casement with only this:] Essential to make the Convention a bold anti-English affair & have the report of it sent over to Germany thro Bernstorff – He should be forced to acknowledge to his govt. its value to him

[upside down:] R. in Berlin

19. Feb 1916.

Adler Christensen's first wife Sadie Weaver who was a Nansemond Indian

~~I think.~~ – It had been brought by von Papen they said. I nearly laughed – and asked why they had not shown it earlier. What their idea was in now showing me this paper I can scarcely conceive, except that they stupidly thought it would intimidate me to see that Christensen, the man I trusted and sent to America had turned into a ruffian and was found out by Devoy. I read the paper smiling and told them I was already perfectly aware of the whole of the facts there recorded. This preliminary settled, they began telling me of the plans made and what had already been done in the way of getting the rifles, ammunition &c. ready.

Finally there was a lull and it came my turn to say that I had made up my mind <u>not</u> to take the men. From the way they received it I could see that they were perfectly aware of my letter to Wedel and knew well my whole point of view. They argued and expostulated civilly and nicely, pointing out the need of the men until about 4 p.m. Nadolny came in. They explained to him my "new departure" over the men, and immediately the issue was joined. Nadolny began by disputing entirely my right to regard the men as in any way under my power, and said he quite refused to recognise my right to interfere as the Agreement was "dead"!

<u>Monday</u> 3 April 1916
[This paragraph at the page top is stroked out:] Nadolny had 'phoned

for me. V. Haugwitz when I met him at 3 today explained he had been to Zossen to see Monteith and that he did not want me to think he had done anything behind my back. I absolved him.

The conversation this afternoon on Nadolny's part was even more infamous than before. He insisted first – that the Agreement of 23-28 December 1914 was now null and void – and he declined to recognize my right to interfere in any way in regard to the Irish soldiers at Zossen. The "Irish Brigade" had not materialized and therefore the agreement had not come into existence! He could do as he pleased with the soldiers at Zossen and send them to Ireland if he chose and they agreed. I said laconically "try it."

I pointed out that while the purpose of the Agreement had not been attained the pledge to the men certainly held good, if the German govt. regarded its honour.

He called the agreement a Contract[171] – very well, a contract between two parties. One party could not interpret it as he pleased. I had as much right as the German govt. in the matter to put my interpretation on it – and this was clear that the pledge of the German govt. applied as fully to <u>one</u> Irish soldier who had come at my call, on faith of that agreement, as to 500 or 5000. If the Agreement were dead, non-existent, I asked him what then was the status of these men at Zossen?

"Oh!" he said – "Deserters!" "Deserters!" I exclaimed – "and <u>who</u> made them desert, you? I? – did the Imperial German govt. actually descend to tempting men to desert? and does it now propose to despatch deserters to Ireland against their will – or with their will for that matter?

And if they are "deserters" – <u>what</u> is Lt. Monteith the officer in command, with the sanction of your war office?"

I had the cad there. He blushed, looked down and stopped.

"Oh well" he said: "Let us view it this way – those men are Irish patriots, they wish to fight for their country, we offer them a chance, we are sending help to Ireland and they are <u>vitally</u> necessary to the success of the undertaking to have the machine guns ready for instant use on landing. You are not a soldier. You oppose this vital military requirement on a theory, a doctrine – we shall appeal to the men direct over your head and ask them if they are willing to go to Ireland under these circumstances."

I said I could not prevent him doing so if he insisted since I was so obviously a prisoner here in Germany (I did not say in the coils of a serpent!) but that I could and should still prevent him getting the men, unless he took them by force and as prisoners on board.

He said "<u>How?</u>" I said "because you do not understand the minds of free

---

[171] The German word 'Vertrag' serves for both contract and treaty.

men! The men will respond to your appeal to fight for Ireland with alacrity, I know – and then they will ask – the first question – what about Sir Roger Casement and Lt. Monteith, our officer – <u>Where are they</u>? <u>Are they not coming</u>?

Monday 3 April 1916

And if you do that, and try by this method to entrap these men against my will, then I don't go – and Lt. Monteith does not go – and once the men know our view, <u>they</u> will not go – unless you kidnap them."

He glared, and bit his lips – "Then" he said "I shall telegraph to the Irish Committee in America and ask them if they will require the men to go?" I said again "You may do so – but I should demand the right to telegraph too and put my views forward." "No" he said – "you shall not telegraph." "Very well" I said "try that course if you like but don't think it will succeed either for you will surely find that in anything you try to do with these men you will have to come back to me, and my mind is made up. Nothing you can say or do will alter it, or budge me one inch. You may take me out there and shoot me" and I pointed to the Spree Bank outside the window of Zimmer 178III – "but I'll never agree to those young men going. They trusted in my honour and good faith – as I in yours – or that of the German govt. – and while I am not responsible for <u>your</u> point of view, I am for mine."

The only gentleman on their side was young von Haugwitz. He agreed with me on all points except that the military necessity of the case required the men as gunners.

I said I should let no plea of military necessity or any other necessity override my sense of honour. They said – collectively – "you argue for a theory – a principle – we, as soldiers for a vital military need. Do you wish the thing to succeed or fail?"

I said I should not wish for any success founded on a dishonourable and cowardly act and that I feared we had "been brought up in two different schools of thought." I said this to Nadolny. It was impossible to agree I knew – and our respective views were grounded in a wholly different personal regard for certain things and different estimation of their value.

The fight had been long and exhausting but I saw I had won. Nadolny wound up (about 6 p.m.) by saying: "Well, we will settle it tomorrow, we will refer the matter to Lt. Monteith on military grounds – he is the expert there and you are not – and will abide by his decision – and then if he agrees with you you and he must sign a paper absolving us from all blame on military grounds, for the non-despatch of the men."

That night at 11 p.m., I got a wire from Fr. Crotty[172] he would arrive at 8.44 a.m. on Friday at Frederickshaven.

[Telegram to Casement from Father Crotty:]

Monteith
Telegramm aus Limburg Lahn
komme dienstag morgen friedrichstr berlin
Grotty [sic]
[Casement note:] L. Lim 11-2. Arr. B. 8-44
Dear Sir Roger
From Fr. Crotty – Will you please phone or wire me by what train you are coming so that I can arrange.
RM
3.4.16

Berlin, April 4, Tuesday.

Fr Strasse 8.44 to meet Fr. Crotty from Limburg. Missed him there but found him at Potsdamer Station 9.33 train for Zossen – stopped him and brought him back to hotel – gave him bath and breakfast and then told him all. He was horrified and we talked long as to best course. I told him of my idea of using Krebs[173] perhaps to go over and try to stop the thing. I later took Krebs into our confidence – but he was not able (and rightly I think) to carry out the half thought I had had. But he remains a witness. Fr. Crotty went on to see a certain lady and then to his Dominicans – and returned at 6.30 or 7 – and I kept him here getting him a good room.

Monteith and I went on to G.G.S. in afternoon and got all details for departure on probably Friday night from v. Haugwitz after it had been settled that only Beverley goes with us. The gun men at Zossen go on with their target practice so as not to excite suspicion if it were suddenly stopped with us both gone away.

VH promised me to get poison for us. I begged him to do so – and he agreed.

We will take £100 in gold – paying German money for it – v. Haugwitz gets it for us from bank. We are all there to go to G.G.S. at 6 or so on Friday night – I shave there – we change clothes and emerge by another door and exit (the orderlies all sent away in meantime from the corridors) to the quay by Lehrter Station and take the train to Hamburg in a reserved carriage.

Such is the plan.[174]

---

[172] NYPL Maloney IHP, Box 2, Folio 1
[173] Franz Hugo Krebs. There is a note in NLI 17432, probably by Joe McGarrity, which reads: "Krebs was a newspaper correspondent in Germany and perhaps a spy. I have no evidence of this. He seemed to really admire Sir R."
[174] NLI 17033

Daniel Julien Beverley (Bailey)

[Casement found time that day to write to his schoolboy friend in Bavaria. The envelope was addressed:]
Max Zehndler,
Zögling des Stad. Realschul =
Pensionates,
Landsberg a/Lech.

**[In correct German it should read, "Max Zehndler, Zögling der Städt. Realschule, Pensionat, Landsberg/Lech." i.e. Max Zehndler, Pupil Boarder of the Town Secondary Modern School, at Landsberg on the Lech.
Casement pretty well tells Max in this letter, written a week before his departure to Ireland, that something big is afoot i.e. the Easter Rising.]**
Berlin/
   4.4.16
   My dear Max,
   I hope you are better now and enjoying this good weather at Landsberg. I am

not going back to Ammersee for some time I fear and shall not see you for a long time I think as I have to go away now on a journey that will take up much time.

If I can I will come back to the dear old Ammersee – but if not you will know I am detained.

Meantime I hope for your welfare and success at school and that you may grow good, brave and strong and be very happy.

I hope your Easter holiday this year will be very pleasant and happy – Please remember me very kindly to your Uncle and Aunt – and with all kind thoughts and wishes,

Your sincere friend,
      Roger Casement.

[On a separate scrap of heavy paper:]
– P.S. I send you some old stamps.
Also a small present. Don't answer this letter as I shall not get your reply.
Be a good boy and work hard and make your friends happy by obedience and cheerfulness. R.C.

Back and dinner with Fr. Crotty – and then Gaffney came and talked till 11 nearly, in my room – and talked me asleep. Fr. Crotty enjoyed the change greatly I think, God bless him.

Wednesday, 5 April 1916

Out to Zossen with Fr. Crotty. He confessed most of the men, and then I gave a short address, telling them I had to go away with Lt. Monteith for a time and begging them to go on with everything just the same. It was dreadful. I could not tell them the truth – and I had the vision before me all the time of the dreadful deception being practiced on them – and of the callous treatment they would have once we were gone and all pretence of an "Irish Brigade" finished – God forgive me – and God protect these poor boys. I am writing the Chancellor direct about them. We (Lt. Monteith and Fr. Crotty and I) came back to Berlin at 5.30 and I met Krebs there. He has a copy of my letter to Wedel of 30 March and a few other things – for use <u>after the war only</u> – and only then if I am dead.

Fr. Crotty left for Limburg at 9.17 p.m. and I came back and wrote the long "Exposé" that follows. This I did after talk with Fr. C. – He said to make another effort to impress the serious character of the thing on the German govt. – and I wrote this "Exposé" specifically for <u>their</u> eye. It will go to Noeggerath in morning.

April 5. <u>1916</u>
  "Expose"
Another day gone, and another last page to my Diary! Today I went to

Private Charles James McCarthy in Irish Brigade uniform,
Zossen Camp, 1916

Zossen, ostensibly with the Priest who confessed the men, really to bid them goodbye. At least I have saved them! The whole thing appals me as a piece of the most ghastly folly – or rather one of the most criminal attempts ever perpetrated. And I am debarred from saying so and taking the needed steps to prevent it by fear of incurring a personal reproach of cowardice (already grossly implied by some of those who are handling the matter at the G.G. Staff).

[Written down the side of the page:] Or worse still or perhaps, <u>not</u> preventing it but only depriving them of the arms at the critical moment.

Am I not, perhaps, a greater coward in fearing to incur this reproach, or any reproach rather than take the wholly courageous step of protesting in the highest quarter against a scheme that has been considered, I fear, only by underlings and is being rushed to certain failure by men of inferior intelligence at the best, and in this particular matter (Ireland) of no understanding.

How can a scheme so launched and by <u>such</u> methods as those I have had witness of the last week succeed?

On all grounds by which we may consider it, it is a scheme that can only bring failure – and probably something far worse than failure – disaster. Let us – let me put down these grounds as I perceive them. This is a record of my mind and understanding – and I want it to live after me.

1st. Military.

On military grounds the project is beneath contempt. To begin with it is <u>not</u> a military enterprise at all – but a piece of gun-running.

It has no military element about it, except poor Lt. Monteith! He, I, (and perhaps one young soldier) disguised as sailors, (each with a bottle of poison kindly supplied us!) are to invade a Kingdom – bringing with us 20.000 rifles and some cartridges.

As a gun-running enterprise or effort it might pass if attempted say by Walford & Co., of Antwerp or some other notorious firms of that character who make a living by supplying arms to <u>irate</u> savages and semi-civilized South American republics. But for the G.G. Staff of the greatest military power in the world ~~even as a gun-running effort~~ it is an astounding adventure – and as an episode in this world war it will surely be without parallel. I say nothing of the Navy because I am convinced they are doing the thing as well as it can be done and that from the naval point of view, as a "job" entrusted to them for execution they will do everything they can to carry it through successfully.

But on all other grounds of a military character is has not been properly approached and none of the essentials to success are even being applied. I will not discuss here, tonight, these shortcomings – they must be apparent to any soldier who is given the rudiments of the proposal to consider.

On military grounds I am convinced, I could damn it before any staff college in the world. The dangers I foresee are far less from the obvious military shortcomings than due to the absence of political intelligence.

Let us consider it on political grounds.

2. <u>Political</u>

On political grounds, (even if the scheme were susceptible of sound military handling) it involves the gravest dangers to Germany – perhaps far greater than to Ireland.

<u>2</u>. Political   I see dangers enough to Ireland in it at the best. The <u>only</u> reason that justifies it at all on Irish grounds is the argument put forward by John Devoy in his speech on 4-5 March in New York – viz that the Irish Volunteers were going to resist disbandment by force, and this being so their friends in America should help them. That a fight would come in any case – only a scuffle really – and it would be only chivalrous to help them

to put up a better fight.

But the political dangers are so tremendous, when I put aside the natural sentiment of desire to help these young men if they do fight, that I think they far outweigh the possible gain that might come from a successful street scuffle that deferred or hindered greatly the possible recruitment of these young men.

Here are a few of those dangers. The vast bulk of Irishmen are law abiding and peace loving.

They will bitterly resent bloodshed and civil strife in Ireland – forced on them as will then seem apparent by a filibustering expedition launched from Germany for that purpose. And in truth that is just what it is being sent for. Nadolny confessed quite frankly to me that what the German Staff wanted was bloodshed in Ireland – a "diversion" there that might help Germany. The diversion may indeed come! But it will not help Germany I fancy. It may be a last straw the other way.

Once it becomes clear – as it surely will become clear – that Germany tried to incite a revolt or "rising" in Ireland by a paltry gift of second hand rifles put in the hand of excitable young men, all that is solid and respectable in Ireland will be moved to the deepest resentment – "Pro-German" feeling of today will be changed into wrath and contempt.

The object of Asquith's visit to Rome, I believe, (or one of the objects) was to get the Pope to move the Irish clergy to an anti-German attitude. He failed I feel sure, but this "anti-Irish attempt" of the German govt. to embroil Irishmen on their own soil, so that Germany might reap some trifling military advantage from bloodshed in Ireland can redound only to the extreme discredit of Germany, and may easily secure from the Irish Bishops a Declaration that Mr. Asquith failed to obtain from an appeal to the Holy See.

Once the Bishops (who, with the exception of the Archbishop of Tuam have been very fair and just) are moved to denounce a "German plot" against the internal peace of Ireland, then we may find public feeling In Ireland change to the complete detriment of Germany and leave her with no shred of Irish goodwill. The British Recruiting Sergeants will get the reward – not the German military machine.

And certainly that machine does not deserve to get anything but a kick for the way it has tackled this problem.

3. Political

The political results will not be confined to a mere increase of ill feeling in Ireland against Germany – they would I feel confident, in the end, be of a far more widespread character and would probably cross the Atlantic and sway Irish feeling in America just in the opposite way to that hoped for.

The <u>inadequacy</u>, the hopeless inadequacy of the means employed and the absence of any prior precautions to ensure success will convince all thinking Irishmen that the project was not inspired by goodwill to Ireland at all, but sprang solely from a desire to secure profit from <u>any</u> sort of blood-letting in Ireland. Anger, contempt and resentment would be aroused once the <u>facts</u> of the attempt became known, and we may trust the British government for making these very widely known with a colouring and a "colour scheme" all their own.

Not even the "rape" of Belgium was exploited as this attempt to stir up strife, and secure a massacre of half-armed boys in peaceful Ireland will be exploited. And the moral will be a plain one. German "good-will" is as dangerous as that of a mad dog – it bites the friendly hand as impartially as that of its enemy. *Timeo Danaos et dona ferentes.*[175]

If all the facts connected with the ill considered and half thought out enterprise become known – and they will become known within a very few weeks at the latest – then the fair name of Germany, or at least of the German government is tarnished before all neutral countries and chiefly in the United States. Only success could justify an enterprise of this kind – and all the elements to ensure success are wanting so far as I can see – have not, indeed, ever been invoked at all.

If my diary is ever published – as some day it may be – what a figure all these military minds or political minds of this great Empire will cut! From Virgil's Æneid: 'I fear the Greeks even when they bear gifts' i.e. the Trojan Horse.

The excuses put forward to me that it is being undertaken <u>solely</u> at the request of Irishmen themselves and without the moral responsibility of the German government being involved at all will not hold for a moment. I, even I here, with my hands tied (as it were) and my means of communicating with my friends in Ireland or America cut off can see that this statement is only very partially true. The very methods employed to enforce my acquiescence in a project I have expressed my disapproval of convince me that these assurances are wholly insincere.

I am given no chance of a full decision – and when I seek to express the opinion of an honest man I am threatened with a wholly devilish (I can call it nothing else) charge that the blame for failure will be put entirely on me.

4. On moral grounds the thing does not bear inspection at all. As Monteith said to me, referring to how the issue effects myself – "it is dastardly."

How can a scheme of "helping Ireland" that evokes such comment from a wholly unselfish and chivalrous Irishman produce happy results?

Let us look at it on "Moral" grounds. These are closely associated with the

---

[175] From Virgil's Æneid: "I fear the Greeks even when they bear gifts" i.e. the Trojan Horse.

political aspects of the affair – they cannot be dissociated from the political.

On moral grounds I think nothing <u>can</u> be said for the thing, <u>as it is being worked</u>.

Advantage is certainly being taken of me in a wholly unfair and even cowardly way – and if (the inevitable!) I am captured by the British this will be made clear.

It <u>must</u> be made clear.

Nothing I may do, or abstain from doing, can then save the character of the German govt. Most men will charge them with putting me in a dreadful position – with running me into the hands of my enemies – some even, with deliberately handing me over to the British government!

All the circumstances connected with the agreement the German government made concerning the ill-fated "Irish Brigade" will come to light. They are, already, fairly well known in England – and while it suits the English government <u>today</u> to vilify me as a "traitor" – it will suit them far better, once I am safe in their hands, to vilify the German government for having actually betrayed me as they will say, their poor dupe, into the very hands of the government I had defied with the concurrence and support of the German govt.

Whatever wrong I, the individual Irish rebel, may have attempted will be swallowed up in the far graver charge of treachery the British govt. (through its press) will bring against Germany. "Why" – they will say – "they couldn't be loyal even to the wretched man who had sold himself to them!"

And the world will support the charge. I, the "traitor" of today will become the "sacrificed dupe" of tomorrow.

The more the question, thus posed, is inspected, the more pitiable my case will be made out – the more contemptible that of the people who launched me on the road to doom.

No one will seriously assert for a moment that the German government really believed that by sending me on a ship to Ireland, with no support, no help, no possible means of escape, even they were doing a chivalrous thing.

The "murder of Nurse Cavell" will not be in it with the "betrayal of Sir Roger Casement."

The English are quite capable of shutting me up in a lunatic asylum and asking the world what it thinks of the people who handled the lunatic thus!

And the world will give only one answer. My madness may be pardoned – but the cowardice of those who first took advantage of it where they thought they saw some gain, and then flung the madman to destruction, when they had no longer any use for him, will echo through the world as a possibly crowning example of "Hun" methods.

I should not like to be von Falkenhayn when the British govt, having dealt with Sir Roger Casement, turn upon those who planned this "military aid" to Ireland!

(I much prefer to be myself in any case – with all my faults and mistakes. At least no man, or people, or country can say I sold them or gave a friend away.)

This aspect of the affair does not concern me personally – my honour and my courage cannot be questioned, however my intellect may be arraigned – I have not shirked the ordeal – and when, if ever, the facts become public of <u>how</u> I have been forced to act against my judgment in the matter then, indeed, most men will forgive me while they will despise those who put me in the fire.

I am not free here in Germany, forced by ignorance, by the dire necessities of the case (as it is presented to me) to go blindly on, to <u>dictate</u> or prescribe the necessary steps that should be taken if the attempt is to be regarded seriously.

I see what should be done – and I have said so. My clear statement in the two Memoranda I gave the General Staff has not been acted on. I am told it cannot be – for "technical reasons." If technical reasons prohibit the preliminary steps that are essential, from being taken then the thing should not be attempted at all. That is clear. But I am told it must go on in spite of the absence of these essential precautions; and I am forced to assent or incur a shameful reproach. I go on – because I am fool enough, or brave enough or coward enough – I know not which – while I know it is hopeless.

Like Francis I I say "all is lost but honour." The <u>right</u> thing to do even now would be to stop the whole thing – to delay it, until we are quite sure of the condition of things in Ireland, of the means at the disposal of our friends there, both for resistance and for the immediate landing of the arms – and until adequate steps had been taken at this end to afford sufficient help.

That is the right thing to do – obviously. I ought to insist on that. And yet I dare not. If I do – God knows what may be the result. I am so completely in the dark as to what is being really planned in Ireland, in America, that I dare not accept the responsibility – And no one here will accept any responsibility. They put it on me. And threaten me, in an infamous way with responsibility for betraying my friends if I don't fully accept what I know is a half digested project.

I must swallow it at all costs. All I have been able to do has been to save the poor Irish lads at Zossen – and still leave even these to their fate. For, it is clear from what Nadolny said yesterday afternoon that they are going to be treated again as prisoners of war and sent to some detention camp.

That is a gross violation of the pledge of the German govt. Nadolny even called them "deserters" to my face! My God – it is the most abominable position a man was ever put in. Whatever I do is wrong – is hopeless. The thing <u>cannot</u> work out well, conceived in such a spirit as this – planned with a total disregard of the first essentials of military efficiency and launched with a callous indifference to the most obvious consideration of honour and sincerity it can only produce evil. Of that I feel sure.

And the evil will fall on the heads of those who planned it and persisted in carrying it through in violation of all they <u>must</u> know to be right.

Whatever happens to me is a small thing – But what may happen in Ireland is a big thing – and since it <u>can</u> only be evil I feel that the evil after all, will not fall in Ireland, but on those who have ensured it.

This absurd expedition may – Who knows? produce incalculable consequences. It is Germany, I feel certain will reap them in the end – and they will prove a sorry harvest. It may well be the turning point with a vengeance, of German relations with America, and all the Chancellor's wise efforts to retain friendly relations with America may be wholly brought to ruin by this half thought out scheme of soldiers who know as much of Ireland as they do of America.

From a telegram in tonight's paper I see the British fleet is "very busy" on the Norwegian coast these last few days. Here it is.

[Newspaper cutting dated 5 April tipped in, and headlined:] '*Englische Seestreitkräfte an der norwegischen Küste*' ['**English seafighting craft near the Norwegian coast**'].

That is perhaps the most hopeful sign in the whole business as it now stands! Our chances of escaping capture are daily diminishing – and to be captured may be the only way out! who knows.

Well – I can do nothing – the madness is not of my choosing, planning or design – I have done my best to preach sanity and to enforce reason and I am insulted for the effort. Fate may be using me in some inscrutable way to end the war! I sometimes think it. But how?

I who have tried to save Ireland from the horrors of war and to be the friend of Germany may now, by the very act of the German govt. become the very instrument to launch Irishmen into the war – and possibly with them the Americans too.

The whole thing is appalling – and as Saturday approaches and the irreparable step is taken – I feel like a man <u>already</u> damned.

All <u>I</u> can hope for is that, later on, my part will be made clear, and it will be seen how great a victim I was.

Pray God, that Germany be not the far greater victim for the sins of her military counsellors. They have usurped the place of her political advisers, in this matter at all events – and I think she will pay bitterly for the exchange.

I have no time for more than these crude fears tonight – tomorrow is already here – it is 1 a.m. – and I have much to write.

I <u>must</u> write Zimmermann or the Chancellor maybe on the fate of the Irish soldiers left behind at Zossen and insist that as Wedel promised me formally in writing last June, apart from the clear terms of the Agreement itself, they shall not be the victims of the General Staff – even as I am – but that the promises of the German govt.* shall be strictly and honourably fulfilled in their regard – after I am gone. This morning when I spoke to them and pretended I was just going ahead of them on a journey to clear the way for their employment in the East as they think, I could scarcely refrain from crying. I felt that I was leaving them to deception and misery – they who have already sacrificed so much – to be treated as "Deserters" – or disgraced "prisoners of war." It is time I died – for if I looked them in the face again I could not say what I wrote just now "all is lost but honour." I feel that <u>all</u> is indeed lost and the sooner my life is taken away from me the better.

[At bottom of page:] *Note I showed <u>this</u> part of my Diary to Noeggerath. <u>He</u> saw the vital gist of the thing and went to Zimmermann who authorized him to go to G.G.S. and Admiralty. I said no use going to G.G.S. but perhaps to Admiralty for submarine. He went with the result that in the end they gave the submarine – not because it ensured my safety en route so much as their own reputation. It was only that argument appealed to them! Chivalrous! but the German Admiralty is the best part of all this show – a long way the best. 8.4.16.

Thursday, April 6 1916

On getting up I sent for Gaffney, read him my Diary of last night – with every word of which he agrees. I expressed my ever growing anxiety as to the consequences to Ireland. He went up to Noeggerath who came down to see me; having read the Diary he went to Zimmermann the Under Secretary of State (after having come to me) and returned to say that Zimmermann could not go to the Chancellor, who has to speak again today in Reichstag, but authorised him (N) to go to G.G.S. and Admiralty. I told Noeg it was no use going to G.G.S. – they were hopeless and Nadolny a low-minded intriguer but that he might go to the Admiralty.

Georg v. Haugwitz called in forenoon to say that the arrangements were as follows:–

Certain articles of clothing still to be purchased by me he supplying the rest G.G.S. £100 in gold ready (I to give him a cheque) Monteith to come in tomorrow to go to G.G.S. and also to see some more explosives. Sgt. B.

(who goes with us after all) not to be told until tomorrow night, say 6 p.m. and v. Haugwitz will come too. Finally we are all three to "change" at G.G.S. on Saturday afternoon – when I shall change and shave (the last time was in the Hotel Prince George coming to Germany Oct. 17, 1914!) and go off to the station "disguised" as sailors and in charge of the Captain of Marine who is running the show – the man I already met at Admiralty who went with me to G.G.S.

Noeggerath with me several times today and dear old Krebs the faithful one. Krebs is full of fight. Monteith brought Beverley in at 11.30 or so and he went out to see the town. Noeggerath went to the Admiralty he told me and explained the political standpoint – political standpoint – throwing a "bombshell" in he said – They were greatly impressed and said that they "might have to reconsider the whole thing."

Noeg's idea is they had given no consideration to it at all – only a childish incident. The Chief of the Admiralty staff was away but was to be consulted and Noeg was told he would be informed later of the decision come to. What Noeg chiefly impressed on them was that I should be sent to Ireland before by submarine – that it was a fearful risk for them as well as for me to send me by the steamer and they had no right to incur that risk for themselves – if they did not regard mine. Of course personal risks are not considered and cannot be in war – all go out to die – but in this case there were possible consequences (to Germany) on the lines of my diary of last night that they had to consider – <u>and then</u> the grave risk of being "tarred" with responsibility for the whole thing.

This point, viz German responsibility they had none of them considered – so my Bombshell has hit the mark.

Each of the parties I have had anything to do with disclaims responsibility!

First the G.G.S. are "only complying with the request of the Irishmen themselves and have no responsibility in the matter – in which they were not consulted" &c. &c.

2nd The Admiralty are "only carrying out the work entrusted to them by the G.G.S. and have no power of decision on any point of policy" (This is all right and I agree with this – they are the only innocent parties in the business.)

3rd The German F.O. have "no responsibility of any kind"! – they "know nothing of it as it was all arranged between G.G.S. and "my friends" in America! Everyone is clean handed. And yet on 29 February Assessor Meyer is kind enough to send me Robert Emmet's Dying Speech "in these times." It is quite clear they had made up their minds that although they had "no responsibility", and all was between G.G.S. and America – and that America had asked to keep me out – they had decided to bring me in. My mind was to be "prepared" by R. Emmet's speech for the proposals coming after. Now it is absurd to think that Germany had no responsibility in a matter of this supreme importance – viz equipping (quite inadequately) a rebellion in Ireland – which is made contingent really on the arrival of the arms! For it is clear "No revolution no rifles" is the maxim of the whole crowd here – & their fury against me is due to the fact that I am pressing home this argument and <u>compelling</u> them to shoulder some of the responsibility, & that I sent J. McG. [**John McGoey**] out of the country & they fear he may call off the whole thing.

After Noeggerath had come and gone – I was in my room very unhappy until 4 p.m. when I went down to go out for a few minutes – and got in the hall an urgent letter from Wedel of Foreign Office. It was dated today – (see it)[176]

[Wedel letter to Casement:]

[**Casement note:**] R in Berlin 4.15 p.m. <u>1916</u>
Auswärtiges Amt
Berlin, April, 6th 1916.
Dear Sir Roger,
I just received the enclosed letter which your friend handed to our minister at Berne yesterday, requesting him to have it forwarded to you as quickly as possible.
Believe me, dear Sir Roger,
Yours sincerely
        Georg Wedel.

and forwarded to me a letter from Berne of 5 April – signed by "a friend of James Malcolm" with the signs agreed on last June with J.P. This letter said that the writer was sent from Dublin <u>with the urgent message</u> from Ireland[177] –

[Count Plunkett letter to Casement from Berne:]

R in Berlin 4.15 p.m.
Berne, 5th April 1916
Aisling [**Symbol: circle with cross through it**]
Dear Roger Casement,
   I am sent here as Delegate by the President and Supreme Council of the Irish Volunteers and through the courtesy of His Excellency the German Ambassador I am enabled to give you the urgent message from Ireland.

---

[176] NYPL Maloney IHP, Box 2, Folio 1 (original and typescript)
[177] NYPL Maloney IHP, Box 1, Folio 14 (original). "A friend of James Malcolm" was Count George Noble Plunkett, father of Joseph Mary Plunkett, who had in 1915 gone via Switzerland to Germany and seen Casement and the German authorities. He was executed in 1916. The Count in 1917 was elected a Sinn Fein MP at the North Roscommon by-election.

1. The rising is fixed for the evening of next Easter Sunday.
2. The large consignment of arms to be brought into Tralee Bay must arrive there not later than the dawn of Easter Monday.
3. German officers will be necessary for the Volunteer forces. This is imperative.
4. A German Submarine will be required in Dublin harbour.

The time is very short, but it is necessarily so, for we must act of our own choice, and delays are dangerous.

  Yours very sincerely
   A friend of James Malcolm

1st the rising was fixed for Easter Sunday night.

2nd The steamer with the "large consignment" was to come to Tralee Bay not later than dawn of Easter Monday. –

3rd German officers vitally needed – "This is imperative"

4 A submarine to be in Dublin Bay.

I wrote instantly to Noeggerath to come here before 6 and then went to the Admiralty – saw Heydell who took the letter to chief of Staff (he said) and after 20 minutes returned to say they would not give a submarine. This was final! For all the other matters I was referred to the G.G.S. I said that that was useless for I had the measure of their intelligence always and we saw very little in common, or eye to eye – I said even more – for I was angry – not with Heydell, but with the whole of the soulless thing.

Thursday 6 April **[date repeated down side of page]**

I told Heydell some of the things I had written in my Diary as to the danger to Germany from an act of the kind – "treachery" I called it – and I wound up by saying that I had no opinion of the political intelligence of the G.G.S. and that if that was the thing going to rule Germany "it would send it straight to Hell!" I don't know what Heydell thought of me – probably mad. I was for the moment and bitterly angry when I thought of Ireland, and of those poor boys on Easter Sunday and Easter Monday waiting for the steamer – the "rising" already accomplished! – and their one hope the ship with the rifles and the officers – who will not be there – the utter callousness and indifference here – only seeking bloodshed in Ireland – the "rising" is their only hope!

The guns are so timed to arrive as to ensure that the rising must precede them – "no blood no rifles."

I came back to the hotel a horrified man and telephoned at once to von Haugwitz to come and see me urgent. I wrote to Wedel a brief note of thanks and said I'd reply to the message tonight[178]

---

[178] NYPL Maloney IHP, Box 1, Folio 14

[Casement's reply to the messenger (Count Plunkett) in Switzerland:]

Original letter to Berne messenger.
Berlin
6 April 1916
Ashling. **[Symbol: circle with cross through]**
To the friend of James Malcolm
Berne

Your letter of 5th received and submitted to competent authorities.

(1) A steamer is being sent to reach Inishtookert – the north-west of "the Hags" rocks, north of Rough Point – Tralee Bay, not later than Easter Monday dawn.

She will carry 20.000 Russian Rifles, 10 machine guns (German) with 5.000.000 cartridges available for both and 1.000.000 cartridges for Lee Enfield and some more cartridges fitting the rifles already in Ireland.

(2) No German Officers or men are being sent.

(3) No submarine is being sent.

(4) I go with her, accompanied by Lt. Monteith and one soldier of the Irish Corps, to stand and fall with those at home.

(5) The steamer must be met off Inishtookert by a fishing boat for piloting her into Fenit pier. The steamer will fly Norwegian flag, as signal by day. By night cruising at half speed in circles, lights out. The pilot boat by night will show two green lights close together as signals, for a few seconds, then one of the green lights will be covered for about five minutes the pilot boat then only showing one light – then showing two for a few seconds and so on.

If by day the pilot boat will have a man with a green jersey who, on sighting the ship will pull off his jersey and put it in a basket. The steamer will answer by downing the pilot flag & lower the home flag a little & pull it up again & lower it altogether. The pilot boat is imperative, to pilot the steamer in, otherwise she cannot go inside to pier.

The rifles are in boxes of 5 each, with 5 bayonets and 5 bayonet pouches & 900 cartridges in each. The rifles are ~~Lee Enfield~~ **[In another version:** 'Russian rifles with Russian cartridges'**]** & the cartridges 303.

The machine guns are German guns – no English machine guns available. As no artillerymen or gunners are coming from here it is essential you have the best artillerymen ready on shore to take the guns at once into action.

Monteith & the one soldier from this are trained in use of the machine guns. If you could send off some of the gunners from shore in the boat or boats to the steamer they could have the guns ready at once.

The chief danger lies in British cruisers from the sea shelling the ship before she puts the cargo off. High explosive in considerable quantities are going too.

I sent a messenger from this on 19th March, John McGoey, a Clan man from Chicago, to try & reach Dublin to tell them all this, place of landing etc to add surety to the message I was told had been sent via America to you & Committee but McGoey may not arrive, so I repeat his instructions.

If the steamer is arrested en route I fear you will have no means of knowing as the British Authorities may probably not announce the capture for their own ends. She carries no wireless I believe. She is timed to sail next Sunday or Saturday night.

I leave this Saturday night with M & the soldier.

I much regret the absence of the officers and submarine – but am told both are impossible – I have repeatedly urged submarine.

Under all the circumstances I am bound to go with the ship and take all the risks. The steamer will most likely arrive off Inishtookert in the night coming from the N.W. direction probably. It is possible the steamer may arrive Easter Sunday night – Have all ready for that night to hold off troops & put material on shore.

Hurry back Dublin at once and report.
Roger Casement

Brought back by Graf von Haugwitz 7.45 pm. He stopped it when the submarine question was settled by my act. He is delighted at the submarine. He says no use to send this letter now. I ask for the man to be brought here. He demurs – but will see what is best to be done "tomorrow". This letter v. Haugwitz says was already in the carrier's box for Berne, but he got it back just in time. He says the telegram went & in that I asked for answer on various points.

[Casement memo of 10 April about his 7 April telegram to Count Plunkett in Berne:]

~~£15 = M 2010 To morrow~~

This was my original telegram to "the friend of James Malcolm" at Berne – written in G.G.S.

It was sent von Haugwitz tells me but "no reply has been received"! (It is quite clear that it was "held up" by the Minister at Berne, on instructions from this!

Von Haugwitz brought it back to me today (10 April 11.30 am) in reply to my note (see it) and said nothing had been heard from Berne & he thought it unlikely! He suggests it would be unwise to send the messenger back quickly & adds that he could not get to Dublin in time for Easter Sunday? I begged v.H. to wire to Berne & let me know if the messenger still there. He promised to do so – but I think it very unlikely N. will allow even that.

This wire was written by me at 10.30am 7 April.
7 April 1916
When did you leave Dublin & what were you last advised from Germany?
2 point 20,000 rifles
    5,000,000 ctg
    10 machine guns
    1,000,000 ctgs for Lee Enfield rifles being shipped.
    Timed arrive Easter Sunday night 23rd
(3) No German officers or men going – impossible despatch.
(4) No submarines can be sent.

~~a pilot boat must be out~~
Can you reach Dublin before Easter Sunday? a letter with fuller information follows.

– see my reply to Wedel.[179]

[Casement letter to Wedel:]

Hotel Saxonia
Berlin
6 April 1916
Dear Count Wedel,
Thank you for the letter you kindly sent on –
I hope to be able to give a reply to Berne tonight and will be very much obliged if you will send it there for me by special messenger.
It is very urgent.
    Yours sincerely,
     Roger Casement
I have been to the Admiralty: they persist in refusing a Submarine.

Then Noeggerath called and I showed him the letter – and Monteith who came in – and they were reading it when von Haugwitz was announced. I had to prevent him seeing Noeggerath and Monteith cleverly stopped him in nick of time and got him up to my bedroom where I gave him the letters. He said the officers were "impossible." What I knew already – his reasons on military grounds, I admit at once. German officers could not go without some German soldiers – and to command Irish Volunteers with different disciplines &c. &c. – I agreed on all these grounds – but I pointed out then the lamentable state of "the rising." Here they were, with thousands of brave boys, armed very indifferently, without true cohesion, commissariat, baggage, and No officers, going to commit an irreparable act – and be swept down in hundreds – or perhaps thousands – and the world will always hold me responsible for the whole thing – whereas in every single particular my advice was been scorned – and I have not been even consulted until too late and these wholly imperfect "arrangements" made.

One of the things I predicted on 16 Mch when I was dealing with the gun-running aspect of the matter alone was now coming to pass – a check at the eleventh hour – all of us working in the dark – no coherent plan and no communications kept up.

How could a scheme so engineered with the essential preliminaries ne-

---

[179] NYPL Maloney IHP, Box 2, Folio 6 (manuscript copy), *Politisches Archiv des Auswärtigen Amtes* (PA AA) WK 11k secr., vol. 11 (R 21163), also in Doerries pp. 207-8.

glected be successful? Poor young von Haugwitz he is a gentleman – one of the very few I have met here. Heydell too, I like at the Admiralty – but the whole thing is a brazen serpent, lifted up in a wilderness of worshippers – worshippers from fear <u>at bottom</u>. This Prussian system <u>is</u> a curse. I see it clearly.

It represses all the higher sentiments of humanity – they dare not exist beside it – it is the embodiment of "soulless efficiency", in mere military things only, dominating a great people – Here in my case it is absolutely soulless – and not efficient either – because while these poor asses think they are dealing with a military problem it is a political problem of the very highest order they are assailing with such rude hands. An abortive rising in Ireland, <u>inadequately armed and supported by them</u>, yet encouraged and urged on by their promise of support – let them say what they will – is a crime they will pay for bitterly. I have now said it so plainly to them all they must be beginning to tremble. To von Haugwitz I said "<u>the ship must go</u> – nothing can stop her: she is bound to go – you are pledged to that – and I go too – that is all." As regards the man at Berne I tell him that no officers and no submarine can be given – and I will send the letter by Wedel – He said it was absolutely certain no officers could go – and if I was squarely sure from the Admiralty that no submarine could go, then he agreed I might write the letter to Berne at once. I sat down and drafted what I was going to send to Berne.

Thursday 6 April 8.30pm

Noeggerath came again and I kept him to dinner alone – We talked very much. Krebs came and squatted for a spell.

Noeggerath said (when Krebs was gone) that he was quite sure there were "very serious" talks going on over the whole thing. That he hoped still for the submarine. I said yes – but they would not send me in her! "Why" – he said: "You know" I answered – "they fear my intelligence. They know how profoundly I disapprove the rising and they want it – and they fear if I get to Ireland I may be able to stop it. It is that they are afraid of. Their fury over my despatch of John McGoey shows me that they meant to keep me from all communication with my friends – to launch me out in the dark – and let all responsibility fall on me and others." Then there is one ray of hope that John McGoey arrived in time – and that they may listen to him. <u>He</u> knows the true character of German goodwill to Ireland now – He saw how they kept their promises to the poor betrayed handful of men at Zossen and how they treated himself! – no uniform and refusal to release him when I demanded it in February. He told me that he had sized up German militarism and he is heart and soul against it – even as I am!

Later in the evening I told Noeg. that I felt an absolute conviction that the British would seize the ship and that I was praying for it, as probably the best way to avoid the greater evil. If the ship is arrested and the English government <u>publish</u> the fact that they have collared a ship with rifles and R.C. on board, then the mere fact of that publication will stop "the rising" in Ireland. That is clear. Knowing that the steamer is in the enemy's hands and no relief can come they will <u>never</u> go on with it. So I pray God in His mercy to have this the solution. Anyone that saves the situation in Ireland – and saves our young people from being made the victims of this callous conspiracy. Poor Ireland! God save her indeed – only He can.

Von Haugwitz said he would bring me back the Berne letter tonight – but he did not come by midnight. That all shows that there is a very animated fight going on somewhere. Noeg said that the Admiralty people while profoundly impressed with the gravity of the situation revealed by his views (mine of my yesterday diary) were "raging" at my having told him.

He said he thought they all mistrusted me – and I said I felt sure of it – and I repaid them all the compliment with a very clear comprehension of how much they deserved my mistrust.

Even Noeg now agrees that I <u>must</u> go with the arms – that I <u>could</u> not, in honour, stay here and let the guns go, feeling as I do – but that the infamy of the thing is that the German government does not send me in a submarine. He still has hopes. So he said. I don't. He begged me not to send any reply to Berne about submarine until he sees me again tomorrow as the naval men will let him know – I agreed.

We talked of other things till late and he left me worn out and I fell asleep at once. Here I am again.

<u>Friday morning</u>. <u>7</u> April.

Tomorrow is the last day. Today there will be a last fight for the submarine – I know it is futile. Then clothes to buy – a long letter to the Chancellor about the fate of the Irish soldiers at Zossen – to see that Nadolny's infamous intentions are not executed. I can only plead. I dare not threaten – it is not fair to the Chancellor either – yet I know that the machine (he hates it too I fancy) responds only to pressure and fear.

Last night among other things Noeggerath said he was convinced that S. (who took the Findlay letters &c. over on "Kristianiafjord" in February) has been captured!

The letters were to be in Captain's safe – I expect the British got them too! All Gaffney's doing when I was ill to urge me as he did to send them to the Irish convention in New York. No word from S. or Mary MacFadden since they sailed. They both left Berlin on Sunday 20 Feb. and were to sail on the

"K'fjord" on Wednesday 23rd.

The ship was held up 2 days (or more) we know in Kirkwall – and arrived in New York on 7th – two days after the Convention. Mary had letter to (Nina) **['Cohalan only' stroked out and inserted above 'Nina']** from me and S. to Cohalan – but nothing of moment save to ask them if I should try and come over as G. suggested – that I was useless here and ill and it would be far better to try and get to them.

No answer of any kind has come.

I had returned to Munich after this with G. on Sunday 27 Feb. with fever and was in bed for a week nearly and then came Monteith on 7th March and this project – and everything else has paled into insignificance.

What a laugh! There in America they want me to stay here as their "representative", thinking there is an Irish policy here and that I can influence these people – little knowing that they insult me, lie to me, break faith, – and would now, for their own ends, see me hanged, if it served them.

Friday 7 April 1916

Emerson told me on 1 April when I had tea with him at Esplanade that the Turks were now completely disillusioned as to the character of German "goodwill" to Turkey. He said when I told him my opinion of the G.G.S. à pro pos something else – he said – "You should hear the Turks on them"!

Today is really my last day – and I shall be hunted and driven all day. It is still early.

I told that faithful splendid Monteith last night I should be glad to go even to death on the scaffold – to an English jail to get away from Germany and these people I despise so much. He said "Indeed I think I would too." He and Beverley slept here last night. Latter is in old suit of mine. If my papers survive and above all the Treaty and some kind of friend of former years (say E.D.M.) should edit them, there may yet be told a strange chapter of Irish history. In any case it will be shown that I was only a fool – to trust German honour or good will – and never a rogue.

The picture of me in "Graphic" of February 26 "The Voice of the Traitor" Fr. Crotty tells me was sent to many of the soldiers in Limburg. The Kommandantur there asked the N.C.O.s to state on oath that it was false. They refused – altho' as Fr. Crotty said everyone knows it to be a lie. He said the young Nussing (Brother Canethus Warren) is not a Nationalist and said it was a horrid lie against me.

Of course, we all know that Fr. Crotty promised to contradict it in writing – I hope he may, dear soul.

I must get ready for the ordeal of this last awful day –

God keep me straight and help me to go right for Ireland's sake – That is all I now can hope to do.

Berlin Friday April 7<u>th</u> 1916

Monteith went out to Zossen to pay the poor boys and clear all out from bank there.

[Side note:] He returned at 6 or so – with the balance of cash to credit of Brigade Fund = Mks 3878.30 and handed it to me. I then told him the matter was delayed – and that the Admiralty had promised me a submarine to take him, Beverley and myself over to Ireland in time to take part in "<u>operations</u>."

At 10 I got a message from v. Haugwitz asking me to go to G.G.S. I went and found the trio – von Hülsen, Nadolny and the young Count – he always nice and sincere.

N. produced the letter of the Delegate from Berne and we discussed it. They seemed suspicious at first – as usual but I was able to assure them it came from the right quarter.

I telegraphed from G.G.S. as follow: –

"When did you leave Dublin?

(2) Steamer with <u>so much</u> ammunition and rifles (stating quantities) will be off Inishtooskert rock, N.W. Hags on Easter Monday dawn.

(3) <u>No officers can be sent</u>.

(4) <u>No submarine going</u>.

(5) <u>When can you return to Dublin?</u>"

I gave v. Haugwitz a long letter to follow by the special courier leaving today for Berne. (I <u>opened it here</u>.) It was brought back at 7.45 in (the evening).

Then V.H. brought me back to hotel in his car after deciding all about our departure tomorrow night. We three are to go to the G.G.S. in afternoon – change there into other (sailors things) I get shaved and then we go off to Hamburg (I fancy) in a special coupé. Nadolny was very cheery. He said it was impossible to get a submarine and he was sure this way was allright. He asked after Noeggerath putting many questions, saying I had sent him to Z. and the Admiralty and latter were very angry and charged them (G.G.S.) with breach of faith. I said put it all on me. "I am responsible for telling Noeg. and involving his aid to try and get a submarine since all other means had failed." I explained who Noeg. was – a confidential agent of the Foreign Office and entirely in their confidence and they might rest assured there was no danger from his being brought into my confidence.

I added I had told Gaffney a little only as I was leaving him to look after the interests if the Irish soldiers at Zossen and that I was writing to the Chancellor on that subject. They were very anxious to know if I had told anyone else – but I evaded that by talking on Gaffney's share. I was sorry to deceive them – but could not help it.

Noeggerath came to hotel on my return – He had no news from Admiralty or Foreign Office and asked if I had – I had none – Very soon after I got a phone call from Assessor Meyer asking the name of the marine officer I had seen at the Admiralty – I said Heydell and he said "all right."

Soon after I got a phone call from Heydell asking me to go round to the Admiralty at 4 adding it was "over the submarine." I went and he left me with a junior nice young Korvetten Kapitän[180] – where I stayed till 6.30 reading back numbers of English papers.

Then came Heydell in great excitement to say that they had a full dress debate and the thing was settled. I was to go by submarine. Details would be arranged later. I said "but you must promise to land me in time for any fight in good time" and he promised. Captain Stoelzel came breathless from running up stairs and told me it was settled – and repeated the positive assurance I should be landed in good time – I was to return at 1 p.m. tomorrow. I left feeling another victory! Noeggerath I had seen going into the Admiralty just before I did – but we did not greet each other.

When I got to the hotel I told Monteith in a whisper – and then came Noeg. He had been present all through the debate and it was his arguments had swayed them – but they had not told him the decision come to. He learned it only from me and was delighted. While we were talking young von Haugwitz came bringing me back my letter to the Delegate at Berne saying it was no use sending it now and he had stopped it. The telegram had gone he assured me.

I discussed what to do with the Delegate and said I'd like to get him here – or if not to send him back to Dublin post haste – but he demurred and said it was better to wait – until tomorrow at any rate. He congratulated me warmly on the change of plan and said he had been very unhappy about the steamer and that he was delighted I had got the submarine. He added "I will bring the poison all the same." He begged me to keep out of danger in Ireland and said many kind things.

Gaffney came – many times during the day – I told him only that there was a delay – no more, and that we should have more time to arrange things and talk over the proper line for him to take about the affairs of the men at Zossen after I was gone and that I was naming him in my letter to the Chancellor as my representative in their regard.

I dined with Frau Remy-Barsch[181] and Krebs and turned in at 10 p.m.

---

[180] Korvetten Kapitän – Lt. Commander
[181] According to Pásztor Árpád, a Hungarian journalist, who intrepidly interviewed the

Monteith I forgot to say had been sent to Foreign Office by Meyer today at <u>8 p.m.</u> who asked him many questions about the "rising" and what prospect of success there might be – M. had replied that he regarded it as quite hopeless and impossible of success.

I am in further distress about the man at Berne. It <u>may</u> be J.P. – but I think not I know the writing – but cannot remember its owner at the moment. It is <u>perhaps</u> T. MacDonagh.[182]

Were these people or this govt. inspired by any sense of decency fair play or gentleman of soul they would at once have brought him here – or permitted me to communicate frankly with him. They do neither – but carefully keep us apart – at this crisis in our country's affairs! – and it is doubtful if he will be told anything sure at all – or if he will be told I have gone away to Erin.

<u>Saturday</u> 8 <u>April</u>. 1916

I was to have left today – disguised as a sailor at 3 p.m. or 4 with M. & Beverley from the G.G.S. – but yesterday's debate at the Admiralty has changed that. Now I await the fresh developments from Admiralty at 1 p.m. Gaffney called at 10. Showing me this! **[In pencil after gap:]** Not rec'd by Noeg.

[Side note:] All the papers have it. The *Preussische Zeitung* puts asterisks for the <u>name</u> and omits in same way some of Herr L's[183] remarks. *B. Tageblatt* and *Lokalanzeiger* has it in full. R.C.

This is awful! I don't know what they may do now. Surely there <u>is</u> a fate that hurls things on. How Liebknecht got a hold of this goodness only knows. Monteith came at my request and Zerhusen who is here to translate it.[184]

Berlin hotel staff just after the execution, Frau Barsch also lived in the Saxonia Hotel and was very friendly with Casement, often sending him flowers, but there "was no love affair". She was born in Egypt and married to an Austro-Hungarian. The staff thought Casement a kind-hearted, shabbily-dressed gentleman. He did not drink much but liked a Martini cocktail, never smiled and was obsessed with writing about Ireland (NLI 13090).

[182] It was neither Thomas McDonagh nor Joseph Plunkett but his father Count Plunkett.

[183] Herr L.' i.e. Karl Liebknecht; the German socialist leader was charged with attempted war treason because of a speech he had made in the Reichstag on 7 April about Casement. Liebknecht's alleged crime had been reading out the Irish Brigade Treaty in the Reichstag. He had prefaced his remarks by saying that Germany had entered "a treaty with the arch-traitor Sir Roger Casement whereby English soldiers were to be used against England."

[184] Joseph Zerhusen wrote an interesting and lengthy memoir of 117 typed pages, catalogued in NLI 43570 as "Recollections of Herr Zerhusen concerning Roger Casement's Irish Brigade". This was reserved until 1989 "because of adverse comments on Mrs Agnes Grabisch (1875-1948) and Sergeant O'Toole". A shorter, 16-page, version is in NLI 31728. Zerhusen hated Prussians and thought Beverley glib and too compliant. Casement wrote to him on 10 April 1916 saying, "You are one of two men in this country to whom I say goodbye with keen regret". His father-in-law, John Hand, was an Irish Home Rule Councillor in Liverpool.

Z. has two copies he says of the Treaty. So has Hahn. And the soldiers had it for months – and all in Limburg knew of it – and the "Times" long ago brought out a very <u>fair rendering</u> of it.

Noeggerath just phoned to say he was leaving town for a few days and wished to see me – and I told him to come at once. He is coming. He came at 12.30 to bid me good–bye and to ask me to give him a letter of authority to recover the Findlay letter from the Captain of the "Kristianiafjord." He thinks Schirmer was arrested at Kirkwall on the outward voyage of the "K" say 25-26 February.

S. it seems, was not on the passenger list! S. was to have handed the Findlay letter to the Captain to keep in his safe. Noeggerath thinks this was probably done and that the letter may be there, safe and sound, but the Captain does not know what to do with it, as it would have been in an unaddressed envelope. Schirmer was to have given it to D.C.[185] in New York – as no word has come, we presume S. was taken off the boat.

I have written a letter authorizing Noeggerath to get the letter back from the Captain, if it is still in his possession – and have given N. a letter of introduction to D.C., J.D., and J. McG. **[Joe McGarrity]** in America.

I then went on at 1 to the Admiralty and saw Captain Stoelzel the chief of the affair and one of his under Captains. No word had yet come. Heydell had gone to Wilhelmshaven to see about the submarine – but the matter had not been settled at 1 o'clock. I was asked to call again at 3. I have just been there and saw Stoelzel and the message was there just coming by phone as I sat in this sofa. It was that a "U boat" would be at my service from Emden on 12 April. I am to call on Heydell on Monday 10th in the forenoon and get details of departure.

We shall probably leave this for Emden on 11th April (Tuesday) night.

Monteith and Beverley are here. Latter knows nothing yet – but Monteith says he will surely go – and with joy. I think M's real reason for taking Beverley was this – M. was in a fearful state over my going by the steamer (I still don't know her name!) and would have done anything to save me. Seeing it was impossible to get a submarine (as we thought) and that I <u>must</u> go I think he meant to "capture" me at the last moment down at Kiel or wherever the port was – with Beverley's help and tie me up and leave me behind or else, perhaps, as we cruised along the Norwegian coast (in territorial waters all the time) a chance might come to do this and put me on shore.

Old Krebs put the idea before me! He said Monteith was capable of any-

---

Zerhusen's papers were destroyed in a Hamburg air raid in 1943. He visited Ireland in 1966 and was filmed by RTE for the 50th anniversary commemorations.

[185] Daniel Cohalan *op. cit.*

thing to save me – and that – I must get on board that ship "alive or dead." I agreed with K, and laughed. Now since yesterday evg. this "possibility" has gone.

Zerhusen is here and buying things for Beverley "for the journey to the East."

Zerhusen is a fine chap – and his wife a good Irishwoman still.

If I live I hope to see them again – but there is not much chance in this world.

Anyhow there are three days more.

My chief trouble now is the man at Berne. They clearly want me not to see him or communicate with him – and I don't know what to do. I am powerless – in their hands.

[The days from 28 March 1916 to 6 April 1916 are covered for a second time by Casement in NLI 17587/2:]

Rough note of last days in Berlin.

1916
Tuesday 28 March –

Arr. From Munich at 7. Met by Monteith who considers the whole thing "dastardly." Told him I wd. stop it if I could – but saw no way without irreparable injury to others – but that I had decided not to take the men.

Wed. 29 M'ch.

In Admiralty by appointment and explained there the objections to taking the men. – They saw them & one captain to G.G.S with me – where a very furious discussion arose (see my letter to Wedel of 30th)

From the G.G.S. & this row, wherein I saw clearly the character of the thing explained here & the aims these men have – viz. slaughter in Ireland for German military purposes – I met Gaffney & to Noeggerath's by chance really – Latter had said he'd like to see me. I told both there under seal of secrecy the whole situation. Both came to dinner with me.

Meantime Haugwitz from G.G.S. had called – but I was out. I was ill with fever. (Haugwitz went to Zossen next day to try and get Mon[**teith**] to agree to take the men "over my head. He failed.)

Thursday 30. M'ch.

Phone call from Nadolny to see him as soon as possible. Went & he again tried to blackmail me into full acquiescence with his plan. I think him a complete and perfect scoundrel and he knows I do. He is but the instrument

Rudolf Nadolny in civilian clothes

of a policy of scoundrels. Back & told Noeggerath whom I had seen before going to G.G.S. & told him my fears. He to Zimmermann at 12.30 & back at 2 to say Z. interested & would try do something. My views all the time submarine essential if the thing to go on at all – stop it if could – & send more help.

Thursday 30 M'ch

Back to G.G.S at 3 – after seeing Monteith in from Zossen. At G.G.S. I listened to Nadolny & came away more than ever impressed with the horrors of these people.

[Insert stroked out:] He called the Irish soldiers at Zossen "Disasters"! Said he would cable to U.S.A. over my head to take them & tried all he could to get me to give in. I never budged. A record of our conversation would damn the G.G.S.

N's politeness to me today due to Z I fancy & also to the fact that Haugwitz had been out to Zossen to try to detach Monteith from me. On finding he could not (Staunch Monteith!) H. had doubtless phoned in to N & then latter had phoned to me.

I returned from G.G.S. ill & lay down with high temperature. In evg. Monteith came I while I was in bed. I told him I thought of writing to Wedel explaining the whole damnable thing from my point of view & saying at any rate I should not take the men.

I could not sleep – any more than last night – at 1.30 or 2 a.m. (3 really). I got up & wrote rough dft my letter to Wedel of 30 Mch. Lay down & slept 1½ hours all told.

Friday. 31 M'ch.

Finishing my letter to Wedel – fever on me all day. Doctor came. Manager hotel insisted on it. Lying down nearly all day. Gaffney greatly approved it & went on got me copying things to get copies of it. Busy on it & other things. Dr. said <u>must</u> stay in bed.

April 1.
Saturday.

Finished my letter to Wedel with rough copies. Dr. called again. Says threatened congestion of lungs. Told me go out for a few seconds & walk slowly.

Sent letter to Wedel by Monteith, after reading it to him – He approves strongly. He took it & Wedel said it wd. have "his immediate attention."

I was hopeful after sending the letter to Wedel. Wedel is the best of the lot in the F.O.

To Esplanade with Gaffney after my short walk & there met Emerson & Fromme and took tea with them till 6.

Back – Gaffney dined with – the Zerhusens came she is nice Irish woman still in spite of so many years in Germany. Stayed up talking with them until nearly 11 p.m. Sent a second letter to Wedel. 9 today – See it – & learned he had "gone on leave of absence for four days."

April 2. Sunday.

Lovely day. Gaffney called & out with him in Thiergarten & then lunch at hotel with Frau R. B. Dined with G. in evening at Hoffman's Keller and back at 9 p.m. to meet Monteith who stayed with till 11.30. The latest development was that at 6.35 I got a phone call from Assessor Meyer saying they (F.O.) could do nothing and I must call with Nadolny – see my remarks on it.

April 3. Monday.

Called on Ctess. B. Left her copy of the x... and explained a very little only. She thinks I go to Munich. v. Haugwitz phoned begging me to call at 3. important.

I consulted & went. They still wanted the men to go as gun company. I refused and while we were polite differed profoundly. Nadolny came in during our conversation & revealed the Beast again. Matter was still left to be settled tomorrow – they phoned for Monteith to come in and aid.

At 11 p.m. Zerhusens in from Zossen with letter from Monteith to say Fr Crotty coming in morning. I had asked for him to come & M. had wired Limburg.

<u>Tuesday. 4 April</u>
Met Fr. Crotty and brought him to Hotel & after short talk explaining much, he had bath and breakfast. Then told him all in my room. He went on to C'tess Blücher– with a letter from me begging her to secrecy absolute. She replied by him – with a prayer book & confession book.[186]

[Princess Blücher, in her usual self-exculpatory and unreliable manner, wrote in a passage of her book dated seeing Casement on 4 April 1916:]

"I was suddenly rung up on the telephone by Sir Roger Casement, saying he must see me at once. I was somewhat surprised, as I thought he was ill in bed at Munich. He was, a few days ago, when we heard of him last.

However, although I was not keen on seeing him, I telephoned back to say that I would do so for a few minutes. Little did I think what a scene was before me.

The poor man came into the room like one demented, talked in a husky whisper, rushed round examining all the doors, and then said: "I have something to say to you, are you sure no one is listening?"

For one moment I was frightened, I felt I was in the presence of a madman, and worked my way round to sit near the telephone so as to be able to call for help. And then he began: "You were right a year ago when you told me that I had put my head into a noose in coming here. I have tried not to own you were right, and I did not like to tell you when you kept on urging me to get out of the country, that I realised from the moment I landed here what a terrific mistake I had made. And also I did not want to tell you that in reality I was a prisoner here. I could not get away. They will not let me out of the country.

The German Foreign Office have had me shadowed, believing I was a spy in the pay of England, and England has had men spying on me all the time as well.

Now the German Admiralty have asked me to go on an errand which all my being revolts against, and I am going mad at the thought of it, for it will make me appear a traitor to the Irish cause."

And at these words he sat down and sobbed like a child. I saw the man was beside himself with terror and grief, and so I tried to get a few more definite facts out of him, and told him there is a way out of every difficulty if he would only tell me more.

But he said, "If I told you more, it would endanger the lives of many, and as it is, it is only my life that has to be sacrificed." I made all sorts of suggestions, but all he would say was: "They are holding a pistol to my head here if I refuse, and they

---

[186] Princess Blücher, pp. 130-131.

have a hangman's rope ready for me in England; and so the only thing for me to do is to go out and kill myself."

I argued him out of this, and at last he went away after giving me a bundle of farewell letters to be opened after his death. As he went out of the door, he said: "Tell them I was loyal to Ireland, although it will not appear so."

He asked to see me again, but as I am watched like everyone else here, and as there was evidently some political intrigue on, I had to refuse."

Then with M. to G.G.S. where finally <u>they</u> gave in & accepted the inevitable – that the men should not go. We take Beverley at M's wish. Poison arranged for all three! Haugwitz the only gentleman there.

Everything fixed for departure – "probably Friday night." My second victory – I have saved the men. Fr Crotty to the Dominicans & then to dinner with me. He in my room till 10.30 or 11. I fell asleep while they talked.

Wed. 5 April.

Fr Crotty at 10. We go to Zossen at 10.38. Von Haugwitz called with measurements for the sailors' clothes for M., Beverley & myself. I am convinced the thing was largely inspired by von Papen – who filled J.D. with assurances of German goodwill & support, possibly honestly enough. <u>He</u> did not know his G.G.S. either. Spent day at Zossen talking to men a word of farewell – Breaking heart. I have been crying all the morning.

Back with Fr. C. at 5.30 and Krebs to whom I had given Wedel's letter to copy. I took Krebs into confidence under strictest promise of secrecy – as I want another witness after death. I have not told him all only the blackguardism of the G.G.S. which he sees very clearly – & the other things – But J.D.'s letter explains much. Fr Crotty left for Limburg at 9.17 train. Saw him off. Wrote diary till 1.30 a.m. after Fr Crotty who begged me to make fresh attempt.

<u>Thursday</u> 6 <u>April.</u>

Haugwitz several times. Also N. after reading my diary – He went to Z. "greatly impressed" & on to Admiralty he told me.

At 4.15 I got letter from Wedel, inclosing one from Berne 5 April – Awful. Off to Admiralty, rang up Haugwitz who came at 6. Gave him the letter & he to Nadolny – promising return. Did not come. I expect a great row on.

[Casement's 'A final word' letter to Dr Curry:][187]

A final word   6 April 1916

Take the original Irish verses to Reute & bury them safe and sound.

Go carefully through Graf Wedel's letters to me. There are two I want very much preserved.

One is of June 28 1915. I think –

In it the Count says the G. Govt. will scrupulously respect and observe all their obligations & promises to me and the men of the Irish Brigade – In another letter of August 1915 or Sept 1915 possibly – he says that he regards me "as a hero" &c. &c.

Wholly private letters – or business letters, from publishers &c. &c. you need never read thro – only glance at. The important letters are those of the German Govt. to me, & my drafts of letters to them – &c. &c.

The parcel of letters from John Devoy, J. McGarrity & my sister in America – you need not read. They are wholly personal & need never be published or dealt with at all. Those of Devoy & McGarrity are not intended for any eyes but mine I think.

I am giving Gaffney a big bundle of papers &c. &c. here – collected by Monteith & myself. They are important – because a lot of them are my closing pages of my diary here now & deal with the last fatal situation of the last three weeks or so – since 16. March to be exact.

There is the copy of a letter of 30 M'ch to Count Wedel of supreme importance – it is as important as the Irish verses almost. It states my position so clearly & will cover my honour & responsibility for ever I think. It should go with the Irish verses into the same place Of course I mean always the Original Treaty when I speak of the Irish verses. Let no one know you have it - & never part with it save on my order, or to the people named after I am dead.

6 April 1916
A final word. contd.

If, during the course of the war I should send for it to you then you must send it to me by the course I suggest. It and other papers I might name. It is just possible I could find a means of sending to you for it & even of getting it out of the country - & if I do this you must give it up no matter what the circumstances might be. I may be put on trial & might want to have it - & I should certainly want the letter to Wedel of 30 March 1916 (It is in with my Diary).

I am relying on you very much indeed in the strange situation I am put in by the action of others – for altho' Gaffney knows (I had to tell him) I don't rely on his discretion or ability. He is well-meaning – but very loquacious & I fear always he may say things without thinking. This is a case that cannot ever at any time be helped by loose talking, or denouncing or gabbling. It is a case for clear thought, and clear

---

[187] Casement's letter to Dr Curry entitled 'A final word' and dated 6 April 1916 is in NLI 17027. It is written on one 2-sided sheet while 'A final word contd.' is written over two 4-sided sheets.

precise, written statements when, if ever, the time should come to state it to the world in my defence. In that event not even you can help. You are only the custodian. It must be stated by some one who knows all the facts (1ˢᵗ) - Knows me too. (2) and is a master of English (3) E.D. Morel would be the best – a Mrs. Green of 36 Grosvenor Road London SW – still better. Or they, two, together collaborating

They are both my dearest friends.

If I die – or other things (no matter what) happen to me, then I think, on thinking it all over – you should try & see Mrs. Green.

She would welcome you. Tell her everything. She is an Irishwoman to the core altho' probably today anti-German. So am I – in some things. I am anti-General Staff to the core – and to some extent - but not much anti-Foreign Office – But I am wholly pro German always for the sake & cause of the German people. The evils of their system of military rule they must deal with from within –

I see those evils – but they are primarily a German question and have not caused Europe alarm. The attack on the German people on the pretence of overthrowing Prussian militarism is both a crime & a mistake. It can't succeed in the first case - & it only drives the German people more resolutely into the military machine's clutches. After the war, if all the brave Germans are not killed in defending the Fatherland, the People themselves, I am convinced will deal with the evils of the system of rule begotten in the Prussian state system and transferred thence to all Germany.

This is a digression. - -

See Mrs. Green if you can, as soon as the war is over & you are free to travel. Write her at once. Ask her, too, to bring you into touch with Professor Eoin MacNeill of the National University of Ireland – Dublin – a historian and scholar.

See my "Romance of Irish History" & the remarks of his I quote.

These two heads are clear & sound – his and Mrs. Green. & so is E.D. Morel and all firm friends to the death.

It is not my own honour is at stake alone – but the cause of Irish nationality in the extreme form I have stood for. The Br. Govt. will seek to injure both - & one thro' the other. By assailing me & my character they will hope to blacken my cause too – at any rate to gravely weaken it.

Gaffney will tell you details of my forthcoming departure. It is all arranged for tomorrow night - - Friday! – unlucky omen! –

Lt. Monteith comes with me He insists. I am sorry – but I can't stop him – & one brave man of the corps.

It is Monteith's wish to take this man. He has not been told yet but will be today & I am sure he will volunteer & go with joy.

I stopped all the others after fearful fight & truly disgusting efforts by the G. Staff (Political Dept.) to force me to take them. There only hours?? I won.

I gave them no option there – and after trying bullying, blackmailing, (there is no other word for it) & threats of various kinds I dropped it - & I go alone, save for that noble Monteith & the one man he chose.

This man is a young soldier named Julian Beverley. Devoted to Monteith.

As for Monteith, he is really a hero – I am not. I am a coward at heart I feel it – for I should be brave enough to stop the whole thing & take the full responsibility for doing so & face the jeers & jibes and curses too of my own Countrymen. It is this last dread sways me. If I stop it – this "relief expedition" I incur the awful responsibility of depriving them of the only aid offered at the hour of their fate. So it would seem. And yet I feel it is all wrong & mad & that instead of helping them the safe arrival by the steamer & the attempt to land the guns (foredoomed to failure) will be the signal for a futile rising in Ireland. & wretched effusion of blood.

Instead of helping Ireland it may do it infinite harm – & possibly Germany too.

I am distracted – wherever I turn is hopelessness.

Only God can save the situation – some Almighty power that moves thro' men & their acts & failures & stumbling efforts to do right in spite of all the inherent evils of their imperfect natures.

I am such a one today – and while I go with a brain appalled and a heart sick to death & longing for death I sometimes feel with a throb of hope that the whole situation will be saved & the evil I foresee averted.

If only these people here had carried out my entreaty – to send me ahead in a submarine. Then the facts of the situation wd. have been known & we should know exactly where we were going and what doing.

I hope with all my heart – sincerely that I may be killed quickly in this mad attempt – for I don't want to go on bearing this wretched burden of life, and being assailed on all sides – If only a lucky shot puts me out quickly I'll be very glad – and then my part in the whole madness can be brought to light without my having to show what it was.

Were I put on "trial" (a queer trial it would be!) & I defended myself by <u>telling all</u> I put this Govt. (Germany) in a terrible position before the world.

<u>Their</u> character would be gone for ever – that is certain - & instead of helping them <u>or</u> Ireland – I should again hurt both. For it is evident the Irish would <u>then</u> be furious with Germany & so England would get them into her recruiting net evils - & Germany would have been shown to have practically sent me to my doom on an absurd & disgraceful expedition (from a military standpoint) in order to reap some possible advantage to herself from bloodshed in Ireland. Altogether it is the most extraordinary laugh?? was ever set one to unwind.

The one thing I see clearer & clearer is that the G. General Staff here are criminally guilty – from every point of view. They plotted & planned this thing <u>I am convinced</u>, thro' von Papen in New York with old John Devoy – a furious hater of England - & carefully behind my back because they knew I should oppose it on <u>such</u> <u>lines</u>. And then when the home strikes?? for the thing to go I am brought on the scene in order to take the responsibility off their shoulders. They <u>know</u> I can't refuse to go. That if the thing goes I must go – otherwise incur the damning reproach of being afraid to face the music <u>I</u> had set going. & so forth.

9-11 April 1916 – Casement's last three days in Berlin[188]

Sunday 9 April 1916

Dies non. Spent day with Gaffney and walked all night nearly to try and got sleep – but none.[189]

[Casement letter of 9 April 1916 to Dr Curry and a second related, but undated:]

HOTEL SAXONIA
Delayed at last moment
BERLIN W.9.
9.4.16
Dear Dr Curry
Bury the Irish verses. Let no one know about them. Other papers keep at Riederau or in your rooms.
You remember the box of photo plates I left at Riederau? They are of the Treaty - Later on (much later on) they may be useful – also that plate of the Findlay Letter I gave you in Munich.
I want you to send the photograph of the Treaty I left with the papers I gave you at Munich lately to Franz Hugo Krebs at the Hotel Bristol, Berlin but not by post. It should go by hand - a friend – and no one should know what is in it. I have told Mr Krebs it will come to him.
Please try and get it to him fairly soon – in a week or so.
I think that is all.
    Yours ever,
      Roger Casement,
P.S.
The best thing to do after the war, if you can manage it, wd be to try and see Mrs Green 36. Grosvenor Road, Westminster. S.W. Of course the Irish verses are Ireland's and can not be given to anyone except the friend I told you of in the U.S.A. – but she could be consulted on many things – especially diaries and letters.
The Diaries are very poor stuff very poorly written and hastily put together - and would need much editing by a friend – for I often say things in them I should not like to stand for ever.
It is so hard to see straight even when one is well and not troubled – and I am not well in body and have not been for long and then greatly troubled too in mind – so that my remarks are often unjust and hasty and ill considered.
The last days are all a nightmare – I have only a confused memory of them and some periods are quite blank in my mind – only a sense of horror and repugnance to life –

---

[188] NLI 17587/1

[189] Casement letter of 9 April 1916 to Dr Curry (also in NYPL partially) and an undated second. Photocopies of the originals are in PRONI T3787/21/7-8 and were provided to Hugh Casement by Marion Bembé, Curry's granddaughter.

But I daresay clouds will break and brighter skies dawn – at least for poor old Ireland.
>Kindest thoughts for Your Mother.
>>Yours R. C.

HOTEL SAXONIA
BERLIN W.9.
[beginning lost]
Please keep this along with all other documents of mine. Mr G will find means later on of sending it to the men at Zossen – or perhaps of reading it himself to them.
Above all things, save the "Irish verses". Let no man or woman know you have them. Hide them effectually and give only to the man appointed.
Don't forget to send Krebs at the Bristol a copy of the Treaty – but don't let Gaffney know anything about it. Never tell him – I fear he may speak unguardedly. Better take the photo of the Treaty you have among the last papers I left with you at Munich to Krebs and give to him personally letting no one know of it. The precaution is very essential.
I go tonight with Monteith and one man only of "the boys" – and I am quite sure it is the most desperate piece of folly ever committed but I go gladly. It is only right and if those poor lads at home are to be in the fire then my place is with them.
Keep all my papers safe - let no know you have them or they may be seized or stolen - and don't let Gaffney talk – Love to all of you and may God bless you.
>Yours always,
>>Roger Casement

P.S. Don't forget my sister Mrs Newman, c/o John Devoy Gaelic American New York City
She is my nearest one – and she will be heart broken. Try and see her some day and cheer her up.
>Adieu.
>R.C.
P.S
Keep the little agate pen box as a souvenir I've had it 20 years and more out on the Congo and everywhere – The writing pad – brown canvas keep too. Mrs Green made it for me herself, when I was going to the Putumayo in 1910 - and I wrote on it - the Putumayo Report and later the Treaty of Dec 1914.
It is a little souvenir.
>R.C

Monday 10 April
>Sent Monteith[190] to G.G.S. (with Beverley)

---

[190] http://www.irishbrigade.eu/recruits/monteith/monteith-germany-diary.html

[Monteith's diary entry for 10 April 1916:]

I must move quickly as my time is short. I am now driven, I can use no other word, to embark on what I believe to be the wildest enterprise in the history of Europe, and it is in my opinion a deliberate cold blooded attempt to get rid of Sir Roger Casement and myself, under the pretense of helping our country. A record of details of this enterprise has been left in other hands and in other minds, so I shall not go into the matter here. There is no way out of the difficulties. We are cut off from communication with Ireland and America, and the whole transaction amounts to this, that I believe Sir Roger Casement, Sgt. Beverly and myself are going straight to our death with our hands tied, without even hope of being able to raise a hand to defend ourselves, and fools think we cannot see through their treachery—or let me be charitable, want of foresight. We go well knowing what is in front of us, but we go without fear and without reproach. Without me and perhaps without Beverly the world will move along in the same way, but in Sir Roger Casement, the world loses one of her best and greatest men.
R. Monteith
10/4/16 Berlin

& a note to Count von Haugwitz – attached hereto[191]

[Casement note to Count von Haugwitz:]

Hotel Saxonia
Berlin W.9
Monday, 10 April. 1916

[In Casement's handwriting:] sent by Monteith 10.30 a.m.
Dear Count von Haugwitz
I shall be very glad to know what answer came from Berne – and also if you will be so kind as to give me a copy of my telegram to Berne of 7th. Something must be done today about the messenger there and his departure.
I should wish to send him a letter today. It is a great pity he was not brought here. It should have been done.
Please let me know how much German money is needed for the English gold you are letting me have. I think £75 will be enough instead of £100. I will give you the German money and not a cheque, as I have closed my bank a/c.
[crossed out:] I wait final instructions to start with impatience
Lt. Monteith and Sergeant Beverley were waiting yesterday in obedience to your request for them to revisit the explosion place.
   Yours very truly
    R. Casement

and then at 11 to Reichsmarineamt and saw Captain Stoelzel and Heydell.

---
[191] Not attached in NLI but in NYPL Maloney IHP, Box 1, Folio 5

Former told me the "U boat" would go either from Emden or Wilhelmshaven – not yet settled which – and we should be ready to go tomorrow night (Tuesday 11 April) at 11 p.m. from Zoological Garden station. Captain–Leut Kirchheim will accompany us. All details of departure to be arranged by G.G.S. – a coupé will be reserved.

I asked if the steamer had gone – Yes – & if there would be any chance of our meeting her & Stoelzel said that was not certain – he was not sure!!

Neither am I!

We shall start I think with sealed orders & even after the Commander of the "U boat" has them I wonder if <u>we</u> three men in a boat shall ever learn our destination?

I doubt it. More I think it highly probable that if the "U Boat" find no revolution in Ireland we shall be brought back for God knows what sort of fate in Germany. If the revolution does not come off it will be put up to me and John McG! **[McGoey]**

Monteith sent for Kavanagh today to give him some information about Quinlisk who has been saying strange things of late Monteith says – M. says it is better to know what the thing is & Kavanagh says he will not tell it save to me. So he is brought in and waiting here with Unteroff. Hahn the return of Monteith from the G.G. Staff. He went there about 10.15 and it is now 11.40 – I was not long at the Admiralty only a few minutes. Both Stoelzer and Heydell very cordial.

My chief concern now is for the man at Berne – What a shame not to have brought him here! Just think of it – he has come all that way and I can not communicate with him or learn anything at first hand about the true state of affairs in Ireland.

I do not think for a moment they gave him my telegram comm! It was sent but probably censored by the Legation at Berne.

It looks clear to me that they don't want him to leave Berne until it is quite out of the question he should reach Dublin in time to stop "proceedings."

They argue possibly thus – Our people <u>still</u> hope for the officers and a submarine – perhaps if they were told neither was being found there would be no "revolution" or "revolt" I mean.

So, MacDonagh, if it indeed be he, is kicking his heels out at Berne waiting for word from me – & I am unable to send it to him.

The right thing would be to bring him here, let us talk frankly – & if he could send him, too by the submarine to Ireland!

They treat me all the time just as they think suits them and their needs – & I am really a prisoner altho' I go to an almost certain death.

I tread the pavement with joy – my last day in Berlin, city of dreadful night and most "forbidding society." How I loathe the place!

I felt the day I arrived here 31 Oct 1914 that I had walked into a trap – I heard the jail door close behind me – and it has indeed been my prison and my doom.

Oh! To see the misted hills of Kerry and the coast and to tread the fair strand of Tralee!

Monday. 10 April

Monteith and Br. back from G.G.S. with the same information roughly as I got at the Admiralty except that they did not know the station or hour of train departure tomorrow night. Then v. H. called bringing me back the original <u>telegram to Berne which clearly has not been delivered to the messenger.</u> (See my remarks on back of it) or else he has hurried off again home after sending his letter to me on 5 April.

What a fearful business! They will certainly be convinced in Dublin that the officers are coming – <u>"this is imperative"</u> – & yet the scoundrels have deliberately gone on with the enterprise, pushing those poor boys into the fire, knowing they need officers <u>imperatively</u> & that none could or would be sent.

Von Haugwitz says I must pay Mks <u>2010</u> for £75 gold – before the war it would have been about Mks <u>1500</u>.

I was with Frau Remy-Barsch and Krebs a little in afternoon – & feeling most upset. She gave me some sleeping draught & I slept after dinner.

<u>Tuesday</u> <u>11 April</u>

My last day in Berlin! Thank God – tomorrow my last day in Germany – again thank God, an English jail or – scaffold would be better than to dwell with these people longer.

All deception – all self-interest – all "on the make."

Haugwitz called at 10 – and we interviewed Beverley and put it up to him. He comes gladly. I pointed out all the dangers & horrors & even impossibility of it – but he said he would gladly come.

So that is settled. Haugwitz was there and Monteith.

Now for some clothing for the voyage – I have only one thin suit – too cold – the suit Mr J.E. L.[192] crossed in in Oct 1914!

Gaffney several times & Krebs – & Emerson to luncheon – He & Krebs fought or sparred. Differing types of American that is all.

I wrote a letter to the Chancellor about the Irish soldiers[193]

---

[192] James E. Landy - Casement's alias for his transatlantic voyage and arrival in Germany.
[193] Casement to Bethmann-Hollweg typescript in NYPL Maloney IHP, Box 1, Folio 5. See also NLI 13085 "Documents relating to Roger Casement's negotiations in Germany and the Irish Brigade, including letters from J. M. Plunkett, 1914-1916."

[Casement letter to Chancellor Bethmann-Hollweg:]

Berlin,
11 April 1916
Excellency,

On the point of leaving Germany on a mission that will probably cut me off from further communication with this country - at least during the course of the war, I venture to bring to your Excellency's notice the situation of the small body of Irish soldiers who volunteered to form an Irish corps, to fight for Irish freedom, with the whole hearted support and approval of the Imperial German Government.

The terms on which they agreed to serve and to observance of which the Imperial Government pledged its good faith in the most formal way are embodied in the agreement drawn up by myself on 23 December 1914 and accepted by the Under Secretary of State on 28 December 1914.

I need not refer your Excellency to that document, since it was so fully within your Excellency's cognizance following the interview on the subject of German policy towards Ireland I had the honour to have with your Excellency on 18 December 1914.

Now that I am leaving Germany, as I hope for Ireland in order to help in the very critical circumstances in which events seem to push my country, I cannot depart without recalling the situation of these Irish soldiers who volunteered for the cause of Ireland under the pledge of that agreement, and begging that nothing should be allowed to interfere with its strict fulfillment in their regard.

These men remain a charge confided to the honour of the German Government and German people.

They are guests of Germany in the highest sense of the word and are entitled to the scrupulous fulfilment of the terms of the agreement under which they threw off their allegiance and entered into rebellion.

The German Government was a full consenting party to that act of theirs and did all in its power, through its military chiefs, to assure these men that their "treason" was honourable in itself, since it was for their oppressed country and assured them that they should be most honourably treated during the period of their stay on German soil.

Today, through the channel of the Political Section of the Gr. General Staff I am informed that the Agreement of 23-28 December 1914 is null and void, and has no binding force in relation to the men; that the Irish soldiers now at Zossen, to the number of some 53, are "Deserters" or "Prisoners of War" and may be treated in any way that seems fitting to the military authorities.

Dissenting profoundly from this point of view, I am forced to refer the treatment of these Irish volunteers to your Excellency as the highest representative of the Imperial German Government, in the firm conviction that every stipulation of the agreement of 23-28 December 1914, in so far as it affects the men, their status here in Germany and their ultimate disposal on the conclusion of peace will be faithfully fulfilled by the Government of this great Country.

I have requested my friend Mr. St. J. Gaffney, former U.S. Consul General at Munich, to have a kindly interest in the men so far as this may be possible and am recommending him in this capacity to Count Georg von Wedel of the German Foreign Office, whose assurances to me on behalf of the men I recall with gratitude and confidence.

I have the honour to be, Excellency,
    with the greatest respect,
        Your Excellency's most obedient humble servant
        Roger Casement.

– also to Count Wedel about Gaffney and the men[194]

[Casement letter to von Wedel:]

Berlin 11 April 1916.
Dear Count von Wedel,

I am asking Mr. St. John Gaffney to do what he can on behalf of the Irish soldiers still at Zossen, and have written today a letter to the Imperial Chancellor on the subject.

Such money as I still have left I am handing to Mr. Gaffney to expend on the men in the way already established since they took up their quarters at Zossen.

I think the best thing to do would be to put them to some useful occupation here in Germany until the war is over, and then to send them to America where Father Nicholson is already doing what is possible to provide for their future there.

As the money I leave with Mr. Gaffney will not go very far, I fear, I am forced to recall your letter to me of 11th December last in which you stated that the sum I had refunded (Mks. 8000) would be held at my disposal should I require it at any time for Irish affairs.

It is always probable and indeed very likely that further remittances from my friends in America will be received here in the usual way.

If so, I beg that they may be handed to Mr. Gaffney who will expend them as seems best in the interest of the men.

In any case I wish whatever sum you may hand to Mr. Gaffney from the Fund you and your friends so kindly raised for the Irish cause to be ultimately refunded to you by my friends in America.

I am instructing Mr. Gaffney in this sense.

I should like Mr. Gaffney to have access to the men at Zossen, and beg you as a last act of personal regard to do all in your power for them, to mitigate the cruel disappointment they will surely labour under and to make clear ultimately to them

---

[194] NLI 13085/9/i-x "Copy letters by Roger Casement principally to members of the German government and German Officers viz Count von Wedel, Capt. Boehm, Capt. Nadolny etc., a few to Adler Christensen, Joe McGarrity, H.J. Reilly, J. [O'H in Rome] and re T. St. John Gaffney. With some copy memoranda and diary extracts, c. 186p. Dec. 1915- April 1916."

how I left them without any explanation and apparently abandoned them.

I have acted throughout, in what seemed to be their best interests, and now in leaving them behind I feel I am still trying to do my duty to them.

I am concerned about the messenger at Berne too.

I telegraphed to him on the 7th instant asking several questions and wrote a letter of instructions.

The telegram remains without answer; and the letter was returned to me by the General Staff on the evening of the 7th as owing to the change of plan come to at the last moment as to my own means of departure, the General Staff thought the letter need not be sent

I leave Berlin tonight and I should much like the messenger at Berne to be informed.

I enclose a list of the remaining Irish soldiers at Zossen, a copy of which is also given to Mr. Gaffney.

With renewed expressions of warm personal regard,
    Believe me,
        Dear Count Wedel,
            Yours sincerely,
                Roger Casement.

– & a farewell to the men to be left with Gaffney& handed to them.[195]

[Casement note to Gaffney:]

10 April 1916
For Mr. Gaffney
Note on the 53 men Still at Zossen

There were originally 55 – but Holohan is dead & Beverley (I presume) going away – John McGoey was a Volunteer from U.S.A. & brought the total up to 56. He too, is gone.

The 2 lists joined are.

1st Complete list of names & their previous condition before they enlisted.

2nd List of Volunteers who were willing to go to Egypt or India or "anywhere to get a whack at England"! – as one of them said.

Taking Lt. Monteith, John McG. & myself away, it shows 37 Volunteers of the originally 55 who joined at Limburg. These 37 are better men than the 18 who refused to volunteer for the East – and greater attention, in the end, should be paid to them.

It is quite certain to my mind, that the Gr. Grl Staff and the War Office will not keep the 53 men in their present quarters at Zossen, or in their uniforms, once we have gone (Lt. M. & I.). The question is what is best to be done.

They cannot be sent into a Gefangenelaager or treated as prisoners of war – that would be a gross breach of faith with the men which I am sure the German Foreign

---

[195] NLI 17580

Office will not assent to. On the other hand the G.G. Staff will certainly want to get rid of them – & there will be a fight over their future status during the rest of the war.

Once peace comes it may well be that the Br. Govt. would pardon them – but their comrades never! Their position in Ireland, (for some time to come at any rate) would be intolerable – the butt of jibes and jeers.

So there is nothing for it, even if England did pardon their treason, but to send them to U.S.A. with <u>at least</u> £10. in pocket. That sum the German Govt. is pledged to give them – at least that sum in order to land in conformity with the Immigration Laws. My view is that, say a <u>month</u> after we are away – or when it is <u>known</u> we have landed safe & sound – the Germans should put the men to some useful trade or labour where they wd. be occupied & earning money.

The letter accompanying this should be sent to the men thro' Zerhusen.[196] But it would be far better if you – Mr. Gaffney – could yourself take it out to Zossen and read it to them.

You could explain how it was we <u>had</u> to go away – and without being able to tell them – and that it was really to save them from the great danger of capture.

If a miracle should happen & we <u>were</u> to succeed at all, in Erin then these men might be delighted to try & come over with a relief ship.

Burn this paper after you have mastered its contents but keep the Lists of men very carefully – and do all you can for those poor fellows.

Under Secry Zimmermann will do what he can – the trouble will be the Kriegsministerium & the G.G. Staff.

Of course any success in Erin will put these men in a much better position here in Germany.

Let us hope for it.
    R.C.
11 April <u>1916.</u>

Paid my bill at Saxonia – very dear – and they have swindled me over the doctor – <u>two visits 60 mks</u>!

These people are all swindlers.[197]

Emerson's story of the 6 mark lunch <u>is</u> the best I've heard. Guests to a private <u>house</u> here & then the host asked them to pay for their lunch. They

---

[196] Zerhusen later told Gaffney about the Irish Brigade troubles, saying, "In some towns the police and magistrates have begged us to take the Irishmen away, as there is always some trouble, swindling, debts, burglaries, selling stolen goods, beating policemen, found living with *Kriegerfrauen* when the husbands came home…In some factories they will not employ Irishmen, because they work too irregular, one day and the next day gone, or keep away in the afternoon, get advances on weeks pay and disappear. In short on the average they are a disgrace on the name of Irish." (NLI 13085/1/iv, 20 May 1918)

[197] NLI 13085/14: Casement was so outraged he also wrote on the back of the Hotel Saxonia bill, "an example of the swindling in this country. The doctor visited me twice! And charges 60 marks" while against the doctor's charge on the front of the bill, he continued, "X a swindler".

offered 2 marks and he said it had cost so much so they paid 6 marks.

Haugwitz say the train goes at 9.30 tonight – and we are to go to G.G Staff before hand to get some final instructions – code for more arms etc. etc. Poison too.

Haugwitz assured Beverley in my presence and M's that we should be put on <u>shore in Ireland</u>.

Nous verrons.

We shall be 12 days I reckon in the submarine – round by Orkneys probably. It will be a dreadful voyage – confined and airless and full of oil smells I fear.

My <u>first</u> fear is that we shall never land – but be kept off the shore until the "rebellion" breaks out,[198] and if that does not materialise then taken back again to this land of Crooks.[199]

Captain – Lieut. Kirchheim will come down with us.

This is my last chance of writing. I have lost my spectacles yesterday – but as there will be nothing to read – or do on the submarine – the 12 days will pass very slowly and <u>blindly</u> in any case.

I told Emerson I was going to Munich! Alas! It is dreadful the lying I am put to.

---

[198] From here to the end is omitted by Angus Mitchell in his *Berlin Diary* (p. 233).
[199] There is a different ending in the NLI 17587/4 typescript. After "this land of Crooks.", appears, "I long only for peace and forgiveness and reconciliation. All my life is one of that – and yet I've turned it into a nest of Serpents at the end – oh! what a fate!" The manuscript source for this alternative additional ending is unknown. Angus Mitchell included it in a *Berlin Diary* extract published in the Irish Times on 30 April 2016 but not in his book.

APPENDIX 1

The Nation 1921-1922

Extracts from Dr Charles Curry's book *Sir Roger Casement's Diaries – His Mission to Germany and the Findlay Affair* were published in a series of eleven chapters in *The Nation* in 1921-22 under the general title *The Diary of Sir Roger Casement*. The first item appeared on 30 November 1921 and the last in the edition of 8 February 1922.

Dr Curry's introduction and preface in *The Nation* read:

> Dedication
> To Alice Stopford Green – Roger Casement's ideal of a friend

My acquaintance with Sir Roger Casement dates from his first sojourn at Munich the latter half of 1915. I was presented to the Irish patriot by an Egyptian friend – Prince Mouhamed Ali Hassan, the day after his arrival – at the hotel "Bayerischer Hof", where Sir Roger had taken rooms. From our first meeting I did everything in my power to make his sojourn in a strange country, the language of which he did not speak as agreeable as possible. We soon became such intimate friends that, when I moved out with my family to the Ammersee for the summer vacation at the end of May, Sir Roger requested me to engage quarters for him there. I succeeded in securing two comfortable rooms for my friend in the country inn at Riederau; whereupon Sir Roger left Munich and joined us on the rural shores of the great lake. He was so happy and contented in his new environments – away from the noise and bustle of the city, that he remained in Riederau till late into the autumn. When we all returned to town at the end of the summer vacation. Sir Roger still kept his rooms in the little country inn, that he might spend, at least, the week-end there. It was, in fact, not until after Christmas, when Sir Roger broke down completely in health, that he could be induced to give up his summer quarters on the lake.

Before Sir Roger's final departure the end of March 1916 for Berlin, where all preparations were being made for his fatal voyage to Ireland, he entrusted to me all he possessed in this world, his personal effects and writings, and left me various written instructions chiefly regarding his diaries and their publication upon the close of the war. I deemed it from the outset a grave but sacred duty to a deceased friend to carry out those instructions to the best of my ability and with as little delay as the circumstances permitted...

Casement photograph on Ammersee pier with hat (not in New York as suggested by Angus Mitchell). The version in Magherintemple reads on the back, "Taken on the banks of the 'Ammersee' Bavaria 1915 when he was well." The printed inscription reads, "Sir Roger Casement who laid down his life for Ireland August 3, 1916." Alongside (right) is a photograph of kinsman Hugh Casement on the same jetty some 75 years later.

"With this issue *The Nation* begins publication of part of the diary of Sir Roger Casement, laying bare the soul of a man who, having done much to win for the peoples of the rubber–growing regions of the Belgian Congo and the Putumayo district of Peru whatever freedom from slavery they now enjoy, renounced all his British honours and, for the sake of Ireland, embarked upon the course which led to his execution. The manuscript was edited, and the preface written, by Charles E. Curry of Boston, to whom Sir Roger entrusted "all he possessed, both personal effects and writing."

Preface

In August 3, 1916, I unveiled a memorial slab to Sir Roger Casement, in the little hotel he frequented, at Riederau by the Ammer See, in the presence of several hundred mourning villagers, to whom Sir Roger had become a familiar figure during his holiday walks among their hills.

It was not necessary to know him much to love him much. These simple peasants, in sums ranging from a few pfennigs to an occasional mark, had raised the price of the slab among them in little more than a week. The postman of a village five miles away had walked over the hills to bring his fifty pfennigs "for the Irishman whom the children loved."

Close-up of Riederau house plaque which reads:
Hier wohnte im Sommer 1915
Sir Roger Casement,
*ein **Märtyrer für Jrland**'s Freiheit,*
ein hochherziger Freund
Deutschlands in schwere Zeit.
Er besiegelte die Liebe
zur Heimat mit seinem Blute.

When Sir Roger Casement was a public servant in matters where English interests derived that moral profit so eagerly demanded by the British temperament he was lauded as "one of the noblest figures in our imperial history." His services in the exposure of the Belgian cruelties on the Congo and of the barbarities in the Putumayo, as the London Daily News recently stated, stand "among the most unselfish acts" of a career that has been largely devoted to the welfare of the weak and the oppressed. The London Times, in one of its editorials in 1911, said of his fearless action in the Putumayo, in destroying a band of pirates controlled by a London company "he had deserved the thanks of the nation." Lord Fitzmaurice used almost identical words in the House of Lords on an earlier occasion (1906) when eulogizing the service Sir Roger Casement had rendered to the cause of humanity by his exposure of the Belgian atrocities on the Congo.

In transmitting to the Powers signatory to the Berlin Act (1884) Sir Roger Casement's indictment of the infamous system created by King Leopold II and carried out by Belgian officials on the Congo, Lord Lansdowne, then the British Minister of Foreign Affairs, claimed the earnest consideration of the governments addressed for this document, on the ground that it was the production of an official of "wide African experience." In spite of the sustained attacks made upon Sir Roger Casement's report against the Congo administration, the truth of his charges was amply demonstrated by the findings of the Special Commission of Inquiry sent out to the Congo in 1904 by the late – King Leopold. That commission of three carefully selected officers, dispatched by the Congo sovereign in the firm hope that they would curse the man who had exposed the infamies of Belgian administration, returned to bless the accuser.

The report was so damaging to the Belgian Congo administration that despite their pledge to publish it, given before the dispatch of the commission, it was withheld for many months from the public, and was only finally issued (but with the evidence on which it rested carefully withheld) when to keep it back became more dangerous than to issue it.

Perhaps the best testimony to the careful mind that had directed Sir Roger's impeachment of Congo misgovernment is to be found in a dispatch from Sir Edward Grey himself. Writing to the British Minister at Brussels on January 9, 1906, Sir E. Grey pointed out: "The Commission of the Inquiry has confirmed the statements made in Consul Casement's Report on the condition of the natives in the Congo. His Majesty's Government consider it unnecessary, therefore, to insist further on the existence of abuses which call for administrative reform."

When the war broke out Sir Roger Casement was in the United States.

He had gone there openly to enlist the sympathies of Irishmen in America with the Irish Volunteer movement, in which he had taken so active a part. He could have returned to Great Britain. His name as a wholly disinterested man, his reputation as a fearless public servant were assets to the cause of "public morality," which Great Britain avowedly sustained when she took up arms in defence of Belgian neutrality. Sir Roger had only to call at the British Embassy in Washington, to step on board the first Cunarder bound for Liverpool, and he would have been hailed on landing as one of the "brightest figures in our imperial history" and offered some post of distinction in the public service – perhaps to arraign Germany, in turn, for "atrocities in Belgium"! Letters to this effect had reached him from more than one quarter. The Patriotic League of Britons Overseas, in the person of Lord Aldenham, wrote in October, 1914, on behalf of this movement to invite him to join the Central Committee in London, then in process of formation, to which the following had already notified their adhesion: the Right Honourable Earl Selborne, K.G.; Lord Aldenham; Sir R. Balfour, M.P.; Admiral the Honourable Sir E. Freemantle, G.C.B.; Sir Charles Addis.

But ere this John Redmond had issued his appeal to Irishmen "to flock to the colours," and Sir Roger had replied to it in the following open letter to the Irish press:

New York,
17 September, 1914

As an Irishman and one who has been identified with the Irish Volunteer movement since it began, I feel it my duty to protest against the claim now put forward by the British Government that, because that Government has agreed with its political opponents to "place the Home Rule Bill on the Statute Book," and to defer its operation until after the war and until an "Amending Bill" to profoundly modify its provisions has been introduced and passed, Irishmen in return should enlist in the British Army and aid the allied Asiatic and European Powers in a war against a people who have never wronged Ireland. The British Liberal Party has been publicly pledged for twenty-eight years to give self–government to Ireland. It has not yet fulfilled that pledge. Instead it now offers to sell, at a very high price, a wholly hypothetical and indefinite form of partial internal control of certain specified Irish services if, in return for this promissory note (payable after death), the Irish people will contribute their blood, their honour, and their manhood in a war that in no wise concerns them. Ireland has no quarrel with the German people or just cause of offence against them in this war, beyond saying that the public profession under which it was begun, namely, to defend the violated neutrality of Belgium, is being daily controverted by the official spokesmen of Great Britain. The London *Times*, in its issue of the 14th instant, declared that Great Britain would not consent to peace on any terms that did not involve the "dismantling of the German Navy" and the permanent impairment of Germany's place in the world as a great seafaring nation. That may or may not be a worthy end for British statesmanship to set before it and a warrant for the use of British arms against Germany, but it is no warrant for Irish honour or common sense to be involved in this conflict. There is no gain, moral or material, Irishmen can draw from assailing Germany. The destruction of the German navy or the sweeping of German commerce from the seas will bring no profit to a people whose own commerce was long since swept from land and sea. Ireland has no blood to give to any land, to any cause but that of Ireland. Our duty as a Christian people is to abstain from bloodshed; and our duty as Irishmen is to give our lives for Ireland. Ireland needs all her sons. In the space of sixty-eight years her population has fallen by far over 4.000.000 souls, and in every particular of national life she shows a steady decline of vitality. Were the Home Rule Bill all that is claimed for it, and were it freely given today to come into operation tomorrow, instead of being offered for sale on terms of exchange that only a fool would accept, it would be the duty of Irishmen to save their strength and manhood for the trying tasks before them, to build up from a depleted population the fabric of a ruined national life. Ireland has suffered at the hands of British administrators a more prolonged series of evils, deliberately inflicted, than any other community of civilized men. Today, when no margin of vital strength remains for vital tasks at home, when its fertile fields are reduced by set design to producing animals and not men; the remnant of our people are being urged, to lay down their lives on foreign fields, in order that great and inordinately wealthy communities may grow greater and richer by the destruction of a rival's trade and industry. Had this war the highest moral aim in view, as its originators claim*for it, it would still be the duty of *Irishmen to keep out of it. If Irish blood is to be "the seal that will bring all Ireland together in one nation and in liberties equal – and common to all," then let that blood be shed in Ireland where alone it can be righteously shed – to secure those liberties. It was not Germany destroyed the national liberties of the Irish people, and we cannot recover the national life struck down in our own land by carrying fire and sword into another land.... Speaking as one of those who helped to found the Irish Volunteers, I say, in their name, that no Irishman fit to bear arms in the cause of his country's freedom can join the Allied millions now attacking Germany in a war 'hat, at the best, concerns Ireland not at all and that can only add fresh burdens and establish a new drain, in the interest of another community, upon a people that has already been bled to the verge of death.

This appeal to Irish patriotism brought from Sir Edward Grey the following official demand:

Foreign Office,
October 26, 1914

Sir: The attention of the Secretary of State has been called to a letter dated New York, September 16th, which appeared in the Irish Independent of October 5th over your signature. The letter urges that Irish sympathies should be with Germany rather than

with Great Britain and that Irishmen should not join the British army. As you are still liable, in certain circumstances, to be called upon to Serve under the Crown, I am to request you to state whether you are the author of the letter in question. I am, Sir, your most obedient humble servant,
(Signed) A. Nicolson[200]

Having written his public appeal to Irishmen to remain neutral, events led Sir Roger to set out for Berlin to secure convincing proof that Ireland need not fear a German invasion and that, when Irishmen were told by British Ministers that it was to their interest to join in assailing Germany, they were being misled. This diary tells of these events and the history of his mission to Germany."

[**Curry writing, from Buzzards Bay, Massachusetts, in September 1921, in the foreword to his book said:**[201]] "Upon due and careful consideration I finally concluded to publish only those parts of the diaries that deal with Sir Roger's "Mission to Germany and the Findlay Affair", the title of the present volume."
He also explained why Casement had chosen not to provide his own account: "Sir Roger wrote this Foreword apparently for Christensen's projected publication of the Findlay Affair, to which he had at one time given his consent."

[**The Casement foreword opened:**[202]] "I have been asked by many persons to write some account of the circumstances attending my journey from America to Europe and of the very peculiar incidents that followed my arrival at Christiania on 28-29 October [**1914**] and of my subsequent stay in Germany. While I feel that these matters are of sufficient public interest to warrant a clear statement of the facts, I have decided to refrain from dealing with them myself on the lines of a book. I prefer to meet those who plotted against me on another field; and to reserve a full exposure of the criminal attempt to intercept my coming to Germany to a later stage of my fight for Irish nationality against the greedy system of world exploitation termed "the British Empire." As a matter of fact the term "Empire" is misapplied. The thing that threatens today the existence of the German people, and has already throttled the people of Ireland and is in course of throttling the people of India, Egypt, Malaya, and a score of other dependencies of the London market is not an "Empire" but an Emporium. England fights only for profit, just as the tradesman deals only for profit. Her wars have always been wars

---

[200] Letter to Casement from Sir Arthur Nicolson (1st Lord Carnock)
[201] Curry pp. 9-10
[202] Ibid., p. 41

undertaken on a profit and loss account. When the balance lay on the debit side, England sheathed the sword; when it lay on the credit side, she wrapped the whole world in war and from a safe point of observation counted up the gains and assessed the value of her investments in other men's blood..."
[Curry added (by way of excuse):] "At Sir Roger's consent Christensen attempted to write up a full account of the Findlay affair in the early spring of 1915 with the intention of publishing it in the form of a book in both English and German, but finding the task beyond him – his English was too deficient and his knowledge of German very limited – he was obliged to have recourse to friends, "internationalist" of an inferior type, whose acquaintance he had little difficulty making during his sojourn in Berlin. Their sole interest in the enterprise was a mercenary one, as is evident from the several contracts they had drawn up and had induced Christensen to sign. When Sir Roger was finally consulted on the matter by Christensen, he became so disgusted, that he withdrew his consent to any publication or statement whatever, by these "friends" of his faithful companion. Moreover their knowledge of both English and German was of a most inferior sort as they were given to understand by Sir Roger himself. Most of the scandalous reports that were circulated later in Berlin on the authenticity of the Findlay affair can be traced to those "international" friends[203] of Christensen, who then turned on Sir Roger for upsetting their little business scheme."

THE NATION

Chapter I – 30 November 1921 opens as this diary does above:
'Berlin, 7 November, 1914
Now that I am safely in Berlin, having arrived here on Saturday evening, 31 October, 1914, from Christiania via Traelleborg and Ruegen-Stralsund route...'

[Chapters II to IV deal with Adler Christensen and the Findlay affair, illustrating Casement's obsession with this episode, something which so

---

[203] Georges Chatterton-Hill (born in Ceylon of an Anglo-Irish father and native mother) was one of those who admitted hearing Adler Christensen described as a swindler and who "thought you [Casement] had too much confidence in him." In a letter of 20 April 1915, however, he retracted, calling Adler "a loyal and noble character who has been grossly libelled" and "a good and faithful and generous-minded character" (Curry pp. 219-226). Chatterton-Hill was released from internment in 1915 after agreeing to work for the Germans. He described himself in a letter to Casement as "a Catholic and an Irishman" and someone who recognised that "England is the only Enemy of Ireland" (Doerries p. 96); author of *Irland and seine Bedeutung für Europa* ('Ireland and its significance for Europe'), Berlin, 1917, with a foreword by Eduard Meyer. He wrote frequently in the *Continental Times* and briefly worked for the Irish diplomatic service in Germany in the 1920s.

concerned his American friends, especially John Devoy, and made them start to question his judgement.]

Chapter II – 7 December 1921
'Early Spring, 1915'[204]

The reasons that induced me to come to Germany to urge certain proposals I had already placed before the German Ambassador at Washington are known[205] and I need only say here that, after I had decided on the course now taken, I looked only ahead. The immediate difficulty was to reach Germany from America. The British Authorities in U.S.A. have been accustomed, for many years, to watch the movements of all prominent Irishmen at home, in Ireland, and of all the leading Irish Americans in the United States. I was aware, during my stay in America (from July 20 to October 15), that I shared these attentions and was the object of a certain amount of espionage. Accordingly, when my decision to come to Germany was taken, I was forced to adopt a disguise and a false name and identity in order to cross the ocean. This was speedily effected through the good offices of some leading Irish Americans, who procured for me a passport and a letter of recommendation for a certain Mr. James ....[206], whom it was decided I should personate until the safety of the German frontier was reached.

As a double precaution I engaged a man, whom I had already helped[207] when in difficulties and who was grateful for this help, to carry the few papers I thought it essential to bring with me.

This man, by name Adler Christensen, was a native of Norway, had been for some years a sailor and latterly at work in America. He booked his passage in second class to return to Norway to visit his parents at Moss. Mr. James's ticket was procured by an agent of the Austrian Consulate, and the real Mr. James accompanied me on board the "Oscar II" at Hoboken on Thursday, 15th October.

Adler Christensen had already taken my baggage on board, paid my bill at the hotel, where, for two days, "Mr. R. Smythe" of London had been staying and then I had shaved myself completely and slipped down the back stairs and out of the hotel by an entrance into another street.

Thus Mr. R. Smythe disappeared "for Chicago"; Sir R. Casement had already

---

[204] The extract 'The reasons that induced me to come to Germany' is from Curry, Chapter 2, pp. 29-40: 'Preparations for departure from New York. Voyage from New York to Christiania on "Oskar II" in October 1914 – from a Letter of Sir Roger to his Sister.'
[205] [cf. Sir Roger's Essay "Why I came to Germany"] This is a 12-page document in NLI 13085/11 dated 16 December 1915.
[206] Landy
[207] [cf. Chapter I (p. 18)]

telegraphed for rooms in the La Salle Hotel there and his imminent arrival in Chicago had been given out to the local press; and at noon on the 15th October Mr. James ... of Orange County, State of New York, arrived on board the "Oskar II"; and at 2 p.m. that vessel sailed for Christiansand, Norway, as her first port of call, with Christiania and Copenhagen as her destinations.

"Mr. James" had a part of some difficulty to play on board as there were three genuine Americans among the passengers and Mr. James's English was, by no means, that of New York or any State of the American Union. However, he accounted for various discrepancies of speech and bearing by referring at times to his foreign education (he had even been "at school in England") and prolonged sojourn in Europe.

The majority of the passengers took him for "an English spy", and a certain emotion was frequently visible, when he approached stout Dutch gentlemen or Danish families recalled to Europe by family affairs.

[**Curry then writes:**] Sir Roger's diary of his last voyage across the Atlantic, together with other papers and documents that are not to be found among his posthumous papers, was thrown overboard in the neighbourhood of the Faroe Islands, where the "Oskar II" was overhauled by the British warship "Hibernia" and taken into Stornoway (cf. footnote p. 18 and p. 32.) Were it not for an extant letter of 44 pages Sir Roger wrote later to his sister but never sent off we should have no record whatever of this eventful voyage, the two weeks subsequent to his final decision to come to Germany in behalf of the Irish cause...

Chapter III – 14 December 1921
'Last week's instalment of the Diary closed by telling how Sir Roger's confidential man, Adler Christensen, returned to the hotel in Christiania and threw down some money which he said had been given to him at the British Legation.
The Diary itself does not tell more of this incident, but it is set forth in detail below from memoranda written by Sir Roger late in 1914 and early in 1915. The story, in brief, was this: When Adler had had his breakfast after leaving me about 9 a.m., he had been in the large hall of the hotel, when a stranger brushed against him and said quickly: "Go to the telephone booth and call up No. 11460 and you will hear something good."...'

Chapter IV – 21 December 1921
'Berlin, 2 November, 1914
Meyer called for me at 11, took me on foot to Unter den Linden, close at hand, and down it to the Wilhelmstrasse in which, at No. 76, is the Foreign Office...'

Chapter V – 28 December 1921, text roughly as in original above
'Berlin, 24 November, 1914
Today I was to go to the Baroness von W. [**Nordenflycht**] but got a 'phone to say she was in bed with cold; and just then a 'phone came from Blücher at the Esplanade Hotel–to my great joy–and I hurried off to lunch with him there. After lunch I talked with the Countess. She is in great distress for her young brother, left with two broken legs in a captured trench…'

Chapter VI – 4 January 1922, text roughly as in original above
'Berlin, 12 December, 1914
Went to Foreign Office at 1:30 yesterday and saw von Wedel. We agreed first that I should proceed as I thought best about Christiania. He had forwarded my letter from Limburg to Adler through the post, telling the police to allow it to go through in the ordinary way…'

Chapter VII – 11 January 1922
'Berlin, 18 December, 1914'

Chapter VIII – 18 January 1922
'Limburg, 15 Janry, 1915
LAST night I got a letter from Meyer. Meyer said nothing of Christiania, so I am as much in the dark as ever as to the meaning for Adler's sudden return and telegram to me and equally sudden return next day. What was the plot? The German F.O. are very peculiar people and one never knows where one is with them.
My own course is not at all clear. Now that I have practically abandoned the idea of the Irish brigade, there seems little object in remaining in Germany…'

Chapter IX – 25 January 1922, opens as in original above
'Berlin, 11 February, 1915'

Chapter X – 1 February 1922, opens as in original above
'Berlin, 29 Janry, 1915'

Chapter XI – 8 February 1922
'February 11, 1915, is the date of the last entry in the regular Diary kept by Sir Roger from the time of his arrival in Berlin. This Diary fills four quarto notebooks of 180 pages each. The last notebook contains, however, an entry of later date, March 28, 1916, at Berlin. It begins "'My Diary' ended here"; this entry gives a retrospect of the period from the last entry of the regular Diary up to the end of December, 1915. It deals almost exclusively with the Irish Brigade.

Sir Roger began a third and final Diary (*The Nation* is negotiating for the right to publish part of these subsequent records) shortly before his departure for Ireland in a German submarine in April, 1916. The first entry, March 17, 1916, at Berlin, gives a retrospect of the period from the beginning of 1916, during the greater part of which time Sir Roger was ill at the Sanatorium Neu-Wittelsbach in Munich. The subsequent entries, from March 27, at Munich, till April 8, at Berlin, deal exclusively and in detail with his various interviews with the different authorities at Berlin on his fatal expedition to Ireland, which was undertaken against his will and judgment and ended in placing him at the mercy of the British, who hanged him.'

Postscript

Sir Roger having escaped the physical assassination plotted by M. de C. Findlay, the British Minister to Norway, was next assailed by character assassins in the British service. Against the universally organized British press control Sir Roger was, in his isolation, helpless, except for such aid as the incapable and uninterested German Foreign Office might vouchsafe. The statement he prepared on March 15 (printed in last week's issue of *The Nation*) was not published, and Sir Roger attempted no further public defence of his name… *The Nation's* Irish Issue announced for February 15 will be postponed[208] in order to include important new material. Further announcement will be made later.

---

[208] No such 'Irish Issue' appears to have been published in *The Nation*.

APPENDIX 2

John Devoy's 1924 articles in the *Gaelic American* on Casement's actions at Easter 1916

Roger Casement and John Devoy in New York, August 1914

John Devoy wrote several explanatory (and critical) articles on Casement's actions in 1916 in the *Gaelic American* newspaper in October 1924[209] and in letters to colleagues such as Laurence de Lacy.[210] The 4th and 11th October articles are transcribed below from cuttings in the NYPL. That for 18th October has only the headline.

Issues for October 1924 are not to be found in the NLI nor on the NYPL microfilm (a copy of which is also in NLI). 1924 is the only missing year. Devoy also wrote an article entitled 'Sir Roger Casement and the Irish Brigade in Germany' in the issue of 28 June 1924.

---

[209] NYPL Maloney IHP, Box 3, Folios 6, 7-12
[210] *Documents Relative to the Sinn Fein Movement* 20 July 1916, p.19

GAELIC AMERICAN 4 OCTOBER 1924

CASEMENT RETURNED TO IRELAND, NOT TO TAKE PART IN FIGHT, BUT TO URGE ITS POSTPONEMENT

TRIP HAD NO CONNECTION WITH THE SAILING OF THE *AUD* AND HE DECEIVED THE GERMANS INTO BELIEF HE WOULD TAKE PART IN RISING, SO THEY PLACED SUBMARINE AT HIS DISPOSAL – CAPTURE DUE TO THE INDECISION OF AUSTIN STACK.[211]

BY JOHN DEVOY

The fact that the submarine with Casement, Monteith and Bailey on board arrived at Tralee almost simultaneously with the shipload of arms led to the general belief that both vessels were part of the same expedition. Such was not the fact, however. They were both on separate errands. The *Aud* came to aid the projected insurrection by supplying arms to fight the English; Casement came to stop the insurrection if he could, believing that a fight at that time must end in disaster and that it ought to be postponed to a better opportunity.

Inexperienced as he was in the Irish movement, he put his own opinions above those of the men in Dublin who had fixed the date for the rising and thought they could hold on till a better chance would come. He left the British Government out of account. The men in Dublin knew the Government had made up its mind to crush the intended revolt by arresting all the leaders, so that there would be nobody left to take care of the movement and make other plans. It was a question of fighting at the time or having the organisation smashed and losing the German arms. Postponement would be more disastrous than defeat in the field.

Casement admitted that he deceived the Germans into the belief that he wanted to go to take part in the fight but that his real purpose was to reach the leaders and get them to put off the rising and that if he failed in this he would "go out and die with them." He had no military knowledge whatever and his judgment in this matter was wholly valueless and his presense would have added nothing to the force of the insurgents.

The Germans gave him a submarine, with a Captain who was friendly to him and of a genial disposition, but before she got far on her way her machinery broke down and she had to put into Heligoland for repairs and Casement was supplied with another submarine, the Captain of which was a gruff man and unwilling to oblige Casement. He knew the southern coast of

---

[211] *Gaelic American* 4 October 1924, p. 2

Ireland very well, and insisted on landing the Irishmen there when Casement wanted to be put ashore at Galway, in order to get to Dublin more quickly. The Captain's decision to land the men in Tralee made the coincidence of the *Aud* and the submarine arriving practically at the same time.

Knowing that the men in Dublin had irrevocably fixed the date for the rising and that Casement would surely endeavour to get them to alter their plans and thus confusion, I asked the German Government to request him to remain in Germany to look after Irish interests when the expedition started. He was then in the Sanatorium in Munich and the news of the decision to fight on Easter Sunday was brought to him by Monteith. He laboured under the false impression that the Germans (with probably air raid) had forced the hand of the men in Dublin for the mere purpose of making a military diversion.

Nothing could be further from the truth. The decision was made in Dublin early in February and took us completely by surprise, while the Germans knew nothing whatever of it until we transmitted them a copy of the announcement we had received from the Supreme Council of the I.R.B. But Casement's feelings were undoubtedly hurt by the making of such an important decision without his knowledge or consent, and personal pique must have, in part at least, influenced his action. He was undoubtedly filled with the notion that he was the Director General of the Irish Movement, but the Dublin men did not take kindly to the idea and resented his part in the surrender of the Volunteers to Redmond. In fact they would not have agreed to his going to Germany at all and sent Joseph Plunkett to Berlin to get first hand information of the situation.

The circumstances of Casement's being put ashore in a collapsible boat off Tralee by the submarine need not be dwelt on further than to say that he was physically and mentally unfit for the operation. When captured by the police in the old fort where his companions had to leave him while they went into Tralee to open communications, he was in a state of almost complete collapse and he at once asked to see a priest. Father Murphy was brought in to him and Casement trusted him with the despatch of the fatal letter to Eoin MacNeill which wrought havoc with the insurrection. Its contents have never been published, but there is no doubt as to their general purport.

Casement impugned the good faith of the German as to the quantity and quality of military supplies and asked that the Rising be postponed. The charge of bad faith was wholly unfounded. The exact number of rifles and machine guns they had offered to send, in response to the request from Dublin were on board the *Aud* according to the testimony of the English diver sent to examine the vessel after she had been sunk by her crew. This evidence is on record in the Blue Book containing the Report of the Royal Commission which investigated the Rebellion. And she arrived exactly on time, on the first of the four days named in the original Dublin message and repeated in the German answer.

Mr. MacNeill had a genuine grievance in not having been informed until a few days before Easter Sunday of the decision to fight on that day. He is a fine scholar and a patriotic Irishman, but wholly lacking in the qualities required of a military commander. This I knew to be the opinion of Tom Clarke and Sean MacDermott, who, besides, deeply resented his joining with Casement in bringing about the surrender to Redmond. But he was the regularly chosen Commander of the Volunteers and ought to have been taken into their confidence.

On the other hand, MacNeill having agreed to the Rising, as I was informed at the time he had, was not justified in taking upon himself the responsibility of countermanding the order for the manoevers set for Easter Sunday – which was the plan agreed on for getting out the Volunteers. The Conference he called at Rathfarnham on Saturday night (of which I was informed soon after Easter Week by a member of the Provisional Committee who was present and who approved of MacNeill's action), had no right whatever to interfere with the Volunteers, much less to revoke a decision already made. Only a few of them were members of the Provisional Committee, and most of them, including one or two women, were outsiders. And the information on which they based their action (or their approval of MacNeill's action) was wholly wrong. It was Casement's wrongheaded opinion, not a statement of fact.

According to my informant, MacNeill, usually a mild mannered man, was very emphatic, thumped the table, and said with strong emphasis "I tell you we've been betrayed" – evidently meaning by the Germans. He did not say how he had received the information – though he may have done so before my informant reached the meeting – but his reference was plainly to Casement's letter from Tralee. Of course, also, the news of the capture and sinking of the *Aud* had by that time reached Dublin and influenced the action of MacNeill and his friends. But that was the result **[not so]** of the treacherous action of the Wilson Administration in communicating to the British Government the contents of the despatch from Dublin seized in the illegal raid on the Wall Street Branch Office of the German Embassy, on Tuesday, April 18, referring to the landing of arms on "the night of Sunday, 23". It was as disgraceful an act as that of the English Postmaster General, Sir George Graham, in betraying the Bandiera brothers by opening Italian letters in the post office.

The seizure of the *Aud* and her precious cargo was really the decisive factor in defeating the Rising, but she would not have been captured if there had been a man of decision, of character in Tralee, instead of Austin Stack. Monteith informed me after his arrival in New York that when he finally reached Stack (through a Jew news dealer), and informed him that the vessel laden with German arms was ready to discharge her cargo, Stack replied, "My orders are for Sunday night." The men who issued those orders certainly never intended the vessel should run the risk of capture by lying off the Irish coast for three days after her arrival. It is true that other men than Stack were sent down from Dublin to take charge of the landing, and that they were drowned by their automobile tumbling over the rocks into the sea through their Limerick driver taking the wrong road, but the ship and the arms were there for twenty-two hours if there was anyone to take charge of landing them. But there was not even a man to get into communication with the German Captain, although the German government had requested that "Irish pilots should wait north of Inishtookert Island from between dawn of April 20, displaying at intervals three green lights." The responsibility for the failure at Tralee must, of course, be divided between individuals, but the fact remains that the failure was wholly Irish, not German.

Casement was so intent on preventing the fight at the time that he got Monteith to write to Connolly (with whom he was connected in the Labor movement) to the same effect as his own letter to MacNeill, and I was informed that Connolly replied promptly "Germans or no Germans, we'll fight tomorrow." Connolly, Clarke and MacDermott were men of indomitable resolution and had their plans not been upset by weaker, but equally well meaning men, the fight of Easter Week would probably have had a different ending.

The man who told me of the Rathfarnham meeting, at which the countermand of the Easter Sunday manoevers was approved, spoke disparagingly of their lack of sense of proportion in thinking they could overthrow the British Empire with a few hundred **[page torn]** not conversant have spoken in the same strain since then. But it was the critics who were really lacking in sense of proportion. England was fighting for her life with the greatest military power in the world, which had her on the very verge of defeat when Wilson threw the great power of the United States on her side and averted the destruction of her Empire. Had the "Aud" landed her arms, small as the quantity was, the supplies would have been supplemented by submarine, competent German officers would have been sent over, and England would have been obliged to detach large forces from the Western Front and thus ensured a German victory before Wilson could have come to her aid. At that time while he was boasting that he "kept us out of war", and facing a

Presidential Election, he dared not make the change of policy of which he was determined from the beginning, while Hughes, a weak man formally committed privately to peace and confronted by a Democratic Congress, could not possibly have thrown the United States into the war. Wilson had a venal press subsidized by England, browbeat Congress into declaring war, but Hughes in the very probable event of his election, had not the force, even if he had the will, to do that. It was the Irish women of San Francisco, who gave California's electoral vote to Wilson on a plea that he had "kept us out of war", and they would have reversed their action and made Hughes President if Ireland were in arms and the Germans winning the war.

Thus history again repeated itself and comparatively small incidents proved the decisive factor in great events.

Casement's trial and conviction, decided by a prejudiced jury on irrelevant evidence and his tragic end on the scaffold were the inevitable result of the panic and hysteria brought on in England by the fight of Easter Week and must be dealt with in another chapter.

GAELIC AMERICAN 11 OCTOBER 1924

CLAN-NA GAEL PAID FOR SIR ROGER CASEMENTS DEFENSE
IRISH MARTYR SENT TO HIS DOOM ON FOUL AND
LOATHSOME TESTIMONY
WAS CONVICTED BEFORE HE WAS TRIED

JOHN DEVOY ADVANCED $5,000 FROM PROCEEDS OF
BROTHER'S
ESTATE TO MICHAEL FRANCIS DOYLE OF PHILADELPHIA,
FOR
CASEMENT – THE PATRIOT'S EYES FILLED WITH TEARS
WHEN LAWYER ENTERED HIS PRISON CELL WITH TOKEN OF
THE FAITH OF IRISH IN
AMERICA[212]

The British Government brought Casement to London for trial to make a more spectacular impression on the world, not because it was not sure of a partisan judge and a packed jury to convict in Dublin. But the impression on the world was the reverse of what was expected. It showed that England was in a panic and that Ireland was still a danger to the Empire.

Casement's plea that he was an Irishman and entitled to be tried by a

---

[212] *Gaelic American* 11 October 1924, p. 1

jury of his own countrymen was sound enough, but it would have made no difference whether the Government's orders were carried out in London or Dublin: the result would have been the same except for the effect on the public opinion of the world. If convicted and hanged in Ireland, the uninformed portion of the world (always the greater part) would have placed the responsibility on the Irish people, whereas trying him in London was a tacit admission that it was a risk to put his case before an Irish jury. Of course, the Government knew there was no such risk. Robert Emmet, the Sheares brothers, Thomas Russell, William Orr, and other United Irishmen were hanged on the verdicts of packed Irish juries, and the Young Ireland leaders and the Fenians were sent to penal servitude by the same sure process, and there would have been no difficulty about Casement. But the Government wanted to fix the eyes of the world on London for the spectacle presented of her savage and relentless punishment of her revolting subjects and other enemies in Ireland.

But England's panic stricken statesmen missed their mark. The record of Casement's trial shows a straining of England's own law and the substitution of slanderous abuse for argument on the evidence presented. The evidence went far short of proving treason, and even an English jury in normal times might have failed to convict on it. But the English people were then war mad and must be appeased by Irish blood, so Casement was offered up as a sacrifice.

But the government depended more on foul and loathsome propaganda than on the testimony presented. Leaders who were notorious degenerates sent to America men trained in colleges, which are nurseries of unnatural vice, and who were themselves more than suspected, to give broad hints on public platforms and retail manufactured details in private among the Anglomaniacs who practice aristocratic vices and have none of the robust qualities of the English race.

From a legal point of view there was little worthy of notice in the trial of Casement. He was brought to London to be sentenced to death and hanged and the purpose was relentlessly carried out. The part of the trial with which I am most concerned is the effort we in America made to defend him. We knew, of course, that conviction and execution were a foregone conclusion, but we were determined nevertheless to provide as best we could for a decent defense. All the leaders of the movement in Ireland had either been executed or were in English prisons. The Government had filled the jails in Ireland with over 3,000 suspects and was endeavoring to terrorize the people into abject submission. While they failed in that, they succeeded in dislocating the movement for the moment, so that organized effort in any direction was rendered extremely difficult. The defense must be financed from America or there would be no defense at all. The treasury of the Clann-na Gael was exhausted by the sending of $25,000 to Dublin for Easter Week. It was our last dollar and the money must be procured at once.

McGarrity and I met in a hotel across the street from the bank in which I had deposited the proceeds of the sale of my brother's estate in New Mexico and he brought with him from Philadelphia Michael Francis Doyle, who was ready to go to London at once to do what he could for Casement without charging a fee. We agreed to send to Casement by Doyle $5,000 and I immediately drew the money. We gave it to Doyle and he at once got a draft for the amount, telling Doyle to inform the lawyers that we had no more funds and that they must keep their fees and expenses down to that figure.

Doyle started for London by the next steamer, was allowed to visit Casement in prison, presented him with the money and got his receipt for it. Facsimiles of that receipt and of Doyle's receipt, given when we handed him the $5,000 in cash are herewith reproduced.

[Extract from *Roger Casement: The Black Diaries*[213] on Michael Francis Doyle's stewardship of Devoy's $5000:]

Ironically, given Casement's scrupulous refusal to take German money, the equivalent of £1,000 was ultimately forwarded from Berlin to Bernstorff in America for his defence. It was to repay John Devoy who had provided $5000 of his own money in emergency (from his brother's estate). It was brought over by Michael Francis Doyle, apparently in the form of a cheque made out to Casement.

Devoy later wrote,[214] "After the trial the lawyers were constantly insisting that Doyle should get more money from us for them, although he had conveyed our message that we could pay no more than the $5,000 he had brought over…

Indeed on 5 July, Doyle was actually telegraphing the US to seek an additional amount, immediately, by cable, saying, "COUNSEL ASK FIVE HUNDRED POUNDS".[215] In the event Sullivan charged £530 for the case and said in July, "Fifty guineas is quite enough for the appeal"[216] (There is some confusion over Doyles since Arthur Conan Doyle, recorded simply as 'Doyle', gave £700 to the defence fund, as accounted by Gavan Duffy on 21 June.[217])

Harford Montgomery Hyde, who interviewed Michael Francis Doyle, failed to draw any malign conclusion from the contradictory evidence as to the draft's eventual disbursement. The meticulous Gavan Duffy never accounted for any of it, despite Doyle telling Hyde he gave the cheque to him. This was done, Doyle said, after he

---

[213] Dudgeon (2nd edition 2016), pp. 504-5
[214] *Gaelic American*, 11 October 1924, p. 1
[215] NLI 18081/13
[216] NLI 10763/15, Sullivan to Gavan Duffy, 7 July 1916
[217] NLI 10763/16

had seen Casement to get it endorsed. Doyle told Hyde that he had then been given £250 of it by Gavan Duffy. Hyde asked to see the receipt but Doyle said he could not locate the "photographic copy of the check".[218]

However Doyle did not see Casement alone – his solicitor, always accompanied him and a warder had to be present. Indeed the Brixton governor sat in on the visit of 15 June and sent a report of what he heard to the Home Office, including that Doyle was giving the impression of being uninvolved in Irish political matters.

In several pages of his book,[219] Hyde innocently explained how it was difficult to understand Gavan Duffy's concerns about a lack of funds, given the American money. Curiously, with his Unionist politics and their contrary views on the diaries, Hyde dedicated his 1964 trial book to the memory of Michael Francis Doyle, "Late of the American Bar: Defender of Sir Roger Casement no less after his execution than during his trial."

Gavan Duffy wrote to Doyle in 1917 with the final trial accounts. Costs totalled £1750, with counsels' fees being £1086. His own fees, for a huge amount of methodical work, were £800 but there was only £500 available to pay them, so he was out of pocket to the tune of £300.[220]

On this evidence, it would seem that Michael Francis Doyle pocketed the whole £1000 provided by Devoy and managed to deceive everyone about it, to the point where Sullivan in particular, but also Gavan Duffy, were blamed for being greedy, profligate and ungrateful.

A final word on the shortfall went to Gavan Duffy. Telling off Doyle, he wrote: "Your friends there have not treated me well in the matter. I suppose they believe in payments by results."[221]

Even the ablest American lawyer would have been of no service to Casement except in an advisory capacity. He could not plead or take any open part in the defense. It was the demonstration afforded by Doyle's presence that the Clann-na-Gael was standing by Casement and the knowledge that the organization was paying for his defense that had a favorable effect on Casement's spirits. He looked surprised when Doyle handed him the money and tears came into his eyes. He had been forming hasty and wholly unjustifiable conclusions about us and the Germans, which the receipt of the money dissipated so far as we were concerned.

After the trial the lawyers were constantly insisting that Doyle should get more money from us for them, although he had conveyed our message that we could pay no more than the $5,000 he had brought over. I believe it was Mr. Sullivan who made the demands. He wanted to appeal the case to

---

[218] Michael Francis Doyle letters to Hyde, 4 November 1958 and 6 December 1958 refer. Series 1.23 Harry Ransom Humanities Research Center Austin, Texas
[219] Montgomery Hyde 1964, pp. 183-5
[220] NLI 10763/27, 27 January 1917
[221] NLI 10763/27, 8 December 1916

the House of Lords, but that would be only prolonging Casement's agony. The Lords would certainly confirm the sentence. I was informed that Mr. Sullivan showed a considerable temper in his criticisms of us for not sending the money which he had been told we had not got. Everybody in Ireland expects money from America and seems to think there is no limit to the amount available.

I could not afford to draw any more money from the bank and had to wait until the next Convention of the Clann-na Gael, in 1919, to get my $5,000 back, and we could not divert any of the funds collected for the relief of the wives and children of the victims of Easter Week. But £1,000 was a comfortable fee.

One of his first questions was "Did you bring Agnes over?" referring to his sister Mrs. Newman. When Doyle answered in the negative Casement said "Thank God." His cousins, residents of London, asked the same question and also said "Thank God" when they got the same answer.

We had been providing for Mrs. Newman at a higher rate than her brother was able to do at his request, and he promised to pay back the money we gave her when he reached America again. She repaid us with insult and vile abuse, and I have a large collection of her abusive and incoherent letters, which continued to reach me up to my departure from Ireland at the conclusion of my recent trip. If necessary they can all be produced – the early complimentary ones, as well as the crazy effusions which followed.

I may add here that Mrs. Newman had no inside knowledge whatever of her brother's relations with us, or of his work in Germany, and that in these matters she is the victim of malignant men and women who play on her irascible temper and use her as an instrument of their ignoble personal animosities.

Counting the $3,500 we gave Casement in America, the Clann-na Gael furnished him in all $16,000. I hold the receipts furnished me by Captain Von Papen, the German military attaché, and Mr. George von Skal (who acted for him in his absence). During our relentless persecution by Woodrow Wilson these and a number of other important papers had to be put away for safe keeping and transferred in a hurry more than once to other places. When finally it was safe to examine them they were in confusion and some missing, but the latter doubtless will turn up when my eyes are in a condition to permit a more thorough search.

I have in addition a very long and unnecessarily minute statement of his expenditures by Casement while in Germany, but it would take up too much space to print it, and it would be wholly unnecessary to do so.

It is proper to add here that the money we gave to Christensen and the amount spent in the attempt to send men from New York to reinforce the "Brigade" are not included in the $16,000. A sum of $500 sent to relieve the wants of the men on the eve of the departure of Count von Bernstorff and his staff is also omitted.

GAELIC AMERICAN 18 OCTOBER 1924[222]

SIR ROGER CASEMENT'S SISTER BELIEVES LYING STORIES TOLD HER BY JOHN DEVOY'S FOES.

ACCUSES HIM OF SENDING THE MARTYRED JOSEPH PLUNKETT TO GERMANY TO IMPERSONATE HER BROTHER – SINCERE AND PATRIOTIC, SINISTER INFLUENCES ARE WORKING ON HER NEUROTIC TEMPERMENT – THE STORY OF HER STAY IN THE UNITED STATES

Devoy apparently quotes a letter from Casement's sister, Mrs Nina Newman, dated 3 September 1924 that accuses Devoy of sending Joseph Plunkett to Berlin to impersonate Casement and of telling a Miss Gilford **[actually Gifford]** in New York at the end of 1916 of Birkenhead **[F.E. Smith]** calling Casement an "Oscar Wilde".

Devoy later said "Well it's <u>all true</u>. I know it myself." These words were spoken to the two Gifford sisters, as said by Nina to her cousin Gertrude Parry in a letter of 1 November 1924.[223] Devoy refutes the palpably false Plunkett impersonation story at length, and goes on at length on how the Clann helped the ungrateful Mrs. Newman. He does not contradict Birkenhead's "Oscar Wilde" epithet.

---

[222] No original is available, only the headline and some notes.
[223] NLI 13075/4

APPENDIX 3

Casement's War in Germany and Ireland 1914-16

Jeffrey Dudgeon response to Angus Mitchell articles on Germany in *Field Day Review* 8. 2012

Part I [224]

Field Day Review
- *'A Strange Chapter of Irish History': Sir Roger Casement, Germany and the 1916 Rising* by Angus Mitchell.
- *Diary of Roger Casement, 1914-16, Part I: 'My Journey to the German Headquarters at Charleville'*, annotated by Angus Mitchell.
- *'A last Page of My Diary,' 17 March to 8 April 1916*, with an introduction by Angus Mitchell.
- *'Phases of a Dishonourable Phantasy'* by Angus Mitchell. **[See Part II]**

This edition of the *Field Day Review*[225] is beautifully presented and exceptionally well produced. On the cover and flyleaf are evocative photographs of Banna Strand where Casement landed in April 1916 and of Murlough Bay in the 1890s, and 1953 during Eamon de Valera's visit.

Murlough Bay was to be Casement's final resting place, a mile from his adopted home near Ballycastle but, short of partition ending, cannot be. Despite his efforts, the division of Ireland is nearly a century old, Northern Ireland's frontier being one of the longest standing in Europe. The memorial cross to Casement (and others) at Murlough's "green hill" was torn down in 1957 during the IRA border campaign which was quite eventful in the area. Little of it remains.

The four items under review are two transcriptions from Casement's German diaries, introduced and annotated by Angus Mitchell, and two substantive articles by him on the German episode and the diary authenticity debate and its history. Together they run to 125 pages.

Mitchell has not entered the authenticity debate before at such length, previously publishing books on Casement's 1910 and 1911 Peruvian Amazon

---
[224] Originally published as Part I in *drb* (Dublin Review of Books), Issue 31 dated 25 March 2013, http://www.drb.ie/essays/casement-s-war.
Part II below, in Issue 36, 4 June 2013, was entitled *Casement Wars*, http://www.drb.ie/essays/casement-wars
[225] Field Day Review 8. 2012, pp. 4-125, University of Notre Dame, Indiana

investigations – in the form of transcribed documentation, and a short biography which avoided the diary issue. Indeed he has been largely silent since 2000, when, "acting on the advice of several senior Irish academics I had decided to remove myself from the controversy rather than engage with every new polemical development".[226] This came just after reviewing "the McCormack and Dudgeon books" in, it has to be said, in my case anyway, a highly dismissive manner, as a "queer reading…serving the cause of gay unionism."

The imminent centenary may be the reason for discarding that censorious and career minded admonition, but off the leash Mitchell certainly is, after a decade of relative silence.

From the off, he asserts that, "Independent Ireland has found it hard to incorporate into its foundational history the [Casement] narrative."[227] However this is difficult to credit given Casement's state funeral and reburial in 1965 and the fact that Ireland has fairly faithfully pursued his foreign policy ideas since 1921. The diaries have obviously created difficulties but until the advent of modern deniers they had been glided over.

The first transcription[228] following an introduction[229] is Casement's report of a brief trip into Belgium, ostensibly to discuss the suborning of Irish POWs with Baron Kurt von Lersner, a diplomat he had met in New York. And secondly, Baron Wilhelm von Stumm a pro-war diplomat, who was at the Belgian outpost of the German Foreign Office in Charleville. The German difficulty, never quite resolved, was that they could not distinguish between Irish and English prisoners.

Casement's diary is like an article by an embedded war correspondent, readable and packed with telling detail. He honestly reports seeing the graves at Andenne where the German Army in August had executed 350 Belgian civilians in a semi-disciplined operation, partly prompted by panic over *francs tireurs*.

Why he was shown these sights is not clear. Mitchell says Casement's guide, Count von Lüttichau of the German General Staff (GGS) "had orders" to take him on a detour to witness conditions. However a more intriguing explanation is that his companions chose to display these embarrassing scenes in the (vain) hope that he would grasp the dreadful nature of the war.

This is borne out by Casement writing:[230] "Lüttichau begged me to try and

---

[226] Ibid., p. 110
[227] Ibid., p. 6
[228] Ibid., pp. 22-46
[229] Ibid., pp. 5-21
[230] Ibid., p. 30

get thro' my interview with von Stumm by 10.30 a.m. so that we might return by Dinant, Namur and Liège. This, a much longer route back to Cologne would be far more interesting as we should pass thro' some of the most famous spots of the opening stages of the war." Again, later, his English-speaking chauffeur Meckel, "a well known German automobilist and aviator" simply "stopped the car to show me a gruesome sight and tell a horrible story."

Casement also notes the devastation of large parts of Liège and Louvain by German forces and details the many destroyed bridges in France and Belgium, adding that sometimes the damage was self-inflicted or the bridges were wrecked by the retreating armies. He tries to justify his new ally, the German Empire, by expatiating on how the Belgians were getting just reward for their war crimes in the Congo:[231] "Sometimes I must confess when the present 'Agony of Belgium' confronts me – and it cannot well be minimised it is in truth a national agony – I feel that there may be in their awful lesson to the Belgian people a repayment. All that they now suffer and far more, they, or their king, his government and his officers wreaked on the well nigh defenceless people of the Congo basin. And with no such reason as the Germans. Germany offered Belgium fair terms – she asked only a "right of way" to meet her foemen face to face on French soil. Belgium refused – at the instigation of England and preferred the arbitrament of arms."[232]

And of course this is the essence of Casement's endlessly repeated standpoint, of British war guilt – a case worth arguing and one Mitchell does take forward but not by describing it as "Casement instinctively dismantling the colonial hierarchy of humanity". When couched in Casement's and Mitchell's moral and Anglophobic tones, it loses its force and audience. There is however useful mention of the issue of secret treaties as a cause of the war on which Casement's great political ally, E.D. Morel, campaigned in the Union of Democratic Control.[233]

Angus Mitchell discusses clearly, if in a partisan manner, the 'Rape of Belgium', the German atrocity issue, averring that Casement was uniquely well placed "to critically evaluate the official investigative practices into German atrocities in Belgium." (Casement did evasively concede in his diary, "Wrongs were undoubtedly committed in Belgium but they were not all committed by Germans upon Belgians."[234])

He then picks on Professor J.H. Morgan, a lawyer soldier and prolific war author and investigator for London. Because he (openly) advised Case-

---

[231] Ibid., p. 15
[232] Ibid., pp. 15 & 37
[233] Ibid., p. 31, n. 21
[234] Ibid., p. 18

ment's legal team in 1916, he is seen as part of the "secret history of Casement's trial." Morgan, like the Ulsterman James Bryce who reported for the government on the German actions in Belgium, was a Liberal patriot. People can have mixed or layered opinions without being in a conspiracy.

The author cannot resist adding the claim that King Leopold's casualties were "as high as the death toll of the 1st World War."[235] He of course references Adam Hochschild book for this ludicrous claim but not the work of Professor Roger Louis, a Congo population-loss sceptic (no census was taken), or the recent work of Aldwin Roes, particularly *Towards a History of Mass Violence in the Etat Indépendant du Congo, 1885–1908* which views Leopoldian rule critically but fairly.[236]

In discussion with Baron von Stumm,[237] Casement tellingly explained, "I told him of my larger hope – 'a dream if you will' – of an independent Ireland emerging from this war and he at once said it would be to Germany's interest to have an independent Ireland. I said 'Yes – to the interest of Europe at large.'"

Casement linked the matter pithily to London's offer of Home Rule: "In return for a partial promise to allow Ireland to erect a debating society on the banks of the Liffey at some wholly unspecified future date, Irishmen today are to give 300.000 men to the shambles in France and Flanders in order that the Englishmen, who is too valuable himself to be put in danger may "capture the German trade.""

Co-incidentally, or perhaps because we travel the same narrow street, albeit on opposite sides, I have also transcribed the same German documents as Mitchell, but in their entirety – while interpolating some of Casement's correspondence.

I too recognise Casement's time in Germany, the months of nervous breakdown aside, as hugely significant for Ireland and England, and especially apposite now the 1914-16 centenary years are approaching.

The German episode has great dramatic potential which the rest of his too varied, and too sexual life militates against, the trial aside, and that lacked a certain tension, with the verdict a foregone conclusion. At the same time most *parti pris* Casement art and writing has been marred by too sugary a treatment, one that frequently is, or becomes, religious.

The issue of war guilt and war avoidance, not to mention how to end wars also looms large but these articles bring no guidance and little insight. Mitchell none the less performs a valuable service through the transcrip-

---

[235] Ibid., p. 15, n. 25
[236] Aldwin Roes, http://eprints.whiterose.ac.uk/74340/2/roesAW2.pdf
[237] Field Day Review 8. 2012, p. 31

tions by making us address the nature of Casement's actions in Germany and his arming of the Volunteers in 1914 and 1916. He runs through the literature on Ireland and the Great War cogently.

That Casement recoiled from the actual Rising has greater significance than noted. Here he is "despairing of the imminent project of a rising," indeed trying to subvert it. Next he says it will be abortive and "a crime they [the Germans] will pay for bitterly." John Devoy however in the *Gaelic American* of 4 October 1924 judged differently, "Casement impugned the good faith of the Germans as to the quantity and quality of military supplies and asked that the Rising be postponed. The charge of bad faith was wholly unfounded."

Like Edward Carson, perhaps more so, Casement militarised Ireland. Mitchell admits as much, saying that after he retired on ill-health grounds, "His energies were then channelled into the Home Rule crisis and the paramilitarisation of Irish politics",[238] as if that was an achievement. Casement's view here of the Irish Volunteers as "excitable young men" reveals only irresponsibility. Get young men guns and they will use them, and of course they did.

In Ulster's case, the young men went off to the Somme. In later years from 1970, deserted by the upper class and abandoned by the middle they joined paramilitary groups which, thereby, lacked officers, something Casement felt the Irish Volunteers also did. The results were inevitable and not pleasant.

The extracts seriously condemn Casement who latterly rails against a weak German offer of support in endless, inane and silly writing. They also reveal why he wrote the Black Diaries: his writing is a substitute for conversation. It is plainly a process of talking to himself and recording his thinking in ceaseless and increasing self-justifying rage. Mitchell admits[239] "at times Casement's inner reflections border on the paranoiac."

Not so. Not paranoid, but hysterical, and I think the behaviour of someone who can only be oppositional, until doubt sets in and they become conflicted.

Or was he all emotion as Joseph Conrad memorably wrote of him in May 1916 (to John Quinn)? "He was a good companion but already in Africa I judged that he was a man, properly speaking, of no mind at all. I don't mean stupid. I mean that he was all emotion. By emotional force (Congo report, Putumayo – etc) he made his way, and sheer emotionalism has undone him. A creature of sheer temperament – a truly tragic personality, all but the greatness of which he had not a trace. Only vanity."

There is a central gap or flaw in Casement's reasoning which made him

---
[238] Ibid., p. 7
[239] Ibid., p. 10

a limited thinker. He here denies Germany the right to interests, just as he, previously, and Republican dissidents today, deny England its interests. Ireland, in contrast is above having interests and Casement like modern anti-revisionists is self-righteously and unyieldingly critical of its enemies for such a sin. Every state has interests, even the Irish, but Casement (and his crony Alice Stopford Green) was relentless in denying England any; everything is exploitation of the weaker by the strong, nobody has free will.

Casement's greatest achievement in his first months was the statement or declaration he obtained from the German Chancellor on 20 November 1914 which in particular stated, "Should the fortune of this great war, that was not of Germany's seeking ever bring in its course German troops to the shores of Ireland, they would land there not as an army of invaders to pillage and destroy but as the forces of a Government that is inspired by goodwill towards a country and people for whom Germany desires only *national prosperity and national freedom*."[240]

Within three weeks of his arrival in Germany, he had effected the greatest of diplomatic advances, one similar to Wolfe Tone's in Paris – diplomatic recognition of an independent Ireland.

In his birthday congratulations to the Kaiser of 29 January 1915, Casement was expressing his gratitude by praying "for the righteous triumph of German arms" and earlier when voicing annoyance at the then comparatively low level (57,000) of British losses.[241]

But later in the extract he complains of the "curse of Prussian militarism," that the Prussian system was the "embodiment of soulless efficiency," of the "coarse and selfish heads of this Prussian abortion," virtual blockheads who were "incapable of understanding the minds of other men…collectively a great nation, individually – an undesirable one."

Mitchell under-explains all this by saying that the Germans had "lost sympathy with his cause," although Casement wrote "their only interest in me lay in exploiting me & the Irish cause." As if it wouldn't be.

This Declaration was followed on 28 December 1914 by the Treaty with Zimmermann which opened, "With a view to securing the national freedom of Ireland, with the moral and material assistance of the Imperial German Government, an Irish Brigade shall be formed from among the Irish soldiers, or other natives of Ireland, now prisoners of war in Germany."

It is ironic and remarkable that the same man should, only fifteen years earlier, have been advising the Prime Minister, Lord Salisbury, in March 1900, of "frequent allusions to 'downtrodden Ireland' which appeared from

---

[240] *The Continental Times*, 20 November 1914
[241] Field Day Review 8. 2012, p. 41

time to time in the *Standard & Diggers News* in connection with the so called 'Irish Brigade' ... a runlet of Johannesburg tapsters and cornerboys swelled by driblets of Continental ruffianism." This was a possible reference to his future colleague in 1916, Major John McBride.[242]

Formation of the Irish Brigade in Germany, which took up the next year, was however a disaster. Casement managed to get only 50 recruits and they were in no sense reliable while his foolish attempts to get the Brigade to Syria (and thence Egypt) were viewed with horror by John Devoy in New York: "Fighting for the Turks would be a fatal cry in Ireland." He was also concerned with Casement's "indiscreet talk"[243]. Amongst others made aware of the coming Rising was the "politically biased English-born"[244] Princess Blücher. In her case, she voluntarily handed Casement's incriminating papers over to British Intelligence after the war.

The second transcription[245] is entitled 'A Last Page of My Diary,' being in the original 134 pages long. It tells of Casement's final three weeks from 17 March before he, Lt. Monteith and one other Irish POW, Sgt. Daniel Beverley (chosen by Monteith) leave for Ireland. Those weeks were spent in a state of rage, depression, frenetic writing and bitter arguments with the GGS. His army contact, Rudolf Nadolny was, understandably, apoplectic[246] when he discovered that Casement, with the assistance of the Admiralty, had sent John McGoey (who had recently arrived from the US) via Denmark to try and get the Rising called off because of poor German support.

It is actually quite remarkable that Casement was not immediately arrested, as was his old colleague Bulmer Hobson in Dublin in April when the IRB feared he was up to the same trick. Hobson was never forgiven unlike Casement. And it is even more amazing that the German Admiralty "the best part of all this show – a long way the best"[247] finally provided a submarine to transport him to Ireland to arrive in time, as he thought, to block the Rising.

Had the Admiralty not been so silly as to provide a submarine – persuaded Casement said for German reputational reasons – he would have survived the war and entered Irish politics in 1918 on a par at least with Eoin MacNeill and probably much more significantly, and certainly by 1921 a negotiator in chief. Unfortunately this aspect of the last days in Berlin goes largely without comment or analysis by Mitchell. Irish revolutionaries on German submarines, one notes, have a poor outcome.

---

[242] TNA FO 2/368/280-283
[243] Field Day Review 8, 2012, p. 51
[244] Ibid., p. 11
[245] Ibid., pp. 47-83
[246] Ibid., p. 61
[247] Ibid., p. 75

U-19, the first ever German diesel submarine, was to arrive in Tralee Bay just a few hours after the arms ship *Aud*. It also failed to find the promised pilot. What Casement apparently never knew was that Captain Weisbach had been ordered, as the *Aud's* Captain Spindler wrote, that "under no circumstances however must a landing occur before April 20th [Thursday] in the event of a premature arrival." Thus Casement would only ever have had hours to get to Dublin to persuade MacNeill (and the IRB) to abandon the action. The Germans seem to have tricked Casement as there was no point in sending him separately if the vessels' timings were designed only to ensure he made a rendezvous with the *Aud* in Tralee Bay. It seems the two German services, as ever with armies and navies, were not acting in concert but this key puzzle goes unanalysed by Mitchell. Perhaps the most interesting part of this story is the fate of Casement's companions on U-19, and of John McGoey. Robert Monteith, who was a Cavan Protestant farmer's son, and a Connolly socialist, managed to evade capture in Kerry, making it back to the US. Not unreasonably, he did not participate further in the Rising but did in US socialist politics.

Beverley was using a nom de guerre. He was actually Daniel Julien (sometimes Julian) Bailey, a Dubliner from St Michans with a French mother (named Berthelier). He evaded capture in Kerry a day longer than Casement and after giving various other names offered a statement to the RIC. He was eventually charged and brought to trial at the Old Bailey.

His fate was not settled until after sentence of death was passed on Casement. Contrary to Mitchell's note[248] that Bailey/Beverley "turned King's Evidence," he didn't give court evidence, or reveal much more than the British knew or what Casement himself told the Kerry police and Scotland Yard.

Bailey's statement denied personal culpability and foreknowledge of the operation. Omitting most salient facts, he said he had only participated with a view to getting home. His most significant remark, duly ignored by the authorities, was, "I heard that Dublin Castle was to be raided." His statement was however read out in court by F.E. Smith, the Attorney General and Carson's 'Galloper.'

After Casement had been taken down, Smith surprised the court by dropping the charges against Bailey. He said he "was a private soldier of humble origin" who had made a statement on his arrest when he said that he was not, and never had been, a traitor to this country or the Army. "He had joined the Irish Brigade with one object only – namely, to return by a subterfuge to the Army. He wanted to escape from the hardship and inactivity of his captivity. It was impossible to know what the motives might be which actu-

---

[248] Ibid., p. 69

ated a man – inference and conjecture were the only guides."

The Attorney added he had come to the conclusion that the evidence was inconclusive; therefore it was necessary to look at his Army record. "Bailey had served nine years, six of them abroad. His record was uniformly good. In these circumstances he had taken on himself the responsibility of deciding not to test the defence which the accused would have put forward. He did not think it right merely to enter a nolle prosequi, but to offer no evidence, so that the jury might enter a verdict of acquittal."

This seems very much a personal decision by the Galloper, probably to ensure the focus on Casement was not lost or diffused, and otherwise to prove his humanity in relation to the common soldier. Bailey then disappears from view, that is until a recently released record in Kew.[249] It dealt with a concern expressed in 1918 by the Hon. Miss Anne MacDonnell of the Irish Woman's Association that Bailey had become a Captain in the British Army!

The rumour was stated to be "groundless and mischievous [as] Bailey is now a Private in the Railway Operations Department, Royal Engineers and serving in Egypt." Earlier in a peculiarly English mode, there is a record of the police in 1916 watching a Mrs O'Dea, a widow "educated in Germany" described as engaged to Bailey and "a fast woman." She had two sons in the Army and it was ascertained that her sympathies were "entirely British."

Full and further details of Bailey (and his medals) have since been made available on David Grant's website, one oddly unmentioned by Mitchell.[250] It carries an amazing amount of Irish Brigade documentation particularly in the form of birth, marriage and death certification, war records and news cuttings. Bailey died in Ontario in 1968 having migrated to Canada in 1921, but only after another marriage, in 1926, to 18-year-old Clara Nash. His first wife, Katherina O'Dea died in 1924 aged fifty.

John McGoey's story is even stranger. Stated by nationalist writers to have been executed by the British in Scotland, he never resurfaced after leaving Germany. Mitchell says[251] that he remained "something of a mystery" and that "different rumours surround his fate." He conceded however that "more recent research [unspecified] suggests he survived the war."

The question that remains is whether he was too late getting out of Denmark or, more likely, decided to disobey Casement's orders. He had the power to stymie the Rising but didn't. Which is not to say he couldn't be a quick worker. Last seen en route to Denmark in late March, by September 1916 he was marrying a Miss Ethel Wells in Essex while serving on an armed

---

[249] TNA MEPO 2/10668
[250] http://www.irishbrigade.eu/recruits/bailey.html
[251] Field Day Review 8. 2012, p. 54

merchant cruiser, HMS Kildonan.

Perhaps McGoey believed the Rising should go ahead and he was disillusioned with Casement's demoralising machinations, despite telling him "he had sized up German militarism." Or perhaps because of that militarism, he had decided to cross over to the other side while securing and preserving his own freedom. He certainly never sent the card marked 'off' from Denmark that Casement so desperately awaited.

Sadly McGoey was to die in a building accident on the Chicago Tribune Tower in 1925, leaving Ethel a widow with one child.[252]

Lives lived are often more complicated and interesting than conspiracy theories. What Angus Mitchell cannot say however is that British Intelligence was really quite flatfooted, something "the archive" tellingly reveals.

At the end of his first article, he reminds the reader "of the suspect nature of official evidence and of the vulnerability of the historical record to such typical acts of intellectual treason."[253]

He has become Casement.

---

[252] See David Grant's website for more on John McGoey http://www.irishbrigade.eu/othermen/goey/goey.html

[253] Field Day Review 8. 2012, p. 21

APPENDIX 4

Casement Wars (over the Black Diaries)

Jeffrey Dudgeon response to Angus Mitchell article in *Field Day Review* 'Phases of a Dishonourable Phantasy'

Part II [254]

In Part I of this essay entitled *Casement's War*,[255] we saw how Roger Casement had spent his first weeks in Imperial Germany in 1914, successfully working to gain recognition of an independent state of Ireland, and, attempting, ineffectively, to raise an Irish Brigade. His last days in Berlin in March and April 1916 were then observed as he obtained a shipment of arms for Ireland while seeking to leave separately in a submarine. His intention however was to get the Easter Rising called off because of inadequate German support.

Now we come to responding to *Phases of a Dishonourable Phantasy*, Angus Mitchell's most substantive work on the Black Diaries since *The Riddle of the Two Casements,* his contribution to the 2005 Royal Irish Academy (RIA) publication *Roger Casement in Irish and World History*. This book purported to be the proceedings of the RIA Symposium that had been mounted by the Irish Government in 2000. He honourably points out that the RIA "volume also excluded an overtly gay voice." In fact my Symposium presentation was missing from the proceedings while his was one not even delivered at the event.

The book offered him the opportunity to further develop his thinking on the diaries after the relatively small number of discrepancies he had highlighted in his 1998 *Amazon Journal of Roger Casement.* These, in turn, were addressed succinctly by Séamas Ó Síocháin in his 656-page biography, *Roger Casement: Imperialist, Rebel, Revolutionary* (2008) which I reviewed in the *drb* in October 2008, under the title *He Could Tell You Things.*

In his harsh review of Ó Síocháin's book[256] he wrote that Casement's "evolution into a revolutionary however and the deep veneration his name commanded in IRA ranks prevent him from achieving the legitimacy his life deserves." This is just not true. It was Casement's separatist revolutionism

---

[254] Part II, *drb* Issue 36, 4 June 2013, http://www.drb.ie/essays/casement-wars
[255] Part I, *drb* Issue 31, 25 March 2013, http://www.drb.ie/essays/casement-s-war,
[256] Angus Mitchell, *History Ireland*, July 2008

– stunningly successful within five years of his execution – that gives him enormous legitimacy and which justified his political and military work from 1914-16 in Ireland and Germany.

He was not left out of the discourse, as his state funeral and reburial in Dublin so reveal. But Mitchell believes otherwise, saying only,[257] "The return of his body to Ireland in 1965 temporarily calmed the bitter controversy that has raged over his life and death for the preceding half century." This comes after asserting that[258] "all discussion of the Black Diaries was closed down in 1965 at an official level." As if the Irish government was going to encourage discussion about that subject at a moment of state solemnity.

In this main *Field Day Review* article[259] – from the batch of four – Mitchell returns to the field as a 'Casement Wars' combatant, telling a tale replete with mystery, deceit and conspiracy. And that isn't just when it comes to Casement's own machinations. It is a well-researched, well-told narrative peppered with a good, often modish, turn of phrase. He has certainly unearthed and references – some might say obsessively – many new articles on Casement and his controversies, alongside every twist and turn in the authenticity debate for nearly a century.

Well-notated, it offers an in-depth and interesting, if dense, account of the decades of dispute and argument, and of very recent events, in the context of Irish, English, and, to a degree, global politics. However he dulls the story with a mood of conspiracy and victimhood. Indeed it is pervaded by a tone of resentment while, at times, the text seems a vehicle for revenge for sins of lèse majesté and for too many slights.

Significantly the writer hardly addresses the outstanding and contemporary issues of Ulster and the Irish nation, else he might reveal Casement, and his representatives on earth today, have little original or useful to say on that subject beyond *bien pensant* peace process remarks and the slagging off of England.

We are told that "Casement always saw the bigger picture for humanity and fought against the bitter pettiness born of sectarian posturing." But he saw no bigger picture where the north was concerned. As stated, "He organised gun running into Ireland" (twice) yet did not conceptualise the consequences. He, like Redmond, had believed Carson and Craig were bluffing and he was horribly wrong, despite reality staring him in the face by 1914 in the form of the Covenant, the UVF and their German guns. Not that Asquith wasn't also. No analysis of Casement's failure and the fact that partition has

---

[257] Field Day Review 8. 2012, p. 86
[258] Ibid., p. 90
[259] Ibid., pp. 84-126

lasted for nearly a century is to be found here nor, sadly, would I expect to have seen one.

What does Mitchell tell us that is new or convincing about diary authenticity or forgery, and why are we bothered, if we are not voyeurs, of which some here are accused? He assumes other historians work in tandem, and there is some degree of truth in that, although many learn and advance their ideas through the clash of argument and dispute. Not so where diary forgery theory is concerned. Facts are rarely adduced and issues always disputed, as in republican lawyering, until most other writers, especially English ones, despair and leave the field. This writer doesn't, having a dog or two in the fight. Throughout Mitchell writes more like a defender than an historian.

So why is he taking up the cudgels on behalf of the forgery theorists, again and now? The school was formerly more united, being composed of himself, the Roger Casement Foundation, various unreconstructed old-time nationalists (who could not always be relied upon to curb their anti-homosexual sentiments), and the nexus of the IPR/BICO/Athol Books under Brendan Clifford.

That combination had gone its separate ways and Mitchell, having, as he says, taken advice from his mentors, perhaps wisely, set out on an academic and global path. Yet after being told for the sake of his career to keep out of the controversy, he seems released from that advice. One clue may be that the piece is a precursor to a big international conference on Casement in Tralee in October 2013 run by the University of Notre Dame, one that, in turn, may be linked to *The Gathering*.

The British and Irish Communist Organisation (BICO, formerly the ICO) with its HQ in Athol Street, Belfast used to have a different view on the diaries and Casement's homosexual activities, but now appreciate him only for his anti-English, anti-war writings and activities. Unwisely, they linked up with the forgery theorists, seriously subverting their own case on the origins of First World War, one that is now underpinned and sustained by a monocular Anglophobia.

For the record, in February 1984, *The Irish Communist* said:

"The great Irish homosexual is <u>Roger Casement</u>. The great English homosexual is Oscar Wilde. Casement was of the Keynes variety and Wilde of the Quentin Crisp variety. Casement never got into trouble over his apparently rampant sexual activity while he was a British imperialist agent, but his diaries were used after his conviction for treason in order to dampen down the demand for a reprieve. And Wilde wouldn't have got into trouble if his sense of humour has not failed him at a critical moment. The most outrageous humourist in the English language struck a high moral attitude when it was vital that he should have made a joke. He insisted on going to court, and he ended up doing hard labour for unnatural practices.

Irish national culture could only cope with Casement by declaring the allegation of homosexuality to be an imperialist slander and insisting that the diaries had been forged by Scotland Yard. It was tacitly conceded that if the diaries were not forged, then Casement was an abominable person. But Wilde, unnatural practices notwithstanding, became part of the fabric of English culture – both in his own proper person, and through the Gilbert and Sullivan opera, "Patience".

Official tolerance of homosexuality in England came after a long period of de facto tolerance connected with the growth of liberal culture. Perhaps that is why many English homosexuals can take queer jokes in their stride, and even contribute to them.

The culture of nationalist Ireland was not tolerant of sexual perversion and its classification of perversions was very extensive indeed. In the good old anti-imperialist days, a demand for *"gay rights"* would have been given short shrift.

The de facto tolerance of "gay liberation" in recent years is not the product of a growth of liberal culture. It is a product of cultural collapse.

For half a century after independence nationalist Ireland embarked on a line of cultural development diverging from that of Britain. But that line of development was cut short by the influence of the Second Vatican Council. The past decade has seen a collapse in the value system which the society had been cultivating since the mid 19th century. The old convictions are giving way to mere confusion. The society is beginning to follow on behind Britain for want of anything else to do, but the strongly developed liberal convictions of the British are absent.

"Gay liberation" has sprung into being in this vacuum. Perhaps that is why it is so thin-skinned."

(This article followed a dispute over a comic squib in the *Irish Communist's* December 1983 issue entitled "Gay Noise" which prompted the Cork Quay Co-op to withdraw all ICO publications from sale.)

Mitchell offers, early, an interesting fact that Casement's name is absent from "the principal historiographic collection analysing Irish revisionism, *Interpreting Irish History*, edited by Ciaran Brady (2004)". He follows this by writing[260] when discussing the Casement biographies by Brian Inglis and B.L. Reid (of 1973 and 1976 respectively):

"The medico-psychiatric vocabulary masqueraded as a form of analysis, and it remained a favoured element of the new propaganda offensive against

---

[260] Ibid., p. 92

Irish republicanism and nationalism in Northern Ireland, an obsessive determination by people, who were usually woefully undereducated, to identify nationalism as a pathology. These biographies were widely reviewed in both academic and mainstream journals as part of a strategy of depoliticising and criminalizing the broader republican movement. In terms of their interpretative trajectory, the Black Diaries comply with what Kevin Whelan (2004) has defined as the second and third phases of Irish revisionism from the late 1950s to 1990s."

This is Mitchell trying to turn Casement into the prevailing wind, but Inglis and Reid were researching before the 1970s Troubles, and writing some time before the anti-revisionist movement set sail. He also adds,[261] in something of a non-sequitur, that Brian Inglis's acceptance of authenticity masked his lack of consideration of "the Diaries as documents of historical record" and thus ignored "what they were intended to reveal about the crimes against humanity under investigation."[262] Both writers, he remarks, saw Casement "as a disaffected consul with tendencies to psychosis and erotomania."

In 2002, I wrote of the two: "Reid attempts, evidentially, if not always accurately, to prove the diaries genuine and psychologically consistent. He deals with the homosexuality issue in an interesting and amusing mode, clearing away his own prejudices and treating Casement very much as a human sexual being with all the absurdity that can appear to involve for the outsider looking in. This novelised history was overshadowed by that of Brian Inglis. The two authors' paths frequently crossed in those source rooms of *Casementia* – the National Library of Ireland in Dublin's Kildare Street, and the Public Record Office in London."

I would repeat that B. L. Reid, a prize-winning American journalist, did try too hard to find evidence of Casement being homosexual. The recently rediscovered (in the NLI) 1881 "Scribbling Diary" has undone another of his assumptions about the teenage Casement's desire for a "Sweet boy of Dublin," one whom he saw in his dreams. It appears he was innocently quoting lines from a song – *Colleen dhas cruthen na moe*.

Mitchell's view of a corroding, cruel revisionism exploiting medical terminology on the Troubles does not fit the facts. It is based on the idea of the 1916 Rising and the War of Independence – which did become an unassailable founding myth for the first fifty years of independence – as the settled and single view of the Irish people. In truth, that view was imposed on top of a variety of outlooks. It was inevitably to wear out, allowing for older, more complex outlooks such as Redmondism to resurface, like Fermanagh's dreary steeples.

---
[261] Ibid., p. 93
[262] Ibid., p. 92

The Bolshevik revolution in Russia in 1917 bears great similarity to the Easter Rising, each being a well organised conspiracy and putsch that changed everything for decades, suppressing all that went before, but failing to stay the course. Although in Ireland's case, the unintended victor from the struggle, the English-speaking Catholic Free State, became the target. It is currently more vulnerable than separatism or Sinn Féin.

Casement's policies of European Union (without England), and the Commonwealth as a replacement for Empire, have stayed the course despite the destabilisation caused by Dublin overplaying its economic hand in the Celtic Tiger years. Perhaps even the Blairite idea of an ethical foreign policy and the adoption of benign, global and transnational strategies can also be traced back to Casement.

However revisionism hardly got a look-in in post-1968 Northern Ireland. The IRA operated within the separatist founding myth and neither the British nor the Unionists bothered to query or undermine it, a few admirable exceptions aside like BICO, Jim Kemmy of the Democratic Socialist Party and Conor Cruise O'Brien.

Mitchell fancifully tries to locate Casement far closer to modern realities than he merits when he says[263] "Release of the diaries [in 1959] co-incided with various political and cultural changes in Ireland. A new era in Anglo-Irish relations dawned, and with it the promotion of 'transparency' in government. On 31 August 1994 the Provisional IRA announced a complete cessation of military operations and negotiations opened between Westminster, Leinster House and the Sinn Fein leadership. In October 1995, a further 200 closed Casement files were declassified."

There was no "new propaganda offensive against Irish republicanism and nationalism in Northern Ireland [nor] an obsessive determination…to identify nationalism as a pathology." There was however an understandable aversion to the extreme violence of the IRA and INLA, and a separate attempt to suggest that Ulster Protestants had rights, within or without the single Irish nation.

Neither managed to gain much purchase and the war ran its long course, until the spoils of Northern Ireland came to be split after 1998 in a consociational Stormont. This process only happened because Sinn Fein/IRA chose, at last, to cash in their large accumulation of political chips, won by a titanic military campaign, essentially of armed Hibernians, not Republicans. It succeeded otherwise only in decimating the Unionist population, literally, but then that is not a human rights issue concerning Mitchell. Casement hardly figured in the Troubles although his diaries became a part of the loosening

---

[263] Ibid., p. 94

of the Catholic state in the south that he inadvertently created.

Within a limited number of committed separatists, notably James Connolly, he stood largely apart from Irish political sentiment. Their pro-Germanism also put them at odds with both British socialists and radicals like Ramsay MacDonald and Casement's close friend, E.D. Morel, and the German Communist Party leader Karl Liebknecht, all of whom maintained a due distance from their countries' patriotic wars.

The arrest on 1 May 1916 of Liebknecht tells an unmentioned tale. As I wrote, "He was charged with attempted war treason because of a speech he had made in the Reichstag on 8 April about Casement. While still in Germany, Casement had been advised of the speech. The charging was reported on 16 May in the *Daily Chronicle* and Casement sent the cutting to Gavan Duffy, scribbling alongside it, 'I am still anxious on this matter.' It could be dangerous for several reasons, but the most obvious and immediate was that Liebknecht's alleged crime had been reading out the Irish Brigade Treaty in the Reichstag. He had prefaced his remarks by saying that Germany had entered 'a treaty with the arch-traitor Sir Roger Casement whereby English soldiers were to be used against England.' Luckily, Liebknecht's quotation of the actual details had been suppressed in the German newspapers."

Mitchell adds little meat to the diaries issue, just sowing doubt wherever he can, as when reminding readers, "In Derridean terms Casement's ghost is a reminder of an alternative history". Nor does his homage to the archive and its integrity go so far as to allow him to remark on significant gaps in Casement's, otherwise voluminous, manuscript documentation.

Most notably there is a paucity of letters from two of his most frequent correspondents, E.D. Morel and his cousin Gertrude, nor are there inward boyfriend letters, as mentioned in the diaries – a few innocuous Millar Gordon items aside, or indeed other diaries. His Amazon and Congo investigation material including the Black Diaries was left in London and seized in April 1916 although returned, while his German material was eventually brought back from that country.

I presume the missing items were stored in Belfast at F.J. Bigger's house, 'Ardrigh'. The lack of other diaries is interesting but unresolved although it seems to fascinate Mitchell. The most substantive reference to another was when Casement's papers were inspected at Ardrigh (including perhaps a 1913 or 1914 diary) after he left for the U.S and were then burned in panic as realisation dawned about their contents.[264] This was detailed by Bigger's

---

[264] A recently spotted Bureau of Military History witness statement (no. 381) by George Gavan Duffy tells however of the likely destruction of most of Casement's personal papers kept in Belfast. He wrote, "I had in fact received the year before [1915], from a friend of

nephew Senator Joseph Warwick Bigger in warning letters, his memorable remarks being replicated in correspondence between Dr W.J. Maloney, author of *The Forged Casement Diaries*, and the writer Frances Hackett.

I wrote of this[265] (2002) quoting from a Maloney letter:

""Bigger's uncle Francis Joseph, the one who lived at Ardrigh where Shane Leslie used to call, was interested in the boy scout movement about thirty years ago when I occasionally went to Belfast and never had any interest in what he was doing. Yet that did not spare my shocked ears from hearing that the Greeks had a name for Francis Joseph Bigger's habits and that he needed none to show him how to scout for boys. In this rumor he was I am sure misrepresented…As far as I can ascertain his sexual habits were not obtrusive and were presumably normal.

But then no friend's nephew has come forward to tell with correct reluctance and with noble purpose of Bigger [sic] the sodomite's diary secretly burned at a midnight fire in the kitchen stove…I don't place the proper significance on the informer Bigger's statement that he learnt from the cook and his uncle that Casement went out much at night.

Bigger tells you that his uncle, when Casement's activity in Germany became known (which was in October 1914) "feared a search by the military authorities and got rid of his (Casement's) bags and old clothing". As late possibly as September 1915 the nephew "had found in the small room on the right of the hall at Ardrigh which Mr Leslie may remember" a diary telling of anti-British activities in organising the Irish Volunteers, in pitting German against British shipping interests in Ireland and in other spheres as well as exposing myself [sic] as a confirmed sodomist."

Joseph Bigger described his uncle Frank almost fainting on making the discovery adding that the thing was destroyed "immediately in the kitchen fire – it was late at night – everyone but ourselves had gone to bed."

Maloney's commentary intervenes again, "The only collateral statement that can be tested is the reference to Casement's brother being in debt in 1914." Finally, Professor Bigger tried to explain: "My object in writing [to Hackett and Leslie] is to attempt to bring the controversy to an end because I am convinced that the British Government had and probably has diaries of Roger Casement which if published would establish beyond question that

---

his, three cases of his papers which the friend thought it unwise to retain and he wanted to dispose of them. I remember spending an arduous week-end with Art O'Brien, whom I called in, going through these documents to see what might be utterly seditious in them." Tantalisingly, nothing more is stated, but disappear those three cases and their contents did. Their likely destruction explains the lack of whole swathes of correspondence and indeed other diaries. The German material, in contrast, was never culled.

[265] Dudgeon (2nd edition 2016), pp. 571-2

he was a pervert." Bigger's assessment of Casement nonetheless was that "his present position of national hero and martyr is one that is well deserved.""

Casement had indeed sent instructions from Berlin via Washington in November 1914 for things to be hidden: "Also let him tell Bigger solicitor Belfast to conceal everything belonging to me. Roger." There could have been little subversive in the cache as he did not start dealing with Germany until after he left for America so one must assume it was the private letters and diaries that concerned him. MI5, as was their wont and despite Mitchell's talk[266] of the "efficacy of the intelligence services", having deciphered the message, ignored it.

Angus Mitchell does advise of his own view[267] that "the Diaries are skilled forgeries"; their creation involved "rewritten versions of existing journals"; and also that the forgers "interpolated existing Diaries or manufactured a new set with the sex-centred narrative." Regardless of which, he is clear, if it was Casement's writing,[268] "he deliberately authored diaries that executed him, dramatically compromised his work as an investigator of atrocities and betrayed himself as 'a man of no mind,'" (Joseph Conrad's phrasing),[269] adding they are "homophobic documents" portraying "a predatory sex tourist who debased and objectified the native."

Anyway Casement's first extant diary was commenced before he even received the commission for his Congo investigation. Mitchell then offers this unworthy remark, "If the Black Diaries' Casement is the one true Casement, it is right that gay history should claim him as their own, for Casement was the true martyr of the gay rights cause more than Oscar Wilde or John Addington Symonds."

He also repeats his somewhat crazed notion[270] that, "The authorities actually had 43 years to perfect the look of the Black Diaries", these 43 years being from their delivery to Scotland Yard in April 1916 to the Kew release in 1959. However the typed versions effectively stolen by Sir Basil Thomson, from Scotland Yard in the 1920s (he was by then a renegade), are, typos aside, how the documents read that are currently in the National Archives at Kew.

In a few belittling paragraphs, he turns briefly[271] to this author. "Among the many Casement publications to appear during this period, the most deliberately provocative was the stalwart voice of gay activism in Northern Ireland, Jeff Dudgeon. As a devout Unionist and professed Irish non-nationalist

---

[266] Ibid., p. 88
[267] Ibid., p. 100
[268] Ibid., p. 117
[269] Ibid., p. 102
[270] Ibid., p. 120
[271] Ibid., p. 110

and both veteran and architect of Northern Ireland's gay rights movement, Dudgeon took apparent pleasure in antagonizing and enflaming nationalist feeling on the Casement issue."

I actually got no reviews of my book in the northern nationalist press despite provision of multiple copies – even to *An Phoblacht*. It was studiously ignored.

He describes my book (the title is carefully not provided) thus: "His new version of the Black Diaries published privately in the Spring of 2002 (November actually), gained academic approval, following a launch by Professor Lord Bew of Queen's University, Belfast. This somewhat eccentric publication which included extensive passages from all the disputed diaries, along with fresh interpolations, and thoughtful omissions amounted to little more than an updated and camped-up version of the 1959 edition, with a few original insights into Casement's early years in Antrim. Dudgeon upheld the diaries as the heart and soul of Casement's biography and used them provocatively as a means of destabilising (or queering) the martial spirit of Northern Irish Protestant nationalism and representing it as some deviant youth movement. The book baffled academics, and was as unashamedly political as it was scholastically unsound."

Exactly not. I gave equal space to Casement's family and upbringing and his role in Irish and Ulster politics, which role Mitchell seems incapable of engaging with. My book's title tells it precisely: *Roger Casement: The Black Diaries – With a Study of his Background, Sexuality, and Irish Political Life*.

I am no academic but am, I hope, a scholar. If I "gained academic approval" does that not suggest some recognised merit in the work? I even received a commendation for my researches from Brendan Clifford of BICO in his *Irish Political Review* (IPR) review, although the book and its launch was largely mined for ammunition against the revisionist school of Irish history.

I am essentially accused of being 'a gay unionist'.

I am one, but I especially don't like being <u>accused</u> of it by an ersatz Scotsman from London who went to Harrow and won't ever engage on the matter of the Union and partition. If I am a Unionist, Mitchell is a Nationalist, indeed another ersatz Irishman hiding his partisan politics behind a mask of internationalism.

He had written earlier, "Jeff Dudgeon uses the Black Diaries to update the queer geographies of Ulster and to re-imagine Northern Protestant nationalism as some high camp drama driven by a cabal of queer crusaders",[272] and then accuses me of homophobia! If I enflame anyone, it is he, who, like

---

[272] Angus Mitchell, *Beneath the Hieroglyph: Recontextualising the Black Diaries of Roger Casement*, Irish Migration Studies in Latin America, July 2009

Alice Stopford Green, has taken on the mantle of Ireland.

Another stalwart of homosexual politics in the north gets the same, standard treatment. Harford Montgomery Hyde was a Unionist MP in the 1950s and wrote extensively on Oscar Wilde, Casement and espionage. He lost his north Belfast seat in 1959 because of his courageous (politically suicidal?) efforts in the House of Commons, almost alone, to bring about the decriminalisation of homosexuality after the Wolfenden Report.

However all we get in the *Field Day Review* are constant clunky reminders of his period working in MI5 during the war, such as "the hand of British intelligence was again evident in the intervention of the Unionist MP H. Montgomery Hyde".[273] Links between top people in London, in this case Lord Beaverbrook, René MacColl, a popular and racy journalist (who wrote the first critical biography in 1956, *Roger Casement: A New Judgment*), and Hyde, also a journalist and often short of money, are found. But they prove nothing except that Fleet Street was a small world. They fail even to be suggestive.

Mitchell does however mention that Hyde's 1960 Casement trial book carried "passages that were possibly the most explicit descriptions of homosexuality ever to appear in a mainstream publication in Britain." This was a fortnight of entries in the 1911 Black Diary, which I republished in full for the first and, so far, only time in 2002. Even the Maurice Girodias edition of 1959 did not carry them. He, meantime, is rubbished for consorting with elements of the British establishment i.e. Singleton-Gates who provided the text of the diaries (via Basil Thomson). And this despite the nationalist tone of the Irish historical material Girodias carried in his Paris-published volume. (Henry Miller was the most famous of his authors.)

Venom is reserved, at length, for Bill McCormack who had earlier accused Mitchell of "substituting personalized insinuation for argument and evidence" in a review[274] of his book *Roger Casement in Death or Haunting the Free State*. The diary forensics and handwriting tests are then filleted, along with the accompanying BBC film, where it is said "those who argued for forgery were dismissed as atavistic republicans".

McCormack[275] is accused of having "adopted an agenda-driven position, assuming an aggressive malignancy towards the tradition advocating forgery, while affecting a position of calculated neutrality." This was all based on "personal political interests." Good to know that writers can have them! That and a headline-focussed press get condemned, although Professor Eunan

---
[273] Field Day Review 8. 2012, p. 91
[274] IESH Newsletter 15 Spring/Summer 2004
[275] Field Day Review 8. 2012, p. 106

O'Halpin is quoted,[276] helpfully, as saying the forgery theory is "essentially an article of belief not susceptible to conventional historical analysis."

Bravely, Mitchell does then enter the sensitive and difficult area of paedophilia, explaining[277] that as the years passed, "Casement's sexuality was being rebranded. He would emerge by 2005 not as acceptable homosexual, but as unacceptable pederast and/or paedophile." He tells at length of a hostile review of my book in the American *Irish Literary Supplement* by one Coilin Owens who was as unpleasant about Casement's sexual activities with boys as he was about me, and then of an unsparing *Irish Times* article by Vincent Browne in 2004.

He quotes[278] Browne saying of Casement that "almost certainly he abused young boys" although it was "unfair to write off someone because of a perversity". Mary Kenny added to the debate, similarly, by asserting "a good man can also be a paedophile." My responding letter[279] tried to clarify the question:

"Vincent Browne's assertion that Casement "was probably a paedophile" is relatively new. I suspect any evidence to support that allegation comes from my book, published two years ago. In the 1911 diary, not previously available and the biography, readers were enabled to observe several occasions when Casement's behaviour moved into the unacceptable. It involved the importuning and sexualising of two young teenagers, Teddy Biddy in Barbados and José Gonzalez in Peru. Otherwise his self-recorded penchant was for young men who were plainly eager for sexual contact.

If one must categorise a person's sexual mode at a hundred years' distance, Casement was not a paedophile but might best be described as a pederast, the casual French expression that, in its particularity, means both homosexual and someone keen on teenage boys. Paedophile is generally taken to mean someone interested in pre-pubescent children. The danger for those who respect and applaud Casement has been that the remaining forgery theorists, having an idealised view of the man, perhaps accept that he was gay but assert instead that the 'forging' diarist was variously "a psychopathic predator" and a "pederastic exploiter" (Angus Mitchell) or someone who "had absolutely no conscience in regard to his own sexual life" (Martin Mansergh). But, as he was the diarist, these descriptions apply to Casement!

It is one thing to argue forgery but another to regard the diarist as a sexual monster; indeed it is quite perilous if that person is proven to be one and the same man who Dr Mansergh has also stated it was "legitimate to co-opt … as a forerunner of Ireland's independent foreign policy".

---

[276] Ibid., p. 109
[277] Ibid., p. 112
[278] Ibid., p. 113
[279] *Irish Times*, 25 August 2004

Of course paedophilia in the last decade has brought down the mighty in Ireland with the mightiest of all, the Catholic Church, still on the ropes because of a near-century of exemption from the laws of independent Ireland and their enforcement. Lesser mortals like Cathal Ó Searchaigh have fallen into the exclusion abyss for misbehaviour with boys in Nepal, written off as 'fair-trade sex tourism', while Senator David Norris came under serious pressure, twice, during the 2011 Presidential election on the matter.

Initially it was for a standard issue (old) interview which touched on the subject of Greek love – the unlikely arrangement in Athens where teenage boys were passed around family friends as part of the maturing process – and then when it emerged he had sought clemency for his former partner after he was convicted in Israel of sex with a fifteen-year-old. One way or another, a national treasure, who had led the opinion polls for the Presidency, was reduced to an also-ran who couldn't achieve the necessary percentage for a refund of his expenses.

Casement, had he survived, untried, would have probably become President of Ireland in 1938, instead of Douglas Hyde, and escaped notice because of the media omerta of the time, but his reputation would have been shredded by the 1980s.

The whole piece is seamed with portentous statements, often bigging-up Casement, which ensure that Angus Mitchell will not be taken as seriously as his abilities probably warrant. He asserts that Michael Collins in 1922[280] "officially accepted the authenticity of the Black Diaries and that this acceptance was part of a secret deal in the diplomatic shadows of the negotiations [explaining] why the Irish government remained so ambiguous about the authenticity of the diaries for many decades afterwards."[281]

Later he avers that, "A process was set in motion in 1916 to shut Casement down through a dangerous act of historical necromancy…This conspiracy was then shared at the birth of the Irish Free State and awkwardly carried through subsequent decades in the sensitive and shadowy negotiations of diplomatic relations between the Republic of Ireland and the United Kingdom & Northern Ireland."

Earlier it was, "Archival releases of the 1990s suggest that Ireland had to embrace the Black Diaries as part of the secret diplomacy behind the Irish Free State treaty. But, as Martin Luther King commented, no lie can live forever."

The only Irish governmental comments I recall, over the decades, were Eamon de Valera's remarks on the Maloney book, "the British allegations against Casement have never been believed by Irishmen and so far as they are

---

[280] Field Day Review 8. 2012, p. 89
[281] Ibid., p. 122

concerned no refutation is needed"; his effective, if ambiguous, answer in the Dail in February 1937, "Roger Casement's reputation is safe in the affections of the Irish people, the only people who mattered to him," and, finally, his expression of relief in 1965, "Now thanks be to God he is back here."

The fact that Casement knew all the founding fathers of the Free State and that they loved him, as they did their own achievement, is disregarded, even disrespected. They saw him as one of their own and instinctively defended him against all comers – the partial exception being John Devoy, the other man from New York.

Later Mitchell also states, "In the 1990s a political transformation in Anglo-Irish relations in turn transformed the image of Casement and the issues surrounding the Black Diaries." And elsewhere he wrote, "The archive has played the crucial role in the privileging of a dominant narrative convenient to Anglo-Irish relations"[282] yet also that Casement's "memory was elevated to a level of devotion among the generations of Irish republicans who fought the War of Independence."[283]

Other writers get short shrift. Colm Tóibín is disposed of in grand style, as someone who, "in his rush to proclaim a gay patriot overrode all methodological, archival and historical concerns."[284]

Mitchell gives no credit to rivals, or other writers and researchers, except those who follow his path, like Jordan Goodman, author of *The Devil and Mr Casement* (2009) of whom he wrote in a *drb* review, "When placed in the environment of the atrocity they claim to describe, the politics of the Black Diaries become deeply suspect. That it has taken non-Irish historians and intellectuals like Goodman to throw the most disinterested and scholarly light on Casement further reveals the abusive nature of the controversy."[285]

However Goodman is not as faultless as Mitchell would have us believe, given that he has praised him for "deliberately avoided using the diaries in his narrative."[286] But Goodman could not resist the colour the diaries provide and several times quotes them as Casement's words - without any reference being given.

Another writer to whom Mitchell is curiously nasty, despite his previous obsequious interview in 2009 and somewhat fawning later articles, is the Peruvian Nobel Prize winner for Literature, Mario Vargas Llosa who did not, could not, write a novel where Casement turned out straight.

---

[282] Angus Mitchell, *History Ireland* review of Ó Síocháin biography, July 2008
[283] Field Day Review 8. 2012, p. 89
[284] Ibid., p. 102
[285] Angus Mitchell, *One Man's Struggle for Human Rights in South America's Heart of Darkness,* Dublin Review of Books, 2009
[286] Sao Paulo conference 2010

In truth, in *Dream of the Celt*, he did the second best thing, so far as Mitchell should be concerned, he portrayed Casement as a guilt-ridden, mother-fixated, sexual incompetent. None of which he was.

One senses a Casement-like mood of betrayal being experienced in this turnabout, when he feels obliged to use phrases like, "The Irish rebel emerges as a man of priapic stamina…not merely sexually deviant but prone to bouts of psychosis and delusional dreaming."[287] The novel itself is described as a heavy handed biographical pastiche with "maladroit sexuality at the core of the story." It is also overloaded with those "sexual antics" Mitchell so often disdains, although the sexual element in the novel was relatively slight and unconvincing.

A sad betrayal, hard-felt, but Mitchell really should be grateful, as I suspect his early influence ensured a poor novel (the riveting Amazon episodes aside) turned out to be a history, one much as an Irish writer in the 1930s would have produced, with Casement as hero, rebel, angel, patriot, martyr and anti-imperialist. Or indeed as Angus Mitchell would produce today.

The issue of whether the British government's circulation of copies of diary pages, particularly to Americans, prevented a reprieve, a view which is now conventional wisdom, gets mention. An article by Elizabeth Jaeger is referenced[288] which is quite convincing in that her researches prove the diaries hardly surfaced in the public debates in the US over a reprieve. However they did get significant circulation in Washington society by means of a "photographic facsimile & transcript."

She writes,[289] "The most recent books on Casement do not concern themselves with the U.S. government's perceptions of Casement. The works by Jeffrey Dudgeon, W.J. McCormack, Angus Mitchell, and Séamas Ó Síocháin focus on Casement's diaries, his trial, and/or his humanitarian work without exploring U.S. involvement." However I don't think she read my text on the diaries and Woodrow Wilson, where I argued it was Casement's documented links to German-inspired and assisted bombings in America that were the strongest reason for Wilson's inaction and silence in the face of a Senate appeal seeking White House support for a reprieve.

And it was certainly not what Manus O'Riordan asserted in the IPR when he wrote that "President Wilson's raw-nerve of pure-and-simple Ulster Presbyterian homophobia had been touched in July 1916."[290] Seeing Wilson

---

[287] Field Day Review 8. 2012, p. 117
[288] Elizabeth Jaeger, *Roger Casement: How Effective Was the British Government's Smear Campaign Exposing the Homosexual "Black Diaries"*, Eire-Ireland p. 89 n. 7, Winter 2011
[289] Ibid., n. 66
[290] IPR October and December 2011, Manus O'Riordan, *Larkin and the German sabotage*; Jeffrey Dudgeon response IPR March 2012.

as an Orange homophobe is not just anachronistic but unpolitical, which is not to say he had not been influenced by Asquith who, as he noted in a contemporary journal entry, had told him "of the unmentionable Casement diary, which shows a degree of perversion and depravity without parallel in modern times."

The reality is that on 18 April 1916, just before Casement landed in Kerry, the American Secret Service raided the New York offices of Wolf von Igel, a German diplomat masquerading as an advertising executive, and gathered up a cache of documents on sabotage operations in the U.S., that implicated Casement and von Papen amongst many others.[291]

I wrote in 2002, "The seized documents were erroneously thought by John Devoy to be the reason for Casement's capture on Good Friday in Kerry. In fact his arrest was a matter of chance as the British had not warned the RIC in Tralee of his imminent arrival. Whether decrypts of Berlin's January 1915 message to von Papen in Washington specifically naming Casement as someone suggesting people "suitable for sabotage in the United States" reached Wilson matters not. He knew enough by April 1916 to be assured Casement = von Papen = US sabotage and thus was someone he was not going to be seeking a reprieve for."

In the upshot, President Wilson told his Irish Catholic secretary, Joseph Tumulty, on 20 July 1916, somewhat obscurely, "It w'd be inexcusable to touch this," adding, "It would involve serious international embarrassment." Earlier, on 2 May, Wilson had told Tumulty in the same vein, "We have no choice in a matter of this sort. It is absolutely necessary to say that I could take no action of any kind regarding it."[292]

The sabotage, along with the sinking of the Lusitania off Cork in May 1915 was to become part of the gathering recognition in Washington that conflict was looming. The proximate *casus belli* was the mindless telegram from the German Foreign Secretary, Arthur Zimmermann, which London deciphered as it headed from Berlin to the German Minister in Mexico. It is worth restating those ten lines which brought America into the war:

"We intend to begin on the first of February unrestricted submarine warfare. We shall endeavor in spite of this to keep the United States of America neutral. In the event of this not succeeding, we make Mexico a proposal of alliance on the following basis: make war together, make peace together, generous financial support and an understanding on our part that Mexico

---

[291] See *The New York Times* news article of 23 September 1917: http://query.nytimes.com/mem/archive-free/ pdf?res=9502E6D9103AE433A25750C2A96F9C946696D6CF

[292] Woodrow Wilson Papers, Library of Congress, Washington, D.C., File 3085

is to reconquer the lost territory in Texas, New Mexico, and Arizona. The settlement in detail is left to you. You will inform the President of the above most secretly as soon as the outbreak of war with the United States of America is certain and add the suggestion that he should, on his own initiative, invite Japan to immediate adherence and at the same time mediate between Japan and ourselves. Please call the President's attention to the fact that the ruthless employment of our submarines now offers the prospect of compelling England in a few months to make peace. Signed, ZIMMERMANN".

How much easier and more efficacious it would have been to forge that than the thousands of lines in Casement's diaries?

A reprieve from the 3 August execution, probably desired by many of Casement's acquaintances in the Cabinet, was politically impossible, not least because of the huge Irish casualties in the Battle of the Somme beginning in July and the execution by the Germans as a *franc-tireur* of Captain Robert Fryatt at the end of the month. (His merchant navy ship had rammed a German submarine.) It is almost as if Imperial Germany wanted Casement dead. Yet had he stayed in Germany as Berlin wanted rather than make a largely pointless, if honourable, journey to Ireland he would have survived the war. It was his choice to go to a certain death.

Which Casement is Angus Mitchell? He is more like the man in the gloom of his last days, seeing opposition and difficulties everywhere, not so much the earlier Roger who was at times positive and enthusiastic, although never sunny. He certainly inhabits and colonises those aspects of Casement I don't appreciate. They think alike and of course blame the same. He would want to have been Casement as I, briefly, was. Indeed he has become Casement in all but matters sexual where I ceased to be, except in the heritage and sexuality departments which may explain the fascination we both have for the man.

One has to ask, as at the end of a trial, how a proper judgment or assessment on the authenticity of the diaries can be made, for that is the issue.

I reckon there are five options:

- Under the criminal trial rule, judgment is by the classic, if confusing, phrase "beyond reasonable doubt." I have proved to my satisfaction the diaries are genuine. I tested a fair number of such doubts and none remain, although the bulk of the evidence, it must be said, is the diaries themselves, alongside circumstantial material, but the diaries, if admissible, as they must surely be, have colossal weight;
- Secondly, the evidential test in a civil case with its lesser burden of proof – "the balance of probabilities." This is the one I would expect most other highly interested parties to use to bring in a positive verdict. Mitchell certainly offers next to no evidence to prevent such

a verdict, just the mood of a mystic victim.

He at one time in a 1997 letter to the *Irish Times* approvingly quoted the probability test: "When writing about the Public Record Office manuscripts, Professor Roger McHugh quoted Montaigne: Historians can decide which of two reports is the more probable. That is what I did."[293] But as the contrary evidence mounts he no longer sticks to that position. He doesn't even go down to the next level.

- Thirdly, for the academic, the historian and the reader of history there is a common sense measure based on the evidence provided so far as it is possible to obtain in the circumstances of passing years and a subject's natural secretiveness. This has to be set against any alternatives presented, but alternatives there have to be, not just assertions or the casting of doubt. Obviously historical judgments in most non-contemporary cases are made on limited or small amounts of evidence. No such alternative evidence, for example of a forging process, has ever been adduced. Mitchell and his colleagues know many are not too fussy about the lack of alternatives given the natural instinct of Irish nationalists to be super sceptical.
- Fourthly, there is the test in the court of common sense where judgment is based on what evidence there is, and then on an understanding of what is likely, given human nature and people's own experiences. This court does not sit often over Casement's diaries, certainly not in many parts of Ireland.
- And finally, there is the test applied by those who believe truth a moveable feast, the Derridean or Foucaultian interpretation, which is also the view of the Irish republican, not to mention the conspiracy theorist and the inconvincible. If there is a scintilla of doubt, then the case is unproven. Indeed as soon as one avenue of doubt is closed down, another is opened up. That is the evidential test that will never be met, short of Casement's resurrection.

Mitchell in his conclusion[294] returns to the First World War, quoting the famous speech from the dock where Casement invoked an alternate and radically different approach: anti-war and separatist, if effectively anti-Unionist. He dared to dream and turned out to be a nation builder, regardless of the foolish attempts of his more enthusiastic supporters to deny the reality of his sexual nature. If it was accepted, his stature would rise. The choice is theirs.

---

[293] Angus Mitchell, *Irish Times*, 5 December 1997
[294] Field Day Review 8. 2012, p. 124

[A raft of newspaper articles, and academic papers, restating the diary forgery thesis has been published in 2016 in the lead up to the centenary of Casement's landing in Kerry and of the Easter Rising itself. The argument against authenticity has also been made extensively in talks, not least by Angus Mitchell. The most lengthy written case comes from Paul Hyde in *Breac* 'Lost to History: An Assessment and Review of the Casement Black Diaries' http://breac.nd.edu/articles/65746-lost-to-history-an-assessment-and-review-of-the-casement-black-diaries/. No novel evidence of forgery has been provided, only a restatement of doubts.]

APPENDIX 5

SEQUEL 1

Casement and the Easter Rising: Berlin, Dublin and British Intelligence
by Jeffrey Dudgeon [295]

The story of who knew what in April 1916, and why pretty well all parties failed in their allotted tasks is worth retelling, even if it deromanticises many of the players, and diminishes some of their reputations.

The main political question is why did British Intelligence fail to avert the Easter Rising, given their intimate foreknowledge, allied to why, if Casement was so determined to get the rebellion, at least, postponed, did the Germans let him go to Ireland at all, knowing what they did?

Failure of course also bred success in revolutionising southern Ireland and developing its founding myth. Without Easter 1916, an Irish Free State would still have been born, but separatism might not have been so radically successful and for so long.

There are a number of other Casement mysteries, or disputed facts in 1916, over and above the authenticity of the diaries. Many questions also surround the second rank players. Some have recently been solved – at least partially, as detailed below.

I instance the increasing information that has come to light on Casement's four key colleagues in Germany and in two cases on the submarine – Adler Christensen (his Norwegian companion and erstwhile lover), Robert Monteith, John McGoey, and Daniel Julien Bailey (using the *nom de guerre* Beverley, a Dubliner with a French mother), all of whom ended their days in north America. Living as they did along the edge of legality, their stories have not surfaced easily.

In Christensen's case, the mystery was initially advanced to 1928 when – as recently advised by a relative – he deserted Hedwig, his third wife. She was a German girl he had married a year earlier in Winnipeg. The first two wives Sadie Weaver, a Nansemond Indian, and the German, Margarette or

---

[295] This is the text largely as provided to the *Dúiche Néill* editor. The article is based on, and expanded from, a lecture given at the *Roger Casement (1864-1916): The Glocal Imperative* conference in Tralee on 25 October 2013.

Margarethe Verschmidt, were probably concurrent as Adler did not seem to bother with divorce. He was last heard of in Vancouver, "in the opium dens" of that city, until researches in 2015 by a Norwegian writer brought the story forward.

It came to a pathetic conclusion with Adler's death in 1935 in a Paris jail at the age of forty-five. He had been convicted of robbery and of avoiding deportation, and given the last of a series of prison sentences in France that dated from 1931.

Sergeant Daniel Bailey of the Irish Brigade – a man captured in Tralee a day after the landing[296] – entered the Old Bailey dock after Lord Chief Justice Isaacs passed sentence of death on Casement. At the surprising request of the Attorney General, F.E. Smith, Bailey was duly found not guilty by the jury. After recall to the British Army and serving in former German East Africa and Egypt, he emigrated to Canada, dying in Ontario in 1968. First however, in London in 1917, he had married a widow, Katerina O'Dea, née Friedrich. She oddly was born in Germany in 1865, he in 1887. It would be wrong to say Bailey betrayed Casement, not least because Casement was informing the authorities in Tralee, and most everyone else, of the imminent Rising. Neither did he give 'King's Evidence' in court. Indeed Bailey was far from frank with his local interrogators about the details and purpose of their mission, despite his, not unreasonable, efforts to escape the gallows. His motives seem mixed, much as McGoey, although he was no sociopath like Adler.

Captain Monteith, a Connolly socialist, having escaped capture in Kerry, and after a lengthy period in hiding – an adventure story well told in his book and as thrilling an account as many of those recently revealed in the Bureau of Military History – made it back to the US, dying in 1956 in Detroit. He remained a faithful admirer of Casement, telling of a meeting in New York in 1917 where he disputed with John Devoy of Clan na Gael:

> When I made the statement that Casement did not sail with the intention of stopping the Rising, Devoy interrupted me with a vehement and vicious denunciation of Casement, charging him with selling-out and unspeakable crimes on the unsupported word of Adler Christensen, whom Devoy himself described as: "One of the worst I ever met and who was in the pay of the English all along."[297]

This is a misinterpretation of Casement's motives by Devoy, while his view that the raid on the New York offices of the German spy, Wolf von Igel, on 18 April yielded the information to enable Casement's capture was also erro-

---

[296] Bailey is simply called "a third man" on the Casement memorial at Banna Strand.
[297] Monteith, p. 232.

neous, as intelligence derived therefrom only reached London after the event.

The greatest mystery surrounds John McGoey, a Scots-Irish man based in the US, who could have changed history had he followed Casement's orders. His mission was to go to Denmark, and thence Dublin to warn Tom Clarke and Bulmer Hobson of the lack of German support for a Rising. Instead McGoey somehow reached England and, of all things, joined the Royal Navy, while managing to marry a Londoner within six months of leaving Berlin.[298] Casement (as above) wrote of the events of 18 March 1916:

> "McGoey was brought in next day – I explained all the situation to him very fully and pointed out the imperative need of trying to get someone into Ireland to warn them there of the wholly inadequate help being given and to say that I strongly urged no "rising." He (like Monteith) was with me here. McGoey said it would be criminal and that he had long suspected the Germans of playing a double game. He would do anything I asked him to. I told him it was necessary for me to keep silent as to my real opinions before the German General Staff (GGS) and that when I took him to the Admiralty he must do the same. We went at 11.30 o'clock and found the three Captains again – all was explained to John McG. He is to go as an added string to our bow (in addition to the telegram to Devoy) to tell the Dublin Council to have the pilot boat ready at Inishtooskert &c. &c. – but he goes really to try and get the Heads in Ireland to call off the rising and merely try to land the arms safely and distribute these."[299]

Ten days after McGoey had left Berlin on 19 March, Casement was cross-examined by the GGS, later diarying:

> "Their fear was that I had sent John McGoey to stop the rising! They asked again and again if I had given him instructions to that effect. I said I was not the master of the Irish Revolutionary body and whatever I might say would only be advice or suggestion. I avowed that John McGoey himself was dead against a rising, and the fury was uncontrolled. Their fear was that I had sent John McGoey to stop the rising! They asked again and again if I had given him instructions to that effect. I said I was not the master of the Irish Revolutionary body and whatever I might say would only be advice or suggestion. I avowed that John McGoey himself was dead against a rising, and the fury was uncontrolled.
>
> How had I dared to send such a man to Ireland without letting them know!
>
> I saw in clear sharp light, the whole devilish game – Devoy was being fooled too – had been fooled I felt convinced by the ass von Papen. Devoy, an old man, of passionate feeling against England, burning for one brave fight before he dies, had been assured of the entire good will of Germany

---

[298] See David Grant's Irish Brigade website http://www.irishbrigade.eu/ for many intriguing details on the brigade and their backgrounds.
[299] NLI 5244. This entry is dated 27 March 1916.

and of strong military aid. His letter of 16.2.16 showed what he expected at least, and asked for.

These people wanted only bloodshed in Ireland for their own ends – and the fatal steamer was to be the price of the rising. I was being shipped by her, merely to get me out of the scene, tear up the Treaty, and having had their "rising" in Ireland, for what it might be worth to them – then they could wash their hands of all further connection or contact with "the Irish." I had possibly spoiled this game by sending John McGoey across, and at any rate gravely imperilled the "rising" coming off – or "the War in Ireland" as Nadolny termed it!"[300]

Whether McGoey was too late getting out of Denmark or decided to disobey Casement's orders remains unclear. He had the power to stymie the Rising but didn't. Which is not to say he couldn't be a quick worker. Last recorded in late March en route to Denmark, by September, in Essex, he was marrying a Miss Ethel Wells, having already joined the Royal Navy. He was serving on HMS Kildonan, an armed merchant cruiser.

So what happened to him between April and September, when, despite Casement's notion and that of many Republicans, he had obviously not been executed by the British at Kirkwall in the Orkneys? Did the Germans prevent him leaving mainland Europe before the Rising? This was something I reasonably assumed, not believing the secret hanging theory, especially as the German Military knew that Casement had despatched McGoey to sabotage their efforts soon after they discovered the Admiralty had enabled him to travel. Did he decide not to jeopardise the Rising and ignore Casement's orders? Did love of an Englishwoman get in the way of his duty? Perhaps he decided to switch sides after experiencing the Germans close at hand. We can deduce his loyalty to Irish separatism must have been – or have become – sufficiently shallow for him to join the Royal Navy, although he was plainly not averse to military involvement. It must be remembered that people are less ideological, more changeable, and more buffeted by events than we perhaps credit.

McGoey died in Chicago in 1925 in a building accident, taking his story to an early grave. However the key question remains, knowing of his mission, and that the German Admiralty had granted Casement's repeated request for a submarine, once the GGS knew on 7 April, why did they allow him to proceed or, at least, ensure the orders about the timing of the landing were not tighter to minimise his ability to thwart matters? Indeed why did the Admiralty give in to Casement's request for a submarine at all? Was it a desperation to get rid of him or did Casement pull sufficient of his many strings in Berlin?

---

[300] Ibid., this entry is dated 29 March 1916.

We do know that the orders for U20 included, "Headquarters attach importance to getting the Irish ashore at the last possible moment."

Karl Spindler indeed emphasised this, remarking:

> Worthy of special attention is Paragraph (5) [of the Captain's orders] according to which no matter what happened, the landing of Sir Roger much in advance of the outbreak of the revolution was to be prevented.[301]

Was the reason a lack of imagination or Prussian blockheadedness, something Casement came to acknowledge within so much of the German High Command, or the fog of war? This question is one that might be answered by closer inspection of the German-language archives.

Another mystery, partially solved, is the precise origin and family background of Casement's mother Anne Jephson. Results of recent research, aided by various digitisation projects, reveal her origins in Dublin. Part of the failure to ascertain Anne's precise ancestry derives from a change in spelling of her surname which is recorded in earlier times as Jepson, not the more upmarket Jephson. She came from a north Dublin Protestant family living at 48 North Strand and later 15 Portland Street. The family were parishioners of St George's Anglican Church in Hardwicke Place, where Anne was baptised in 1832. That she converted to Roman Catholicism in later married life is well attested, and significant, but she was undoubtedly brought up as a Protestant. Her father was James Jepson, 'Gent', her mother Jane Ball.

From 1834, according to Dublin street directories, Jane ran a series of seminaries for young ladies (some from home) under her maiden name – only becoming noted as 'Mrs Jephson' in 1842. They were in Amiens Street, Seville Place, Portland Street and Dorset Street Lower respectively, the last mention being in 1853. What is noteworthy is Anne's own mother's likely influence as a progressive educationist. At that time it was unusual for girls to be schooled. Such an outlook plainly travelled forward two generations to Jane's grandson Roger and his three siblings (not to mention his Bannister cousins). Their parents, Anne and Captain Casement, shared a world view not dissimilar to that of Oscar Wilde's parents, Speranza and Sir William.

Turning back to British intelligence, the events in the week before the Rising took place on the Monday, and the consequences of each change of mind or plan are involved and convoluted. But they all served unexpectedly the interest of the inner junta of the IRB who were determined on a Rising except, initially, for Casement's capture. It was London's intelligence mishandling that in the event minimised the harm his capture was going to do. Hindsight is of course a clear guide.

---

[301] Spindler, pp. 202-3

The decisions of three men, Captain Reginald 'Blinker' Hall, head of Naval Intelligence in Room 40, aided on the day by Basil Thomson of Scotland Yard, and MI5's 'Q', Frank Hall of Narrow Water Castle in Warrenpoint, (former military secretary of the UVF), ensured the Rising happened and ultimately succeeded. In essence, London denied Dublin the necessary knowledge that should have made the Castle take effective precautions against the imminent outbreak of rebellion. Blinker Hall knew through the decoding of German cables going from their Washington Embassy to Berlin, the fact of a rebellion, its date, the despatch of Casement, and of an arms shipment to be landed in the Limerick area.

By taking him immediately to London, Dublin Castle was again deprived of an opportunity to hear of the plans for a Rising. David Ramsay in his hagiographic biography, *'Blinker' Hall: Spymaster* wrote,

> "The inept Chief Secretary for Ireland (Birrell), who had held the post for far too long (nine years) and who reputedly seldom visited Dublin, lost his job. But Hall as the de facto co-ordinator of intelligence and Thomson must share some responsibility for the failure to pass intelligence to the RIC, one of the most serious intelligence breakdowns in British history."[302]

That the author Ramsay wrote such searing criticism proves Hall was far from flawless and when he worked with Thomson and Frank Hall – three good old boys very much of a kind – the danger was compounded. Eunan O'Halpin tells much the same story writing:

> "Hall was anxious above all to avoid disclosing his source, decrypted German messages; in so doing he jeopardised the security of Ireland."[303]

Hall's secrecy in relation to the Rising had another cause – his view that "politicians were as leaky as sieves". He thus restricted the details he had gleaned to naval personnel, in particular.

We have recently learnt that Margot Asquith and of course her husband, the Prime Minister, were aware of the intelligence.[304] Indeed the whole Cabinet may have been informed by Arthur Balfour, the First Lord of the Admiralty, his source being Sir Henry Oliver, the Naval Secretary.[305] This however has not been confirmed and seems unlikely in that Birrell was plainly not *au fait*.

---

[302] Ramsay, p. 135
[303] Eunan O'Halpin, 'British Intelligence in Ireland, 1914-21' in Christopher Andrew and David Dilks (Eds), *The Missing Dimension: Governments and Intelligence Communities in the Twentieth Century* (Illinois, 1984) p. 59
[304] BBC Radio 4 Document programme, The 'Easter Rising' - the Dublin Rebellion of 1916; broadcast 11 March 2013. http://www.bbc.co.uk/programmes/b01r55x9
[305] Ramsay, p. 134

Asquith discounted the intelligence, apparently as he had heard so much of a similar nature. But why bother with intelligence if you simply ignore it? Stopped-up sieves are more useless than leaky ones. And Asquith was notoriously averse to action. George Dangerfield catches it well if from the view of a Liberal apologist:

> "Captain Reginald Hall, possibly deep in Room 40 of the Admiralty may have permitted himself a twinge of uneasiness. If he had allowed Mr Birrell and Sir Matthew Nathan to know what he knew, and by what means he had come to know it, things might have gone differently. But Captain Hall, even if he had wished to speak, was obliged for security reasons to remain silent. And so the Birrell administration was thrown to the wolves."[306]

Dangerfield adds that Birrell and his deputy Nathan, "pursued their policy – on the whole a very sensible one – of "minimum action and maximum inaction" Why stir up trouble in that excitable land?"[307] This masterly inactivity was called by some appeasement, and, as it always does, in time, leads to a crisis.

'Blinker' Hall was a very political intelligence chief, as many are or become. He also lacked common sense and was possessive of his secrets. There is a pattern of him keeping them too secret as at the Battle of Jutland. The one occasion where he broke his own rule was after the deciphering of the Zimmerman telegram, which, by drawing the US into the war, changed everything, and ensured victory for the Entente powers. Blinker knew well this one secret had to be distributed even at the risk of alerting the Germans to his code breaking.

The informational cascade and its variations is complex, with many names and dates. Hall told General McDonagh, Director of Military Intelligence on 22 March of a rebellion due to start on 22 April and of an arms landing. He in turn advised Lord French, Commander in Chief of the Home Forces, citing only "an absolutely reliable source".[308] Dangerfield writes:

> "Lord Wimborne and Mr Birrell, who met with French in London that day, were not told anything at all…On the whole, Captain Hall would have chanced a rising all over Ireland rather than give the Germans an inkling of the truth – that their coded messages were being read."[309]

---

[306] George Dangerfield, *The Damnable Question – a Study in Anglo-Irish Relations*, (Boston, 1976), p. 248
[307] Ibid., p. 161
[308] Ibid., p. 160
[309] Ibid., pp. 160-1

General Lovick Friend, the Army Commander in Chief in Ireland, was then advised on 23 March, a month in advance of the rising, but not of the unimpeachable source. Matthew Nathan, replying to General Friend on 10 April, but without being told of the intelligence, wrote,

> "I do not believe the leaders mean insurrection or that the Volunteers have sufficient arms if the leaders do mean it."[310]

This has the ring of a conversation with Alice Stopford Green, given her significant friendship with Nathan and Birrell. (They judged her low "in the hierarchy of treason."[311])

Sir Matthew was not inclined to listen to southern Unionists who warned him of mounting trouble and advised of a need for drastic measures, as they would, he probably thought. In particular their leader, Lord Midleton, who wanted the Volunteers proscribed was disregarded, yet his sister the Hon. Albinia Broderick (*Gobnait Ní Bhruadair*) lived in Kerry in a Gaelic League and Volunteer milieu and was to be shot by the Black and Tans. Midleton therefore had to have had some better feel for what was developing than the Castle and its complacent or nationalist advisers. He was aware that an administration that permitted an alternative and opposing locus of military power was asking to be subverted. Despite being the political head in Dublin, Nathan was not given direct knowledge of any of the key intercepts until 17 April, the Monday of Holy Week. General Friend, the top soldier in Ireland, showed him a letter that day which he had received from Brigadier-General Stafford in Queenstown (Dún Laoghaire) on foot of a casual conversation with his naval counterpart, Lewis Bayly, the Admiral Commanding the Western Approaches.

John de Courcy Ireland wrote in *The Sea and The Easter Rising*: "Of course, the British Admiralty did not necessarily always think fit or important to tell the British officials governing this country what it knew"; though Admiral Bayly, British Naval Commander in Chief at the time at Queenstown Base, Haulbowline, wrote in his reminiscences, *Pull together,* that "other Government departments" refused to take seriously naval intelligence's hints of coming trouble in Ireland and, that he knew in advance (unfortunately he gives no date) of the *Libau*'s departure and expected arrival on our coast."[312] As Nathan recounted to the Royal Commission, it told of a

> "contemplated landing from a German ship rigged up as a neutral and accompanied by two submarines, of arms and ammunition on

---

[310] Spindler, p. 24 quoting from Leon Ó Broin, *Dublin Castle and the 1916 Rising: The Story of Sir Matthew Nathan* (Dublin, 1970).
[311] Inglis, p. 82
[312] Lewis Bayly, *Pull together ! - The Memoirs of Admiral Sir Lewis Bayly*, London, 1939, pp. 202 and 206.

the south west coast with a view to their reaching Limerick and of a rising timed for Easter."³¹³

The RIC chief was informed while Nathan and General Friend did agree to arrange for "armed pickets of 100 men to be nightly available at each of the four main barracks," a contingency that seems to have provided no cover of any value, if it ever happened. He was still so unconcerned he brought his sister-in-law Estelle and her children over for Easter. They were staying at the Under-Secretary's Lodge in Phoenix Park (along with Dorothy Stopford, Alice Stopford Green's niece. Mrs Nathan was to be trapped there and terrified for five days. General Lovick Friend notoriously went on leave.

The Royal Navy knowing more than the military and the Castle did take precautions although they were not effective. Here, I particularly rely on Xander Clayton's monumental book *Aud*.³¹⁴ Clayton who lives near Tralee has tracked down and published much original naval material, not least the secret orders from Admiral Bayly to the blockading cruiser squadron off the west and northern coasts of Ireland. These warned of "a rising which some say may be expected about Easter" and an arms landing.³¹⁵

The Navy's alertness however was not so keen as to unmask the *Aud*. It was stopped early on Friday morning (21ˢᵗ) by *Setter 2* (or *Shatter* as Spindler wrote), an outpost trawler commanded by a civilian Aberdeen fisherman named John Donaldson. He, and his admittedly outnumbered boarding party, were tricked by Spindler, despite being several hours on the ship – even telling the supposed Norwegians that intelligence had them on the lookout. Drink was usefully provided. Spindler however realised then his mission was doomed. This failure can be regarded as critical since it delayed knowledge of the ship's German origins for twelve more hours. Indeed that certainty only came via the Fenit Base Officer, Lt. A.S. Holmes, after he visited the RIC barracks in Tralee. He, together with Commander Francis Spring-Rice RN (later 4ᵗʰ Lord Monteagle of Brandon and uncle of the gunrunner Mary Spring Rice), wired Queenstown to have the "Norwegian Steamer '*Aud*' […]

---

³¹³ Royal Commission on the Rebellion in Ireland (Cmd. 8279, 26 June 1916) Report of the Commission, Minutes of Evidence and Appendix of Documents (Cmd. 8311), p. 7 of the latter. (HMSO, Westminster, 1916).
http://www.garda.ie/Documents/User/Royal%20Commission%20on%20the%20Rebellion%20in%20Ireland%201916.pdf

See also *Documents Relative to the Sinn Fein Movement*, XXIX (Cmd. 1108, 1921) (London, 1921). These are intercepted and decrypted transatlantic messages and letters, to and from the German embassy in Washington, on Ireland and Casement, during and after the First World War.

³¹⁴ Xander Clayton, *Aud*, "The true and in depth history of the German arms ship, which battled its way into Tralee Bay for the 1916 Easter Rising" – as per book cover.

³¹⁵ Ibid., pp. 68 and 69. Admiral Bayly's orders of 14 and 16 April 1916.

rearrested and taken to port for examination" as they were sure Casement's boat had landed from it.[316] Details from the interrogations of Casement and Bailey filtered only gradually, and late, to Dublin Castle.

As I wrote in *The Black Diaries*, sufficient material to alert Dublin Castle fully was being provided by Casement and to a lesser extent by Bailey:

> "During the evening Casement began a series of self-justificatory conversations. Indeed before the night was out, first one and then another RIC man, Head Constable John Kearney and District Inspector Ambrose Britten respectively, became his confessors. They were responsive listeners, according to Casement's Notes to Counsel,[317] indeed to such a degree he was concerned not to have their nationalist views made known in court. There was apparently little left out: he spoke of the rising, the arms ship, who held his papers in Germany (posterity calling again), even of the messages he had now sent to Dublin through the visitors arranged by Kearney. It is unlikely by morning there was anything except formal doubt as to his identity.
>
> Whether the two officers were as sympathetic as he reckoned can perhaps be deduced by what they reported to Dublin.[318] If even half this information had been relayed the mystery man would surely have been kept in Ireland. Had they had just been stringing Casement along with remarks such as those he attributed to Britten: "I pray to God it won't end the way of Wolfe Tone…We would be with you to a man if there was a chance of success," then they were masterful. Perhaps they toned down what they told their superiors because of the confessional nature of the whole night's talking or perhaps they believed in what they told Casement and left much information out; perhaps nobody at the centre bothered to ask for any detail once it was decided he was to be moved on, and out of Ireland".[319]

Taking Casement (captured on Friday 21 April) to London on Saturday was however the final mistake that ensured the Rising on Easter Monday 24 April was not snuffed out in advance. This and his execution also ensured he would not end up disgraced within the separatist movement, as happened to his ally and fellow rising-sceptic Bulmer Hobson. Some questions have been answered here. Other remain for further research, but the mysteries lessen.

---

[316] Ibid., p. 656
[317] NLI 13088, "Briefs, memoranda, letters, note-books, appeals for clemency etc. relating to the trial of Roger Casement, 1916. 1000 documents". Casement's trial papers came into the NLI in at least two batches, MSS 13088 and 10763-65, being sourced from George Gavan Duffy in 1950 and Gertrude Parry in 1930. Many items are duplicated.
[318] PRONI D1916/3-5 and 9. RIC papers including District Inspector Frederick Ambrose Britten's typed statement of 14 May 1916 about Daniel Bailey's statement which was taken on Saturday 23 April 1916. Britten says he wired "the Admiral at Queenstown and to the military authorities there" about the imminent rebellion.
[319] Dudgeon (2nd edition, 2016), p. 485

Memorial stone with German inscription at McKenna's Fort near Banna Strand where Casement was arrested in 1916

... and with Irish inscription

APPENDIX 6

SEQUEL 2

Roger Casement letter to his cousin, Gertrude Bannister, from Pentonville Prison, written on the reverse of an incoming Cathal O'Byrne letter [320]

20. July 1916.   Ptonville

My dearest, darling wee Gee,
[words stroked out] !

It is from Cathal O'Byrne & the inclosures put with my other papers – I want you to get all the papers I left with Gavan Duffy & bring out, some day, a statement of the case. Dr Curry in Munich has all the papers except the <u>original</u> Findlay letters to Christensen etc & there ought to be with J.E. Noeggerath, 44. Kamminer Strasse, III. Berlin – an American-German friend. I want the Findlay matter published after my death – & the iniquity made clear. Many papers dealing with it are with Dr. Curry.

Today I am served with the notice of my execution for 3 Augt. – this day fortnight – just after I got the notice Mrs. Gavan Duffy came. I did not tell her it wd. have spoiled the interview. The warder hurried her away. I hope Monteith has got to *Oileán Ur* **[America]** – he is a brave, faithful soul – not like Bailey – & true to me. There is another <u>John McGoey</u> – I sent him over from Berlin on 19 March to try and reach Dublin & beg them not to rise as the help coming was insufficient. I got him over the frontier to Copenhagen – but know nothing more of him. If these people collared him on arrival here – it is probable – they had no evidence – & all they could have done would have been to send him to the front in their army. A dreadful fate enough – & God be with him, the brave faithful soul. I want Joe McGarrity told about him – as it was Joe sent him over to me.

You have been far more to me in these awful days than any human being ever before – except my mother. I think of her often now – and now, at the end you dearest have been to me like mother, sister and all – What should I have done had it not been for Eily and you. I should have gone mad in the Tower. <u>Then</u> I wanted to die – I longed and prayed hourly for death – and was

---

[320] NLI 14100, "A collection of letters by or concerning Roger Casement made by Éamon de Valera, including six letters of Mrs. Agnes Newman and photo-copies of two letters of Casement to Mr. de Valera. Early 20th c."

more than ready for it any minute – <u>now</u>, alas, I do not want to die – since the trial, and even before it, the love of you and others had won me back to care to live – and now it is a cruel wrench to go away from you all – and in such a way too. But it is God's will – He has brought me to this – and I often prayed for death for Ireland's sake – and it has come. God give me strength to bear it as I wish to – In the Tower it would have been easy – with my back to the wall & a firing party – here it is gloomier – and my longing to be free and with you is now strong and vital. But go I must – and I can leave you only my blessing – my eternal blessing and my undying love – and I leave you too, dearest, my honour and my name. Defend them and make clear and plain what you can of all this tangled web. Alas! so much of the story dies with me – and Shawn Bwee has won! Once again. The old, old story – and yet the truth and right live on – in the hearts of the brave and lowly. It is better that I die thus – perhaps – on the scaffold. It is a glorious death – for Ireland's sake – with Allen, Larkin & O'Brien and Robert Emmet – and the men of '98 and William Orr – all for the same cause – all in the same way. Surely it is the most glorious cause in history – ever defeated yet undefeated – and it has always found the right women too – I have been the wrong man – but you, dearest, have not been the wrong woman.

I left G.B.S.'s "John Bull's Other Island" at Brixton for you with much writing on the fly leaf for you – It has gone. They seized it at the High Courts, along with a copy of "<u>Life of St. Columban</u>" I was leaving for Eilis – with a brief inscription. Both were at the Courts that last day with the fatal portfolio. <u>That</u> is really my death warrant I think. There are too many things in that to be passed over. I will send you also my little copy of St. Thomas à Kempis some living soul sent me from <u>Bow St</u>.

I think I <u>must</u> become a Catholic before I die. I always wanted to – or felt inclined to I must say. And since beginning of the year I was taking definite steps & was in touch with a good Bavarian priest, Fr. Fischer. I shall be dead before the anniversary (5th Augt <u>1868</u>) of our baptism in the Catholic church at Rhyl. Up to this I have not taken the necessary steps – because I want only to act on clearest acceptance and conviction – not from emotion. And this takes time. I am, and am <u>not</u> convinced. At times I think all is settled – but some fresh doubt arises within and pulls down the fabric – and now with my end so close I don't like galloping.

Give all my friends my deepest love and affection.

<u>21 July</u>. Today it is three months since I was captured on Banna's Strand – three months today – mavrone! I wanted to send you some letters I got at Brixton I had brought with me here on 29 June in my pocket. I asked to be allowed – they have refused. One was a splendid letter signed "Kathleen"

from Indianapolis. I hoped Miceál [**probably Michael Francis Doyle**] wd. come today – but no sign of him – so I am sure they have refused him permission. The Governor has been in to give me a message "of regret" some friend sent through him and thought it part of his duty to assure me of his "horror" at same time of my "crime". Such is the chivalry of the Saxon! He came in to weep on me the other day, his regret at having to hang me – true. I could not help thinking of the Walrus & the Carpenter but it is all so horrible – to be here in their hands – yet it is not they caught me – but God who gave me into this captivity and death – and I kiss the divine hand that leads me to the grave.

For dearest, it has lead me to you, too, and to a knowledge & perception of Him as love I had lost – and so I pay a small price for a great gain – May god bring us again together in his realm with those who have gone before. And may Ireland forgive her faithless son who failed her. If you can see R. E. Monteith – he was like a brother to me. Faithful to the end. I hope he is in *Oileán Ur* [**America**]. If possible have my body some day taken to Ireland – I would love to have my mother's remains there too – from Worthing – but mavrone – they must be lost sight of now – it is so long ago. I hope to have this sent out by a faithful hand – The days are drawing on now and next week will soon be gone and then my last Sunday on earth. See Fr. McCarroll, the curate of Eden Grove, here he is my pastor in the cell of death.

I wonder if some day Ireland will not put a monument to Allen, Larkin and O'Brien. I have been thinking much of them – because their fate and mine are similar & we are both being murdered here in England. The last execution for high treason I think was Robert Emmet's – 113 years ago – And the last public executions those of Allen, Larkin and O'Brien. I shall be done to death in a corner with the Governor weeping over me – It is the supreme act of English hypocrisy. But God forgive my bitter thoughts – and take them all from me – You, dearest heart, shall be with you to the end, you and Eilis and a "host more outside" – & pray for me, then and hereafter too. Let <u>death</u> not separate our spirits. I shall write you public letter again – but this may probably be the last chance I'll have of sending you a private word.

Don't let them send me down to history as "R<u>D</u>C". My name of Roger is enough – & Ruari better still – and remember darling I was always the same – just as you were. You will have a big talk to tell the whole story after I am gone – but I leave it to you as my dying wish – get all the papers and see the friends. See Mrs. Gaffney in Munich – & Frau Wilhelm Kurt Tzlemann, 17. Prager Str. Dresden, (a dear friend of mine & of Mrs. Gaffney's. Mrs. Gaffney will take you to her) & Dr. Curry & his old mother – He, too, is a dear friend. <u>Don't</u> forget John McGoey & tell Joe McGarrity that John was faithful & true & I want him saved & helped. I <u>fear</u> they <u>have</u> him in their clutches.

And, some day, far off, beyond the years, when the Dawn comes to Ireland?? I may not far off – & you & Ide & N. as "hurts" more – there too.

Adieu Thine eternally
    Scodgie

Irish stamps issued in 2016 to mark the centenary of Casement's execution – 70c and €1.05

APPENDIX 7

SEQUEL 3

Casement and Ulster: Seeding Separatism and Misunderstanding

by Jeffrey Dudgeon[321]

The North Began? Ulster and the Irish Revolution 1900-25

I have long argued that the role of Ulster and the northern counties – Tyrone in particular – in the birth of Irish separatism and the making of the Easter Rising, has been insufficiently recognised. Just as it was that the north, in a different, Unionist, configuration, has thwarted the creation of an island state for a century now.

There was no single Irish nation even if, for opposite reasons, Unionists and Nationalists organised a similar armed resistance to London in 1912, and from 1914, respectively.

During the first decade of the twentieth century, the northern separatist nexus involved a web of organisations, and of propagandising. These small groups covered language, culture and sport, linking with progressive Belfast politics and arts, while underneath was the renascent Irish Republican Brotherhood (IRB), led or staffed by Denis McCullough, Bulmer Hobson and Patrick McCartan. They operated and recruited under various front organisations with titles such as the Dungannon Clubs, and through journals like *Uladh*.

Those three names, and their differing trajectories for half a century, tell the story of separatism and how it unfolded. None became leaders, although McCullough was briefly President of Ireland in 1916 as head of the IRB. The north however, for a significant reason, played no role in the Rising, beyond a foray into Coalisland.

---

[321] Edited version of talk given on 20 June 2015 in the 'Influences and Inspirations' section during the conference of the TCD Centre for Contemporary Irish History and St Patrick's College Drumcondra History Department entitled *The North Began? Ulster and the Irish Revolution 1900-25*.

The linking in common cause of Republicans and liberals in the 1900s was not unlike the experience in Northern Ireland in the late 1960s before the firestorm. And indeed in the 1790s before another firestorm.

That northern nurturing moved, physically in some cases, to Dublin, blending with and giving political leadership to the burgeoning intellectual, academic, and socialist organisations moving over to separatism in the south.

This was in the period just before the Irish Volunteers, when the IRB or its inner junta was led by an old Dungannon Fenian, Tom Clarke, ably assisted by another northern political trainee, Sean MacDermott. The Irish American leader Joe McGarrity, the key link to Imperial Germany, who long remained unreconciled to partition, was a Carrickmore man, like Pat McCartan. Major John McBride was educated in Belfast and James Connolly operated there as a trade unionist.

Around this Irish ferment and in an overarching role, was a further Ulsterman, Roger Casement. He was Hobson's mentor and with F.J. Bigger, the solicitor antiquarian and United Irish romantic, they maintained at Bigger's Belfast house, Ardrigh, something of a university for the city's young nationalists – a number of them radical Protestants. Herbert Hughes, Alice Milligan and Joseph Campbell however developed in more respects artistically. With Casement throughout, was his early mentor and collaborator, Alice Stopford Green.

Casement in his extensive writings, and with his indefatigability and organisational skills, played a significant role in the provision of coherent political analysis for the separatists. And this despite working in South America for a number of the key years.

He was an ersatz Ulsterman, but that is how he saw and defined himself. Coming as he did, from a rootless London-based family with a radical edge, Ireland was to become his child, and anglophobia his ideology. Ultimately he was to provide the core of independent Ireland's foreign policy with his treaty with Germany in November 1914. Backing this view up, Martin Mansergh, in 2000, said of Casement that he was someone, "legitimate to co-opt as a forerunner of Ireland's independent foreign policy tradition."

Casement was totally embedded within the nationalist and separatist camp, indeed more than most who were, in 1916, to crash into armed politics. With a history dating back a decade, he was on intimate terms with the personnel in Belfast and, increasingly, with the revolutionary wing of the movement in Dublin from 1912 to 1914. Indeed he was outranked in seniority by few if any who were not also members of the IRB, a group he never joined or appears to have been asked to join.

A couple of examples of his correspondence tell of his impatience with the

IPP and his ideas for a future Ireland: On 10 August 1905[322] he wrote to Bulmer Hobson saying, "If the "Party" were not so hopelessly in the quagmire of Parliamentary waiting – waiting but not doing – expecting something to "turn up", now from the Liberals, now from the Conservatives, – it might be possible to form a national executive within and from them. They should have a Cabinet – a Prime Minister, a Secretary of Foreign Affairs, of Agriculture, of Home (& Police) of Education, and so through the list. Those men should make a special study of the departments of Irish life they were to overlook. If, instead of wasting their time and energies at Westminster they met in session and had their office in Ireland, they could do more in five years to build up an Irish State, and to create a confident reliant national mind in the country than by all the Parliamentary "successes" they will achieve in 50 years."

And on 7 September 1909[323] it was, "I presume the Daily "Sinn Fein" is out. Is it any use? I cannot believe it can be. Griffith has not been able for over 2 years now to make that tiny weekly Sinn Fein of any weight or real feeling – I often wondered which was the poorest production "Sinn Fein" or "The Peasant" – and it certainly does seem as if our claim to possess any national character was indeed a poor one with such solitary exponents of it. I sent Griffith £50 for shares in the Daily Sinn Fein but I fear it is money thrown away – only I had promised it long ago – and wished for his sake I could have made it more. I have never felt confidence in him as a leader I may tell you, but I did not like to say a word to anyone that would weaken their faith. The meeting I attended in Dublin in December last convinced me of his narrowness – and that we cannot stand in our far too narrow Ireland."

Casement was to bring guns into Ireland twice, something nobody else could boast. Once he started down the military road few others did more, which is not to say that he had the necessary ruthlessness to prosecute a war or encourage a Rising for its own sake.

As it turned out, neither did Bulmer Hobson nor Eoin MacNeill, another Antrim man. Casement came to Ireland from Germany, and as we know, trying desperately to stop the Easter Rising starting because it had no chance of success. He went so far as to tell his captors of the plans.

He also had no ability to judge the Craig and Carson Unionists. Being so out of sympathy with them (and in reality not an Ulster Protestant), he could only sneer or make the selfdeceptive error, common to most nationalists to this day, that Unionists were misguided Irishmen and, given their suspicion of England, people who would easily turn into Irish patriots – even into Irish Irelanders like him.

---

[322] NLI 13158/2/1
[323] NLI 13158/6/34

Eoin MacNeill was not greatly different. As well known, he published an article entitled *The North Began*, in a Gaelic League journal edited by Pearse, *An Claidheamh Soluis*, on 1 November 1913 calling for an historical repeat of the organising of the Volunteers of the 1780s.

They had effected legislative independence for Ireland, an early form of devolution or home rule, although only for the Irish Anglican caste, the Protestant Ascendancy.

MacNeill wrote in the article, "history shows and observation confirms that the Orange democracy and the Presbyterian rural party are home rulers in principle and essence." He ended by remarking, "Some years ago, speaking at the Toome Feis, in the heart of 'homogeneous Ulster', I said that the day would come when men of every creed and party would join in celebrating the Defence of Derry and the Battle of Benburb. That day is nearer than I then expected."

He was not a revolutionary or a separatist. Significantly he was averse to any adventures in the north, indicating that Ulster Catholics were too prone to violent responses. He knew the world of the Woodkern and the Ribbonmen, and later the nature of Hibernianism, too well.

However he could not have been more wrong in his grasp of Unionism but his view prevailed throughout nationalist Ireland, and to this very day in Sinn Fein. It was and is delusional for if it was ever believed the Protestants were not Irish, the essence of Republicanism would be removed turning it into little more than militant nationalism.

MacNeill's assessment may have been faulty but creating a counterweight to the UVF was not. The fact remains that the Volunteers are with us in the form of the IRA, that is Oglaigh na hÉireann.

What MacNeill did get obliquely right was understanding that element in Presbyterian i.e. Scottish Ulster that values devolution more than integration and that keeps Ulster intransigent. David Trimble expanded that view, once saying Unionism could have it both ways. I don't necessarily agree but the loyalty of Queen's Rebels is the driver.

Casement veered between thinking Carson and the Unionists 'home rulers in principle and essence' or bluffers. He rarely treated them seriously, much as Redmond and the IPP failed to do. The Ulsters' Britishness however was not skin deep, rather it was, and is, conditional. A century later, the Union remains the reality and Northern Ireland a place apart.

Another, southern Protestant response, much favoured by women – Oscar Wilde's mother Speranza being an early example – was to link into the coming power, at first only into the Gaelic cultural and language revival, but slowly from there into nationalism, separatism and thence Catholicism, by conversion or marriage. This was true of the many northern Protestant women who surrounded Casement although they were not the marrying kind, and it remains true to this day. Oddly gay men are not so susceptible, perhaps because of a metropolitan outlook, one Casement did not share.

Bulmer Hobson was not so sanguine about the Ulster Protestants. As perhaps the earliest military-minded separatist, and since 1911 on the IRB's Supreme Council, he had proposed in July 1913 to the Dublin Board of which he was chairman, a plan of action in response to the UVF. As he wrote, "It was decided, that the members of the IRB in Dublin should commence drilling immediately." Largely under the instruction of his Fianna, this began in a National Foresters Hall on Dublin's Parnell Square. But what Hobson was noising abroad, in particular, was a unified national force inaugurated by someone of prominence who could become the focal point of a movement. He was also concerned "that the IRB must not show its hand." He seized the opportunity MacNeill's article presented. After discussions with him, facilitated by The O'Rahilly, a giant public meeting was arranged to establish a modern version of those earlier Volunteers.

The thirty-man Provisional Committee of the Irish Volunteers included Hobson, MacNeill, Casement, MacDermott, Joseph Campbell, Pearse, The O'Rahilly, and Tom Kettle of the United Ireland League. Col. Maurice Moore (brother of the writer George Moore), also a member of the League, was to become the Volunteers' Inspector General. Hobson ensured his own people, such as Joseph Campbell, were involved and that Casement became Treasurer. Although Arthur Griffith chose not to join, the new organisation did represent a wide range of opinion and bodies. But the core was separatist.

The North may have begun the process of separation but it was not the Unionists, rather the work of the IRB, assisted by Asquith and his government, that led inexorably to partition. The brief war in Northern Ireland from 1920 to 1922 left 500 dead in Belfast and 100 police fatalities in the north, showing the IRA's power, then and since.

What the North began and saw effected was something of an aberration, obviously distorted like much else by the First World War. Irish separatism was and is a minority pursuit.

It has taken the best part of a century to unravel history back to where we were in 1910–1916.

BIBLIOGRAPHY

[In alphabetical order by author; German-language publications are not included.]

Christopher ANDREW *The Defence of the Realm: The Authorized History of MI5*, Allen Lane, London 2009.

Evelyn BLÜCHER *An English Wife in Berlin: A Private Memoir of Events, Politics, and Daily Life in Germany Throughout the War and the Social Revolution of 1918*, Constable, New York, 1920.

Breac: **A Digital Journal of Irish Studies**, Keough-Naughton Institute for Irish Studies, University of Notre Dame, Indiana, April 2016, http://breac.nd.edu/. Supposed proceedings of the Tralee conference *Roger Casement: The Glocal Imperative* in October 2013 with many articles added, and a few suppressed. Scripts by Patrick Mason and John Banville are usefully included. Several of the multitude of papers relate to the German period.[324]

British Government Reports (Command Papers)
Documents Relative to the Sinn Fein Movement, XXIX (Cmd. 1108, 1921); intercepted and decrypted transatlantic messages and letters to and from the German embassy in Washington, on Ireland and Casement, during and after the First World War
http://digitalcollections.tcd.ie/home/index.php?DRIS_ID=SamuelsBox3_197;

---

[324] *Breac* articles also include Introduction: "The ghost of Roger Casement is beating on the door", John Gibney, Michael Griffin, and Brian Ó Conchubhair; The Three Lives of the Casement Report: Its Impact on Official Reactions and Popular Opinion in Belgium, Pierre-Luc Plasman (Université Catholique de Louvain, Belgium) and Catherine Thewissen (Université Catholique de Louvain, Belgium); Ireland, Empire, and British Foreign Policy: Roger Casement and the First World War, Margaret O'Callaghan (Queen's University, Belfast); The Afterlife of Roger Casement's Irish Brigade, 1916-1922, Justin Dolan Stover (Idaho State University); Roger Casement and America, Robert Schmuhl (University of Notre Dame); Guns in the Water: Quilty's Car, Spindler's *Aud*, and the First Casualties of the Easter Rising of 1916, Eoin Shanahan (Hibernia College); From Fragments to a Whole: Homosexuality and Partition in *Cries from Casement as his Bones are Brought to Dublin*, by David Rudkin, Mariana Bolfarine (University of São Paulo); Lost to History: An Assessment and Review of the Casement Black Diaries, Paul Hyde; A Note on the Casement Papers in the Benjamin Iveagh Library, Farmleigh House, Dublin, John Gibney; *Casement* (An Original Screenplay), John Banville, with an introduction by Bridget English; *The Dreaming of Roger Casement*: A Play, Patrick Mason; Angus Mitchell, In Conversation with John Gibney, Angus Mitchell, with John Gibney; A Review of Angus Mitchell's *Roger Casement: 16 Lives*, Gearóid Ó Tuathaigh (NUI Galway). http://breac.nd.edu/

Royal Commission on the Rebellion in Ireland (Cmd. 8279, 26 June 1916) with *Minutes of Evidence and Appendix of Documents* (Cmd. 8311).
See also the, now digitised, Casement KV2 files in The National Archives in Kew with their extensive and frank accounts by returning POWs, repatriated for health and medical reasons, of their treatment in the camps and the Irish Brigade recruitment, also concerning the Findlay affair; especially KV2-6-1, 4 & 5, and KV2-8-2.

Xander CLAYTON *Aud*, publisher George Alexander Clayton, Plymouth, 2007, 896 pp., paperback. Extensive account, with naval documentation, of the Casement arms ship and the landing in Kerry.

Charles CURRY *Sir Roger Casement's Diaries – His Mission in Germany and the Findlay Affair*, Arche, Munich 1922. These diaries commence in 1914 and cover much of his time in Germany. They were not private diaries and were edited by a close American friend who was the custodian of Casement's German papers.

Reinhard R. DOERRIES *Prelude to the Easter Rising: Sir Roger Casement in Imperial Germany*, Frank Cass, London & Portland 2000: Translating and publishing original German Foreign Office material amongst 159 documents, Professor Doerries, a distinguished US/German diplomatic historian, provided Berlin's view of Casement for the first time.
Also *Sir Roger Casement's mission in the German Empire*, 1914-1916 *Historische Zeitschrift* vol. 222 no. 3 (1976), pp. 578-625.

Jeffrey DUDGEON *Roger Casement: The Black Diaries – With a Study of his Background, Sexuality, and Irish Political Life*, Belfast Press, Belfast, November 2002 (1st edition), 679 pp. See especially chapters 14-16 which deal with Germany.
2nd edition paperback (728 pp.), January 2016,[325] http://www.amazon.co.uk/dp/095392873X, and Kindle, http://www.amazon.co.uk/dp/B01AXB9754.

---

[325] *Irish Times*, 29 April 2016. *Writing Roger Casement – the long and winding road to McKenna's Fort* – Arnold Thomas Fanning, author of the play *McKenna's Fort*, explores the many sources he drew on to paint a full picture of one of Irish history's most controversial figures: "The final source I used was Jeffrey Dudgeon's monumental Roger Casement: The Black Diaries: With a Study of his Background, Sexuality, and Irish Political Life (Belfast Press, 2002, paperback re-issue 2016). This extraordinary book is a minute dissection and decoding of the Black Diaries, and the fullest and most thorough exploration of Casement's private life as a gay man. As such, it is essential reading to get the full picture of who Casement was and how he thought, and became a key text in my journey of reading so as to prepare for writing my play."

Jeffrey DUDGEON *Cult of the Sexless Casement with Special Reference to the Novel 'The Dream of the Celt' by Mario Vargas Llosa (Nobel Prize Winner for Literature 2010)*, Studi irlandesi. A Journal of Irish Studies, n. 3 (2013), pp. 35-58 ISSN 2239-3978 (online) Firenze http://www.fupress.net/index.php/bsfm-sijis/article/view/13792

Jeffrey DUDGEON *Casement and the Easter Rising: Berlin, Dublin and British Intelligence*, Dúiche Néill (Journal of The O Neill Country Historical Society), Benburb 2016 (see Appendix 5).

Roy FOSTER *Vivid Faces: The Revolutionary Generation in Ireland 1890-1923*, Allen Lane, London 2014, 496 pp. Emblematic book on the, largely disappointed, progenitors of the intellectual side to Irish independence. Deals extensively with Casement and F.J. Bigger in the *Loving* and *Arming* chapters.

H. (Harford) Montgomery HYDE *Trial of Roger Casement*, William Hodge, London 1960, in the *Notable British Trials* series: introduced with an account of the arrest and execution by the former Unionist MP for North Belfast. Hyde also reproduced, only in the revised 1964 Penguin edition, entitled **Famous Trials 9: Roger Casement**, a fortnight's extract from the 1911 Black Diary. The MP's parliamentary efforts to get the diaries examined by experts form another appendix. An earlier, censored, transcript of the trial proper was published, in 1917, in the same series, edited by G.H. Knott.

Brian INGLIS *Roger Casement*, Hodder and Stoughton, London 1973, 448pp. Well-written, extensive, historical and political biography by a former *Irish Times* journalist who accepted the Black Diaries were not forged, having held a different view earlier. Inglis is cheerful about Casement's sexuality, seeing him as an effective patriot and Irish nationalist, if a bit of an hysteric. He concentrates on the African, Irish and German aspects. Three paperback editions have also been published since the hardback; by Coronet in 1974; Blackstaff in 1993; with a third, a *Penguin Classic*, in 2002.

John DE COURCY IRELAND *The Sea and The Easter Rising 1916*, Maritime Institute of Ireland, Dublin 1966: a pamphlet largely concerned with Casement's voyage(s) to Ireland from Germany by submarine, and that of the arms ship. It is memorable for the first publication of a photograph depicting Casement without his torpedo beard and revealing his conspicuous elongated jaw. One can see why the beard never came off – except as an attempt at a disguise.

René MacCOLL *Roger Casement: A New Judgment*, Hamish Hamilton, London 1956, 328pp. and Four Square paperback, 1960 and 1965: matter-of-fact biography, first modern professional attempt at a comprehensive and definitive life, accepting truth of the Black Diaries, antagonistic to Casement, the person – windy and unstable – but praising of his humanitarian efforts and Irish patriotic activity. Brisk, journalistic and judgmental, it was written at a time when witnesses were still living, and was consequently informed by MacColl's interviews, especially with Serjeant Sullivan. Somewhat reliant on Princess Blücher's self-serving memory.

Roger McHUGH *Dublin 1916*, Arlington Books, London 1966: with chapters entitled *Dilemma in Berlin: From Casement's last diary*, *Casement's Last Expedition* (Robert Monteith's story), *Arms off the Kerry Coast* (the story of Captain Spindler of the *Aud*), and *the Last Days of Roger Casement* by Gertrude Parry.

Angus MITCHELL *Field Day Review* 8. 2012, University of Notre Dame, Indiana
- 'A Strange Chapter of Irish History': Sir Roger Casement, Germany and the 1916 Rising, interesting and well-researched article with the usual touch of conspiracy.
- Diary of Roger Casement, 1914-16, Part I: 'My Journey to the German Headquarters at Charleville', annotated by Angus Mitchell.
- Roger Casement 'A last Page of My Diary' 17 March to 8 April 1916, with an introduction by Angus Mitchell.
- 'Phases of a Dishonourable Phantasy', extensive discussion of the Black Diary controversy to date with a myriad of references.

Response by **Jeffrey DUDGEON**, Dublin Review of Books (*drb*), March and June 2013, in two parts replying to the *Field Day Review* articles on Germany and the Black Diaries respectively.
- Part I, *Casement's War*, Issue 31, 25 March 2013 http://www.drb.ie/essays/casement-s-war (see Appendix 3).
- Part II *Casement Wars*, Issue 36, 4 June 2013 http://www.drb.ie/essays/casement-wars (see Appendix 4).

Angus MITCHELL *16 Lives: Roger Casement*, The O'Brien Press, Dublin 2013, 414 pp. Mitchell's first substantive work on Casement, placing him in a modern globalist, human rights-oriented setting, in opposition to 'western hegemony'; anti-imperialist yet pro-German, and nationalist. Martin Mansergh in his *History Ireland* review of May 2014 concurs with Mitchell's "scepticism" over the diaries: "Few who accept the 'Black' content as genuine believe it to be literally credible. As the Hitler diaries show, people can go to great lengths to construct something so plausible as to take in the greatest expert." This author responded, especially on Michael Francis Doyle's dubious report of a discussion with Casement in Brixton Prison where he "emphatically" repudiated the Black Diaries. http://www.historyireland.com/uncategorized/roger-casement/ Casement actually kept silent on the issue.

Angus MITCHELL (ed.) *One Bold Deed of Open Treason: The Berlin Diary of Roger Casement 1914-1916*, Merrion Press, Sallins, Co. Kildare, 2016: 280pp., abridged version of this German diary with some 20,000 words or one fifth cut out, dedicated to Dr Charles Curry. Reviewed in *The Irish Catholic* by W.J. McCormack:
http://www.irishcatholic.ie/article/
odd-thoughts-republic%E2%80%99s-man-berlin

Robert MONTEITH *Casement's Last Adventure,* Chicago, 1932; revised with a foreword by Franz von Papen, Moynihan, Dublin 1953. A loyal and thoughtful account of the author's involvement with the Irish Volunteers and Casement's Irish Brigade in Germany. Having landed off the submarine in Kerry in 1916 and evaded capture, Monteith also tells something of his later involvements.

Pól Ó DOCHARTAIGH *Julius Pokorny, 1887–1970: Germans, Celts and Nationalism,* Four Courts Press, Dublin, 2004.

Séamas Ó SÍOCHÁIN *Roger Casement: Imperialist, Rebel, Revolutionary*, Lilliput Press, Dublin, 2008, 656pp., the definitive biography with a succinct 40-page account of Casement in Imperial Germany 1914-16 and the problems of the Irish Brigade.

David RAMSAY *'Blinker' Hall – Spymaster,* Spellmount, Stroud, 2008, pp. 130-138, hagiography with less than accurate segment on Casement.

B.L. REID *The Lives of Roger Casement*, Yale University Press, New Haven and London 1976, 532 pp. This is a little-known, thoroughly researched and brisk biography that majors on the German episode. The book is written in a literary and immensely readable style. In some 150 pages Reid gives a tight commentary, based on many sources, of Casement's time in Germany pointing out the flaws and foolishness in so many of his actions and so much of his rhetoric. Reid who died in 1990 was a Humanities Professor at Mount Holyoke College in Massachusetts and had already published a book on the Irish-American lawyer John Quinn. He attempts, evidentially, if not always accurately, to prove the diaries genuine and psychologically consistent. Reid deals with the homosexuality issue in an interesting and amusing mode, clearing away his own prejudices and treating Casement very much as a human sexual being with all the absurdity that can appear to involve for the outsider looking in. His novelised history was overshadowed by Brian Inglis's biography.

Roger SAWYER *Casement: The Flawed Hero*, Routledge & Kegan Paul, London 1984: biography dealing for the first time, at some length, with Casement's family background and upbringing. Sawyer majors also on the Belgian Congo and South American investigations on rubber slavery for the Foreign Office. The consular service, and Casement's role in it, is a key part of this work which enters much new territory. Sawyer is now the doyen of the Casement authors, with a probably, unequalled, private, documentary archive.

Karl SPINDLER *The Mystery of the Casement Ship – by its Commander*, with a foreword by Florence O'Donoghue, Anvil Books, Tralee, Co. Kerry, 1965 (first published by Kribe Verlag, Berlin 1931). A good naval yarn that also includes dramatic POW-escape accounts from camps in England although some of the author's facts have been disputed by other Germans involved.

INDEX

Abteilung IIIb (German Military Intelligence), 169, 187, 193, 210, 216
Albert I, King of Belgium, 38, 45-6
Andenne atrocity, 37-9, 43-4, 294
Árpád, Pásztor, 249
Asquith, Herbert Henry, 7, 17, 41, 43, 98, 120, 152, 233, 304, 318, 327-8, 341
Aud, 283-7, 300, 330, 342-3, 345
Auswärtiges Amt (*AA*, German Foreign Office), 20, 142, 158, 208, 218-9, 240, 244
Baerle, Major F. von, 202, 212-3
Bailey, Daniel Julien, see Beverley.
Ballin, Albert, 69-70, 73, 98, 104, 156
Bannister, Gertrude, see Parry.
Barsch, Frau Remy, 249-50, 264
Beeck, Müller, 5
Behrens Mrs (Hamburg), 98, 101, 104, 156
Belgium, *x*, 3, 8, 18, 24, 26, 32, 35-40, 44-7, 54, 72, 96, 99, 104, 116-7, 120, 234, 274-5, 294-6, 342
Berckheim, Graf Philipp von, 18, 20-21, 25
Berkessel, Father Johann (Balduinstein), 126, 130, 133
Bernstorff, Theobald von, *vi*, 63-5, 75, 98, 122, 167-8, 189, 197, 224, 289, 292
Bethmann-Hollweg, Count Johann Heinrich, 5, 23, 48, 83-4, 92, 99, 105, 109, 115, 264-5
Beverley (Bailey), Daniel Julien, *vii*, 181, 283, 301, 322-3, 331, 333, 188, 228-9, 239, 247-8, 250-2, 256, 258, 261-2, 264, 267, 269, 299-300, 322
BICO, 305, 308, 312
Bigger, F.J. (Francis Joseph), 309-11, 338, 344
Blücher von Wahlstatt, Count, later Prince, Gebhard, 54, 60, 63, 65, 67, 69, 73, 84-5, 97-104, 113, 116, 141, 144, 146-7, 149-50, 154-6, 160, 280
Blücher von Wahlstatt (*née* Stapleton-Bretherton), Countess, later Princess, Evelyn, *vi*, *xii*, 54, 56, 65, 72, 221, 225, 280, 299, 342, 345
Blücher (German cruiser), 152
Boehm, Captain Hans W., 80, 161, 163-4, 167, 216, 266
Boy-Ed, Karl, 58, 64
Brezien (or Bresien), Professor, 79-80, 88
Browne, Vincent, 314
Bryce, James, 296
Campbell, Joseph, 338, 341
Carson, Sir Edward, 297, 300, 304, 339-40
Casement, Hugh, *vii*, 206, 260, 271
Cavell, Nurse Edith, 235
Charleville visit to German Military HQ on Western Front, *x*, 5, 18, 21, 26-30, 33-4, 39-40, 47-9, 103, 115, 293-4, 345
Chatterton-Hill, Dr Georges, *xii*, 154, 277
Christensen (Olsen), Adler Eivind, *vi-viii*, *xii-xiii*, 2-6, 9, 14-15, 21,

25, 31, 48, 53-4, 60, 62, 71-3, 84-5, 88, 97, 105-9, 111-16, 121, 123-4, 126, 128, 131-3, 135, 141-4, 147-51, 153-8, 165, 171, 174, 199, 223-5, 266, 276-80, 291, 322-3, 333

Clarke, Tom, 204, 285-6, 324, 338

Clayton, George Alexander (Xander, *Aud* author), 330, 343

Clifford, Brendan, 305, 312

Cockran, Bourke, 15-16

Cohalan, Judge Daniel, 53, 63, 75, 98, 106, 117, 183, 247, 251

Conrad, Joseph, 297, 311

Crotty, Father John Thomas, 49, 65-6, 82, 87, 91, 98, 118, 126, 129-30, 132-3, 140-1, 201-2, 228, 230, 247, 255-6

Curry, Dr Charles Emerson, *iii, vi, x-xii*, 2, 7, 11, 18, 48-9, 66, 70, 72, 109, 114, 116-7, 174-5, 191, 198-9, 206, 222, 257, 260, 270-1, 276-9, 333, 335, 343, 346

Declaration of Goodwill to Ireland (20 November 1914), 8-9, 24, 33, 48-50, 53, 54, 56, 59, 61-6, 70, 75, 77, 98-9, 103, 121, 125, 129, 160, 298, 338

Dernburg, Bernhard, 100, 134

De Valera, Eamon, 136, 193, 293, 315, 333

Devoy, John, *iii, vii, xii*, 15, 17, 117, 143, 145, 155, 161, 188-90, 194-6, 200-3, 207-10, 212, 214-5, 218-9, 222-5, 232, 257, 254, 261, 278, 282-92, 297, 299, 316, 318, 323-4

Doerries, Professor Reinhard (Casement author), 181, 193-5, 218, 244, 277, 343

D'Oleire, Heinrich (Heini), 6, 26

Donnersmarck, Graf Henckel von, 160

Dowling, Sergeant Joseph, 161, 188

Doyle, Michael Francis, 287, 289-91, 335, 346

Dudgeon, Jeffrey (author), *iii-vi, ix*, 198, 289, 293-4, 303, 310-3, 317, 322, 331, 337, 343-5

Duffy, George Gavan, 199, 289-90, 309, 331, 333

Emerson, Col. Edwin, *vi*, 109, 116-7, 217, 247, 254, 264, 268-9

Erzberger, Matthias, 99, 154

Exner, Major General Paul, 76, 78, 83, 87-9, 130, 140-1

Falkenhayn, General Erich von (Chief of the GGS), 221, 236

Fenit (also Fennet and Fennit, Co. Kerry), 187, 190, 200, 202, 207, 242, 330

Findlay, Sir Mansfeldt de Cardonnel, *vi, x-xi, xiii*, 18, 25, 31, 48, 53, 62, 73, 84-5, 87, 106-9, 111-14, 116, 121, 123-4, 126, 132, 135, 142-4, 146-54, 160-1, 183-4, 198-9, 246, 251, 260, 270, 276-7, 281, 333, 343

Friend, General Lovick, 329-30

Fromme, Franz, 217, 254

Fryatt, Captain Robert, 319

Gaelic American newspaper, *iii*, 15, 54, 99, 132-4, 261, 282-92, 297

Gaffney, Thomas St. John (and wife), *vi*, 104, 106-8, 110, 117, 154, 167, 182-5, 187, 198, 205, 213, 217-9, 222, 230, 238, 246, 248-50, 252, 254, 257-8, 260-1, 264, 266-8, 335

Gerard, James W. (US Ambassador in Berlin), 53

Godøy, Bjørn (biographer of Adler Christensen), *viii*
Goodman, Jordan (Casement author), 316
Grabisch, Agnes Bullitt, 250
Graeff, General de (usually spelt Graaff by Casement but twice Graaf), 73, 75-6, 78-85, 87, 89-90, 119, 126, 128-9, 141
Grant, David (Irish Brigade website), 177, 301-2, 324
Green, Alice Stopford, 11-12, 16, 105, 115, 121, 125, 258, 260-1, 270, 298, 313, 329-30, 338
Gregory, John Duncan, 105
Grey, Sir Edward, later 1st Viscount Grey of Fallodon, 12, 30, 39, 42, 52, 54-5, 62-3, 131, 141, 149, 273, 275-6
Griffith, Arthur, 339, 341
Groeben, Countess, 53, 99
Grünert, Major Richard, 78, 80, 89
Grunewald Sanatorium, Berlin, 147, 157-8
Hahn, Countess Tessa, 97-8, 101, 122, 156, 160
Hahn, Unteroffizier (translator), 251, 263
Hammond, Mr (Casement's *nom de guerre* in Germany as an American), 4, 9, 18-19, 25, 29, 48, 62, 121, 128, 131, 154, 157-8, 174, 208
Harden, Maximilian, 5
Hassan, Prince Mouhamed Ali, 270
Haugwitz-Hardenberg-Reventlow, Count Curt von, *vii*, 193, 210-11, 213, 215-6, 222, 224, 226-8, 238-9, 241, 243-6, 248-9, 252-4, 256, 262, 264, 269
Herwarth von Bittenfeld, Hans-Wolfgang, 109, 216

Heydell (or Heidel), Captain Eberhard, 147, 198-200, 202, 208-10, 241, 245, 249, 251, 262-3
Hindenburg, President Paul von, *vi*, 21-23, 64, 108-9, 134, 147
Hobson, Bulmer, *vi*, 16, 90, 145, 204, 299, 324, 331, 337-9, 341
Hochschild, Adam, 45, 296
Hoesslin, Dr Rudolf von, 191
Hohenlohe, Princess, 122, 160
Holohan, Private Patrick, 205, 267
Howard, Sir Henry, 63, 65, 101, 105, 130
Hülsen (Huelsen), Bernhard von, 193, 210, 222, 248
Hyde, President Douglas, 136, 315
Hyde, Harford Montgomery, 289-90, 313, 344
Hyde, Paul (diary sceptic), 321, 342
Isendahl, Konteradmiral Walther, 120-1, 142, 147, 152, 200, 203
Jagow, Gottlieb von, 5, 23-4, 48, 54, 69, 73, 83-5, 87, 98-100, 103, 105
Jephson (or Jepson), Anne (later Casement), 326
Kavanagh, Corporal John, 188, 263
Kelly, Bryan A., 105, 107, 118-9, 126, 128-9, 135, 144
Keogh (also Kehoe), Sergeant-Major Michael, 162-3, 171, 188
Klicks, Herr (Continental Hotel Manager), 21, 157
Krebs, Franz Hugo, 228, 230, 239, 245, 249, 251-2, 256, 260-1, 264
Kuranstalt Sanatorium, Neuwittelsbach, Munich, 182-5, 190-1, 201
Landy, James E. (Casement's American *nom de guerre*), 3-4, 53, 62, 106, 264, 278

Leiningen, Prince Emich, 76, 78-9, 82-4, 87, 126
Leopold II, King of Belgium, 11-12, 38, 45-6, 104, 273, 296
Lersner, Baron Kurt von, 18-19, 27-9, 294
Liebknecht, Karl, 250, 309
Limburg, 67, 73, 75-9, 81-3, 87-90, 92, 94-7, 105-6, 113, 118-9, 124, 126, 129-133, 135-6, 139-143, 146, 148-9, 153, 161-4, 167, 171, 173, 206, 228, 230, 247, 251, 255-6, 267, 280
Lody, Carl, 58
Lothes, Major, 5, 40, 119
Lübbers, Captain S. von, 162, 216
Ludendorff, General Erich, *vi*, 22-3, 64
Lüttichau, Graf Siegfried von, 25-30, 33, 36, 44, 46, 48, 81, 294
Lynch, Col. Arthur, 10
MacColl, René (Casement author), *xii*, 313, 345
MacDermott, Sean, 238, 246, 285-6, 341
MacFadden, Mary, 183-4
MacMurrough, Sergeant Francis, 80-2, 85-6, 88-9
MacNeill, Eoin, 80, 115, 125, 136, 258, 284-6, 299-300, 339-41
Macran, Professor Henry S., 122, 124, 144
Maloney, Dr. William J. (Casement author), 175, 310, 315
McCartan, Patrick, 337-8
McCormack, W.J. (Bill) (Casement author), 294, 313, 317, 346,
McGarrity, Joseph, *vi*, 15-17, 93, 117, 171, 182, 203, 205, 228, 251, 257, 266, 289, 333, 335, 338

McGoey, John, *vii*, 176-7, 198, 200, 202-4, 207-8, 210-3, 240, 242-3, 245, 263, 267, 299-302, 322-5, 333, 335
Meckel (or Meckle), Paul, 25-8, 33, 37, 43-5, 48, 81, 295
Meyer, Fräulein Antonie (Toni), 22, 101, 105, 122, 157
Meyer, Professor Eduard, 121, 154, 277
Meyer, Kuno, 22-4, 59, 75, 105-7, 117-8, 122, 136
Meyer, Richard (F.O. Assessor), *vi*, 2-6, 8-9, 19-23, 25-30, 33, 36, 44-5, 47-8, 54, 59-60, 63, 65, 67, 73, 84, 98-9, 104, 107, 109, 122-4, 128, 132-3, 135, 141-3, 147-8, 150-1, 153-5, 157-8, 161, 163-4, 187, 201, 213, 218-21, 239, 249-50, 254, 279-80
Milligan, Alice, 338
Monteith, Captain Robert, *vii*, *xii*, 171, 173, 175, 181, 183-96, 200-9, 212-7, 219-22, 226-8, 230, 232, 234, 238-9, 242, 244, 247-55, 257-64, 267, 283-4, 286, 299-300, 322-4, 333, 335, 345-6
Montgelas, Graf Max von, 122, 153
Morel, E.D., 11, 258, 295, 309
Morgan, Professor J.H., 295-6
Morten, Richard, 6, 25-6
Munster, Count Alexander von, 160
Nadolny, Captain Rudolf, *vii*, 161, 168-9, 173, 192-5, 200-2, 205-6, 210, 212-6, 220-2, 225-7, 235-6, 238, 246, 248, 252-4, 256, 266, 299, 325
Nathan, Sir Matthew, 105, 328-30
Newman, Nina (also Agnes, *née* Casement), *xi-xii*, 125, 247, 261, 291-2, 333

Nicholson, Father John Thomas (Philadelphia), 109, 114, 130, 133, 141, 145-9, 153, 161-2, 266

Nicolson, Sir Arthur (1st Lord Carnock), 275-6

Noeggerath ('Noeg'), Jacob E., 184, 187, 213-5, 230, 238-41, 244-6, 248-53, 333

Nordenflycht, Baron Ferdinand von, 53-4, 155-6

Nordenflycht (née Mühlig), Baroness Adelheid von, 53-4, 61, 149, 155-6, 162, 179, 280

Nordenflycht, Gussie (daughter), 53-4, 149

O'Byrne, Cathal, 333

O'Callaghan, Corporal Michael, *vii*, 127, 188, 191-2

O'Connor, Frank, *xii*

O'Connor, T.P., 12

O'Gorman, Father Canice, 49, 65-6, 82, 91, 126, 129-30, 132, 135, 141, 155

O'Laughlin, John Callan, 117

O'Riordan, Manus, 317

O'Riordan, Monsignor Michael (Rome), 49, 91, 130, 155,

Oppersdorff, Count Hans von, 53, 99, 144

Papen, Franz von, 64, 212, 224-5, 256, 259, 291, 318, 324, 346

Parry (née Bannister), Gertrude (Gee), *iii*, *x*, 292, 326, 331, 333, 345

Pasha, Enver, 181

Pless, Princess Daisy, 65, 69

Plunkett, Count George, 175, 240, 242-3, 250

Plunkett, Joseph Mary, 161, 240, 250, 264, 284, 292

Poison, 209, 228, 232, 249, 256, 269

Pokorny, Professor Julius, *vi*, 135-7, 346

Pond, James B., 14

Praschma, Graf Hans, 69

Purser, Sarah, *vi*, 125

Puttkamer, Jesco von, 108-9, 119

Quinlisk, Sergeant Timothy Henry (Harry Quinliss), 80-2, 85, 88-9, 96, 129-30, 135, 162, 181, 263

Quinn, John, 15, 117, 297, 346

Redmond, John, 7, 31, 50, 61, 90-3, 102, 107, 115, 117-8, 122, 130-1, 140, 145, 159, 274, 284-5, 304, 307, 340

Reid, B. L. (Casement author), *xii*, 48, 306-7, 346-7

Reuss, Princess Hermine, 160

Riederau am Ammersee (Bavaria), *vii*, *x*, 180, 190, 206, 260, 270-2

Roeder, Baron Ernst von, 72-3, 98-9, 144, 150, 155, 160

Roes, Aldwin, 296

Roosevelt, Theodore, 104

Ruhleben Camp, 97, 105, 107, 118, 124, 126, 132, 144, 149, 152

Sawyer, Roger (Casement author), *xii*, 347

Schiemann, Professor Theodor, 20-1, 23, 57, 59-60, 72-3, 75, 84-5, 99, 102-3, 106, 108, 113, 148, 154

Schröder, Kurt von, 160

Skal, Georg von, 5, 291

Solf, Dr Wilhelm Heinrich, 102-3

Spindler, Captain Karl, 300, 326, 329-30, 342, 345, 347

Stack, Austin, 283, 286

Stalleys (Staples), Ponsonby, 219-20

Stanhope, Aubrey, 104, 106, 108, 157-8

Stölzel ('Stultzer'), Captain Albert, 210
Stumm, Baron Wilhelm von, 24, 29-30, 33, 39-40, 46-7, 52, 294-6
Submarine U-19 and U-20, 176, 188-90, 193, 196-8, 200, 206, 215-6, 238-9, 241-6, 248-9, 251, 253, 259, 263, 269, 281, 283-4, 286, 299-300, 303, 319, 322, 325-6, 329, 344, 346
Submarine warfare, 23-4, 32, 55, 64, 99, 102, 133, 138, 146, 151, 154, 318-9
Tirpitz, Alfred von, 24, 134
Treaty on the Irish Brigade of 28 December 1914 ('*The Irish Verses*'), 24, 125, 159, 161-2, 164, 167-8, 171, 195, 197, 201, 205, 207-9, 212, 220, 247, 250-1, 257, 260-1, 298, 309, 325
Vatican, 49, 55-6, 59, 63, 66, 101, 105, 130
Verschmidt (later Christensen), Margarethe or Margarette, 322-3
Victoria, Queen, 139-40
Vollmoeller, Karl, 119
Warren, Brother Canethus, 247
Weaver, Sadie (later Christensen), *vii*, 223, 225, 322
Wedel, Count Georg von, *vi*, 6, 8-9, 19, 21, 23-5, 49, 53-4, 59, 63, 73, 83-4, 87-8, 97-8, 100, 106, 109-12, 116, 118-9, 122, 132, 141-4, 146, 148-50, 152-4, 161, 163-4, 167-8, 171, 175, 216-20, 225, 230, 238, 240-1, 244-5, 252-4, 256-7, 266-7, 280
Weisbach, Captain Raimund, 300
White, Mrs (Continental Times), 103, 108-9, 116, 118, 157-8
Wiegand, Karl Henry von (journalist), 104, 108, 121, 157-8

Wiegand, Theodor (archaeologist), 121
Wilde, Oscar, 199, 292, 305-6, 311, 313, 326, 341
Wilhelm II, Kaiser, *vi*, 5, 23, 45, 63, 64, 67-9, 102, 106, 112, 136, 160, 298
Wilson, President Woodrow, 23, 58, 63, 119, 122, 197, 285-7, 291, 317-8
Zehndler, Max, 229-30
Zerhusen, Ellen (*née* Hand), 217, 250, 252, 254
Zerhusen, Joseph, 217, 250-2, 254-5, 268
Zimmermann, Arthur, 2, 5-8, 23, 125, 157, 163, 214-5, 238, 253, 268, 298, 318-9, 328
Zittel, Nelly, 98, 118-9
Zossen Camp, *vi*, 168, 171, 173, 180-2, 187, 189, 194, 196, 202-3, 205-7, 212-3, 215-7, 219, 221, 226, 228, 230-1, 236, 238, 245-6, 248-9, 252-3, 255-6, 261, 265-8

www.ingramcontent.com/pod-product-compliance
Lightning Source LLC
Chambersburg PA
CBHW051813090426
42736CB00011B/1457